ANTI-INFLAMMATORY DIET COOKBOOK FOR BEGINNERS 2022

How To Heal The Immune System, Weight Loss and Drastically Lower The Chances Of Contracting Diseases. +500 Recipes and 7 Week-Meal Plan Included

LARA BRANDON

Table of Contents

INTRODUCTION 1

MY STORY 3

CHAPTER 1: WHAT IS INFLAMMATION? 5

WHAT IS THE DIFFERENCE BETWEEN INFLAMMATION
AND ACUTE INFLAMMATION? 5
WHAT DOES CHRONIC INFLAMMATION CONSIST OF? 6
WHAT CAUSES DISCOMFORT CAUSED BY CHRONIC
INFLAMMATION? 6
WHAT CAUSES CHRONIC INFLAMMATION?..................7
SYMPTOMS OF CHRONIC INFLAMMATION 7
HEALTH RISK OF ANTI-INFLAMMATION 8
THE GUIDELINES FOR THE ANTI-INFLAMMATORY DIET 9
TIPS FOR THE ANTI-INFLAMMATORY DIET....................10
FOODS TO EAT AND TO AVOID 12

CHAPTER 2: IMMUNE SYSTEM 15

THE OSTEOARTICULAR SYSTEM..............................15
ARTHROSIS, ARTHRITIS, GOUT AND PAIN. 16
WEIGHT LOSS - PROBLEMS AND SOLUTIONS
(HEALING) 17

CHAPTER 3: BREAKFAST................................... 19

1. ANTI-INFLAMMATORY MUFFINS 19
2. SAVORY BREAKFAST PANCAKES 19
3. SPINACH BREAKFAST 20
4. HEALTHY BREAKFAST CHOCOLATE DONUTS 20
5. BAKED EGGS WITH PORTOBELLO MUSHROOMS..20
6. BREAKFAST SPINACH MUSHROOM
    TOMATO FRY UP 21
7. SWEET CHERRY ALMOND CHIA PUDDING 21
8. PINEAPPLE GINGER SMOOTHIE..................21
9. BEET AND CHERRY SMOOTHIE 22
10. SPICY PINEAPPLE SMOOTHIE....................22
11. BREAKFAST CHERRY MUFFINS 22
12. BREAKFAST SHAKSHUKA 22
13. ANTI-INFLAMMATORY CREPES....................23
14. NO-BAKE TURMERIC PROTEIN DONUTS..........23
15. GOLDEN MILK....................................23
16. GRANOLA 24
17. OVERNIGHT COCONUT CHIA OATS 24
18. BLUEBERRY HEMP SEED SMOOTHIE 25
19. SPICED MORNING CHIA PUDDING 25
20. GREEN SMOOTHIE 25
21. OATMEAL PANCAKES..............................25
22. ANTI-INFLAMMATORY PORRIDGE 26
23. CHERRY SMOOTHIE................................26
24. GINGERBREAD OATMEAL 26
25. ROASTED ALMONDS 27
26. APPLE, GINGER, AND RHUBARB MUFFINS 27

27. ALMOND SCONES..................................28
28. CRANBERRY AND RAISINS GRANOLA 28
29. BREAKFAST ARROZCALDO 28
30. APPLE BRUSCHETTA WITH ALMONDS AND
    BLACKBERRIES 29
31. OAT PORRIDGE WITH CHERRY & COCONUT........29
32. GINGERBREAD OATMEAL BREAKFAST 29
33. YUMMY STEAK MUFFINS..........................30
34. WHITE AND GREEN QUICHE 30
35. BEEF BREAKFAST CASSEROLE 30
36. HAM AND VEGGIE FRITTATA MUFFINS 31
37. TOMATO AND AVOCADO OMELET 31
38. OATS WITH BERRIES 31
39. SPINACH AVOCADO SMOOTHIE....................32
40. ROASTED CHICKPEAS 32
41. SPICED POPCORN 32
42. CUCUMBER BITES 33
43. SPINACH FRITTERS 33
44. CRISPY CHICKEN FINGERS 33
45. QUINOA & VEGGIE CROQUETTES 34
46. SWEET POTATO CRANBERRY BREAKFAST BARS ...34
47. BREAKFAST STIR FRY 34
48. OVEN-POACHED EGGS 35
49. TURKEY BURGERS 35
50. ANTI-INFLAMMATORY BREAKFAST FRITTATA 36
51. MEDITERRANEAN FRITTATA 36
52. SPICY MARBLE EGGS 36
53. TUNA & SWEET POTATO CROQUETTES 37
54. VEGGIE BALLS 37
55. SALMON BURGERS 38
56. FENNEL SEEDS COOKIES 38
57. SUN-DRIED TOMATO GARLIC BRUSCHETTA 38
58. COCONUT & BANANA COOKIES....................39
59. HASH BROWNS 39
60. MUSHROOM CRÊPES 39
61. BAKE APPLE TURNOVER 40
62. ALMOND PANCAKES WITH COCONUT FLAKES 40
63. BREAKFAST SAUSAGE AND MUSHROOM CASSEROLE
   41
64. MAPLE OATMEAL 42

CHAPTER 4: LUNCH **44**

65. GRILLED AVOCADO SANDWICH 44
66. CAULIFLOWER STEAKS WITH TAMARIND AND BEANS
    44
67. HEALTHY CHICKEN MARSALA 45
68. TUNA STEAKS 45
69. AIR FRYER SALMON 46
70. ROSEMARY GARLIC LAMB CHOPS 46
71. MUSHROOM FARRO RISOTTO......................46
72. INSTANT POT BLACK BEANS 47
73. POPCORN CHICKEN 47
74. SPICY CHICKEN AND CAULIFLOWER 48
75. SALMON AND SWEET POTATO MIX 48
76. LEMON ONION MASH 48
77. BROWN RICE AND CHICKEN MIX..................49

78. CURRIED SHRIMP AND VEGETABLES 49
79. BUTTERED SPROUTS 49
80. SHEET PAN ROSEMARY MUSHROOMS 50
81. CHICKEN BREASTS AND MUSHROOMS 50
82. CABBAGE WITH APPLE 50
83. ROASTED SUMMER SQUASH & FENNEL BULB 51
84. ROASTED BRUSSELS SPROUTS & SWEET POTATO . 51
85. POTATO MASH 51
86. CREAMY SWEET POTATO MASH 52
87. GINGERED CAULIFLOWER RICE 52
88. SPICY CAULIFLOWER RICE 52
89. SIMPLE BROWN RICE 53
90. QUINOA WITH APRICOTS 53
91. SIMPLE CARROTS MIX 53
92. TASTY GRILLED ASPARAGUS 53
93. EASY ROASTED CARROTS 54
94. DILL HADDOCK 54
95. TROUT AND SALSA 54
96. SHRIMP CAKES 54
97. ITALIAN CALAMARI 55
98. CHILI SNAPPER 55
99. MASHED CHICKPEA BRUSCHETTA 55
100. PUTTANESCA-STYLE GREENS AND BEANS 56
101. MEDITERRANEAN QUINOA BOWLS 56
102. PINEAPPLE THREE BEAN SALAD 57
103. LEEK AND CHARD FRITTATA 57
104. GREEK TURKEY BURGERS WITH TZATZIKI 57
105. SEARED AHI TUNA POKE SALAD 58
106. ONE-PAN EGGS WITH ASPARAGUS AND TOMATOES 59
107. ANTI-INFLAMMATORY BUDDHA BOWL 59
108. HONEY GINGER SHRIMP BOWLS 59
109. BAKE CHICKEN TOP-UP WITH OLIVES, TOMATOES, AND BASIL 60
110. RATATOUILLE 60
111. CHICKEN MEATBALL SOUP 61
112. CABBAGE ORANGE SALAD WITH CITRUSY VINAIGRETTE 61
113. GREEN SOUP 61
114. PEPPERONI PIZZA LOAF 62
115. BEETS GAZPACHO 62
116. BAKED BUTTERNUT SQUASH RIGATONI 62
117. CAPELLINI SOUP WITH TOFU AND SHRIMP 63
118. LEMON BUTTERY SHRIMP RICE 63
119. CAULIFLOWER SOUP 63
120. APPLE AND TOMATO DIPPING SAUCE 64
121. HOT TUNA STEAK 64
122. IRISH STYLE CLAMS 64
123. ITALIAN HALIBUT CHOWDER 65
124. KETO SALMON TANDOORI WITH CUCUMBER SAUCE 65
125. KETO ZOODLES WITH WHITE CLAM SAUCE 66
126. LEMON-CAPER TROUT WITH CARAMELIZED SHALLOTS 66
127. LEMONY MACKEREL 67
128. LEMONY TROUT 67
129. LIME COD MIX 67
130. MACKEREL BOMBS 68

CHAPTER 5: DINNER 70

131. TURMERIC RICE BOWL WITH GARAM MASALA ROOT VEGETABLE AND CHICKPEAS 70
132. ROASTED ROOT VEGGIES AND GREENS OVER SPICED LENTIL 70
133. WALNUT ROSEMARY CRUSTED SALMON 71
134. ROASTED SALMON WITH SPICY CRANBERRY RELISH 71
135. ROASTED CAULIFLOWER AND POTATO CURRY SOUP 72
136. DIJON SALMON WITH GREEN BEAN PILAF 73
137. VEGAN COCONUT CHICKPEA CURRY 73
138. CAULIFLOWER TIKKA MASALA WITH CHICKPEAS 73
139. SHEET-PAN CHICKEN AND VEGETABLES WITH ROMESCO SAUCE 74
140. GLUTEN-FREE TERIYAKI SALMON 74
141. GLUTEN-FREE PINEAPPLE BURGERS 75
142. VEGAN MUSHROOMS IN BROTH 75
143. VEGAN AND MEDITERRANEAN MANGO AND BEAN STEW 75
144. COD AND PEAS 76
145. ROASTED VEGETABLES AND SWEET POTATOES WITH WHITE BEANS 76
146. ROASTED TOFU AND GREENS 76
147. TOFU AND ITALIAN-SEASONED SUMMER VEGETABLES 77
148. SPICED BROCCOLI, CAULIFLOWER WITH TOFU AND RED ONION 77
149. TEMPEH AND ROOT VEGETABLE BAKE 77
150. GARLICKY CHICKEN AND VEGETABLES 78
151. TURMERIC-SPICED SWEET POTATOES, APPLE, AND ONION WITH CHICKEN 78
152. HONEY-ROASTED CHICKEN THIGHS WITH CARROTS 78
153. SESAME-TAMARI BAKED CHICKEN WITH GREEN BEANS 79
154. SHEET PAN TURKEY BREAST WITH GOLDEN VEGETABLES 79
155. SHEET PAN STEAK AND BRUSSELS SPROUTS WITH RED WINE 79
156. MISO SALMON AND GREEN BEANS 80
157. TILAPIA WITH ASPARAGUS AND ACORN SQUASH. 80
158. SHRIMP-LIME BAKE WITH ZUCCHINI AND CORN 80
159. BROCCOLINI WITH ALMONDS 81
160. VEGETABLE AND CHICKEN STIR FRY 81
161. BAKED TILAPIA WITH ROSEMARY AND PECAN 81
162. TOASTED BROWN RICE WITH THYME AND MUSHROOMS 82
163. ITALIAN STUFFED PEPPERS 82
164. CHICKEN WITH HERB PARMESAN SPAGHETTI SQUASH 83
165. CHICKEN CURRY WITH TAMARIND & PUMPKINS. 83
166. ZUCCHINI AND LEMON HERB SALMON 84
167. PARMESAN AND LEMON FISH 84
168. CHICKEN LEMON PICCATA 85
169. BLACKENED CHICKEN BREAST 85
170. CHICKEN MARRAKESH 85
171. SHRIMP AND VEGETABLE CURRY 86
172. BANANA AND PEANUT BUTTER DETOX 86
173. ESCAROLE, PINEAPPLE, AND APPLE SMOOTHIE .. 86
174. GREEN AND LEAFY GINGER-APPLE DRINK 87

175. NUTTY PINA COLADA 87
176. CHAI TEA DRINK 87
177. LEMON-MINT GREEN TEA 87
178. SPICY CHICKEN VEGETABLE SOUP 88
179. LEMON AND GARLIC SCALLOPS 88
180. WALNUT ENCRUSTED SALMON 88
181. BROCCOLI AND TILAPIA 89
182. ESPECIAL GLAZED SALMON 89
183. GENEROUS STUFFED SALMON AVOCADO 89
184. CAJUN JAMBALAYA SOUP 89
185. ANTI-INFLAMMATORY TURMERIC GUMMIES 90
186. SPICY TUNA ROLLS 90
187. GINGER DATE BARS 90
188. TASTY ROASTED BROCCOLI 91
189. THE ALMOND BREADED CHICKEN GOODNESS... 91
190. VANILLA TURMERIC ORANGE JUICE 91
191. HIBISCUS GINGER GELATIN 92
192. LEMONY MUSSELS 92
193. TROPICAL FRUIT PARFAIT 92
194. ZUCCHINI PASTA WITH AVOCADO SAUCE 92
195. CHERRIES AND QUINOA 93
196. FRUIT BOWL WITH YOGURT TOPPING 93
197. BROILED WHITE SEA BASS 93
198. CELERY ROOT HASH BROWNS 94
199. BRAISED KALE 94
200. TENDER SALMON IN MUSTARD SAUCE 94
201. BRAISED LEEKS, CAULIFLOWER AND
      ARTICHOKE HEARTS 94
202. SCALLOPS STEW 95
203. SPICY BAKED FISH 95

CHAPTER 6: FISH AND SEAFOOD 97

204. SHRIMP SCAMPI 97
205. SHRIMP WITH SPICY SPINACH 97
206. SHRIMP WITH CINNAMON SAUCE 98
207. PAN-SEARED SCALLOPS WITH LEMON-GINGER
      VINAIGRETTE 98
208. MANHATTAN-STYLE SALMON CHOWDER 98
209. ROASTED SALMON AND ASPARAGUS 98
210. CITRUS SALMON ON A BED OF GREENS 99
211. ORANGE AND MAPLE-GLAZED SALMON 99
212. SALMON CEVICHE 99
213. COD WITH GINGER 100
214. ROSEMARY-LEMON COD 100
215. HALIBUT CURRY 100
216. MARINATED FISH STEAKS 101
217. BAKED TOMATO HAKE 101
218. CHEESY TUNA PASTA 101
219. SALMON AND ROASTED PEPPERS 102
220. SHRIMP AND BEETS 102
221. SHRIMP AND CORN 102
222. CHILI SHRIMP AND PINEAPPLE 102
223. BALSAMIC SCALLOPS 103
224. WHITEFISH CURRY 103
225. SWORDFISH WITH PINEAPPLE AND CILANTRO ...103
226. SESAME-TUNA SKEWERS 104
227. TROUT WITH CHARD 104
228. SOLE WITH VEGETABLES 104
229. POACHED HALIBUT AND MUSHROOMS 105
230. HALIBUT STIR FRY 105
231. STEAMED GARLIC-DILL HALIBUT 105
232. HONEY CRUSTED SALMON WITH PECANS 106

CHAPTER 7: MEAT 108

233. PORK WITH BALSAMIC ONION SAUCE 108
234. PORK WITH OLIVES 108
235. PORK WITH TOMATO SALSA 108
236. BEEF WITH CARROT & BROCCOLI 109
237. BEEF WITH MUSHROOM & BROCCOLI 109
238. CITRUS BEEF WITH BOK CHOY 110
239. BEEF WITH ZUCCHINI NOODLES 110
240. BEEF WITH ASPARAGUS & BELL PEPPER 111
241. SPICED GROUND BEEF 111
242. GROUND BEEF WITH CABBAGE 112
243. GROUND BEEF WITH VEGGIES 112
244. GROUND BEEF WITH CASHEWS & VEGGIES 112
245. GROUND BEEF WITH GREENS & TOMATOES 113
246. BEEF & VEGGIES CHILI 113
247. GROUND BEEF & VEGGIES CURRY 113
248. SPICY & CREAMY GROUND BEEF CURRY 114
249. CURRIED BEEF MEATBALLS 114
250. BEEF MEATBALLS IN TOMATO GRAVY 115
251. PORK WITH LEMONGRASS 116
252. PORK CHOPS WITH TOMATO SALSA 116

CHAPTER 8: POULTRY 118

253. TURKEY SLOPPY JOES 118
254. HIDDEN VALLEY CHICKEN DUMMIES 118
255. CHICKEN DIVAN 119
256. APRICOT CHICKEN WINGS 119
257. CHAMPION CHICKEN POCKETS 119
258. CHICKEN-BELL PEPPER SAUTÉ 119
259. HONEY CHICKEN TAGINE 120
260. ROASTED CHICKEN 120
261. CHICKEN IN PITA BREAD 121
262. SKILLET CHICKEN WITH BRUSSELS
      SPROUTS MIX 121
263. SPICY CHIPOTLE CHICKEN 121
264. CHICKEN WITH FENNEL 122
265. ADOBO LIME CHICKEN MIX 122
266. CAJUN CHICKEN & PRAWN 122
267. HEALTHY TURKEY GUMBO 123
268. CHINESE-ORANGE SPICED DUCK BREASTS 123
269. SUPER SESAME CHICKEN NOODLES 124
270. LEBANESE CHICKEN KEBABS AND HUMMUS 124
271. NUTTY PESTO CHICKEN SUPREME 124
272. DELICIOUS ROASTED DUCK 125
273. DUCK BREAST WITH APRICOT SAUCE 125
274. DUCK BREAST SALAD 126
275. DUCK BREAST AND BLACKBERRIES MIX 126
276. CHICKEN PICCATA 127
277. HONEY-MUSTARD LEMON MARINATED
      CHICKEN 127
278. SPICY ALMOND CHICKEN STRIPS WITH GARLIC LIME
      TARTAR SAUCE 127
279. CHICKEN SCARPARIELLO WITH SPICY SAUSAGE 128
280. ALMOND CHICKEN CUTLETS 128
281. CHEESY CHICKEN SUN-DRIED TOMATO
      PACKETS 129
282. TUSCAN CHICKEN SAUTE 129
283. TURKEY HAM AND MOZZARELLA PATE 130
284. AVOCADO-ORANGE GRILLED CHICKEN 130
285. BACON-WRAPPED CHICKEN WITH CHEDDAR
      CHEESE 130

286. BAKED CHICKEN MEATBALLS - HABANERO & GREEN CHILI 131
287. BALSAMIC-GLAZED TURKEY WINGS 131
288. BASIC "ROTISSERIE" CHICKEN 131
289. BASIL CHICKEN SAUTÉ 132
290. BBQ CHICKEN ZUCCHINI BOATS 132
291. BLUE CHEESE BUFFALO CHICKEN BALLS 132

CHAPTER 9: SOUP 135

292. VEGETABLE SOUP 135
293. LENTIL SOUP 135
294. PEA SOUP 135
295. CABBAGE SOUP 136
296. GERMAN CREAM-SOUP 136
297. ASIAN SOUP 136
298. CHICKEN SOUP 137
299. ARIGATO SOUP 137
300. ANTI-INFLAMMATORY SPRING PEA SOUP 137
301. ANTI-INFLAMMATORY SWEET POTATO SOUP 138
302. BACON & CHEESE SOUP 138
303. BEEF AND VEGGIE SOUP 139
304. BROCCOLI CHEDDAR & BACON SOUP 139
305. BROCCOLI SOUP WITH GORGONZOLA CHEESE ..139
306. BROWN RICE WITH SHITAKE MISO SOUP AND SCALLION 140
307. BUFFALO SAUCE AND TURKEY SOUP 140
308. BUTTERNUT SQUASH SOUP WITH SHRIMP 141
309. CANNELLINI BEAN SOUP 141
310. CARROT BROCCOLI STEW 141
311. CARROT, GINGER & TURMERIC SOUP 142
312. CAULIFLOWER AND CLAM CHOWDER 142
313. CAULIFLOWER, COCONUT MILK, AND SHRIMP SOUP 142
314. CELERY SOUP 143
315. GREEK SPRING SOUP 143
316. MOROCCAN LENTIL SOUP 143
317. ZUCCHINI SOUP 144
318. ROASTED CAULIFLOWER AND CHEDDAR SOUP ..144
319. WHITE BEAN SOUP 144
320. HALIBUT CHOWDER 145
321. BEEF BARLEY SOUP 145
322. CABBAGE AND SMOKED SAUSAGE SOUP 145
323. EGGPLANT CHICKPEA STEW 146
324. RED PEPPER AND TOMATO SOUP 146
325. TUSCANY VEGETABLE SOUP 146
326. CHEESY CAULIFLOWER SOUP 147
327. CREOLE CHICKEN GUMBO 147
328. QUINOA CHILI 147
329. TOMATO BASIL CHICKEN STEW 147
330. MINESTRONE 148
331. PASTA FAGGIOLI 148

CHAPTER 10: VEGETABLE 150

332. BEETS AND CARROTS BOWLS 150
333. ITALIAN STYLE VEGETABLE MIX 150
334. WILD RICE PILAF 150
335. APPLES MIX 151
336. ASPARAGUS MIX 151
337. ASPARAGUS AND EGGS MIX 151
338. CLASSIC VEGETABLE MEALS 151
339. OKRA AND MUSHROOMS SIDE DISH 152
340. OKRA AND TOMATO SAUCE MIX 152

341. STEWED OKRA WITH CAYENNE PEPPER 152
342. OKRA AND CORN BOWLS 152
343. ROASTED BEETS WITH OLIVE OIL 153
344. THYME BEETS WITH GARLIC 153
345. BEETS AND HONEY SIDE SALAD 153
346. LEMONY BEETS WITH WHITE VINEGAR 153
347. CARROT SIDE SALAD 154
348. CAULIFLOWER GRATIN 154
349. TARRAGON BEETS 154
350. SUMMER MIX 154
351. INSTANT POT COLLARD GREENS 155
352. BRAISED KALE AND CARROTS 155
353. INSTANT POT SAAG ALOO 155
354. 3-MINUTE INSTANT POT KALE 156
355. INSTANT POT TURNIP GREENS 156
356. SARSON KA SAAG (SPICED MUSTARD GREENS) .156
357. SPICY TURNIP GREENS 156
358. SAUTÉED SWISS CHARD WITH GARLIC AND LEMON 157
359. DANDELION GREENS WITH CURRANTS AND PINE NUTS 157
360. RADICCHIO AND ONIONS 157
361. ESCAROLE AND BEAN SOUP 158
362. MISO SOUP WITH SHITAKE AND BOK CHOY 158
363. LENTILS WITH TOMATOES AND TURMERIC 158
364. WHOLE-WHEAT PASTA WITH TOMATO-BASIL SAUCE 159
365. FRIED RICE WITH KALE 159
366. NUTTY AND FRUITY GARDEN SALAD 159
367. STIR-FRIED BRUSSELS SPROUTS AND CARROTS ..160
368. CURRIED VEGGIES AND POACHED EGGS 160
369. BRAISED CARROTS AND KALE 161
370. STIR-FRIED GINGERY VEGGIES 161
371. CAULIFLOWER FRITTERS 161
372. STIR-FRIED SQUASH 162
373. CAULIFLOWER HASH BROWN 162
374. SWEET POTATO PUREE 162
375. CURRIED OKRA 162
376. VEGETABLE POTPIE 163
377. GRILLED EGGPLANT ROLL-UPS 163

CHAPTER 11: VEGAN 165

378. EGGPLANT GRATIN 165
379. VEGGIE STUFFED PEPPERS 165
380. CHEESY GRATIN ZUCCHINI 166
381. KOREAN BARBECUE TOFU 166
382. COLLARD GREEN WRAP 166
383. ZUCCHINI GARLIC FRIES 167
384. STIR-FRIED EGGPLANT 167
385. SAUTÉED GARLIC MUSHROOMS 167
386. STIR-FRIED ASPARAGUS AND BELL PEPPER 168
387. WILD RICE WITH SPICY CHICKPEAS 168
388. CASHEW PESTO & PARSLEY WITH VEGGIES 168
389. SPICY CHICKPEAS WITH ROASTED VEGETABLES .169
390. SPECIAL VEGETABLE KITCHREE 169
391. MASHED SWEET POTATO BURRITOS 170

CHAPTER 12: SNACK 172

392. HOMEMADE GUACAMOLE 172
393. LEMONY BERRY GUMMIES 172
394. CARROT AND PUMPKIN SEED CRACKERS 172
395. ZUCCHINI CHIPS 173

396.	Butternut Squash Fries	173
397.	White Fish Ceviche with Avocado	173
398.	Massaged Kale Chips	174
399.	Almond Yogurt, Berry, and Walnut Parfait	174
400.	Buckwheat Waffles	174
401.	Simple Coconut Pancakes	175
402.	Coconut Rice with Dates, Almonds, and Blueberries	175
403.	Mandarin Cottage Cheese	175
404.	Candied Dates	176
405.	Berry Delight	176
406.	Blueberry & Chia Flax Seed Pudding	176
407.	Spicy Roasted Chickpeas	176
408.	Berry Energy Bites	177
409.	Roasted Beets	177
410.	Bruschetta	177
411.	Cashew Cheese	177
412.	Low Cholesterol-Low Calorie Blueberry Muffin	178
413.	Carrot Sticks with Avocado Dip	178
414.	Boiled Okra and Squash	178
415.	Oven Crisp Sweet Potato	178
416.	Olive and Tomato Balls	179
417.	Mini Pepper Nachos	179
418.	Avocado Hummus	180
419.	Flavorsome Almonds	180
420.	Chewy Blackberry Leather	180
421.	Party-Time Chicken Nuggets	181
422.	Protein-Packed Croquettes	181
423.	Energy Dates Balls	181
424.	Energetic Oat Bars	182
425.	Bell Pepper Veggie Wraps	182
426.	Vegetable Nuggets	182
427.	Turmeric Muffins	183
428.	Quinoa Tortillas	183
429.	Steamed Cauliflower	184
430.	Saucy Brussels Sprouts and Carrots	184
431.	Steamed Purple Sweet Potatoes	184
432.	Mexican Veggie Meat	184
433.	Flaxseed Crackers	185
434.	Buckwheat Crackers	185
435.	Zucchini Slices	185
436.	Easy Zucchini Snack	186
437.	Cumin Zucchini Spread	186
438.	Celery Spread	186
439.	Stuffed Mushrooms	186
440.	Simple Mango Salsa	187
441.	Spicy Kale Chips	187
442.	Green Bean Snack	187
443.	Avocado and Pepper Hummus	187
444.	Easy Veggie Stuffed Mushrooms	188
445.	Sesame Spread	188
446.	Easy Eggplant Spread	188
447.	Creamy Artichoke Spread	188
448.	Balsamic Onion Snack	189
449.	Lentil and Mushrooms Cakes	189

CHAPTER 13: DESSERT 191

450.	After's Apple Cinnamon Chips	191
451.	Avocado Choco Cake	191
452.	Sweet Strawberry Sorbet	192
453.	Rum Butter Cookies	192
454.	Sherbet Pineapple	192
455.	Spicy Popper Mug Cake	192
456.	Strawberry Granita	193
457.	Strawberry Ice Cream	193
458.	Strawberry Orange Sorbet	193
459.	Strawberry Shortcake	194
460.	Sweet Almond and Coconut Fat Bombs	194
461.	The Most Elegant Parsley Soufflé Ever	194
462.	Tropical Fruit Crisp	194
463.	Tropical Popsicles	195
464.	Turmeric Milkshake	195
465.	Vanilla Cakes	195
466.	Yummy Fruity Ice-Cream	196
467.	Refreshing Raspberry Jelly	196
468.	Citrus Strawberry Granita	196
469.	Coconut Butter Fudge	197
470.	Comforting Baked Rice Pudding	197
471.	Cookie Dough Bites	197
472.	Creamy Frozen Yogurt	197
473.	Lemon Vegan Cake	198
474.	Dark Chocolate Granola Bars	198
475.	Blueberry Crisp	199
476.	Chocolate Chip Quinoa Granola Bars	199
477.	Apple Fritters	199
478.	Roasted Bananas	200
479.	Berry-Banana Yogurt	200
480.	Avocado Chocolate Mousse	200
481.	Anti-Inflammatory Apricot Squares	200
482.	Raw Black Forest Brownies	201
483.	Berry Parfait	201
484.	Easy Peach Cobbler	201
485.	Salts Peanut Butter Cookies	201
486.	Almond Butter Balls Vegan	202
487.	Coffee Cream	202
488.	Almond Cookies	202
489.	Chocolate Mousse	203
490.	Raspberry Diluted Frozen Sorbet	203
491.	Chocolate Covered Strawberries	203
492.	Coconut Muffins	203
493.	Chocolate Cherry Chia Pudding	204
494.	Pineapple Cake	204
495.	Mediterranean Rolled Baklava with Walnuts	204
496.	Mint Chocolate Chip Ice Cream	205
497.	Flourless Sweet Potato Brownies	205
498.	Paleo Raspberry Cream Pie	206
499.	Caramelized Pears	206
500.	Berry Ice Pops	207

7 WEEKS (49 DAYS) MEAL PLAN 209

BONUS: INTRODUCTION TO 15 TOP ANTI-INFLAMMATORY HERBS 214

CONCLUSION 216

Introduction

Do you suffer from inflammation? Did you know that the diet choices you make can have a huge impact on how your body deals with extreme stress? Anti-Inflammation Diet is a Lifestyle.

The results can be life-changing. For example, we recently discovered that the quality of your sleep is totally affected by how healthy your gut is. We also learned that choosing to eat a high-quality diet is the only way you can have complete control over inflammation. Not only are meals high in anti-inflammatory foods designed to improve your health, but they are also designed to help you achieve the best night's sleep of your life.

Diet has been directly linked to a person's health. If you are looking for ways to improve your diet and reduce the inflammation in your body, an anti-inflammatory diet might be the solution that works best for you.

An anti-inflammatory diet is made up of foods that have been proven to reduce inflammation while still providing all essential nutrients. These include vegetables, fruits, nuts and seeds, whole grains and beans, healthy proteins like fish or poultry, herbs, and spices that may help fight inflammation, such as turmeric or ginger. It also includes spices like salt or pepper, which have been shown to be anti-inflammatory.

You probably don't even know what the term "inflammation" means, but if you suffer from joint pain or are trying to reduce your risk of heart disease, it's a good idea to be familiar with this word. When you injure yourself, or an external strain (like a tight muscle) causes damage to your body, a chemical reaction occurs that is known as inflammation. This allows blood vessels to dilate so that the injured area can be supplied with blood by the body's circulation system. The resulting heat and swelling are signals for the immune system to send enzymes and white blood cells to fight off infection or repair damaged cells.

Inflammation is an important indicator of the body's status. It indicates when something's wrong, but it can also be a response to a lot of foods and lifestyle changes that normal healthy people encounter every day.

The most extreme form of inflammation is Critical Diffuse Inflammatory Demyelination Disease (CDID), a rare condition in which areas of the nervous system are affected, causing problems with memory, coordination, and mood. Most people don't suffer from CDID, but there are some diseases that cause chronic inflammation that you may want to avoid. They include rheumatoid arthritis, lupus, multiple sclerosis, and irritable bowel syndrome.

Inflammation and the resulting pain are thought to be one of the factors that cause depression. And, finally – in case you didn't already know this – inflammation is a big part of weight gain, too. As I've said a number of times throughout this website (the most recent being here), excess fat cells in your body release inflammatory cytokines that can cause oxidative stress and damage your DNA. The damage caused by these chemicals is then passed down through your cell's DNA, which can lead to an increased risk of degenerative diseases.

To make matters worse, the inflammatory response is also tied to your body's stress response. When your body recognizes a stressful situation, it sends out chemicals called glucocorticoids into the bloodstream. This causes inflammation throughout the body in an attempt to increase fighting capacities by reducing pain sensitivity and increasing alertness.

Inflammation and stress go hand-in-hand. If you reduce one, you can mitigate the other.

In general, foods that are rich in pro-inflammatory agents are those that are high in fats and simple sugars. Processed foods, refined carbs, and non-organic dairy products are also extremely inflammatory. On the other hand, foods loaded with anti-inflammatory agents are those that are anti-oxidant rich (like grapefruits and blueberries), have anti-inflammatory properties (like ginger), or contain a lot of omega-3 fatty acids.

For the most part, diet is one of the best ways to decrease inflammation. Not only do you avoid eating inflammatory foods like refined sugar, but you can also substitute foods that contain ingredients that invoke an anti-inflammatory response in your body. Combined with a regular exercise routine, you can expect to see an improvement in your overall health.

Introduction

As I've already mentioned, there are certain foods that have properties that fight inflammation. In the following list of foods, you'll find examples of foods high in omega-3s (like salmon), anti-oxidants (like blueberries), and anti-inflammatory spices (like ginger).

My Story

The Anti-Inflammatory Diet, an Elixir of Long Life!

In my first Dash Diet Cookbook, I explain how I improved my health and body weight and solved many problems after meeting Amanda, a life coach, at a seminar. I was 26 years old at the time. This extraordinary woman turned out to be a wellspring of knowledge, not only in the DASH Diet but especially in natural diets that strengthen the immune system, and reduce inflammation and muscle and joint pain such as the Anti-Inflammatory Diet, an extremely healthy evergreen diet that if understood and applied correctly can be considered a real elixir of life!

The Meeting That Changed My Life!

Amanda, who was 47 at the time, told me how her success was due to balancing her emotions and food. She often told me that conflicting emotions such as fear and conflict are 'food' that we create unconsciously and that they have a detrimental impact on our choice of junk food (inflammatory) and therefore on our health, including the weakening of the immune system with its associated bone, joint, digestive and genito-urinary problems. Rebalancing the emotional state, combined with healthy, expertly prepared food, is the key to optimal health that lasts. Amanda, as well as being a highly trained Life Coach in different types of diets and recipes, is also an expert in yoga, meditation and mindful breathing.

The Anti-Inflammatory Diet, a Solution to Many Health Problems

In fact, after becoming well established with the DASH Diet, I decided to learn more about the benefits of the Anti-Inflammatory Diet, not only by studying in books but also by traveling abroad and attending schools and seminars. The reason for this choice was due both to a personal need to improve my health and prevent many ailments, especially as I get older (I am 50), and to help many of my relatives, friends, and clients who were suffering from immune deficiency, osteoarticular problems such as gout, arthritis, arthritis and rheumatic pain, inflammatory stomach and genito-urinary disorders. Seeing them suffer made me sad, especially when they told me their stories of wandering around for years in clinics and specialists and not having their problems solved. On the contrary, the problems persisted, affecting their sleep, mood, motor activity and fear of degenerative diseases, with harmful consequences on their lives.

Well, I am happy to have helped so many of these people who have turned to me, trusting me and scrupulously following my dietary and lifestyle advice. Many of them have not only solved most of their health problems but have also ignited that inner flame of LIFE that now makes them confident and more loving towards themselves and their loved ones. In short, those who have persevered, despite the initial difficulties, have transformed their lives into something wonderful. In fact, the true concept of health is not just having a healthy body and mind, but having healthy relationships with those who love to share the same experiences in a loving way.

Tasty Recipes and Natural Herbs Also for Weight Loss

Thanks in part to Amanda, with whom I have maintained friendly and professional relationships for years now, I have succeeded over time in creating tasty and healthy recipes, many of which I can consider real superfoods, aimed at nourishing, detoxifying and regenerating the immune system and all related organs, and promoting weight loss. I have combined these simple, tasty and healthy recipes with 15 TOP natural anti-inflammatory herbs that can boost and accelerate the beneficial effects of the recipes. This last idea I wanted to give you as a BONUS, as it is the result of the experience I have gained over the years in the field of herbal medicine and which I would like you to use for your health. In fact, some of these herbs naturally activate the metabolism, helping you to lose weight and get into great shape if they are combined correctly with the recipes, as I recommend in the book!

Take Good Care of Your Body!

Mens sana in corpore sano! This is a statement by the ancient Latins that shows us that to heal the body well, you must also heal the mind well. In fact, my journey with the Anti-Inflammatory Diet has also strengthened my mind. The body is the mirror of the mind and vice versa. Both produce healthy emotions when they are in balance. And emotions are 'food' for the body and the mind. And this is why I have introduced meditation and conscious breathing into my lifestyle, as well as moderate but constant physical activity, such as long walks in contact with nature, in parks, in the hills, in the mountains, and by the sea to feel one with Mother Nature. This is our natural dimension, to live healthy and happy!

Chapter 1
What Is Inflammation?

Inflammation is the body's reaction when we get an injury or infection. It is the body's way of protecting itself from further damage and invading organisms by creating an inflammatory response. Inflammation, at its worst, can have a minor inconvenience as it relates to injuries, but at its best can help us fight sickness and disease.

It is the body's natural response to tissue damage caused by infections or foreign substances that enter the body. The inflammatory process is intended to promote healing and fight against the disease. However, in some cases, it can cause severe pain, disable movement, and result in loss of organs or tissue damage if not treated correctly.

Inflammation is caused by the immune system, the system that detects and attacks harmful organisms. When an injury occurs, minor or severe, the body will begin to form an inflammatory response. This response aids in healing itself; however, if left unchecked, it can cause further damage to other tissues in the body.

Types of inflammation include:

- Acute inflammation: it is the initial response to any harmful foreign agent. It starts with blood platelets and white blood cells, then neutrophils which can kill bacteria. As the body heals, the neutrophils begin to clean up the wound, and it is ultimately replaced with macrophages that form scar tissue.

- Chronic inflammation: This occurs when acute inflammation drags on for too long or is not treated correctly. As bacteria and other foreign agents enter the body, the body produces substances that cause inflammation. The outcome is that the white blood cells begin to react, increasing their number and leading to more complications.

- Chronic inflammatory diseases: Diseases such as rheumatoid arthritis, lupus, and multiple sclerosis are characterized by chronic inflammation. Anti-inflammatory drugs can treat chronic inflammation with anti-inflammatory drugs; medical advice should always be taken as the severity of these conditions differs from case to case.

What Is the Difference Between Inflammation and Acute Inflammation?

The reaction of the body to a dangerous stimulus is called inflammation. There are four types of inflammatory response: bronchitis, dermatitis, gastritis, and proctitis.

Acute inflammation reacts to an irritant, such as a chemical or a bacterial or viral infection. It can generally be resolved using anti-inflammatory medications. Chronic inflammation is caused by repetitive physical force and injury, leading to back pain and other discomforts. In addition, chronic inflammation can lead to other severe conditions, such as fibromyalgia and arthritis, where you may need to see a physician for treatment options that aid in healing and pain relief.

Acute inflammation can lead to chronic inflammation, meaning that the body will react by forming scar tissue. For example, scar tissue may develop in the lungs, heart muscle, or blood vessels, preventing them from functioning correctly.

Acute inflammation occurs because of a dangerous foreign agent, and chronic inflammation occurs when the body is injured too many times and does not properly heal. As a result, the body will eventually scar, causing damage to other parts of the body where it is located.

The body's natural defense system causes inflammation and acute inflammation. It is the body's way of protecting itself from foreign agents and bacteria while at the same time creating scar tissue that prevents further damage to other parts of the body.

What Does Chronic Inflammation Consist Of?

The term chronic inflammation refers to a process that occurs when inflammation is long-term. It's characterized by swelling, pain, redness, and heat. The most common types are caused by the body fighting off infections or foreign objects. However, there are examples of long-term chronic inflammation outside these examples as well.

Chronic inflammation can lead to severe illnesses such as heart disease, depending on the severity of what's causing it. In addition, chronic inflammation causes further tissue damage, gut disorders, hormonal disorders, and genetic predisposition.

The causes of chronic inflammation involve a variety of different factors. While the inflammatory response is a good thing for the body to fight off infection, it can become a problem when it occurs incorrectly or lasts too long. While avoiding conditions is one thing, other factors can cause chronic inflammation.

Chronic inflammation is often associated with an increase in the levels of the inflammatory marker, C-reactive protein (CRP). It occurs when there is an immune response outside of a typical injury or tissue damage within the body. When this happens, inflammation can become chronic by causing multiple tissue damages over time.

Chronic inflammation can occur if no injuries are sustained. It is because inflammation causes damage to blood vessels and tissues by causing angiogenic (blood vessel) injury and tissue cell death. It can cause chronic inflammation to occur over time. When this happens, the immune system will see damaged tissue or no tissue, causing inflammation to become long-term.

Tissue damages caused by chronic inflammation are not the only causes of chronic inflammation. So is an underlying disease that can cause inflammation too. It can be due to certain diseases that lead to chronic inflammatory conditions, or it can be because certain foods impact how the immune system reacts within the body.

There are many causes of chronic inflammation. Some of them can occur because of a response to injury or injury within the body. Other causes of chronic inflammation include:

- Injury: Any changes in tissue structures can cause an inflammatory reaction. When this happens, the body produces chemicals that trigger inflammation. It often occurs when the body repairs itself from an injury within tissue or cells that cause an immune reaction.

- Gut disorders: When the body is trying to repair itself after an injury, inflammation can occur because of some gut disorders or changes in gut flora (gut bacteria). These can cause chronic inflammation to occur.

- Hormones: These are chemicals that the body makes by glands throughout the body. When a hormone is produced, it can cause an inflammatory reaction within the body. It often occurs within the following circumstances: When there is excessive hormone production – such as chronic stress – or an infection that causes inflammation – such as bacterial vaginosis – the immune system calls for help from certain chemicals to heal itself.

What Causes Discomfort Caused By Chronic Inflammation?

Inflammation responses if we get injury or illness naturally. It's meant to help the body heal. Acute inflammation is usually temporary, but chronic inflammation is different because it can last for months, even years. It can flare up at seemingly random times and cause persistent pain, swelling, redness, or other symptoms that are often ignored until they are too severe to ignore any longer.

The problem with chronic inflammatory diseases—aside from the obvious fact that they hurt—is that they don't always leave behind apparent clues about what's causing them.

Mild, low-grade inflammation is relatively standard. Even a healthy organ may have a bit of inflammation going on at all times. But if the cause of the rash does not go away, it eventually causes chronic inflammation.

Chronic inflammation can take all sorts of problems, including heart disease, osteoarthritis, and various cancers. If left untreated, it can also cause autoimmune diseases such as lupus and rheumatoid arthritis.

Chronic inflammation does not have to be serious. This type of inflammation can cause mild discomfort, but it can also cause more severe conditions, such as heart disease, Crohn's disease, or arthritis.

What Causes Chronic Inflammation?

Understanding chronic inflammation can be complicated because it's different for each person. The cause of the rash may not be the same in every case. It is one reason why there is no specific medication that can treat it.

Some people who have allergies may feel pain when they are allergic to certain things, like pollen, dust, mold, or animal hair. People who have seasonal allergies may experience this type of pain in their eyes or nose during allergy season.

People who have arthritis may have flare-ups in the winter when their bodies produce more inflammatory chemicals. They may also have flare-ups around the same time every year. Seasonal allergies and arthritis are two examples of inflammatory conditions caused by environmental factors.

In other cases, chronic inflammation is caused by a medical condition. For example, in people with Crohn's disease or ulcerative colitis, food allergies can be a factor in causing inflammation that causes pain in the intestines. Other causes may include a medical condition, such as lupus or rheumatoid arthritis.

One of the most underrated causes is stress, affecting the immune system and leading to inflammation. People affected by chronic stress may notice that flare-ups happen around the same time every year, which is when they are most stressed out. It can be caused by changes in seasons, holidays, death in the family, relationship problems, work issues, or financial problems.

The common symptoms of acute and chronic inflammation are pain and fever. The difference between the two is that fevers usually go away after a few days, while pain may last longer.

Swelling is another symptom of inflammation. Joints, such as the knees and elbows, often swell in people with arthritis. This can be particularly painful for people who move their joints often or exercise at the gym.

Skin rashes are another symptom that affects several different inflammatory conditions, including allergies and skin irritations to food or other substances. The most usual skin rashes are caused by irritation from insect bites, plant allergy, poison ivy, poison oak, or poison sumac. Less common are skin rashes caused by asthma or some other type of chronic illness.

Symptoms of Chronic Inflammation

Inflammation is a chronic condition that causes redness, swelling, and pain. Although inflammation is usually a healthy response to injury, the process may get out of hand, leading to an increased risk for heart disease and tissue damage. We will explore the symptoms of chronic inflammation and ways to control it through lifestyle changes.

Many of the symptoms associated with chronic inflammation can be hard to deal with. They may include things like fatigue, persistent aches, pain, or swelling that does not go away, or they can be more serious. In addition, many of the symptoms of chronic inflammation become progressively worse. As a result, people with these symptoms can feel significant fatigue after a short period or think they are getting worse.

Symptoms of chronic inflammation include:

- Canker sores, common mouth sores caused by the herpes simplex virus
- Rheumatoid arthritis, a disease that causes pain and swelling in multiple joints and tissue throughout the body
- Fatigue and loss of energy, which often lead to poor health and weight gain
- High cholesterol levels, which may lead to heart disease or stroke
- Headaches and migraines
- Mood swings, irritability, or difficulty concentrating
- Stomach aches or abdominal pain, which can also indicate irritable bowel syndrome (IBS)
- Skin conditions such as eczema or psoriasis
- Joint pain in the hands, feet, knees, hips, elbows, shoulders, back, or neck
- Breathing problems such as asthma or chronic obstructive pulmonary disorder (COPD)
- Rashes
- Dizziness, nausea, or joint pain
- Difficulty swallowing
- Unexplained weight loss

- Trouble eating or a change in eating habits
- Unusual feelings of tiredness or "brain fog"
- More frequent or intense dreams, nightmares, or unusual desires
- Strange or unpleasant body odor
- Unusual hair loss
- Changes to the shape, size, or position of body parts
- Changes in menstruation or fertility
- Swelling in the legs that are hard to move, numbness, tingling, or pain that's worse when you're standing up
- Joint stiffness, especially after exercise or injury
- Bone fractures
- The development of a tumor
- Redness, swelling, warmth, or pain in any part of the body
- Blood in the stool
- Rectal bleeding or bloody stools
- Muscle aches or cramps that are usually worse when you wake up or after exercise
- Intense thirst or dry mouth
- Metallic taste in your mouth
- White patches inside your mouth or on your tongue

Fatigue

If the inflammation is continuous, the fatigue can be debilitating, and many people cannot work or study because of their lack of energy. They may also feel chronically run down, generally without the motivation to do much at all.

Chronic Pain

Chronic inflammatory disorders are often accompanied by inflammation throughout the body, leading to pain in various body parts at different times. The pain may be continual, or it may come and go.

Thin Skin

Skin inflammation can lead to the formation of scales or sores on the surface of the skin. Psoriasis can be an example of this in which small red bumps appear, develop into plaques that are covered with silvery scales, and then dry up and form crusty patches on the skin.

Abdominal Pain

In its most critical form, it can lead to severe abdomen swelling that impedes movement and breathing. It may also lead to a severe intestinal infection that requires hospitalization or urgent surgical treatment.

When the inflammation is sustained over an extended time, the ability to work may be significantly limited. It may dramatically reduce the quality of life of a person due to chronic fatigue or pain.

Health Risk of Anti-Inflammation

Anti-inflammatory medications are prescribed to reduce symptoms of inflammation in the body. The medication works by blocking or neutralizing factors that cause inflammation in various parts of the body. However, it is essential to know that anti-inflammation drugs are not without risks, most notably an increased risk for heart attack and stroke.

The health risks associated with anti-inflammatories include:

- Heart attack: Taking anti-inflammatory drugs increases your risk of having a heart attack by 18%. If you've been taking anti-inflammatories for three years, you have a 23% higher risk for heart disease. In addition, doctors say that the heart protection offered by aspirin is less effective in people who regularly take anti-inflammatory drugs.

- Stroke: People who take one type of anti-inflammatory medication called a COX 2 inhibitor have a 24% higher risk for stroke. Additionally, people who take corticosteroids are at risk for hemorrhagic stroke.

- Kidney damage: A study of almost 90,000 patients found that those taking anti-inflammatories were 25% more likely to develop kidney damage.

- Pneumonia: A study of people who had recently been hospitalized for pneumonia shows that those who took anti-inflammatory medications were 34% more likely to die from the illness within six months.

- Impaired wound healing: A recent study of people who had undergone colon surgery found that those taking COX 2 inhibitors were twice as likely to have an incisional surgical site infection. Another recent study of people with gout showed that those who took ibuprofen for three weeks after surgery had slower healing times, with more than twice as much pain on movement.

- Congestive heart failure: When our heart is unable to pump blood effectively—more than half of people who have this illness die within five years. A recent study shows that those with chronic heart failure are prescribed anti-inflammatories more than twice as often as those without.

- Rheumatoid arthritis: People with rheumatoid arthritis are more likely to take anti-inflammatories for pain than those with other types of arthritis. Moreover, they are expected to be hospitalized for gastrointestinal reflux when the stomach acid backs up the throat or esophagus.

- Eye damage: A recent study of over 100,000 patients found that people who took anti-inflammatories for arthritis or asthma were 60% more likely to develop cataracts. Similarly, people who take high doses of NSAIDs are almost twice as likely to develop macular degeneration, which is damage to the macula in the eye.

- Blood clots: Anti-inflammatories increase your risk for blood clots by anywhere from 50% to 400%. Those who take anti-inflammatories have a three times greater risk of developing a blood clot in the leg or arm.

- Infections: Anti-inflammatories can damage your natural defenses against infections by somehow inhibiting the immune system. A recent study of cancer patients found that those who take antimicrobial drugs have much higher hospitalization rates due to urinary tract infections and pneumonia.

- Weight gain: Weight gain can be caused by taking anti-inflammatories for arthritis or asthma. The most commonly prescribed anti-inflammatories are NSAIDs (non-steroidal anti-inflammatory drugs), including over 30 different medications. Over 50% of all adults in the US take an NSAID for at least one week every year.

- Blood Sugar: Taking anti-inflammatories can cause blood sugar to either rise or fall by as much as 40 mg within one week of taking them.

- Pregnancy complications: Women who take aspirin or other anti-inflammatories during pregnancy increase their risk of miscarriage. Additionally, the use of anti-inflammatories during pregnancy causes preterm birth and low birth weight.

- Cognitive deficits: Older adults who take NSAIDs are almost twice as likely to develop Alzheimer's disease. This risk is compounded when people take high doses of the medications every day for long periods.

- Headaches: Headaches are a usual neurological disorder that affects a large percentage of the population. Headaches can be classified in many different ways, such as when it occurs (such as primary or secondary), when pain is experienced (acute or chronic), and the severity (mild, moderate, or severe).

The Guidelines for the Anti-Inflammatory Diet

The anti-inflammatory diet is designed to reduce the levels of inflammation in your body by eating whole foods rich in omega-three fats, vitamins, ginger, turmeric, and other spices.

The primary basis of this diet is to eliminate or reduce the intake of foods that may cause inflammation, such as dairy products (milk, cheese, yogurt), gluten (wheat, spelled, rye and barley), and some refined sugar, coffee, and alcohol.

Anti-Inflammatory Diet Guidelines

1. Avoid Sugar and Processed Foods

Sugar can be very inflammatory to the body because it releases stress hormones like cortisol. Sugar and processed foods can also increase systemic inflammation by spiking insulin levels and altering hormone function.

2. Eat More

- Fish: Wild salmon, mackerel, herring, and others that contain omega-3 fatty acids.
- Leafy greens: Kale, spinach, collard greens, and others.
- Nuts: Walnuts or pecans are especially heart-healthy.
- Flaxseed: Ground up and sprinkled on yogurt or in baking recipes.
- Vegetables: Broccoli, cauliflower, and Brussels sprouts.
- Whole grains: Barley, rye, and oat bran are perfect for reducing inflammation.
- Beans: Lentils, chickpeas, beans, and others are known to boost antioxidants in the body.
- Herbs: Rosemary, turmeric (known to reduce pain), and others.

3. Drink More Water

Water is the most acceptable way to flush out toxins and cleanse your body. Water can also help the absorption of nutrients in foods, which helps feed all your cells and keep your metabolism running at an efficient pace. Another reason to drink plenty of water is that it helps to dilute the salts in your food, which doesn't help much with inflammation (The Arthritis Foundation).

4. Avoid Processed Foods

Processed foods contain preservatives that are associated with inflammation, especially in the joints. These additives can include sodium nitrate, sodium benzoate, and others (Harvard Health Publications). These preservatives kill off good bacteria, leading to an overall increase in inflammation.

5. Eat More Omega-3 Fats

Having an omega-3 intake that's high enough to reduce symptoms of the disease is often difficult because you need to consume at least two servings of fish per week. However, you can still increase your intake by eating more nuts and seeds and using flaxseed and ground-up flaxseed in recipes. You can as well take a fish oil or flaxseed supplement to ensure that you're getting enough omega-3 fatty acids.

6. Eat More Whole Grains

Whole grains such as barley, rye, and oat bran contain soluble fiber, which helps reduce cholesterol levels in the body.

7. Eat More Beans

Not only do beans contain a lot of fiber, but they also contain antioxidants and soluble fiber. They're also deficient in fat and calories.

8. Drink Herbal Teas

Some herbal teas like turmeric tea (known to reduce pain) and rosemary tea (known to relieve inflammation) can be consumed as often as you like (The Arthritis Foundation).

9. Eat More Fruit

Fruit is an anti-inflammatory, antioxidant food because it's high in antioxidants. It can also have a powerful detoxifying effect on the body, which is important because inflammation can be a source of toxins that need to be purged from your system.

Tips for the Anti-Inflammatory Diet

The anti-inflammatory diet: A way of eating that reduces inflammation and promotes gut health. It's not a fad diet but rather a mindful approach to what we eat, one that strives to correct digestive problems and reduce pain while maintaining a healthy weight. In addition, this approach offers relief from chronic conditions such as arthritis, acne, psoriasis, asthma, and even cancer.

The diet provides relief for many conditions without the use of drugs. It is also a diet where you don't have to count calories, weigh portions or track food choices. It makes it easy to follow compared to most other diets. It's simply about eating the right foods that heal, not hurt your body.

The diet also benefits individuals who suffer from food sensitivities and allergies and those with digestive disorders such as diarrhea. Here, we'll go over some tips for navigating the anti-inflammatory diet lifestyle.

Avoid White Food

Avoiding white food such as sugar, salt, etc., can help maintain and control the average blood sugar level. Instead, try to add more lean proteins and high-fiber food to your daily diet. It can be thin types of meat, brown rice, and whole grains.

An Apple a Day Keeps the Doctors Away

Add vegetables, fruits, nuts, and spices to your daily meal plan. For example, garlic, ginger, cinnamon, and lemon will help to boost your immune system and reduce inflammation.

Do Sport Daily

Regular sports activities can help to prevent inflammation. Make 5 to 10-minute sports exercises daily to feel healthier.

Balance Your Mind

Everyday stress leads to the most chronic diseases. Meditation or biofeedback are excellent ways to balance your mind and manage stress.

Choose Suitable Proteins

Lean red meat can be served as a protein source, but it is still high in cholesterol and salt. Instead of it, choose fish such as halibut, salmon, tuna, cod, or seabass. They are rich in omega-3 fatty acids.

Drink Antioxidant Beverages

Herbs are a substantial source of antioxidants and promote faster treatment. Basil, thyme, oregano, chili pepper, and curcumin have high anti-inflammatory features and serve as natural painkillers.

Control the Sleeping Time

8 to 9 hours for sleeping should be a rule for you. Less sleep and oversleeping are the primary triggers for heart disease and 2-type diabetes.

Cross Out Alcohol from Your Diet

Refusing alcohol helps to make the body calm and reduces the risk of inflammation.

Choose Green Tea Instead of Coffee and Tea

Green tea can fight free radical damage. For example, regular drinking of green tea lowers the risk of cancer and Alzheimer's disease.

Take Probiotics

Probiotics are a type of bacteria that can naturally colonize the intestinal tract and regulate the immune system. They have a positive effect on both gastrointestinal and immune health.

Add Spices to Your Food

Spices such as cinnamon help to promote healthy digestion through their anti-inflammatory components, as well as their painkilling properties, for example, black pepper, and ginger root.

Eat More Plant-Based Foods

The anti-inflammatory diet focuses on the consumption of fresh vegetables and fruit, which are rich in antioxidants and nutrients.

Be a Bit Kinder to Yourself

The anti-inflammatory diet can be a bit limiting, but it's not about going to extremes. If you're going to take a walk, go for a brisk walk rather than power walking for 30 minutes.

Take Probiotics for Anti-Inflammatory Purposes

Antioxidants found in certain probiotics can help to reduce the levels of inflammatory proteins that cause joint pain and joint inflammation.

Freshness Matters More than the Color of the Vegetable

The leading causes of inflammation are unhealthy storage of food, excessive exposure to light, and exposure to pesticides. For this reason, buy locally grown foods as much as possible, preferably organic or even biodynamic sprouts or berries if possible.

Foods to Eat and to Avoid

It's no secret that diet is a significant influence on the development of inflammation. Chronic inflammation may be a leading cause of many different diseases such as cancer, heart disease, and diabetes. An anti-inflammatory diet aims to help fight off these chronic illnesses by limiting food items that may cause inflammation in the body. These foods could include sugar, processed foods, and red meat, among others. Sugar increases the risk of inflammation in the body by making insulin less effective and reducing its potency. Sugar also causes an increase in sugar production that ultimately leads to a spike in inflammation.

Red meat is considered a red flag for increasing inflammation because it contains compounds called saturated fats and cholesterol, which can both promote inflammation. In addition, these two types of fats are often associated with other health problems such as high cholesterol and heart disease, leading to heart attack or stroke.

Do you suffer from chronic inflammation? It's possible that what you're eating could be causing it. Many different foods can trigger inflammation, and it might be a good idea to cut them out of your diet to start feeling better. Below is a handy list of foods that have been known to cause inflammation and ones that have anti-inflammatory properties.

Inflammation can be caused by various factors, ranging from stress to infections to the kind of food you're eating. So, the doctors recommend to people with chronic inflammatory conditions, like rheumatoid arthritis, receive anti-inflammatory drugs to help their bodies heal. Occasionally it can be hard to determine which foods are causing inflammation, though.

Foods to Eat

An anti-inflammatory diet helps to calm down our body's immune response to allergic reactions. As a result, it combats the harmful effects triggered by exposure to toxins, allergens, bacteria, viruses, and fungi. Following is the list of inflammation-fighting ingredients.

- Omega-3 fatty acids (healthy fats). They are found in eggs, wild-caught fish, and grass-fed or pasture-raised meat cuts.
- Nuts and seeds, sunflower seeds, pumpkin seeds, chia seeds, almonds, walnuts, cashews, pistachio.
- Onions, ginger, garlic, bell peppers, pumpkin, and leeks.
- Leafy vegetables such as spinach, cauliflower, broccoli, kale, asparagus, Bok Choy, etc.
- Herbs such as rosemary, basil, oregano, parsley, etc.
- All types of berries, pineapple, apple, oranges, red grapes, etc.
- Whole grains such as brown rice, millets, quinoa, and oats.
- Healthy oils such as coconut oil, extra-virgin olive oil, avocado oil, and sesame oil.
- Lentils, beets, avocado, green tea, coconut, mushrooms, zucchini, and beans.
- Spices such as turmeric, cinnamon, black pepper, cumin, etc.
- Non-dairy milk products such as almond milk, coconut milk, etc.
- Red wine (In moderation).
- Honey, maple syrup, dark chocolate, and cacao powder.

Foods to Avoid

These are the following foods that trigger inflammation. Eliminate them from your everyday diet and clear them off your pantry shelves.

- Processed meats: They are loaded with saturated fats (sausage, hot dogs, burgers, steaks, etc.)
- Unhealthy fats including lard, margarine, and shortening.

- Sugar-added products (except for natural fruits): All canned products with added sugars such as soups, canned fruits, yogurts, bars, etc. Unsweetened canned fruits, tomatoes, etc., should be consumed in moderation.

- Sugar-based commercial drinks, beverages, and fruit juices.

- All processed and packaged foods: They are high in additives, artificial colors, and preservatives.

- Refined carbohydrates, including white bread, white pasta, and noodles.

- Foods containing trans fats: Commercially processed foods, fried foods, candies, ice creams, and baked items (cookies, crackers, pastries, cakes, muffins, etc.)

- Alcoholic beverages.

Chapter 2
Immune System

The immune system is central in preventing anti-inflammatory processes that also cause problems in the osteoarticular system such as osteoarthritis, arthritis, gout, rheumatism, chronic pain, and metabolic (weight gain).

The immune system can be divided into different systems:

- The humoral system involves antibodies. The body creates antibodies by itself to fight against infections (such as viruses, bacteria, parasites, and cancer) and to attack foreign molecules in the body. Antibodies are either secreted into the blood or stored in the spleen, bone marrow or lymph nodes.

- The adaptive immune system involves cells that are able to recognize specific molecules (antigens) on their surface. These self-composed receptors activate T-cell and B-cell cells that produce immunoglobulin which helps to prevent diseases and fight infections.

- The innate immune system is the first line of defense against all kinds of diseases and infections that your body is exposed to. This protection system is found in all organisms and consists of different kinds of cells, such as leukocytes, macrophages and dendritic cells. Innate immunity mainly responds to pathogen-associated molecular patterns (PAMPs) that are found in structures like bacteria or viruses (such as PAMPs from fungal cell walls). Innate immunity also includes the "natural killer" cells. In this role, NK cells destroy virally infected cells by releasing perforins which help to form pores in the cell membrane leading to programmed cell death (apoptosis) of cancer cells.

The adaptive immune system is also able to recognize PAMPs. Dysregulated adaptive immune responses are associated with type 1 diabetes mellitus, multiple sclerosis, and rheumatoid arthritis.

Immune-regulating cytokines bind to their receptors on the surface of certain immune cells and regulate the activity of those cells. These cytokines suppress or stimulate immune cell functions such as inflammation or hypersensitivity reactions.

The Osteoarticular System

The osteoarticular system is the junction of bones, joints, ligaments, and tendons which support our body's movement. It is an important component of our ability to function as well as maintain good health. The system also consists of other tissues such as cartilage and synovium in between movable joints. The ligaments and tendons are responsible for holding the bones together. The cartilage pads each joint to avoid friction while the synovium provides ample lubrication through a thick, slippery substance to aid movement.

Problems of the osteoarticular system include:

- Osteoarthritis
- Ankylosing spondylitis
- Fibromyalgia
- Rheumatoid arthritis.
- Gout

The osteoarticular system is one of the most important components of the body. It plays an important role in supporting bones and joints by preventing injuries. The joint cartilage aids in the absorption of shocks, like when a person falls down, which makes the bones less likely to break. The osteoarticular system is also responsible for maintaining mobility and flexibility. If any part of this system gets damaged, it will have an effect on movement and flexibility which can eventually lead to permanent changes in motion or even pain. When it comes to different types of osteoarticular pathologies, many people think that only rheumatologists should be able to identify them.

Solutions to the osteoarticular system include:

- Diet: The most important diet is to control hypertension and high cholesterol which can lead to osteoarticular problems. Low levels of sodium, potassium, and calcium are also causes of osteoarthritis. Eating more protein and iron can help with weight loss and blood pressure control.

- Exercise: In order for joints to work properly a person needs proper exercise, exercise prevents pain by providing needed oxygen supply to the muscles as well as maintaining flexibility. Even with proper exercise balance is needed so that the body doesn't fall over when walking or running, if this happens then it will affect movement in some way which may lead to further injury or pain.

- Medication: The main kind of medication for the osteoarticular system is painkillers. These medications reduce pain by blocking the chemical signals which carry pain between nerve endings in the body.

- Surgery: Surgery is only performed in extreme cases like where a person has dislocated a joint or if one of the bones is severely broken, before every surgery doctor will take proper x-rays to see what treatment is best for that person.

The osteoarticular system plays an important role in maintaining health and is a vital component for the proper functioning of the body as well as movement and flexibility.

Arthrosis, Arthritis, Gout and Pain.

No one likes to talk about gout, but this perhaps lesser-known disease can be as debilitating as it is painful. Arthritis and pain are often associated with aging, but they don't have to become a way of life. A healthy lifestyle and diet can help reduce the risk of contracting arthritis or gout later in life, as well as provide relief for those who already suffer from these chronic conditions. Here's what you need to know about arthrosis, arthritis, and gout.

Arthrosis is a general term used to describe joint pain. One symptom of arthrosis is arthritis. The two terms are often used interchangeably, but in fact, are different. Arthritis can also be called osteoarthritis or degenerative arthritis; it is a chronic condition that affects the joints and causes pain and stiffness. Gout is not a disease, but one of the symptoms of uric acid buildup in the blood. Gout attacks usually result from an accumulation of uric acid crystals in the joints, causing severe pain, inflammation and swelling.

Arthrosis forms when articular cartilage wears down over time, causing bones to rub against each other and become inflamed because there is no cushioning force between them. The simplest form of arthrosis is common arthritis but more severe forms can also result in a gout attack.

Gout attacks come on suddenly, with night sweats, fever, joint pain and swelling. While the symptoms are similar to those of arthrosis, gout is actually caused by a buildup of uric acid crystals in the joint. Acute gout attacks often present as acute arthritis that resolves with the elevation of the joint (joint mobilization) and/or with medications such as steroids or colchicine. Chronic gout may be present for many months or years before an attack occurs. Early recognition and treatment of gout attacks can prevent the long-term damage seen in acute gout.

You don't have to spend your life in pain. There are some easy lifestyle changes you can make that can reduce the risk of developing arthrosis, arthritis, or gout later in life, as well as help, reduce symptoms and discomfort if you already have one or more of these conditions.

How to Relieve Arthrosis, Arthritis and Gout

Arthrosis and gout can be eliminated by following the suggestions given on natural cures or supplements. It is necessary to take precautions when drinking alcohol or eating large amounts of red meat to avoid gout. It may also be wise not to eat pasta, bread or other grains that have been treated with chemicals of any kind. If you are suffering from arthrosis you should try to avoid all forms of stress as much as possible because it can contribute to inflammation and even trigger an attack.

Weight Loss - Problems and Solutions (Healing)

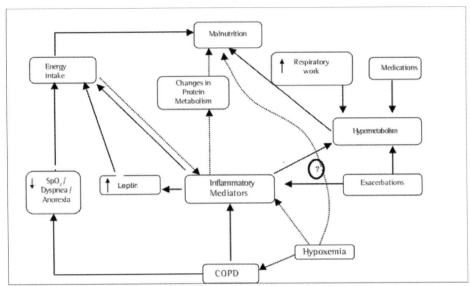

Weight loss and dieting are some of the most popular subjects on the internet and so it's no surprise that there are many misconceptions about how to lose weight. This blog post will go through some of the most common problems people have when trying to lose weight, as well as some practical solutions.

The first problem is that people often don't know what they're supposed to eat in order to lose weight. There is a lot of conflicting information out there, including tips like counting calories or restricting carbohydrates. But what actually matters if you want to lose weight? The answer is surprisingly easy: eat less than your body needs and move more than it does.

This is true for all three macronutrients (carbohydrates, proteins, and fats), but the exact needs differ depending on your age and activity level.

The second problem is that people get obsessed with losing weight and become emotionally attached to it. Some people try really hard to lose weight, but they fail and then get frustrated or angry. They may feel that their whole world has come crashing down around them or that they will never be able to wear certain clothes again. If you're going through this, it's important to remember that it's not the end of the world. Try to move on and keep thinking positively. If you find that a weight loss program isn't working, don't give up.

The third problem is that people refuse to accept advice from others or try a diet or exercise plan that has been recommended by someone else. It is a good idea to get advice from other people that have the same goals as you do. If you want to lose weight, there are probably some people out there who have had success losing weight and are willing to help.

The fourth problem is that people lose interest in their weight loss program if they aren't achieving their goal quickly enough. This makes it more likely that they will stop trying and start suffering other negative consequences of not losing weight.

Solutions

Some people have tried a diet or exercise program and achieved their weight loss goals. For some of these people, it was successful because they had a good eating plan with the right balance of carbohydrates, fats and proteins. This was enough to fuel them while they were losing weight, rather than starving themselves to lose weight. Another reason that diets work well is that there are people who will support you as you lose weight by encouraging you, giving tips or even offering extra help. A diet can also work well if it has a combination of healthy food and exercise that is tailored to your needs. If you need help with choosing the right diet for your situation, ask someone else for advice.

Stress Management

Stress management to counteract the anxiety that causes inflammatory processes, such as long walks in the open air, deep breathing and meditation; keep the body in gentle motion, consistently, to oxygenate it, along with the brain.

Chapter 3
Breakfast

1. Anti-Inflammatory Muffins

Preparation Time: 15 minutes

Cooking Time: 25 minutes

Servings: 12

Ingredients:

- 2 glasses almond flour
- ½ tsp sea salt
- 2 tsp aluminum-free baking powder
- 4 organic pasture-raised eggs
- 2 ripe bananas, mashed
- 1 cup organic-canned sweet potatoes
- ¼ cup essential olive oil
- 1 tsp ground turmeric
- 1 tsp ground ginger
- 1 tsp ground cinnamon

Directions:

1. Start by preheating the oven to 400°F and lining a muffin pan with 12 muffin liners.
2. Whisk the eggs and mix them with the extra virgin olive oil.
3. Mash the bananas and add them to the egg mixture.
4. Add the canned sweet potatoes.
5. Combine the almond flour with sea salt, baking powder, and spices in a separate bowl and stir.
6. Add the flour mixture to the wet ingredients while stirring until it smoothens.
7. Subdivide the amalgamation between the muffin liners.
8. Bake them for 20 to 25 minutes or until a toothpick is released clean.

Nutrition: Total Carbs: 14 g, Fiber: 4 g, Protein: 7 g, Total Fat: 17 g, Calories: 235

2. Savory Breakfast Pancakes

Preparation Time: 5 minutes

Cooking Time: 6 minutes

Servings: 4

Ingredients:

- ½ cup almond flour
- ½ cup tapioca flour
- 1 cup coconut milk
- ½ tsp chili powder
- ¼ tsp turmeric powder
- ½ red onion, chopped
- 1 handful cilantro leaves, chopped
- ½ inch ginger, grated
- 1 tsp salt
- ¼ tsp ground black pepper

Directions:

1. In a mixing bowl, mix all ingredients until well-combined.
2. Heat a pan on low medium heat and grease with oil.
3. Pour ¼ cup of batter onto the pan and spread the mixture to create a pancake.
4. Fry for 3 minutes per side.
5. Repeat until the batter is done.

Nutrition: Calories: 108, Total Fat: 2 g, Saturated Fat: 1 g, Total Carbs: 20 g, Net Carbs: 19.5 g, Protein: 2 g, Sugar: 4 g, Fiber: 0.5 g, Sodium: 37 mg, Potassium: 95 mg

3. Spinach Breakfast

Preparation Time: 10 minutes

Cooking Time: 35 minutes

Servings: 4

Ingredients:

- 2 sweet potatoes, peeled and diced
- 2 tbsp olive oil
- ½ tsp onion powder
- ½ tsp garlic powder
- ¼ tsp paprika
- 4 eggs, pasture-raised
- ½ onion, sliced
- ½ cup mushrooms, sliced
- 2 cups fresh baby spinach
- Salt and pepper to taste
- Coconut oil for greasing

Directions:

1. Preheat the oven to 425°F.

2. Place the potatoes in a baking dish and drizzle with olive oil. Season with onion powder, garlic powder, paprika, salt, and pepper to taste. Once cooked, set aside.

3. Bake in the oven for 30 minutes while turning the sweet potatoes halfway through the cooking time.

4. Heat skillet and grease with coconut oil.

5. Sauté the onion for 30 seconds until fragrant.

6. Add in the mushrooms and egg. Season with salt and pepper to taste.

7. Scramble the eggs.

8. Before the eggs have set, stir in the baby spinach until wilted.

9. Plate the potatoes and top with the egg mixture.

Nutrition: Calories: 252, Total Fat: 17 g, Saturated Fat: 4 g, Total Carbs: 15 g, Net Carbs: 13 g, Protein: 11 g, Sugar: 4g, Fiber: 2g, Sodium: 151 mg, Potassium: 472 mg

4. Healthy Breakfast Chocolate Donuts

Preparation Time: 10 minutes

Cooking Time: 15 minutes

Servings: 12

Ingredients:

- 1 cup coconut flour
- ¼ cup raw cacao powder
- ½ tsp baking soda
- 4 eggs, pasture-raised
- ¼ cup coconut oil, melted
- ¼ cup unsweetened applesauce
- 1 tsp vanilla
- ¼ cup honey
- ¼ tsp salt

Directions:

1. Preheat the oven to 350°F.

2. In a mixing bowl, mix the coconut flour, cacao, baking soda, and salt. Set aside.

3. In another bowl, mix the eggs, coconut oil, and applesauce. Stir in the vanilla and honey.

4. Fold the dry ingredients gradually into the wet ingredients until well combined.

5. Grease the donut pan with coconut oil.

6. Press down the dough into the pan.

7. Bake for 15 minutes or until the dough is cooked through.

8. Remove from the oven and allow cooling before removing it from the donut pan.

Nutrition: Calories: 115, Total Fat: 7 g, Saturated Fat: 4 g, Total Carbs: 9 g, Net Carbs: 8.2 g, Protein: 4 g, Sugar: 7 g, Fiber: 0.7 g, Sodium: 108 mg, Potassium: 255 mg

5. Baked Eggs with Portobello Mushrooms

Preparation Time: 10 minutes

Cooking Time: 20 minutes

Servings: 4

Ingredients:

- 4 Portobello mushroom caps
- 1 cup arugula
- 1 medium tomato, chopped
- 4 large eggs, pasture-raised
- Salt and pepper to taste

Directions:

1. Preheat the oven to 350°F and line a baking sheet with parchment paper.

2. Scoop out the gills from the mushrooms using a spoon. Discard the gills and set them aside.

3. Place the mushrooms on the baking sheet inverted (gill side up) and fill each cap with arugula and tomato.

4. Carefully crack an egg on each mushroom cap.

5. Bake in the oven for 20 minutes or until the eggs have been set.

Nutrition: Calories: 80, Total Fat: 5 g, Saturated Fat: 2 g, Total Carbs: 5 g, Net Carbs: 3 g, Protein: 5 g, Sugar: 3 g, Fiber: 2 g, Sodium: 19 mg, Potassium: 416 mg

6. Breakfast Spinach Mushroom Tomato Fry Up

Preparation Time: 5 minutes

Cooking Time: 10 minutes

Servings: 2

Ingredients:

- 1 tsp olive oil
- 1 red onion, sliced
- 6 button mushrooms, sliced
- ½ cup cherry tomatoes, halved
- ½ tsp diced lemon rind
- 3 large handfuls baby spinach
- Salt and pepper to taste

Directions:

1. Heat oil in a skillet over medium-low heat.

2. Sauté the onion until fragrant.

3. Add in the mushrooms and tomatoes. Season with lemon rind, salt and pepper. Cook for another 5 minutes.

4. Stir in the baby spinach until wilted.

Nutrition: Calories: 38, Total Fat: 3 g, Saturated Fat: 0 g, Total Carbs: 3 g, Net Carbs: 1.5 g, Protein: 2 g, Sugar: 1 g, Fiber: 1.5 g, Sodium: 37 mg, Potassium: 321 mg

7. Sweet Cherry Almond Chia Pudding

Preparation Time: 3 hours

Cooking Time: 0 minutes

Servings: 4

Ingredients:

- 2 cups whole sweet cherries, pitted
- 2 cups coconut milk
- ¼ cup maple syrup, organic
- 1 tsp vanilla extract
- ¾ cup chia seeds
- ½ cup hemp seeds
- ⅛ tsp salt

Directions:

1. In the blender, combine the cherries, coconut milk, maple syrup, and vanilla extract. Season with salt. Pulse until smooth.

2. Distribute the chia seeds and hemp seeds in 4 glasses and pour in the cherry and milk mixture.

3. Allow chilling in the fridge for 3 hours before serving.

Nutrition: Calories: 302, Total Fat: 17 g, Saturated Fat: 4 g, Total Carbs: 29 g, Net Carbs: 22 g, Protein: 10 g, Sugar: 20 g, Fiber: 7 g, Sodium: 59mg, Potassium: 384mg

8. Pineapple Ginger Smoothie

Preparation Time: 5 minutes

Cooking Time: 0 minutes

Servings: 1

Ingredients:

- 1 cup pineapple slice
- ½ inch thick ginger, sliced
- 1 cup coconut milk

Directions:

1. Place all ingredients in a blender.

2. Pulse until smooth.

3. Chill before serving.

Nutrition: Calories: 299, Total Fat: 7 g, Saturated Fat: 5 g, Total Carbs: 51 g, Net Carbs: 49 g, Protein: 9 g, Sugar: 47 g, Fiber: 2 g, Sodium: 108 mg, Potassium: 630 mg

9.   Beet and Cherry Smoothie

Preparation Time: 5 minutes

Cooking Time: 0 minutes

Servings: 4

Ingredients:

- 10 oz almond milk, unsweetened
- 2 small beets, peeled and cut into quarters
- ½ cup frozen cherries, pitted
- ½ tsp frozen banana
- 1 tbsp almond butter

Directions:

1. Add all ingredients into a blender.
2. Blend until smooth.

Nutrition: Calories: 470, Total Fat: 37 g, Saturated Fat: 6 g, Total Carbs: 24 g, Net Carbs: 14 g, Protein: 16 g, Sugar: 10g, Fiber: 10g, Sodium: 67mg, Potassium: 733mg

10.   Spicy Pineapple Smoothie

Preparation Time: 5 minutes

Cooking Time: 0 minutes

Servings: 1

Ingredients:

- 1 tbsp chia seeds
- 1 tsp black pepper powder
- 1 orange, peeled
- 1½ cups frozen pineapple chunks
- 1 cup coconut water
- 1 tsp ground turmeric

Directions:

1. Place all ingredients in a blender.
2. Pulse until smooth.
3. Serve chilled.

Nutrition: Calories: 378, Total Fat: 10 g, Saturated Fat: 2 g, Total Carbs: 73 g, Net Carbs: 53 g, Protein: 9 g, Sugar: 42 g, Fiber: 20 g, Sodium: 261 mg, Potassium: 1281 mg

11.   Breakfast Cherry Muffins

Preparation Time: 10 minutes

Cooking Time: 30 minutes

Servings: 6

Ingredients:

- 1½ cup almond flour
- ¼ cup arrowroot flour
- ¼ cup coconut oil
- ¼ cup maple syrup
- 3 whole eggs
- 2 tsp vanilla extract
- 1½ tsp almond extract
- 1 tsp baking powder
- 1 cup fresh cherry, pitted and chopped
- ¼ tsp salt

Directions:

1. Preheat the oven to 350°F.
2. In a mixing bowl, combine all ingredients except for the cherries. Mix until well-combined.
3. Add the cherries last.
4. Fill muffin liners with the batter and bake for 30 minutes or until a toothpick inserted comes out clean.

Nutrition: Calories: 528, Total Fat: 39 g, Saturated Fat: 5 g, Total Carbs: 36 g, Net Carbs: 29 g, Protein: 13 g, Sugar: 15g, Fiber: 7g, Sodium: 177mg, Potassium: 679mg

12.   Breakfast Shakshuka

Preparation Time: 5 minutes

Cooking Time: 10 minutes

Servings: 6

Ingredients:

- 1 tbsp olive oil
- ½ onion, chopped
- 1 garlic clove, minced
- 1 red bell pepper, seeded and chopped
- 4 cups tomatoes, diced
- 1 tsp chili powder
- 1 tsp paprika
- 6 eggs, pasture-raised
- ½ tbsp fresh parsley, chopped
- Salt and pepper to taste

Directions:

1. Heat oil in a skillet over medium flame.

2. Sauté the onion and garlic for 30 seconds or until fragrant.

3. Add in the red bell pepper and tomatoes. Season with salt and pepper to taste. Stir in the chili powder and paprika. Allow simmering until the tomatoes are soft.

4. Reduce the heat and create 6 wells in the skillet.

5. Crack 1 egg in each well and increase the heat.

6. Cover and allow to simmer for 5 minutes.

7. Garnish with parsley last.

Nutrition: Calories: 177, Total Fat: 12 g, Saturated Fat: 3 g, Total Carbs: 7 g, Net Carbs: 5 g, Protein: 10 g, Sugar: 4 g, Fiber: 2 g, Sodium: 109mg, Potassium: 445mg

13. Anti-Inflammatory Crepes

Preparation Time: 5 minutes

Cooking Time: 4 minutes

Servings: 4

Ingredients:

- 2 tbsp coconut flour
- 4 large eggs, pasture-raised
- 1 tbsp coconut oil
- 1 cup hazelnuts, soaked in water overnight
- ⅔ cup dark chocolates
- ½ tsp vanilla extract
- 2 tbsp maple syrup
- ½ cup water

Directions:

1. Preheat the oven to 350°F.

2. In a bowl, mix the coconut flour, eggs, and water until well-combined.

3. Heat oil in a skillet over medium flame and grease the skillet with coconut oil.

4. Scoop ⅓ cup of the crepe mixture into the skillet and cook for 4 minutes while flipping halfway through the cooking time.

5. Repeat until all batter is made into crepes.

6. Make the hazelnut sauce by combining the hazelnuts, dark chocolates, vanilla extract, and maple syrup in a blender.

7. Pulse until smooth.

8. Spread the Nutella sauce over the crepes before serving.

Nutrition: Calories: 465, Total Fat: 29 g, Saturated Fat: 6 g, Total Carbs: 46 g, Net Carbs: g, Protein: 9 g, Sugar: 32 g, Fiber: 5 g, Sodium: 53 mg, Potassium: 401 mg

14. No-Bake Turmeric Protein Donuts

Preparation Time: 50 minutes

Cooking Time: 0 minutes

Servings: 8

Ingredients:

- 1½ cup raw cashews
- ½ cup Medjool dates, pitted
- 1 tbsp vanilla protein powder
- ½ cup shredded coconut
- 2 tbsp maple syrup
- ¼ tsp vanilla extract
- 1 tsp turmeric powder
- ¼ cup dark chocolate

Directions:

1. Combine all ingredients except for the chocolate in a food processor.

2. Pulse until smooth.

3. Roll batter into 8 balls and press into a silicone donut mold.

4. Place in the freezer for 30 minutes to set.

5. Meanwhile, make the chocolate topping by melting the chocolate in a double boiler.

6. Once the donuts have been set, remove the donuts from the mold and drizzle them with chocolate.

Nutrition: Calories: 320, Total Fat: 26 g, Saturated Fat: 5 g, Total Carbs: 20 g, Net Carbs: 17 g, Protein: 7 g, Sugar: 9 g, Fiber: 2 g, Sodium: 163mg, Potassium: 297mg

15. Golden Milk

Preparation Time: 5 minutes

Cooking Time: 5 minutes

Servings: 2

Ingredients:

- 1 tbsp coconut oil
- 1½ cups coconut milk, light
- Pinch pepper
- 1½ cups almond milk, unsweetened

- ¼ tsp ginger, grated
- 1½ tsp turmeric, grounded
- ¼ tsp cinnamon, grounded
- Sweetener of your choice, as needed

Directions:

1. To make this healthy beverage, you need to place all the ingredients in a medium-sized saucepan and mix them well.

2. After that, heat it over medium heat for 3 to 4 minutes or until it is hot but not boiling. Stir continuously.

3. Taste for seasoning. Add more sweetener or spice as required by you.

4. Finally, transfer the milk to the serving glass and enjoy it.

Tip: Instead of cinnamon powder, you can also use the cinnamon stick, which can be discarded at the end if you prefer a much more intense flavor.

Nutrition: Calories: 205, Protein: 3.2 g, Carbs: 8.9 g, Fat: 19.5 g

16. Granola

Preparation Time: 10 minutes

Cooking Time: 60 minutes

Servings: 2

Ingredients:

- ½ cup ground flax seeds
- 1 cup almonds, whole & raw
- ½ cup ginger, grated
- 1 cup pumpkin seeds, raw
- ½ tsp salt
- 1 cup shredded coconut, unsweetened
- ¾ cup water
- 1 cup oat bran
- ½ cup coconut oil, melted
- 1 cup dried cherries, pitted
- 4 tsp turmeric powder

Directions:

1. First, preheat the oven to 300°F.

2. Next, combine dried cherries, almonds, grounded flax, pumpkin seeds, coconut, salt, and turmeric in a large mixing bowl until mixed well.

3. After that, mix ginger, coconut oil, and water in the blender and blend for 30 to 40 seconds or until well incorporated.

4. Now, spoon the coconut oil mixture into the nut mixture. Mix well.

5. Then, transfer the mixture to a parchment paper-lined baking sheet and spread it across evenly.

6. Bake for 50 to 60 minutes while checking on it once or twice.

7. Allow it to cool completely and enjoy it.

Tip: Substitute dried cherries with raisins if preferred.

Nutrition: Calories: 225, Protein: 6 g, Carbs: 17 g, Fat: 16 g

17. Overnight Coconut Chia Oats

Preparation Time: 10 minutes

Cooking Time: 0 minutes

Servings: 1 to 2

Ingredients:

- ½ cup coconut milk, unsweetened
- 2 tsp chia seeds
- 1½ cups old fashioned oats, whole grain
- ½ tsp cinnamon, grounded
- 1 cup almond milk, unsweetened
- ½ tsp cinnamon, grounded
- 2 tsp date syrup
- ½ tsp black pepper, grounded
- 1 tsp turmeric, grounded

Directions:

1. To start with, keep the oats in the Mason jar.

2. After that, mix the rest of the ingredients in a medium bowl until combined well.

3. Then, pour the mixture into the jars and stir well.

4. Now, close the jar and place it in the refrigerator overnight.

5. In the morning, stir the mixture and then enjoy it.

Tip: You can top it with toasted nuts or berries.

Nutrition: Calories: 335, Protein: 7 g, Carbs: 34.1 g, Fat: 19.9 g

18.   Blueberry Hemp Seed Smoothie

Preparation Time: 10 minutes

Cooking Time: 0 minutes

Servings: 1

Ingredients:

- 1¼ cup blueberries, frozen
- 1¼ cup Plant-Based Milk of your choice
- 2 tbsp hemp seeds
- 1 tsp Spirulina
- 1 scoop protein powder

Directions:

1. First, place all the ingredients needed to make the smoothie in a high-speed blender and blend them for 2 minutes or until smooth.

2. Transfer the mixture to a serving glass and enjoy it.

Tip: Instead of blueberries, you can use any berries of your choice.

Nutrition: Calories: 493, Protein: 37.7 g, Carbs: 46.3 g, Fat: 19.6 g

19.   Spiced Morning Chia Pudding

Preparation Time: 10 minutes

Cooking Time: 0 minutes

Servings: 1

Ingredients:

- ½ tsp cinnamon
- 1½ cups cashew milk
- ⅛ tsp cardamom, grounded
- ⅓ cup chia seeds
- ⅛ tsp cloves, grounded
- 2 tbsp maple syrup
- 1 tsp turmeric

Directions:

1. To begin with, combine all the ingredients in a medium bowl until well mixed.

2. Next, spoon the mixture into a container and allow it to sit overnight.

3. In the morning, transfer to a cup and serve with toppings of your choice.

Tip: You can top it with toppings of your choice like coconut flakes or seeds etc.

Nutrition: Calories: 237, Protein: 8.1 g, Carbs: 28.9 g, Fat: 8.1 g

20.   Green Smoothie

Preparation Time: 10 minutes

Cooking Time: 0 minutes

Servings: 1

Ingredients:

- 2 cups kale
- 1 tbsp chia seeds
- 1 banana
- 1 cup pineapple chunks, frozen
- ¼ tsp turmeric
- 1 cup green tea, brewed & cooled
- 1 scoop protein powder
- ⅔ cup cucumber, cut into chunks
- 3 Mint leaves
- ½ cup mango, cut into chunks
- ½-inch ginger, sliced
- Ice cubes, if needed

Directions:

1. To start with, place all the ingredients in a high-speed blender, excluding the chia seeds and blend them for 2 to 3 minutes or until smooth.

2. Next, put in the chia seeds and blend them for a further 1 minute.

3. Finally, transfer it to a serving glass and enjoy it.

Tip: You can substitute kale with spinach if desired.

Nutrition: Calories: 445, Protein: 31.9 g, Carbs: 73.7 g, Fat: 7.2 g

21.   Oatmeal Pancakes

Preparation Time: 10 minutes

Cooking Time: 10 minutes

Servings: 2

Ingredients:

- 1½ cup rolled oats, whole-grain
- 2 eggs, large & pastured
- 2 tsp Baking Powder
- 1 banana, ripe
- 2 tbsp water
- ¼ cup maple syrup
- 1 tsp vanilla extract
- 2 tbsp extra virgin olive oil

Directions:

1. To make this delicious breakfast dish, you need to first blend all the ingredients in a high-speed blender for a minute or two or until you get a smooth batter. Tip: To blend easily, pour egg, banana, and all other liquid ingredients first and finally add oats at the end.

2. Now, take a large skillet and heat it over medium-low heat.

3. Once the skillet is hot, ¼ cup of the batter into it and cook it for 3 to 4 minutes per side or until bubbles start appearing in the middle portion.

4. Turn the pancake and cook the other side also.

5. Serve warm.

Tip: You can pair it with maple syrup and fruits.

Nutrition: Calories: 201, Protein: 5g, Carbs: 27g, Fat: 7g

22. Anti-inflammatory Porridge

Preparation Time: 10 minutes

Cooking Time: 25 minutes

Servings: 2

Ingredients:

- ¾ cup almond milk, unsweetened
- 2 tbsp hemp seeds
- 2 tbsp chia seeds, whole
- ¼ cup walnuts, halved
- ¼ cup almond Butter
- ¼ cup coconut flakes, unsweetened & toasted
- ¼ cup coconut milk
- ½ tsp turmeric powder
- Dash of black pepper, grounded, as needed
- 1 tbsp coconut oil

Directions:

1. To start with, heat a large saucepan over medium heat.

2. To this, put in the hemp seeds, flaked coconut, and chopped walnuts.

3. Roast for 2 minutes or until toasted.

4. Once the coconut-seed mixture is roasted, transfer it to a bowl and set it aside.

5. Then, heat almond milk and coconut milk in a wide saucepan over medium heat.

6. Once it becomes hot but not boiling, remove it from the heat. Stir in almond butter and coconut oil to it. Mix.

7. Now, add chia seeds, black pepper, turmeric powder, and salt to the milk. Combine.

8. Keep it aside for 5 minutes and then add half of the roasted coconut mixture. Mix.

9. Finally, transfer to a serving bowl and top with the remaining coconut mixture.

10. Serve immediately.

Tip: If possible, try adding bee pollen for enhanced taste.

Nutrition: Calories: 575, Protein: 14.7 g, Carbs: 6 g, Fat: 50.2 g

23. Cherry Smoothie

Preparation Time: 5 minutes

Cooking Time: 0 minutes

Servings: 1

Ingredients:

- ½ cup cherries, pitted & frozen
- 1 banana, frozen
- 10 oz almond milk, unsweetened
- 1 tbsp almonds
- 1 beet, small & quartered

Directions:

1. To make this delightful smoothie, you need to blend all the ingredients in a high-speed blender for 3 minutes or until smooth.

2. Pour into a serving glass and enjoy it.

Tip: If you wish, you can add an extra beet.

Nutrition: Calories: 208, Protein: 5.2 g, Carbs: 34.4 g, Fat: 7.1 g

24. Gingerbread Oatmeal

Preparation Time: 10 minutes

Cooking Time: 10 minutes

Servings: 4

Ingredients:

- ¼ tsp cardamom, grounded
- 4 cups water
- ¼ tsp allspice
- 1 cup steel-cut oats
- ⅛ tsp nutmeg
- 1½ tbsp cinnamon, grounded
- ¼ tsp ginger, grounded

- ¼ tsp coriander, grounded
- Maple syrup, if desired
- ¼ tsp cloves

Directions:

1. First, place all the ingredients in a large saucepan over medium-high heat and stir well.

2. Next, cook them for 6 to 7 minutes or until cooked.

3. Once finished, add the maple syrup.

4. Top it with dried fruits of your choice if desired.

5. Serve it hot or cold.

Tip: Avoid those spices which you don't prefer.

Nutrition: Calories: 175, Protein: 6 g, Carbs: 32 g, Fat: 32 g

25. Roasted Almonds

Preparation Time: 5 minutes

Cooking Time: 10 minutes

Servings: 32

Ingredients:

- 2 cups whole almonds
- 1 tbsp chili powder
- ½ tsp ground cinnamon
- ½ tsp ground cumin
- ½ tsp ground coriander
- Salt and freshly ground black pepper, to taste
- 1 tbsp extra-virgin organic olive oil

Directions:

1. Preheat the oven to 350°F. Line a baking dish with parchment paper.

2. In a bowl, add all ingredients and toss to coat well.

3. Transfer the almond mixture into a prepared baking dish in a single layer.

4. Roast for around 10 minutes, flipping twice inside the middle way.

5. Remove from oven and make aside to cool down completely before serving.

6. You can preserve these roasted almonds in an airtight jar.

Nutrition: Calories: 62, Fat: 5 g, Carbs: 12 g, Protein: 2 g, Fiber: 6 g

26. Apple, Ginger, and Rhubarb Muffins

Preparation Time: 15 minutes

Cooking Time: 25 minutes

Servings: 4

Ingredients:

- ½ cup finely ground almonds
- ¼ cup brown rice flour
- ½ cup buckwheat flour
- ⅛ cup unrefined raw sugar
- 2 tbsp arrowroot flour
- 1 tbsp linseed meal
- 2 tbsp crystallized ginger, finely chopped
- ½ tsp ground ginger
- ½ tsp ground cinnamon
- 2 tsp gluten-free baking powder
- A pinch of fine sea salt
- 1 small apple, peeled and finely diced
- 1 cup finely chopped rhubarb
- ⅓ cup almond/rice milk
- 1 large egg
- ¼ cup extra virgin olive oil
- 1 tsp pure vanilla extract

Directions:

1. Set your oven to 350°F grease an 8-cup muffin tin and line with paper cases.

2. Combine the almond flour, linseed meal, ginger, and sugar in a mixing bowl. Sieve this mixture over the other flours, spices, and baking powder and use a whisk to combine well.

3. Stir in the apple and rhubarb in the flour mixture until evenly coated.

4. Whisk the milk, vanilla, and egg in a separate bowl, then pour it into the dry mixture. Stir until just combined – don't overwork the batter as this can yield very tough muffins.

5. Scoop the mixture into the arranged muffin tin and top with a few slices of rhubarb. Bake for at least 25 minutes, till they start turning golden or when an inserted toothpick emerges clean.

6. Take off from the oven and let sit for at least 5 minutes before transferring the muffins to a wire rack for further cooling.

7. Serve warm with a glass of squeezed juice.

8. Enjoy!

Nutrition: Calories: 325, Protein: 6.32 g, Fat: 9.82 g, Carbs: 55.71 g

27. Almond Scones

Preparation Time: 10 minutes

Cooking Time: 20 minutes

Servings: 6

Ingredients:

- 1 cup almonds
- 1 ⅓ cup almond flour
- ¼ cup arrowroot flour
- 1 tbsp coconut flour
- 1 tsp ground turmeric
- Salt, to taste
- Freshly ground black pepper, to taste
- 1 egg
- ¼ cup essential olive oil
- 3 tbsp raw honey
- 1 tsp vanilla flavoring

Directions:

1. In a mixer, put almonds, then pulse till chopped roughly.

2. Move the chopped almonds to a big bowl.

3. Put flours and spices and mix well.

4. In another bowl, put the remaining ingredients and beat till well combined.

5. Put the flour mixture into the egg mixture, then mix till well combined.

6. Arrange a plastic wrap over the cutting board.

7. Place the dough over the cutting board.

8. Using both of your hands, pat into a 1-inch thick circle.

9. Cut the circle into 6 wedges.

10. Set the scones onto a cookie sheet in a single layer.

11. Bake for at least 15 to 20 minutes.

Nutrition: Calories: 304, Fat: 3 g, Carbs: 22 g, Fiber: 6 g, Protein: 20 g

28. Cranberry and Raisins Granola

Preparation Time: 15 minutes

Cooking Time: 55 minutes

Servings: 4

Ingredients:

- 4 cups old-fashioned rolled oats

- ¼ cup sesame seeds
- 1 cup dried cranberries
- 1 cup golden raisins
- ⅛ tsp nutmeg
- 2 tbsp olive oil
- ½ cup almonds, slivered
- 2 tbsp warm water
- 1 tsp vanilla extract
- 1 tsp cinnamon
- ¼ tsp salt
- 6 tbsp maple syrup
- ⅓ cup honey

Directions:

1. Mix the sesame seeds, nutmeg, almonds, oats, salt, and cinnamon in a bowl.

2. In another bowl, mix the oil, water, vanilla, honey, and syrup. Gradually pour the mixture into the oats mixture. Toss to combine. Spread the mixture into a greased jelly-roll pan. Bake in the oven at 300°F for at least 55 minutes. Stir and break the clumps every 10 minutes.

3. Once you get it from the oven, stir the cranberries and raisins. Allow cooling. This will last for a week when stored in an airtight container and up to a month when stored in the fridge.

Nutrition: Calories: 698, Protein: 21.34 g, Fat: 20.99 g, Carbs: 148.59 g

29. Breakfast Arrozcaldo

Preparation Time: 20 minutes

Cooking Time: 20 minutes

Servings: 5

Ingredients:

- 6 eggs, white only
- 1½ cups brown rice, cooked

For the filling:

- ¼ cup raisins
- ½ cup frozen peas, thawed
- 1 white onion, minced
- 1 garlic clove, minced
- Oil, for greasing

Directions:

1. For the filling, spray a small amount of oil into a skillet set over medium heat. Add in onion and

garlic. Stir-fry until the former is limp and transparent.

2. Stir-fry while breaking up clumps, about 2 minutes. Add in the remaining ingredients. Stir-fry for another minute.

3. Turn down the heat, and let the filling cook for 10 to 15 minutes, or until the juices are greatly reduced. Stir often. Turn off the heat. Divide into 6 equal portions.

4. For the eggs, spray a small amount of oil into a smaller skillet set over medium heat. Cook eggs. Discard yolk. Transfer to holding the plate.

5. To serve, place 1 portion of rice on a plate, 1 portion of filling, and 1 egg white. Serve warm.

Nutrition: Calories: 53, Protein: 6.28 g, Fat: 1.35 g, Carbs: 3.59 g

30. Apple Bruschetta with Almonds and Blackberries

Preparation Time: 20 minutes

Cooking Time: 0 minutes

Servings: 5

Ingredients:

- 1 apple, sliced into ¼-inch thick half-moons
- ¼ cup blackberries, thawed, lightly mashed
- ½ tsp fresh lemon juice
- ⅛ cup almond slivers, toasted
- Sea salt

Directions:

1. Drizzle lemon juice on apple slices. Put these on a tray lined with parchment paper.

2. Spread a small number of mashed berries on top of each slice. Top these off with the desired amount of almond slivers.

3. Sprinkle sea salt on "bruschetta" just before serving.

Nutrition: Calories: 56, Protein: 1.53 g, Fat: 1.43 g, Carbs: 9.87 g

31. Oat Porridge with Cherry & Coconut

Preparation Time: 10 minutes

Cooking Time: 15 minutes

Servings: 3

Ingredients:

- 1½ cups regular oats
- 3 cups coconut milk
- 3 tbsp raw cacao
- Coconut shavings
- Dark chocolate shavings
- Fresh or frozen tart cherries
- A pinch of stevia, optional
- Maple syrup, to taste (optional)

Directions:

1. Combine the oats, milk, stevia, and cacao in a medium saucepan over medium heat and bring to a boil. Lower the heat, then simmer until the oats are cooked to desired doneness.

2. Divide the porridge among 3 serving bowls and top with dark chocolate and coconut shavings, cherries, and a little drizzle of maple syrup.

Nutrition: Calories: 343, Protein: 15.64 g, Fat: 12.78 g, Carbs: 41.63 g

32. Gingerbread Oatmeal Breakfast

Preparation Time: 10 minutes

Cooking Time: 10 minutes

Servings: 4

Ingredients:

- 1 cup steel-cut oats
- 4 cups water
- Organic maple syrup, to taste
- 1 tsp ground cloves
- 1½ tbsp ground cinnamon
- ⅛ tsp nutmeg
- ¼ tsp ground ginger
- ¼ tsp ground coriander
- ¼ tsp ground allspice
- ¼ tsp ground cardamom
- Fresh mixed berries

Directions:

1. Cook the oats based on the package instructions. When it comes to a boil, reduce heat and simmer.

2. Stir in all the spices and continue cooking until cooked to desired doneness.

3. Serve in 4 serving bowls and drizzle with maple syrup and top with fresh berries.

4. Enjoy!

Nutrition: Calories: 87, Protein: 5.82 g, Fat: 3.26 g

33. Yummy Steak Muffins

Preparation Time: 10 minutes

Cooking Time: 20 minutes

Servings: 4

Ingredients:

- 1 cup red bell pepper, diced
- 2 tbsp water
- 8 oz thin steak, cooked and finely chopped
- ¼ tsp sea salt
- Dash of freshly ground black pepper
- 8 free-range eggs
- 1 cup finely diced onion

Directions:

1. Set the oven to 350°F

2. Take 8 muffin tins and line them with parchment paper liners.

3. Get a large bowl and crack all the eggs in it.

4. Beat the eggs well.

5. Blend in all the remaining ingredients.

6. Spoon the batter into the arranged muffin tins. Fill ¾ of each tin.

7. Put the muffin tins in the preheated oven for about 20 minutes until the muffins are baked and set in the middle.

8. Enjoy!

Nutrition: Calories: 151, Protein: 17.92 g, Fat: 7.32 g, Carbs: 3.75 g

34. White and Green Quiche

Preparation Time: 10 minutes

Cooking Time: 40 minutes

Servings: 3

Ingredients:

- 3 cups fresh spinach, chopped
- 15 large free-range eggs

- 3 garlic cloves, minced
- 5 white mushrooms, sliced
- 1 small sized onion, finely chopped
- 1½ tsp baking powder
- Ground black pepper to taste
- 1½ cups coconut milk
- Ghee, as required to grease the dish
- Sea salt to taste

Directions:

1. Set the oven to 350°F.

2. Get a baking dish, then grease it with organic ghee.

3. Break all the eggs in a huge bowl, then whisk well.

4. Stir in coconut milk. Beat well

5. While you are whisking the eggs, start adding the remaining ingredients to them.

6. When all the ingredients are thoroughly blended, pour all of them into the prepared baking dish.

7. Bake for at least 40 minutes, up to the quiche is set in the middle.

8. Enjoy!

Nutrition: Calories: 608, Protein: 20.28 g, Fat: 53.42 g, Carbs: 16.88 g

35. Beef Breakfast Casserole

Preparation Time: 10 minutes

Cooking Time: 30 minutes

Servings: 5

Ingredients:

- 1 lb ground beef, cooked
- 10 eggs
- ½ cup Pico de Gallo
- 1 cup baby spinach
- ¼ cup sliced black olives
- Freshly ground black pepper

Directions:

1. Preheat the oven to 350°F. Prepare a 9" glass pie plate with non-stick spray.

2. Whisk the eggs until frothy. Season with salt and pepper.

3. Layer the cooked ground beef, Pico de Gallo, and spinach on the pie plate.

4. Slowly pour the eggs over the top.

5. Top with black olives.

6. Bake for at least 30 minutes until firm in the middle.

7. Slice into 5 pieces and serve.

Nutrition: Calories: 479, Protein: 43.54 g, Fat: 30.59 g, Carbs: 4.65 g

36. Ham and Veggie Frittata Muffins

Preparation Time: 10 minutes

Cooking Time: 25 minutes

Servings: 12

Ingredients:

- 5 oz thinly sliced ham
- 8 large eggs
- 4 tbsp coconut oil
- ½ yellow onion, finely diced
- 8 oz frozen spinach, thawed and drained
- 8 oz mushrooms, thinly sliced
- 1 cup cherry tomatoes, halved
- ¼ cup coconut milk (canned)
- 2 tbsp coconut flour
- Sea salt and pepper to taste

Directions:

1. Preheat the oven to 375°F.

2. In a medium skillet, warm the coconut oil on medium heat. Add the onion and cook until softened.

3. Add the mushrooms, spinach, and cherry tomatoes. Season with salt and pepper. Cook until the mushrooms have softened. About 5 minutes. Remove from heat and set aside.

4. In a huge bowl, beat the eggs together with coconut milk and coconut flour. Stir in the cooled veggie mixture.

5. Line each cavity of a 12 cavity muffin tin with the thinly sliced ham. Pour the egg mixture into each one and bake for 20 minutes.

6. Remove from oven and allow to cool for about 5 minutes before transferring to a wire rack.

7. To maximize the benefit of a vegetable-rich diet, it's important to eat a variety of colors, and these veggie-packed frittata muffins do just that. The onion, spinach, mushrooms, and cherry tomatoes provide a wide range of vitamins and nutrients and a healthy dose of fiber.

Nutrition: Calories: 125, Protein: 5.96 g, Fat: 9.84 g, Carbs: 4.48 g

37. Tomato and Avocado Omelet

Preparation Time: 5 minutes

Cooking Time: 5 minutes

Servings: 1

Ingredients:

- 2 eggs
- ¼ avocado, diced
- 4 cherry tomatoes, halved
- 1 tbsp cilantro, chopped
- A squeeze lime juice
- Pinch of salt

Directions:

1. Put together the avocado, tomatoes, cilantro, lime juice, and salt in a small bowl, then mix well and set aside.

2. Warm a medium nonstick skillet on medium heat. Whisk the eggs until frothy and add to the pan. Move the eggs around gently with a rubber spatula until they begin to set.

3. Scatter the avocado mixture over half of the omelet. Remove from heat, and slide the omelet onto a plate as you fold it in half.

4. Serve immediately.

Nutrition: Calories: 433, Protein: 25.55 g, Fat: 32.75 g, Carbs: 10.06 g

38. Oats with Berries

Preparation Time: 10 minutes

Cooking Time: 30 minutes

Servings: 4

Ingredients:

- 1 cup steel-cut oats
- Dash of salt
- 3 cups water

For Toppings:

- ½ cup berries of your choice
- ¼ cup nuts or seeds of your choice like almonds or hemp seeds

Directions:

1. To begin with, place the oats in a small saucepan and heat it over medium-high heat.

2. Now, toast it for 3 minutes while stirring the pan frequently.

3. Next, pour water into the saucepan and mix well.

4. Allow the mixture to boil. Lower the heat.

5. Allow it to cook for 23 to 25 minutes or until the oats are cooked and tender.

6. Once done cooking, transfer the mixture to the serving bowl and top it with the berries and seeds.

7. Serve it warm or cold.

Tip: If you desire, you can add sweeteners like maple syrup or coconut sugar or stevia to it.

Nutrition: Calories: 118, Protein: 4.1 g, Carbs: 16.5 g, Fat: 4.4 g

39. Spinach Avocado Smoothie

Preparation Time: 5 minutes

Cooking Time: 0 minutes

Servings: 1

Ingredients:

- 1 avocado
- 1 cup plain yoghurt, non-fat
- 2 tbsp water
- 1 cup spinach, fresh
- 1 tsp honey
- 1 banana, frozen

Directions:

1. Start by blending all the ingredients needed to make the smoothie in a high-speed blender for 2 to 3 minutes or until you get a smooth and creamy mixture.

2. Next, transfer the mixture to a serving glass.

3. Serve and enjoy.

Tip: If you don't prefer to use yogurt, you can use unsweetened almond milk.

Nutrition: Calories: 357, Protein: 17.7 g, Carbs: 57.7 g, Fat: 8.2 g

40. Roasted Chickpeas

Preparation Time: 10 minutes

Cooking Time: 1 hour

Servings: 8 to 10

Ingredients:

- 3 cups canned chickpeas, rinsed and dried
- 2 tbsp nutritional yeast
- 1 tbsp ground turmeric
- ½ tsp garlic powder
- Pinch of cayenne pepper.
- Salt and freshly ground black pepper, to taste
- 2 tbsp extra-virgin organic olive oil

Directions:

1. Preheat the oven to 400°F.

2. In a bowl, add all ingredients except freshly squeezed lemon juice and toss to coat well.

3. Transfer the almond mixture right into a baking sheet.

4. Roast for around 1 hour, flipping after every 15 minutes.

5. Remove from oven and keep aside for cooling completely before serving.

6. Drizzle with freshly squeezed lemon juice and serve.

Nutrition: Calories: 190, Fat: 5 g, Carbs: 16 g, Fiber: 7 g, Protein: 12 g

41. Spiced Popcorn

Preparation Time: 5 minutes

Cooking Time: 2 minutes

Servings: 2 to 3

Ingredients:

- 3 tbsp coconut oil
- ½ cup popping corn
- 1 tbsp olive oil
- 1 tsp ground turmeric
- ¼ tsp garlic powder
- Salt, to taste

Directions:

1. In a pan, melt coconut oil on medium-high heat.

2. Add popping corn and cover the pan tightly.

3. Cook, shaking the pan occasionally for around 1 to 2 minutes or till corn kernels begin to pop.

4. Remove from heat and transfer right into a large heatproof bowl.

5. Add essential olive oil and spices and mix well.

6. Serve immediately

Nutrition: Calories: 200, Fat: 4 g, Carbs: 12 g, Fiber: 1 g, Protein: 6 g

42. Cucumber Bites

Preparation Time: 15 minutes

Cooking Time: 0 minutes

Servings: 4

Ingredients:

- ½ cup prepared hummus
- ¼-½ tsp ground turmeric
- Pinch of red pepper cayenne
- Pinch of salt
- 1 cucumber, cut diagonally into ¼-½-inch thick slices
- 1 tsp black sesame seeds
- Fresh mint leaves, for garnishing

Directions:

1. In a bowl, mix together hummus, turmeric, cayenne and salt.

2. Transfer the hummus mixture to the pastry bag and pipe on each cucumber slice.

3. Serve while using garnishing of sesame seeds and mint leaves.

Nutrition: Calories: 203, Fat: 4 g, Carbs: 20 g, Fiber: 3 g, Protein: 7 g

43. Spinach Fritters

Preparation Time: 15 minutes

Cooking Time: 5 minutes

Servings: 2 to 3

Ingredients:

- 2 cups chickpea flour
- ¾ tsp white sesame seeds
- ½ tsp garam masala powder
- ½ tsp red chili powder
- ¼ tsp ground cumin
- 2 pinches of baking soda
- Salt, to taste

- 1 cup water
- 12 to 14 fresh spinach leaves
- Olive oil, for frying

Directions:

1. In a sizable bowl, add all ingredients except spinach and oil and mix till an easy mixture forms.

2. In a sizable skillet, heat oil on medium heat.

3. Dip each spinach leaf in the chickpea flour mixture evenly and place in the hot oil in batches.

4. Cook, flipping occasionally for about 3 to 5 minutes or till golden brown from each side.

5. Transfer the fritters onto a paper towel-lined plate.

Nutrition: Calories: 211, Fat: 2 g, Carbs: 13 g, Fiber: 11 g, Protein: 9 g

44. Crispy Chicken Fingers

Preparation Time: 15 minutes

Cooking Time: 18 minutes

Servings: 4 to 6

Ingredients:

- ⅔ cup almond meal
- ½ tsp ground turmeric
- ½ tsp red pepper cayenne
- ½ tsp paprika
- ½ tsp garlic powder
- Salt and freshly ground black pepper, to taste
- 1 egg
- 1 lb skinless, boneless chicken breasts, cut into strips

Directions:

1. Preheat the oven to 375°F. Line a substantial baking sheet with parchment paper.

2. In a shallow dish, beat the egg.

3. In another shallow dish, mix almond meal and spices.

4. Coat each chicken strip with egg after which roll into the spice mixture evenly.

5. Arrange the chicken strips onto the prepared baking sheet in a single layer.

6. Bake for approximately 16 to 18 minutes.

Nutrition: Calories: 236, Fat: 10 g, Carbs: 26 g, Fiber: 5 g, Protein: 37 g

45. Quinoa & Veggie Croquettes

Preparation Time: 15 minutes

Cooking Time: 9 minutes

Servings: 12 to 15

Ingredients:

- 1 tbsp essential olive oil
- ½ cup frozen peas, thawed
- 2 minced garlic cloves
- 1 cup cooked quinoa
- 2 large boiled potatoes, peeled and mashed
- ¼ cup fresh cilantro leaves, chopped
- 2 tsp ground cumin
- 1 tsp garam masala
- ¼ tsp ground turmeric
- Salt and freshly ground black pepper, to taste

Directions:

1. In a frying pan, heat oil on medium heat.
2. Add peas and garlic and sauté for about 1 minute.
3. Transfer the pea mixture into a large bowl.
4. Add remaining ingredients and mix till well combined.
5. Make equal-sized oblong-shaped patties from your mixture.
6. In a large skillet, heat oil on medium-high heat.
7. Add croquettes and fry for about 4 minutes per side.

Nutrition: Calories: 367, Fat: 6 g, Carbs: 17 g, Fiber: 5 g, Protein: 22 g

46. Sweet Potato Cranberry Breakfast Bars

Preparation Time: 10 minutes

Cooking Time: 40 minutes

Servings: 8

Ingredients:

- 1½ cups sweet potato puree
- 2 tbsp coconut oil, melted
- 2 tbsp maple syrup
- 2 eggs, pasture-raised
- 1 cup almond flour
- ⅓ cup coconut flour
- 1½ tsp baking soda
- 1 cup fresh cranberry, pitted and chopped
- ¼ cup water

Directions:

1. Preheat the oven to 350°F.
2. Grease a 9-inch baking pan with coconut oil. Set aside.
3. In a mixing bowl. Combine the sweet potato puree, water, coconut oil, maple syrup, and eggs.
4. In another bowl, sift the almond flour, coconut flour, and baking soda.
5. Gradually add the dry ingredients to the wet ingredients. Use a spatula to fold and mix all ingredients.
6. Pour into the prepared baking pan and press the cranberries on top.
7. Place in the oven and bake for 40 minutes or until a toothpick inserted in the middle comes out clean.
8. Allow to rest or cool before removing from the pan.

Nutrition: Calories: 98, Total Fat: 6 g, Saturated Fat: 1 g, Total Carbs: 9 g, Net Carbs: 8.5 g, Protein: 3 g, Sugar: 7 g, Fiber: 0.5 g, Sodium: 113 mg, Potassium: 274 mg

47. Breakfast Stir Fry

Preparation Time: 20 minutes

Cooking Time: 20 minutes

Servings: 2

Ingredients:

- ½ lb beef meat; minced
- 1 tbsp tamari sauce
- 2 bell peppers; chopped.
- 2 tsp red chili flakes
- 1 tsp chili powder
- 1 tbsp coconut oil
- Salt and black pepper to the taste.

For the Bok Choy:

- 6 bunches bok choy; trimmed and chopped.
- 1 tsp ginger; grated
- 1 tbsp coconut oil
- Salt to the taste.

For the Eggs:

- 2 eggs
- 1 tbsp coconut oil

Directions:

1. Heat up a pan with 1 tbsp coconut oil over medium-high heat; add beef and bell peppers; stir and cook for 10 minutes

2. Add salt, pepper, tamari sauce, chili flakes and chili powder; stir, cook for 4 minutes more and take off the heat.

3. Heat up another pan with 1 tbsp oil over medium heat; add bok choy; stir and cook for 3 minutes

4. Add salt and ginger; stir, cook for 2 minutes more and take off the heat.

5. Heat up the third pan with 1 tbsp oil over medium heat; crack eggs and fry them.

6. Divide beef and bell peppers mix into 2 bowls

7. Divide bok choy and top with eggs

Nutrition: Calories: 248, Fat: 14 g, Fiber: 4 g, Carbs: 10 g, Protein: 14 g

48.   Oven-Poached Eggs

Preparation Time: 2 minutes

Cooking Time: 15 minutes

Servings: 4

Ingredients:

- 6 eggs, at room temperature
- Water
- Ice bath
- 2 cups water, chilled
- 2 cups ice cubes

Directions:

1. Set the oven to 350°F. Put 2 cups of water into a deep roasting tin, and place it on the lowest rack of the oven.

2. Place 1 egg into each cup of cupcake/muffin tins, along with 1 tbsp of water.

3. Carefully place muffin tins into the middle rack of the oven.

4. Bake eggs for 15 minutes.

5. Turn off the heat immediately. Please take the muffin tins from the oven and set them on a cake rack to cool before extracting eggs.

6. Pour ice bath ingredients into a large heat-resistant bowl.

7. Bring the eggs into an ice bath to stop the cooking process. After 10 minutes, drain the eggs well. Use as needed.

Nutrition: Calories: 357, Protein: 17.14 g, Fat: 24.36 g, Carbs: 16.19 g

49.   Turkey Burgers

Preparation Time: 15 minutes

Cooking Time: 8 minutes

Servings: 5

Ingredients:

- 1 ripe pear, peeled, cored, and chopped roughly
- 1 lb lean ground turkey
- 1 tsp fresh ginger, grated finely
- 2 minced garlic cloves
- 1 tsp fresh rosemary, minced
- 1 tsp fresh sage, minced
- Salt, to taste
- Freshly ground black pepper, to taste
- 1 to 2 tbsp coconut oil

Directions:

1. In a blender, add pear and pulse till smooth.

2. Transfer the pear mixture to a large bowl with remaining ingredients except for oil and mix till well combined.

3. Make small equal-sized 10 patties from the mixture.

4. In a heavy-bottomed frying pan, heat oil on medium heat.

5. Add the patties and cook for around 4 to 5 minutes.

6. Flip the inside and cook for approximately 2 to 3 minutes.

Nutrition: Calories: 477, Fat: 15 g, Carbs: 26 g, Fiber: 11 g, Protein: 35 g

50. Anti-Inflammatory Breakfast Frittata

Preparation Time: 10 minutes

Cooking Time: 40 minutes

Servings: 4

Ingredients:

- 4 large eggs
- 6 egg whites
- 450 g button mushrooms
- 450 g baby spinach
- 125 g firm tofu
- 1 onion, chopped
- 1 tbsp minced garlic
- ½ tsp ground turmeric
- ½ tsp cracked black pepper
- ¼ cup water
- Kosher salt to taste

Directions:

1. Set your oven to 350°F.

2. Sauté the mushrooms in a little bit of extra virgin olive oil in a large non-stick ovenproof pan over medium heat. Add the onions once the mushrooms start turning golden and cook for 3 minutes until the onions become soft.

3. Stir in the garlic, then cook for at least 30 seconds until fragrant before adding the spinach. Pour in water, cover, and cook until the spinach becomes wilted for about 2 minutes.

4. Take off the lid and continue cooking up until the water evaporates. Now, combine the eggs, egg whites, tofu, pepper, turmeric, and salt in a bowl. When all the liquid has evaporated, pour in the egg mixture, let cook for about 2 minutes until the edges start setting, transfer to the oven, and bake for about 25 minutes or until cooked.

5. Take off from the oven, then sit for at least 5 minutes before cutting it into quarters and serving.

6. Enjoy!

7. Baby spinach and mushrooms boost the nutrient profile of the eggs to provide you with amazing anti-inflammatory benefits.

Nutrition: Calories: 521, Protein: 29.1 g, Fat: 10.45 g, Carbs: 94.94 g

51. Mediterranean Frittata

Preparation Time: 5 minutes

Cooking Time: 20 minutes

Servings: 6

Ingredients:

- 6 eggs
- ¼ cup feta cheese, crumbled
- ¼ tsp black pepper
- Oil, spray, or olive
- 1 tsp oregano
- ¼ cup milk, almond, or coconut
- 1 tsp sea salt
- ¼ cup black olives, chopped
- ¼ cup green olives, chopped
- ¼ cup tomatoes, diced

Directions:

1. Heat oven to 400°F. Oil one 8x8-inch baking dish. Beat the milk into the eggs, and then add other ingredients. Pour all of this mixture into the baking dish and bake for 20 minutes.

Nutrition: Calories: 107, Sugar: 2 g, Carbs: 3 g, Fat: 7 g, Protein: 7 g

52. Spicy Marble Eggs

Preparation Time: 15 minutes

Cooking Time: 15 minutes

Servings: 12

Ingredients:

- 6 medium-boiled eggs, unpeeled, cooled

For the Marinade:

- 2 oolong black tea bags
- 3 tbsp brown sugar
- 1 thumb-sized fresh ginger, unpeeled, crushed
- 3 dried star anise, whole
- 2 dried bay leaves
- 3 tbsp light soy sauce
- 4 tbsp dark soy sauce
- 4 cups water
- 1 dried cinnamon stick, whole
- 1 tsp salt
- 1 tsp dried Szechuan peppercorns

Directions:

1. Using the back of a metal spoon, crack eggshells in places to create a spider web effect. Do not peel. Set aside until needed.

2. Pour marinade into a large Dutch oven set over high heat. Put lid partially on. Bring water to a rolling boil for about 5 minutes. Turn off the heat.

3. Secure lid. Steep ingredients for 10 minutes.

4. Using a slotted spoon, fish out and discard solids. Cool marinade completely to the room proceeding.

5. Place eggs into an airtight non-reactive container just small enough to snugly fit all this in.

6. Pour in marinade. Eggs should be completely submerged in liquid. Discard leftover marinade, if any. Line container rim with generous layers of saran wrap. Secure container lid.

7. Chill eggs for 24 hours before using.

8. Extract eggs and drain each piece well before using, but keep the rest submerged in the marinade.

Nutrition: Calories: 75, Protein: 4.05 g, Fat: 4.36 g, Carbs: 4.83 g

53. Tuna & Sweet Potato Croquettes

Preparation Time: 15 minutes

Cooking Time: 12 minutes

Servings: 8

Ingredients:

- 1 tbsp coconut oil
- ½ large onion, chopped
- 1 1-inch piece fresh ginger, minced
- 3 garlic cloves, minced
- 1 Serrano pepper, seeded and minced
- ½ tsp ground coriander
- ¼ tsp ground turmeric
- ¼ tsp red chili powder
- ¼ tsp garam masala
- Salt, to taste
- Freshly ground black pepper, to taste
- 2 (5 oz) cans tuna
- 1 cup sweet potato, peeled and mashed
- 1 egg
- ¼ cup tapioca flour
- ¼ cup almond flour
- Olive oil, as required

Directions:

1. In a frying pan, warm the coconut oil on medium heat.

2. Put onion, ginger, garlic, and Serrano pepper and sauté for approximately 5 to 6 minutes.

3. Stir in spices and sauté for approximately 1 minute more.

4. Transfer the onion mixture to a bowl.

5. Add tuna and sweet potato and mix till well combined.

6. Make equal-sized oblong-shaped patties in the mixture.

7. Arrange the croquettes inside a baking sheet in a single layer and refrigerate overnight.

8. In a shallow dish, beat the egg.

9. In another shallow dish, mix both flours.

10. Heat enough oil in a big skillet.

11. Add croquettes in batches and shallow fry for around 2 to 3 minutes per side.

Nutrition: Calories: 404, Fat: 9 g, Carbs: 20 g, Fiber: 4 g, Protein: 30 g

54. Veggie Balls

Preparation Time: 15 minutes

Cooking Time: 25 minutes

Servings: 5 to 6

Ingredients:

- 2 medium sweet potatoes, cubed into ½-inch size
- 2 tbsp coconut milk
- 1 cup fresh kale leaves, trimmed and chopped
- 1 medium shallot, chopped finely
- 1 tsp ground cumin
- ½ tsp granulated garlic
- ¼ tsp ground turmeric
- Salt, to taste
- Freshly ground black pepper, to taste
- Ground flax seeds, as required

Directions:

1. Set the oven to 400°F. Line a baking sheet with parchment paper.

2. In a pan of water, arrange a steamer basket.

3. Bring the sweet potato to a steamer basket and steam for approximately 10 to 15 minutes.

4. In a sizable bowl, put the sweet potato.

5. Add coconut milk and mash well.

6. Add remaining ingredients except for flax seeds and mix till well combined.

7. Make about 1½ to 2-inch balls from your mixture.

8. Arrange the balls onto the prepared baking sheet inside a single layer.

9. Sprinkle with flax seeds.

10. Bake for around 20 to 25 minutes.

Nutrition: Calories: 464, Fat: 12 g, Carbs: 20 g, Fiber: 7 g, Protein: 27 g

55. Salmon Burgers

Preparation Time: 15 minutes

Cooking Time: 8 minutes

Servings: 3

Ingredients:

- 1 (6 oz) can skinless, boneless salmon, drained
- 1 celery rib, chopped
- ½ onion, chopped
- 2 large eggs
- 1 tbsp plus
- 1 tsp coconut flour
- 1 tbsp dried dill, crushed
- 1 tsp lemon
- Salt, to taste
- Freshly ground black pepper, to taste
- 3 tbsp coconut oil

Directions:

1. In a substantial bowl, add salmon and which has a fork, break it into small pieces.

2. Add remaining ingredients, excluding the oil, and mix till well combined.

3. Make 6 equal-sized small patties from the mixture.

4. In a substantial skillet, melt coconut oil on medium-high heat.

5. Cook the patties for around 3 to 4 minutes per side.

Nutrition: Calories: 393, Fat: 12 g, Carbs: 19 g, Fiber: 5 g, Protein: 24 g

56. Fennel Seeds Cookies

Preparation Time: 10 minutes

Cooking Time: 9 minutes

Servings: 5

Ingredients:

- ⅓ cup coconut flour
- ¼ tsp whole fennel seeds
- ½ tsp fresh ginger, grated finely
- ¼ cup coconut oil softened
- 2 tbsp raw honey
- 1 tsp vanilla extract
- Pinch of ground cinnamon
- Pinch of salt
- Pinch freshly ground black pepper

Directions:

1. Set the oven to 360°F. Line a cookie sheet that has parchment paper.

2. In a substantial bowl, add all together with the ingredients and mix till an even dough forms.

3. Form a small ball in the mixture made onto a prepared cookie sheet inside a single layer.

4. Using your fingers, gently press along the balls to create the cookies.

5. Bake for at least 9 minutes or till golden brown.

Nutrition: Calories: 353, Fat: 5 g, Carbs: 19 g, Fiber: 3 g, Protein: 25 g

57. Sun-Dried Tomato Garlic Bruschetta

Preparation Time: 10 minutes

Cooking Time: 5 minutes

Servings: 6

Ingredients:

- 2 slices sourdough bread, toasted
- 1 tsp chives, minced
- 1 garlic clove, peeled
- 2 tsp sun-dried tomatoes in olive oil, minced
- 1 tsp olive oil

Directions:

1. Vigorously rub garlic clove on 1 side of each of the toasted bread slices

2. Spread equal portions of sun-dried tomatoes on the garlic side of the bread. Sprinkle chives and drizzle olive oil on top.

3. Pop both slices into an oven toaster, and cook until well heated through.

4. Place bruschetta on a plate. Serve warm.

Nutrition: Calories: 149, Protein: 6.12 g, Fat: 2.99 g, Carbs: 24.39 g

58. Coconut & Banana Cookies

Preparation Time: 15 minutes

Cooking Time: 20 minutes

Servings: 7

Ingredients:

- 2 cups unsweetened coconut, shredded
- 3 medium bananas, peeled
- ½ tsp ground cinnamon
- ½ tsp ground turmeric
- Pinch of salt, to taste
- Freshly ground black pepper

Directions:

1. Set the oven to 350°F. Line a cookie sheet with lightly greased parchment paper.

2. In a mixer, put all together ingredients and pulse till a dough-like mixture forms.

3. Form small balls through the mixture and set them onto a prepared cookie sheet in a single layer.

4. Using your fingers, press along the balls to create the cookies.

5. Bake for at least 15 to 20 minutes or till golden brown.

Nutrition: Calories: 370, Fat: 4 g, Carbs: 27 g, Fiber: 11 g, Protein: 33 g

59. Hash Browns

Preparation Time: 15 minutes

Cooking Time: 15 minutes

Servings: 4

Ingredients:

- 1 lb Russet potatoes, peeled, processed using a grater
- Pinch of sea salt
- Pinch of black pepper, to taste

- 3 Tbsp olive oil

Directions:

1. Line a microwave-safe dish with paper towels. Spread shredded potatoes on top. Microwave veggies on the highest heat setting for 2 minutes. Remove from heat.

2. Pour 1 tbsp of oil into a non-stick skillet set over medium heat.

3. Cooking in batches, place a generous pinch of potatoes into the hot oil. Press down using the back of a spatula.

4. Cook for 3 minutes on every side, or until brown and crispy. Drain on paper towels. Repeat the step for the remaining potatoes. Add more oil as needed.

5. Season with salt and pepper. Serve.

Nutrition: Calories: 200, Protein: 4.03 g, Fat: 11.73 g, Carbs: 20.49 g

60. Mushroom Crêpes

Preparation Time: 1 hour 30 minutes

Cooking Time: 30 minutes

Servings: 6

Ingredients:

- 2 eggs
- ¾ cup milk
- ½ cup all-purpose flour
- ¼ tsp salt

For the Filling:

- 3 tbsp all-purpose flour
- 2 cups cremini mushrooms, sliced
- ¾ cup chicken broth
- ½ cup Parmesan cheese, grated
- ⅛ tsp cayenne
- ⅛ tsp nutmeg
- ¾ cup milk
- 3 garlic cloves, minced
- 2 tbsp parsley (chopped)
- 6 slices deli-sliced cooked lean ham
- ¼ tsp salt
- Freshly ground pepper

Directions:

1. Put and combine the salt and flour in a bowl. In another bowl, whisk the eggs and milk.

Gradually combine the two mixtures until smooth. Leave for 15 minutes.

2. Spray a skillet using non-stick cooking spray and put it over medium heat. Stir the batter a little. Add ¼ of the batter into the skillet. Tilt the skillet to form a thin and even crêpe. Cook for 1 to 2 minutes or until the bottom is golden and the top is set. Flip and cook for 20 seconds. Transfer to a plate.

3. Repeat the steps with the remaining batter. Loosely cover the cooked crêpes with plastic wrap.

4. For the filling. Put all together with the ingredients for filling in a saucepan on medium heat – flour, milk, cayenne, nutmeg, and pepper. Constantly whisk until thick or around 7 minutes. Remove from the stove. Stir in a tbsp of parsley and cheese. Loosely cover to keep warm.

5. Spray a skillet using non-stick cooking spray and put it over medium heat. Cook the garlic and mushrooms. Season with salt. Cook for 6 minutes or until the mushrooms are soft. Add 2 tbsp of sherry. Cook for a couple of minutes. Remove from the stove. Add the remaining parsley and stir.

6. Put. the crêpes side by side on a flat surface. Spread a tbsp of the sauce and 2 tbsp of the cooked mushrooms. Roll up the crêpes and transfer them to a greased baking dish. Put all the sauce on top. Bake in the oven at 450°F for 15 minutes.

Nutrition: Calories: 232, Protein: 16.51 g, Fat: 10.8 g, Carbs: 16.25 g

61. Bake Apple Turnover

Preparation Time: 30 minutes

Cooking Time: 25 minutes

Servings: 4

Ingredients:

For the Turnovers:

- 4 apples, peeled, cored, diced into bite-sized pieces
- 1 tbsp almond flour
- All-purpose flour for rolling out the dough
- 1 frozen puff pastry, thawed
- ½ cup palm sugar, crumbled by hand to loosen granules

- ½ tsp cinnamon powder

For the Egg Wash:

- 1 egg white, whisked in
- 2 tbsp water

Directions:

1. For the filling: combine almond flour, cinnamon powder, and palm sugar until these resemble coarse meals. Toss in diced apples until well coated. Set aside.

2. On a lightly floured surface, roll the puff pastry until ¼ inch thin. Slice into 8 pieces of 4" x 4" squares.

3. Divide prepared apples into 8 equal portions. Spoon on individual puff pastry squares. Fold in half diagonally. Press edges to seal.

4. Place each filled pastry on a baking tray lined with parchment paper. Make sure there is ample space between pastries.

5. Freeze for at least 20 minutes, or till ready to bake.

6. Preheat the oven to 400°F or 205°C for 10 minutes.

7. Brush frozen pastries with egg wash. Bring in a hot oven, and cook for 12 to 15 minutes, or until these turn golden brown all over.

8. Take off the baking tray in the oven immediately. Cool slightly for easier handling.

9. Place 1 apple turnover on a plate. Serve warm.

Nutrition: Calories: 203, Protein: 5.29 g, Fat: 4.4 g, Carbs: 38.25 g

62. Almond Pancakes with Coconut Flakes

Preparation Time: 5 minutes

Cooking Time: 20 minutes

Servings: 6

Ingredients:

- 1 overripe banana, mashed
- 2 eggs, yolks, and whites separated
- ½ cup unsweetened applesauce
- 1 cup almond flour, finely milled
- ¼ cup water
- ¼ tsp coconut oil

For Garnish:

- 2 tbsp blanched almond flakes
- Dash of cinnamon powder
- ¼ cup coconut flakes, sweetened
- Pinch of sea salt
- Pure maple syrup, used sparingly

Directions:

1. Whisk egg whites until soft peaks form.

2. Except for egg whites and coconut oil, combine the remaining ingredients in another bowl. Mix until batter comes together.

3. Gently fold in egg whites. Be sure not to over mix, or the pancake will become dense and chewy.

4. Pour oil into a nonstick skillet set over medium heat.

5. Wait for the oil to heat up before dropping in approximately ½ cup of batter. Cook until each side is set and bubbles form in the center. Turn on the other side, then cook for another 2 minutes.

6. Transfer flapjacks to a plate. Repeat step until all batter is cooked. Pour more oil into the skillet only if needed. This recipe should yield between 4 to 6 medium-sized pancakes.

7. Stack pancakes. Pour the desired amount of pure maple syrup on top. Garnish each stack with cinnamon-flavored almond-coconut flakes just before serving.

8. For the garnish, set the oven to 350°F for at least 10 minutes before use. Line a baking sheet with parchment paper. Set aside.

9. In a bowl, mix almond and coconut flakes. Spread the mixture evenly on a prepared baking sheet.

10. Bake for 7 to 10 minutes until flakes turn golden brown. Stir almond and coconut flakes once midway through roasting to prevent over-browning.

11. Remove the baking sheet from the oven: cool almond and coconut flakes for at least 10 minutes before sprinkling in cinnamon powder and salt. Toss to combine. Set aside.

Nutrition: Calories: 62, Protein: 2.24 g, Fat: 4.01 g, Carbs: 4.46 g

63. Breakfast Sausage and Mushroom Casserole

Preparation Time: 20 minutes

Cooking Time: 40 minutes

Servings: 4

Ingredients:

- 450 g Italian sausage, cooked and crumbled
- ¾ cup coconut milk
- 8 oz white mushrooms, sliced
- 1 medium onion, finely diced
- 2 tbsp organic ghee
- 6 free-range eggs
- 600 g sweet potatoes
- 1 red bell pepper, roasted
- ¾ tsp ground black pepper, divided
- 1½ tsp sea salt, divided

Directions:

1. Peel and shred the sweet potatoes.

2. Take a bowl, fill it with ice-cold water, and soak the sweet potatoes in it. Set aside.

3. Peel the roasted bell pepper, remove its seeds and finely dice it.

4. Set the oven to 375°F.

5. Get a casserole baking dish and grease it with organic ghee.

6. Put a skillet over medium flame and cook the mushrooms in it. Cook until the mushrooms are crispy and brown.

7. Take the mushrooms out and mix them with the crumbled sausage.

8. Now sauté the onions in the same skillet. Cook up until the onions are soft and golden. This should take about 4 to 5 minutes.

9. Take the onions out and mix them in the sausage-mushroom mixture.

10. Add the diced bell pepper to the same mixture.

11. Mix well and set aside for a while.

12. Now drain the soaked shredded potatoes, put them on a paper towel, and pat dry.

13. Bring the sweet potatoes to a bowl and add about a tsp of salt and half a tsp of ground black pepper to it. Mix well and set aside.

14. Now take a large bowl and crack the eggs in it.

15. Break the eggs and then blend in the coconut milk.

16. Stir in the remaining black pepper and salt.

17. Take the greased casserole dish and spread the seasoned sweet potatoes evenly on the base of the dish.

18. Next, spread the sausage mixture evenly in the dish.

19. Finally, spread the egg mixture.

20. Now cover the casserole dish using a piece of aluminum foil.

21. Bake for 20 to 30 minutes. To check if the casserole is baked properly, insert a tester in the middle of the casserole, and it should come out clean.

22. Uncover the casserole dish and bake it again, uncovered for 5 to 10 minutes, until the casserole is a little golden on the top.

23. Allow it to cool for 10 minutes.

24. Enjoy!

Nutrition: Calories: 598, Protein: 28.65 g, Fat: 36.75 g, Carbs: 48.01 g

64. Maple Oatmeal

Preparation Time: 5 minutes

Cooking Time: 30 minutes

Servings: 4

Ingredients:

- 1 tsp maple flavoring
- 1 tsp cinnamon
- 3 tbsp sunflower seeds
- ½ cup pecans, chopped
- ¼ cup coconut flakes, unsweetened
- ½ cup walnuts, chopped
- ½ cup milk, almond or coconut
- 4 tbsp chia seeds

Directions:

1. Pulse the sunflower seeds, walnuts, and pecans in a food processor to crumble. Or you can just put the nuts in a sturdy plastic bag, wrap the bag with a towel, lay it on a sturdy surface, and beat the towel with a hammer until the nuts are crumbled.

2. Mix the crushed nuts with the rest of the ingredients and pour them into a large pot.

Simmer this mixture over low heat for 30 minutes.

3. Stir often, so the mix does not stick to the bottom. Serve garnished with fresh fruit or a sprinkle of cinnamon if desired.

Nutrition: Calories: 374, Carbs: 3.2 g, Protein: 9.25 g, Fat: 4.59 g

Chapter 4

Lunch

65. Grilled Avocado Sandwich

Preparation Time: 10 minutes

Cooking Time: 15 minutes

Servings: 4

Ingredients:

- 8 slices pumpernickel bread
- 1 cup sauerkraut, drained & rinsed
- 1 cup hummus
- 1 tsp dairy-free margarine
- 1 avocado, peeled & sliced into 16 pieces

Directions:

1. Preheat your oven to 450°F.
2. Apply margarine to one side of your bread slices.
3. Keep 4 slices on your baking sheet. The margarine side should be down.
4. Distribute half of the hummus over the bread slices.
5. Place sauerkraut on the hummus.
6. Keep avocado slices over your sauerkraut.
7. Spread hummus on the remaining slices.
8. Keep the hummus side down on your slices of avocado. Bake for 7 minutes.
9. Flip over and bake for another 6 minutes.

Nutrition: Calories: 340, Total Fat: 16 g, Carbs: 39 g, Protein: 10 g, Fiber: 11 g, Sugar: 1 g, Sodium: 781 mg, Potassium: 552 mg

66. Cauliflower Steaks with Tamarind and Beans

Preparation Time: 5 minutes

Cooking Time: 30 minutes

Servings: 2

Ingredients:

- ½ cup olive oil
- ¼ lb cauliflower head
- 1 tsp black pepper, ground
- 2 tsp kosher salt
- 3 garlic cloves, chopped
- ½ lb green beans, trimmed
- ⅓ cup parsley, chopped
- ¾ tsp lemon zest, grated
- ¼ lb parmesan, grated
- ¼ lb panko breadcrumbs
- ⅓ cup tamarind
- 1 lb white beans, rinsed & drained
- 1 tsp Dijon mustard
- 2 tbsp margarine

Directions:

1. Preheat your oven to 425°F.
2. Take out the leaves and trim the stem ends of your cauliflower.
3. Keep the core side down on your working surface.
4. Slice from the center top to down with a knife.
5. Keep it on a baking sheet.
6. Apply 1 tbsp of oil on both sides. Season with pepper and salt.
7. Roast for 25 minutes. Turn halfway through.
8. Toss the green beans in the meantime with 1 tbsp of oil and pepper.

9. Keep on your baking sheet in a single layer.

10. Whisk the lemon zest, garlic, parsley, salt, pepper, and oil together in a bowl.

11. Keep half of this mix in another bowl.

12. Add Parmesan and panko to the first bowl. Use your hands to mix.

13. Add tamarind and white beans to the second bowl. Coat well by tossing.

14. Now whisk together the mustard and margarine.

15. Spread your margarine mix over the cauliflower.

16. Sprinkle the panko mixture over the cauliflower.

17. Add the white bean mix to the sheet with beans. Combine.

18. Keep the sheet in the oven and roast for 5 minutes.

19. Divide the beans, cauliflower, and tamarind among plates.

Nutrition: Calories: 1366, Total Fat: 67 g, Carbs: 166 g, Protein: 59 g, Fiber: 41 g, Sugar: 20 g, Cholesterol: 6 mg, Sodium: 2561 mg

67. Healthy Chicken Marsala

Preparation Time: 5 minutes

Cooking Time: 15 minutes

Servings: 4

Ingredients:

- 1½ chicken breasts, boneless & skinless
- 2 tbsp dairy-free margarine
- ½ lb shiitake mushrooms, sliced & stemmed
- 1 lb baby Bella mushrooms, sliced & stemmed
- 2 tbsp extra virgin olive oil
- 3 garlic cloves, chopped
- 1 cup shallot, chopped
- 2 cups chicken broth, low-sodium
- ¾ cup dry Marsala wine
- Black pepper, kosher salt, chopped parsley leaves

Directions:

1. Dry your chicken breasts using a paper towel.

2. Slice them horizontally into half.

3. Keep each piece between the parchment paper. Use your meat mallet to pound until you have ¼ inch thickness.

4. Season all sides with black pepper and kosher salt.

5. Dredge in some whole wheat flour. Keep aside.

6. Heat your skillet over medium temperature.

7. Pour olive oil and margarine into your pan.

8. Sauté the chicken for 5 minutes. Work in batches, not overcrowding your pan.

9. Transfer to a baking sheet. Set aside.

10. Wipe off excess cooking from your pan. Bring back to heat.

11. Add the remaining margarine and the mushrooms.

12. Sauté over high temperature. Season with black pepper and salt.

13. Add the garlic and chopped shallot to your pan.

14. Sauté 3 minutes. Include the Marsala wine. Bring down the heat for a minute.

15. Include the chicken broth and cook for 5 minutes.

16. Transfer chicken cutlets to the pan. Spoon over the sauce.

17. Garnish with parsley.

Nutrition: Calories: 546, Total Fat: 37 g, Carbs: 41 g, Protein: 10 g, Fiber: 5 g, Sugar: 6 g, Cholesterol: 31 mg, Sodium: 535 mg

68. Tuna Steaks

Preparation Time: 15 minutes

Cooking Time: 15 minutes

Servings: 2

Ingredients:

- 1½ cup water
- 1 tbsp lemon juice
- Pepper and salt to taste
- 1 tsp cayenne pepper
- 2 tuna steaks
- 3 kumquats, seeded, sliced, rinsed
- ⅓ cup cilantro, chopped

Directions:

1. Mix lemon juice, cayenne pepper and water over medium heat in a saucepan.

2. Season with pepper and salt. Boil.

3. Now include the tuna steaks into this mix.

4. Sprinkle cilantro and kumquats.

5. Cook for 15 minutes. The fish should flake easily with your fork.

Nutrition: Calories: 141, Total Fat: 1 g, Carbs: 6 g, Fiber: 2 g, Protein: 27 g, Sugar: 3 g, Cholesterol: 50 mg

69. Air Fryer Salmon

Preparation Time: 6 minutes

Cooking Time: 5 minutes

Servings: 2

Ingredients:

- ⅓ lb salmon filets
- ¼ cup margarine
- ¼ cup pistachios, chopped finely
- 1½ tbsp minced dill
- 2 tbsp lemon juice

Directions:

1. Preheat your air fryer to 400°F.

2. Spray olive oil on the basket.

3. Season your salmon with pepper to taste. You can also apply all-purpose seasoning.

4. Combine the margarine, lemon juice, and dill in a bowl.

5. Pour a spoonful into the fillets.

6. Top the fillets with chopped pistachios. Be generous.

7. Spray olive oil on the salmon lightly.

8. Air fry your fillets now for 5 minutes.

9. Take out the salmon carefully with a spatula from your air fryer.

10. Keep on a plate. Garnish with dill.

Nutrition: Calories: 305, Total Fat: 21 g, Carbs: 1 g, Protein: 27 g, Fiber: 2 g, Sugar: 3 g, Cholesterol: 43 mg, Sodium: 92 mg

70. Rosemary Garlic Lamb Chops

Preparation Time: 3 minutes

Cooking Time: 10 minutes

Servings: 2

Ingredients:

- 4 chops lamb
- 1 tsp olive oil
- 2 tsp garlic puree
- Fresh garlic
- Fresh rosemary

Directions:

1. Keep your lamb chops in the fryer grill pan.

2. Season the chops with pepper and salt. Brush with some olive oil.

3. Add some garlic puree to each chop.

4. Cover the grill pan gaps with garlic cloves and rosemary sprigs.

5. Refrigerate to marinate.

6. Take out after 1 hour. Keep in the fryer and cook for 5 minutes.

7. Use your spatula to turn the chops over.

8. Add some olive oil and cook for another 5 minutes.

9. Set aside for a minute.

10. Take out the rosemary and garlic before serving.

Nutrition: Calories: 678, Total Fat: 37 g, Carbs: 1 g, Protein: 83 g, Sugar: 0 g, Cholesterol: 257 mg, Sodium: 200 mg

71. Mushroom Farro Risotto

Preparation Time: 2 minutes

Cooking Time: 45 minutes

Servings: 5

Ingredients:

- 3 tbsp melted coconut oil
- 4 cups chicken broth, low sodium
- ¾ lb baby Bella mushrooms, trimmed & sliced
- ½ yellow onion, chopped
- 3 garlic cloves, chopped
- 1 tbsp thyme, chopped
- ¾ cup dry white wine
- 1½ cups organic farro
- 1 tsp lemon juice
- ¾ cup vegan parmesan
- ¾ cup peas
- Ground black pepper, kosher salt, chopped parsley

Directions:

1. Keep your chicken broth in a saucepan. Simmer over low heat.

2. Heat the coconut oil over medium temperature in a pot.

3. Add kosher salt and onion. Sauté for 6 minutes. Stir often.

4. Bring up the heat to high. Now add the mushrooms. Combine by stirring.

5. Cook for another 2 minutes. The mushrooms should become soft.

6. Add the thyme and garlic. Sauté for a minute, stirring occasionally.

7. Include the toast and farro and cook for 1 minute. Keep stirring.

8. Pour in the white wine. Cook for 3 minutes. Stir often. The wine needs to be absorbed completely.

9. Add the hot broth to your pot. Combine well.

10. Bring down the heat and cook for 30 minutes. Stir every 15 minutes.

11. Add the lemon juice and grated parmesan. Stir to combine.

12. Fold in the peas. Season with pepper and salt.

13. Take out the pot from heat. Let it sit covered for 5 minutes.

14. Garnish with thyme leaves and parsley.

Nutrition: Calories: 397, Total Fat: 25 g, Carbs: 29 g, Protein: 14 g, Sugar: 5 g, Fiber: 5 g, Cholesterol: 32 mg, Sodium: 429 mg

72. Instant Pot Black Beans

Preparation Time: 15 minutes

Cooking Time: 15 minutes

Servings: 8

Ingredients:

- 2 cups black beans, rinsed & dried
- 1 yellow onion, chopped
- 2 tbsp extra virgin olive oil
- 2 garlic cloves, smashed
- 1 jalapeno pepper, sliced
- 1 yellow or red bell pepper, stemmed & seeded
- 1 handful cilantro
- ½ tsp red pepper flakes
- 2 tsp cumin, ground
- 2 tsp kosher salt

Directions:

1. Keep the black beans in your saucepan. Cover with cold water for 6 hours.

2. Drain and rinse.

3. Heat oil and add garlic, onions, and salt. Sauté for 5 minutes.

4. Add the jalapeno, bell pepper, red pepper flakes, black pepper, and cumin.

5. Sauté for another 3 minutes. Stir frequently.

6. Now include the cilantro stems, beans, water, and some more salt. Combine well by stirring. Cook for 7 minutes. Release naturally.

Nutrition: Calories: 144, Total Fat: 7 g, Carbs: 14 g, Protein: 4 g, Sugar: 1 g, Fiber: 4 g, Cholesterol: 0 mg, Sodium: 606 mg

73. Popcorn Chicken

Preparation Time: 15 minutes

Cooking Time: 15 minutes

Servings: 4

Ingredients:

- ¼ lb chicken breast halves, boneless and skinless
- ½ tsp paprika
- ¼ tsp mustard, ground
- ¼ tsp garlic powder
- 3 tbsp arrowroot

Directions:

1. Cut the chicken into small pieces and keep it in a bowl.

2. Combine the paprika, garlic powder, mustard, salt, and pepper in another bowl.

3. Reserve a tsp of your seasoning mixture. Sprinkle the other portion on the chicken. Coat evenly by tossing.

4. Combine the reserved seasoning and arrowroot in a plastic bag.

5. Combine well by shaking.

6. Keep your chicken pieces in the bag. Seal it and shake for coating evenly.

7. Now transfer the chicken to a mesh strainer. Shake the excess arrowroot.

8. Keep aside for 5 to 10 minutes. The arrowroot should start to get absorbed into your chicken.

9. Preheat your air fryer to 390°F.

10. Apply some oil to the air fryer basket.

11. Keep the chicken pieces inside. They should not overlap.

12. Apply cooking spray.

13. Cook until the chicken isn't pink anymore.

Nutrition: Calories: 156, Total Fat: 4 g, Carbs: 6 g, Protein: 24 g, Sugar: 0 g, Fiber: 1 g, Cholesterol: 65 mg, Sodium: 493 mg

74. Spicy Chicken and Cauliflower

Preparation Time: 5 minutes

Cooking Time: 25 minutes

Servings: 4

Ingredients:

- 2 lb chicken breasts, skinless, boneless and cubed
- 1 tbsp rice vinegar
- 4 tbsp raw honey
- 6 tbsp coconut aminos
- 2 garlic cloves, minced
- 2 lb cauliflower, florets separated
- ½ cup water
- 1 tbsp whole wheat flour
- 2 tbsp olive oil
- 3 green onions, chopped
- 2 tbsp sesame seeds

Directions:

1. In a bowl, mix 3 tbsp honey with 3 tbsp coconut aminos, garlic, vinegar and the chicken. Heat a pan with half of the oil over medium heat, add cauliflower and stir then cook for 5 minutes and transfer to a bowl.

2. Heat the pan with the rest of the oil over medium heat, Drain the chicken, reserving the marinade, then add it to the pan.

3. Toss and cook for 6 minutes. In a separate bowl, whisk together the rest of the aminos with the remaining honey, water, whole wheat flour and the reserved marinade. Add over the chicken, cover the pan and cook on low heat for 10 minutes, take off the heat, add the cauliflower and toss.

4. Divide between plates, sprinkle green onions and sesame seeds on top and serve. Enjoy!

Nutrition: Calories: 250, Total Fat: 4 g, Carbs: 10 g, Protein: 12 g

75. Salmon and Sweet Potato Mix

Preparation Time: 10 minutes

Cooking Time: 0 minutes

Servings: 4

Ingredients:

- 1½ lb sweet potatoes, baked and cubed
- 1 tbsp olive oil
- 4 oz smoked salmon, chopped
- 1 tbsp chopped chives
- 2 tsp horseradish
- ¼ cup coconut cream
- Salt and black pepper to the taste

Directions:

1. In a bowl, whisk together the coconut cream with salt, pepper, horseradish and chives. Add salmon and potatoes, toss to coat and serve right away.

2. Enjoy!

Nutrition: Calories: 233, Total Fat: 6 g, Carbs: 37 g, Protein: 9 g, Fiber: 5 g

76. Lemon Onion Mash

Preparation Time: 15 minutes

Cooking Time: 15 minutes

Servings: 4

Ingredients:

- 2 white onions
- 4 oz cauliflower
- ¼ cup heavy cream
- 4 oz cheddar cheese, shredded
- ½ tsp pink salt
- 1 tsp white pepper
- ½ tsp lemon zest
- 1 tsp lemon juice
- 1 tsp butter

Directions:

1. Peel the onion and grind it.

2. Put ground onion and butter in the saucepan.

3. Blend cauliflower until you get cauliflower rice.

4. Add cauliflower rice to the saucepan too.

5. Add Pink salt, white pepper, lemon zest, and lemon juice. Stir it.

6. Close the lid and cook the mass for 5 minutes over medium heat.

7. Then add shredded Cheddar cheese and heavy cream.

8. Mix up well and stir until cheese is melted.

9. Close the lid and simmer mash for 5 minutes more over the low heat.

10. Switch off the heat and close the lid.

11. Let the lemon onion mash chill for 10 minutes.

Nutrition: Calories: 171, Total Fat: 13.5 g, Carbs: 6.5 g, Protein: 8.1 g, Fiber: 4 g

77. Brown Rice and Chicken Mix

Preparation Time: 10 minutes

Cooking Time: 15 minutes

Servings: 4

Ingredients:

- 1½ cups brown rice, cooked
- 1½ tbsp coconut sugar
- 1 cup chicken stock
- 2 tbsp coconut aminos
- 4 oz chicken breast boneless, skinless and cut into small pieces
- 1 egg
- 2 egg whites
- 2 scallions, chopped

Directions:

1. Put stock in a pot, heat up over medium-low heat and add coconut aminos and sugar, stir, bring to a boil, add the chicken and toss. In a bowl, mix the egg with egg whites, whisk well then add over the chicken mix.

2. Sprinkle the scallions on top and cook for 3 minutes without stirring. Divide the rice into 4 bowls, add the chicken mix on top and serve. Enjoy!

Nutrition: Calories: 231, Total Fat: 11 g, Carbs: 7 g, Protein: 9 g, Fiber: 7 g

78. Curried Shrimp and Vegetables

Preparation Time: 10 minutes

Cooking Time: 15 minutes

Servings: 4

Ingredients:

- 3 tbsp coconut oil
- 1 onion, sliced
- 2 cups cauliflower, cut into florets
- 1 cup coconut milk
- 1 tbsp curry powder
- ¼ cup fresh parsley, chopped
- 1 lb shrimp, tails removed

Directions:

1. In a large skillet, melt the coconut oil over medium-high heat. Add the onion and cauliflower and cook until they are softened.

2. Add coconut milk, curry, and parsley to the skillet. (Feel free to add any other spices you like. Turmeric will give you an even bigger anti-inflammatory boost.) Cook for 2 to 3 more minutes.

3. Stir the shrimp into the skillet and cook until it is opaque.

Nutrition: Calories: 332, Total Fat: 22 g, Carbs: 11 g, Protein: 24 g, Sodium: 309 mg

79. Buttered Sprouts

Preparation Time: 7 minutes

Cooking Time: 20 minutes

Servings: 4

Ingredients:

- 10 oz Brussels sprouts
- 2 oz prosciutto
- 3 tsp butter
- 1 cup water
- 1 tsp salt

Directions:

1. Chop prosciutto and place in the saucepan.

2. Roast it until it starts to be crispy.

3. Then add water and Brussels sprouts.

4. Bring the mixture to boil and close the lid.

5. Boil the vegetables for 15 minutes.

6. After this, drain ½ part of the liquid and add butter.

7. Mix it up until the butter is melted and bring the meal to boil one more time in the butter liquid.

8. Serve buttered sprouts with the butter liquid.

Nutrition: Calories: 76, Total Fat: 5 g, Carbs: 6.5 g, Protein: 5.1 g, Fiber: 4 g

80. Sheet Pan Rosemary Mushrooms

Preparation Time: 10 minutes

Cooking Time: 15 minutes

Servings: 2

Ingredients:

- 1 cup mushrooms
- 1 tsp minced rosemary
- ½ tsp sea salt
- 1 tbsp sesame oil

Directions:

1. Line the baking tray with baking paper.

2. Slice the mushrooms roughly and put them in the baking tray.

3. Sprinkle mushrooms with minced rosemary, sea salt, and sesame oil.

4. Mix up the vegetables well with the help of the hand palms.

5. Preheat the oven to 360°F.

6. Cook mushrooms for 15 minutes.

Nutrition: Calories: 70, Total Fat: 7 g, Carbs: 1.5 g, Protein: 1.1 g, Fiber: 4 g

81. Chicken Breasts and Mushrooms

Preparation Time: 5 minutes

Cooking Time: 25 minutes

Servings: 6

Ingredients:

- 3 lb chicken breasts, skinless and boneless
- 1 yellow onion, chopped
- 1 garlic clove, minced
- A pinch of salt and black pepper
- 10 mushrooms, chopped
- 1 tbsp olive oil
- 2 red bell peppers, chopped

Directions:

1. Put the chicken in a baking dish, add onion, garlic, salt, pepper, mushrooms, oil and bell peppers. Mix briefly and bake in the oven at 425°F for 25 minutes.

2. Divide between plates and serve. Enjoy!

Nutrition: Calories: 285, Total Fat: 11 g, Carbs: 13 g, Protein: 16 g, Fiber: 1 g

82. Cabbage with Apple

Preparation Time: 15 minutes

Cooking Time: 9 minutes

Servings: 2 to 4

Ingredients:

- 2 tsp coconut oil
- 1 large apple, cored and sliced thinly
- 1 onion, sliced thinly
- 1½ lb cabbage, chopped finely
- 1 tbsp fresh thyme, chopped
- 1 red chili, chopped
- 1 tbsp apple cider vinegar
- ⅔ cup almonds, chopped

Directions:

1. In a nonstick skillet, melt 1 tsp of coconut oil on medium heat.

2. Add apple and stir fry for about 2 to 3 minutes.

3. Transfer the apple into a bowl.

4. In the same skillet, melt 1 tsp of coconut oil on medium heat.

5. Add onion and sauté for about 1 to 2 minutes.

6. Add cabbage and stir fry for about 3 minutes.

7. Add apple, thyme and vinegar and cook, covered for about 1 minute.

8. Serve warm with the garnishing of almonds.

Nutrition: Calories: 106, Protein: 2.68 g, Fat: 2.73 g, Carbs: 21.07 g

83. Roasted Summer Squash & Fennel Bulb

Preparation Time: 15 minutes

Cooking Time: 15 minutes

Servings: 4

Ingredients:

- 2 small summer squash, cubed into 1-inch size
- 1½ cups fennel bulb, sliced
- 1 tbsp fresh thyme, chopped
- 1 tbsp extra-virgin olive oil
- Salt and freshly ground black pepper, to taste
- ¼ cup garlic, sliced thinly
- 1 tbsp fennel fronds, chopped

Directions:

1. Preheat the oven to 450°F.
2. In a large bowl, add all ingredients except garlic and fennel fronds and toss to coat well.
3. Transfer the mixture to a large rimmed baking sheet.
4. Roast for about 10 minutes.
5. Remove from the oven and stir in the sliced garlic.
6. Roast for 5 minutes more.
7. Remove from the oven and stir in the fennel fronds.
8. Serve immediately.

Nutrition: Calories: 66, Fat: 4 g, Carbs: 7 g, Fiber: 2 g, Sugar: 0 g, Protein: 2 g, Sodium: 167 mg

84. Roasted Brussels Sprouts & Sweet Potato

Preparation Time: 15 minutes

Cooking Time: 45 minutes

Servings: 6 to 8

Ingredients:

- 1 large sweet potato, peeled and cut into 1 to 2-inch pieces
- 1 lb Brussels sprouts, trimmed and halved
- 2 minced garlic cloves
- 1 tsp ground cumin
- ½ tsp garlic salt
- Salt and freshly ground black pepper, to taste

- ⅓ cup olive oil
- 1 tbsp apple cider vinegar
- Chopped fresh thyme, for garnishing

Directions:

1. Preheat the oven to 400°F. Grease a sheet pan.
2. In a large bowl, add all ingredients except vinegar and thyme and toss to coat well.
3. Transfer the mixture to the prepared baking pan.
4. Roast for 40 to 45 minutes more.
5. Transfer the vegetable mixture to a serving plate and drizzle with vinegar.
6. Garnish with thyme and serve.

Nutrition: Calories: 127, Protein: 2.48 g, Fat: 9.18 g, Carbs: 10.38 g

85. Potato Mash

Preparation Time: 15 minutes

Cooking Time: 26 minutes

Servings: 32

Ingredients:

- 10 large baking potatoes, peeled and cubed
- 3 tbsp olive oil, divided
- 1 onion, chopped
- 1 tbsp ground turmeric
- ½ tsp ground cumin
- Salt and freshly ground black pepper, to taste

Directions:

1. In a large pan of water, add potatoes and bring to a boil on medium-high heat.
2. Cook for about 20 minutes.
3. Drain well and transfer into a large bowl.
4. With a potato masher, mash the potatoes.
5. Meanwhile in a skillet, heat 1 tbsp of oil on medium-high heat.
6. Add onion and sauté for about 6 minutes.
7. Add onion mixture into the bowl with mashed potatoes.
8. Add turmeric, cumin, salt and black pepper and mash till well combined.
9. Stir in the remaining oil and serve.

Nutrition: Calories: 103, Fat: 4 g, Sat Fat: 2 g, Carbs: 23 g, Fiber: 2 g, Sugar: 1 g, Protein: 7 g, Sodium: 224 mg

86. Creamy Sweet Potato Mash

Preparation Time: 15 minutes

Cooking Time: 21 minutes

Servings: 4

Ingredients:

- 1 tbsp olive oil
- 2 large sweet potatoes, peeled and chopped
- 2 tsp ground turmeric
- 1 garlic clove, minced
- 2 cups vegetable broth
- 2 tbsp unsweetened coconut milk
- Salt and freshly ground black pepper, to taste
- Chopped pistachios, for garnishing

Directions:

1. In a large skillet, heat oil on medium-high heat.
2. Add sweet potato and stir fry for bout 2 to 3 minutes.
3. Add turmeric and stir fry for about 1 minute.
4. Add garlic and stir fry for about 2 minutes.
5. Add broth and bring to a boil.
6. Reduce the heat to low and cook for about 10 to 15 minutes or till all the liquid is absorbed.
7. Transfer the sweet potato mixture into a bowl.
8. Add coconut milk, salt and black pepper and mash it completely.
9. Garnish with pistachio and serve.

Nutrition: Calories: 110, Fat: 5g, Carbs: 16g, Protein: 1g

87. Gingered Cauliflower Rice

Preparation Time: 15 minutes

Cooking Time: 10 minutes

Servings: 3 to 4

Ingredients:

- 3 tbsp coconut oil
- 4 (⅛-inch thick) fresh ginger slices
- 1 small head cauliflower, trimmed and processed into a rice consistency
- 3 garlic cloves, crushed
- 1 tbsp chives, chopped
- 1 tbsp coconut vinegar

- Salt, to taste

Directions:

1. In a skillet, melt coconut oil on medium-high heat.
2. Add ginger and sauté for about 2 to 3 minutes.
3. Discard the ginger slices and stir in cauliflower and garlic.
4. Cook, stirring occasionally for about 7 to 8 minutes.
5. Stir in remaining ingredients and remove from heat.
6. Serve immediately

Nutrition: Calories: 111, Protein: 1.48 g, Fat: 10.42 g, Carbs: 4.49 g

88. Spicy Cauliflower Rice

Preparation Time: 15 minutes

Cooking Time: 10 minutes

Servings: 4

Ingredients:

- 3 tbsp coconut oil
- 1 small white onion, chopped
- 3 garlic cloves, minced
- 1 large head cauliflower, trimmed and processed into the rice consistency
- ½ tsp ground cumin
- ½ tsp paprika
- Salt and freshly ground black pepper, to taste
- 1 large tomato, chopped
- ¼ cup tomato paste
- ¼ cup fresh cilantro, chopped
- Fresh cilantro, chopped for garnishing
- 2 limes, quarters

Directions:

1. In a large skillet, melt coconut oil on medium-high heat.
2. Add onion and sauté for about 2 minutes.
3. Add garlic and sauté for about 1 minute.
4. Stir in cauliflower rice.
5. Add cumin, paprika, salt and black pepper and cook, stirring occasionally for about 2 to 3 minutes.
6. Stir in tomato, tomato paste and cilantro and cook for about 2 to 3 minutes.

7. Garnish with cilantro and serve alongside lime.

Nutrition: Calories: 137, Protein: 2.73 g, Fat: 10.69 g, Carbs: 11.1 g

89. Simple Brown Rice

Preparation Time: 10 minutes

Cooking Time: 50 minutes

Servings: 4

Ingredients:

- 1 cup brown rice
- 2 cups chicken broth
- 1 tbsp ground turmeric
- 1 tbsp olive oil

Directions:

1. In a pan, add rice, broth and turmeric and bring to a boil.
2. Reduce the heat to low.
3. Simmer, covered for about 50 minutes.
4. Add the olive oil and fluff with a fork.
5. Keep aside, covered for about 10 minutes before serving.

Nutrition: Calories: 227, Protein: 26.16 g, Fat: 11.75 g, Carbs: 2.5 g

90. Quinoa with Apricots

Preparation Time: 15 minutes

Cooking Time: 12 minutes

Servings: 4

Ingredients:

- 2 cups water
- 1 cup quinoa
- ½ tsp fresh ginger, grated finely
- ½ cup dried apricots, chopped roughly
- Salt and freshly ground black pepper, to taste

Directions:

1. In a pan, add water on high heat and bring to a boil.
2. Add quinoa and reduce the heat to medium.
3. Cover and reduce the heat to low.
4. Simmer for about 12 minutes.
5. Remove from heat and immediately, stir in ginger and apricots.

6. Keep aside, covered for about 15 minutes before serving.

Nutrition: Calories: 196, Protein: 6.56 g, Fat: 2.66 g, Carbs: 37.49 g

91. Simple Carrots Mix

Preparation Time: 10 minutes

Cooking Time: 40 minutes

Servings: 6

Ingredients:

- 15 carrots, halved lengthwise
- 2 tbsp coconut sugar
- ¼ cup extra virgin organic olive oil
- ½ tsp rosemary, dried
- ½ tsp garlic powder
- A pinch of black pepper

Directions:

1. In a bowl, combine the carrots with the sugar, oil, rosemary, garlic powder and black pepper, toss well, spread with a lined baking sheet, introduce in the oven and bake at 400°F for 40 minutes.
2. Divide between plates and serve as a side dish.
3. Enjoy!

Nutrition: Calories 211, Fat: 2 g, Fiber: 6 g, Carbs: 14 g, Protein: 8 g

92. Tasty Grilled Asparagus

Preparation Time: 10 minutes

Cooking Time: 3 minutes

Servings: 4

Ingredients:

- 2 lb asparagus, trimmed
- 2 tbsp organic olive oil
- A pinch of salt and black pepper

Directions:

1. In a bowl, combine the asparagus with salt, pepper and oil and toss well.
2. Place the asparagus on preheated grill over medium-high heat, cook for 3 minutes with them, divide between plates and serve as a side dish.
3. Enjoy!

Nutrition: Calories: 172, Fat: 4 g, Fiber: 7 g, Carbs: 14 g, Protein: 8 g

93. Easy Roasted Carrots

Preparation Time: 30 minutes

Cooking Time: 30 minutes

Servings: 4

Ingredients:

- 2 lb carrots, quartered
- A pinch of black pepper
- 3 tbsp olive oil
- 2 tbsp parsley, chopped

Directions:

1. Arrange the carrots with a lined baking sheet, add black pepper and oil, toss, introduce them inside the oven and cook at 400°F for about 30 minutes.

2. Add parsley, toss, divide between plates and serve as a side dish.

3. Enjoy!

Nutrition: Calories: 177 g, Fat: 3 g, Fiber: 6 g, Carbs: 14 g, Protein: 6 g

94. Dill Haddock

Preparation Time: 10 minutes

Cooking Time: 30 minutes

Servings: 4

Ingredients:

- 1 lb haddock fillets
- 3 tsp veggie stock
- 2 tbsp lemon juice
- Salt and black pepper to the taste
- 2 tbsp mayonnaise
- 2 tsp chopped dill
- A drizzle of olive oil

Directions:

1. Grease a baking dish with the oil, add the fish, also add stock mixed with lemon juice, salt, pepper, mayo and dill.

2. Toss a bit and place in the oven at 350°F to bake for 30 minutes. Divide between plates and serve.

3. Enjoy!

Nutrition: Calories: 214, Fat: 12 g, Fiber: 4 g, Carbs: 7 g, Protein: 17 g

95. Trout and Salsa

Preparation Time: 10 minutes

Cooking Time: 16 minutes

Servings: 2

Ingredients:

- 2 trout fillets, boneless
- ½ cup chopped yellow onion
- 4 tsp olive oil
- 1 tsp minced garlic
- 1 green bell pepper, chopped
- ½ cup canned tomato salsa
- 2 tbsp kalamata olives, pitted and chopped
- ¼ cup chicken stock
- A pinch of salt and black pepper

Directions:

1. Heat up a pan with 2 tsp oil over medium heat, add bell pepper and onion then stir and cook for 3 minutes. Add garlic, stock, olives and salsa, stir, cook for 5 minutes and transfer to a bowl.

2. Heat up the pan again with the rest of the oil over medium heat, add fish, season with salt and pepper and cook for 2 minutes on each side. Transfer to a baking dish, pour the salsa over the fish and place in the oven to bake at 425°F for 6 minutes. Divide between plates and serve.

3. Enjoy!

Nutrition: Calories: 200, Fat: 5 g, Fiber: 6 g, Carbs: 12 g, Protein: 12 g

96. Shrimp Cakes

Preparation Time: 10 minutes

Cooking Time: 10 minutes

Servings: 24

Ingredients:

- ½ lb tiger shrimp, peeled, deveined and chopped
- A pinch of sea salt and black pepper
- 2 tbsp olive oil
- ½ lb ground pork
- 1 egg, whisked
- 2 tbsp coconut flour
- 2 tbsp chicken stock

- 1 tsp coconut aminos
- 1 green onion stalk, chopped
- 1 tsp fresh grated ginger

Directions:

1. In a bowl, mix the shrimp with the pork, salt, pepper, egg, stock, aminos, onion, ginger and flour. Stir well and shape medium cakes out of this mix.

2. Heat up a pan with the oil over medium-high heat, add the cakes and cook for 5 minutes on each side. Divide between plates and serve with a side salad.

3. Enjoy!

Nutrition: Calories: 281, Fat: 8 g, Fiber: 7 g, Carbs: 19 g, Protein: 8 g

97. Italian Calamari

Preparation Time: 10 minutes

Cooking Time: 30 minutes

Servings: 6

Ingredients:

- 15 oz canned tomatoes, chopped
- 1½ lb calamari, cleaned, tentacles separated and cut into thin strips
- 1 garlic clove, minced
- ½ cup veggie stock
- 1 bunch chopped parsley
- A pinch red pepper flakes
- Juice of lemon
- A drizzle olive oil
- A pinch of sea salt and black pepper

Directions:

1. Heat up a pan with the oil over medium-high heat, add the garlic and pepper flakes, stir and cook for 2 to 3 minutes.

2. Add calamari, stir and cook for 3 minutes more. Add tomatoes, stock, lemon juice, salt and pepper, bring to a simmer then reduce heat to medium and cook for 25 minutes. Add the parsley, stir, divide into bowls and serve.

3. Enjoy!

Nutrition: Calories: 228, Fat: 2 g, Fiber: 4 g, Carbs: 11 g, Protein: 39 g

98. Chili Snapper

Preparation Time: 10 minutes

Cooking Time: 20 minutes

Servings: 2

Ingredients:

- 2 red snapper fillets, boneless and skinless
- 3 tbsp chili paste
- A pinch of sea salt and black pepper
- 1 tbsp coconut aminos
- 1 garlic clove, minced
- ½ tsp fresh grated ginger
- 2 tsp sesame seeds, toasted
- 2 tbsp olive oil
- 1 green onion, chopped
- 2 tbsp chicken stock

Directions:

1. Heat up a pan with the oil over medium-high heat, add the ginger, onion and garlic, stir and cook for 2 minutes.

2. Add chili paste, aminos, salt, pepper and the stock, stir and cook for 3 minutes more. Add the fish fillets, toss gently and cook for 5 to 6 minutes on each side. Divide between plates, sprinkle sesame seeds on top and serve.

3. Enjoy!

Nutrition: Calories: 261, Fat: 10 g, Fiber: 7 g, Carbs: 15 g, Protein: 16 g

99. Mashed Chickpea Bruschetta

Preparation Time: 12 minutes

Cooking Time: 0 minutes

Servings: 4

Ingredients:

- 1 can chickpeas, rinsed and drained
- 1 cup spinach or arugula (loosely packed)
- 2 tbsp spring onion, chopped
- 1 garlic clove
- 10 basil leaves
- 1 small tomato, quartered
- 6 to 7 walnut halves
- ½ lemon, squeezed
- ¼ cup small black olives
- 1 tbsp olive oil

For Serving:

- 1 whole-grain baguette OR lettuce leaves

Directions:

1. Combine the chickpeas, spinach or arugula, onion, garlic, basil, tomato, walnuts, lemon juice, olives, and olive oil in a food processor. Pulse a couple of times to achieve a well-mixed but chunky texture.

2. Slice the whole grain baguette into pieces and toast. Spread chickpea mixture on top, and serve.

3. If you prefer, you can use pita chips or make lettuce wraps.

Nutrition: Calories: 255, Fat: 12 g, Carbs: 31 g, Protein: 8 g, Sodium: 415 mg

100.   Puttanesca-Style Greens and Beans

Preparation Time: 15 minutes

Cooking Time: 55 minutes

Servings: 6

Ingredients:

- 3 cups water
- 1 cup dried baby lima beans, soaked overnight
- ¾ cup pitted kalamata olives
- ½ cup pitted green olives
- ½ cup sundried tomatoes in olive oil (optional)
- 1 small yellow onion
- 2 garlic cloves
- 2 tsp capers
- 2 tbsp extra-virgin olive oil
- 2 cups shredded greens (kale, chard, dandelion greens, or beet greens all work well)
- 4 anchovies, or 1 to 2 tsp anchovy paste (optional)
- ½ tsp black pepper

Directions:

1. Combine the water and lima beans in a large saucepan and bring them to a boil over medium-high heat. After it boils, reduce the heat to low, cover, and simmer for about 45 minutes. You want the beans to be tender. When they are, drain well.

2. Combine the olives, sundried tomatoes, onion, garlic, and capers in a food processor and pulse until roughly chopped.

3. Heat 2 tbsp of oil over medium-high heat in a large skillet. When hot, add the olive mixture and cook for about 5 minutes, or until the onions are soft.

4. Add the greens, anchovies, and black pepper. Stir and cook for about 4 more minutes, and then stir in the beans. Heat through, and serve.

Nutrition: Calories: 314, Fat: 19 g, Carbs: 28 g, Protein: 8 g, Sodium: 927 mg

101.   Mediterranean Quinoa Bowls

Preparation Time: 15 minutes

Cooking Time: 0 minutes

Servings: 6

Ingredients:

Roasted Red Pepper Sauce:

- 1 (16 oz) jar roasted red peppers, drained (or roast your own)
- 1 garlic clove
- ½ tsp salt (more to taste)
- Juice 1 lemon
- ¼ cup olive oil
- ½ cup almonds

For the Bowls:

- 3 cups cooked quinoa
- 3 cups spinach or kale
- 1 cup chopped cucumber
- ½ cup feta cheese
- ½ cup kalamata olives
- 1 cup red onion, thinly sliced

Options:

- Hummus
- Fresh basil or parsley
- Olive oil, lemon juice, salt, pepper

Directions:

1. Prepare the sauce. In a food processor, combine the sauce ingredients and pulse until the mixture is just about smooth. It should be thick.

2. Build the bowls. Start with a serving of the cooked quinoa. Top with red pepper sauce, and then add a portion of the other toppings.

Nutrition: Calories: 407, Fat: 23 g, Carbs: 41 g, Protein: 11 g, Sodium: 853 mg

102. Pineapple Three Bean Salad

Preparation Time: 10 minutes + 2 hours chilling time

Cooking Time: 0 minutes

Servings: 6

Ingredients:

- 1 (15 oz) can black beans, drained and rinsed
- 1 (15 oz) can chickpeas, drained and rinsed
- 1½ cups cherry tomatoes, halved
- 1 cup shelled edamame, thawed if frozen
- 1 cup corn kernels
- 1 cup pineapple, finely chopped
- ½ cup cilantro, finely minced
- 3 garlic cloves, minced
- 2 tbsp extra-virgin olive oil
- 2 tbsp apple cider vinegar
- 1 tsp chili powder
- ½ tsp salt
- ½ tsp red pepper flakes
- ½ tsp cumin
- Chips for serving (optional)

Directions:

1. In a large mixing bowl, combine the black beans, chickpeas, tomatoes, edamame, corn, pineapple, cilantro, and garlic. Mix well.

2. In a separate bowl, combine the olive oil, apple cider vinegar, chili powder, salt, red pepper flakes, and cumin. Drizzle this over the beans and veggies, and fold it in.

3. Refrigerate for 2 hours, stirring occasionally.

4. Serve with chips or make lettuce wraps.

Nutrition: Calories: 287, Fat: 8 g, Carbs: 43 g, Protein: 14 g, Sodium: 209 mg

103. Leek and Chard Frittata

Preparation Time: 5 minutes

Cooking Time: 35 minutes

Servings: 5

Ingredients:

- 1 tbsp olive or avocado oil, more as needed
- 1 leek, finely chopped
- 1½ cup potatoes, diced
- 1 cup chard, chopped
- 1 tsp fine sea salt, divided
- 1 garlic clove, minced
- ½ cup cherry tomatoes
- 10 large eggs
- ½ tsp black pepper
- ½ tsp paprika
- ½ tsp turmeric

Directions:

1. Preheat the oven to 375°F.

2. Heat the oil in an ovenproof skillet.

3. When it is hot, cook the leeks for 1 to 2 minutes, and then add the potatoes and cook for 5 more minutes.

4. Add the chard to the skillet and cook until it is soft. Sprinkle with half of the salt and add the garlic and tomatoes.

5. Whisk together the eggs, remaining salt, pepper, paprika, and turmeric, and pour the mixture into the skillet.

6. Move the skillet to the oven and bake for about 25 minutes, or until set.

Nutrition: Calories: 224, Fat: 12 g, Carbs: 13 g, Protein: 14 g, Sodium: 684 mg

104. Greek Turkey Burgers with Tzatziki

Preparation Time: 20 minutes

Cooking Time: 35 minutes

Servings: 4

Ingredients:

- Turkey burgers
- 1 tbsp extra-virgin olive oil
- ½ cup sweet onion, minced
- 2 garlic cloves, minced
- 1 egg
- ½ cup chopped fresh parsley
- ½ tsp dried oregano
- ¼ tsp red pepper flakes
- 1 lb ground turkey
- ¾ cup bread crumbs
- Salt and freshly ground black pepper to taste
- 1 batch tzatziki sauce, for serving
- 4 hamburger buns, for serving

Directions:

1. Preheat the oven to 375°F.

2. In a small skillet over medium, heat the oil and sauté the onions and garlic until soft. Set aside until they are cool.

3. Once cooled, mix the aromatics with the egg, parsley, oregano, red pepper flakes, and ground turkey. Stir in the breadcrumbs, season with salt and pepper, and mix gently until completely combined. Form the mixture into 4 patties.

4. Spray an ovenproof skillet with non-stick cooking spray, then heat it over medium-high heat. Place the patties in the skillet and sear them on both sides, about 2 minutes on each side.

5. Move the skillet to the oven and cook for about 15 minutes, or until the burgers are cooked through.

6. While waiting for the burgers to cook, prepare the tzatziki sauce by mixing all the ingredients.

7. When burgers are done, top with tzatziki sauce and whatever other toppings you desire.

Nutrition: Calories: 326, Fat: 14 g, Carbs: 22 g, Protein: 27 g, Sodium: 109

105. Seared Ahi Tuna Poke Salad

Preparation Time: 20 minutes

Cooking Time: 20 minutes

Servings: 6

Ingredients:

- 20 square wonton wrappers cut into strips (use corn tortillas to make this gluten-free)
- 2 tbsp olive oil
- ¼ cup soy sauce
- 1 tsp cornstarch
- ¼ cup pineapple juice
- ¼ cup honey
- 1 tsp chili garlic sauce or sriracha
- 2 tbsp toasted sesame oil
- 6 (4 oz) ahi tuna steaks
- 2 tbsp black and white sesame seeds, toasted

For the Salad:

- 4 to 8 cups spring greens
- ½ cup fresh cilantro
- 1 cup fresh pineapple, diced
- 1 avocado, sliced
- 1 jalapeño or red chili, sliced

Hula Ginger Vinaigrette (Makes 1½ cup):

- ½ cup hot chili sesame oil or toasted sesame oil
- ¼ cup soy sauce
- 2 tbsp pineapple juice

- 2 tbsp rice vinegar
- 1 tsp chili garlic sauce or sriracha or more to taste
- 1 tbsp tahini
- 1 lime, zested and juiced
- 2 tsp fresh ginger, grated
- 1 garlic clove, minced
- 1 tbsp black and white sesame seeds, toasted

Directions:

1. Preheat the oven to 400°F.

2. Grease a baking sheet with the olive oil and lay the wonton strips on it in a single layer. Sprinkle them with salt. Bake the strips for about 5 minutes, or until they are golden brown and crispy. Set the finished strips to the side for now.

3. Pour the soy sauce into a small saucepan, then whisk in the cornstarch until incorporated. Stir in the pineapple juice, honey, and chili sauce.

4. Over medium-high heat, bring the mixture to a boil, then reduce the temperature and simmer for 3 to 5 minutes, or until the sauce begins to thicken. Set the thickened sauce aside.

5. Pour the sesame oil into a large skillet, and heat over high heat. Sear the tuna steaks for 1 to 2 minutes on each side. Brush the thickened soy sauce mixture over each side and cook another 1 to 2 minutes. Baste with sauce so each side is well covered. When the steaks are done, sprinkle each side with sesame seeds.

6. Prepare the salad. In a salad bowl, combine the greens, cilantro, pineapple, avocado, and jalapeño pepper. Toss to combine.

7. Make the vinaigrette by combining all the ingredients and whisking well.

8. Plate the greens, and top with seared tuna and wonton crisps. Top with some of the vinaigrette, and serve.

Nutrition:

(Before Adding Vinaigrette): Calories: 447, Fat: 18 g, Carbs: 45 g, Protein: 32 g, Sodium: 856 mg

(Only Vinaigrette): Calories: 103, Fat: 10 g, Carbs: 3 g, Protein: 1 g, Sodium: 346 mg

106. One-Pan Eggs with Asparagus and Tomatoes

Preparation Time: 10 minutes

Cooking Time: 20 minutes

Servings: 4

Ingredients:

- 2 lb asparagus
- 1 pint cherry tomatoes
- 2 tbsp olive oil
- 4 eggs
- 2 tsp chopped fresh thyme
- Salt and pepper to taste

Directions:

1. Preheat the oven to 400°F.
2. Prepare a baking sheet by spraying it with non-stick cooking spray or olive oil.
3. Arrange the asparagus in an even layer on the sheet, and top it with the cherry tomatoes.
4. Pour the olive oil over the vegetables, and season them with salt and pepper.
5. Roast the vegetables until the asparagus is tender and the tomatoes have softened (about 10 minutes).
6. Next, crack the eggs over the cooked vegetables and season with salt and pepper, and thyme.
7. Return the baking tray to the oven and cook until the egg whites are set, but the yolks are still soft.
8. Remove from oven and serve.

Nutrition: Calories: 158, Fat: 11 g, Carbs: 13 g, Protein: 11 g

107. Anti-Inflammatory Buddha Bowl

Preparation Time: 10 minutes

Cooking Time: 30 minutes

Servings: 4

Ingredients:

- 2 lb cauliflower florets, stems removed
- 1 tbsp plus 1 tsp extra-virgin olive oil, divided
- 1 tsp turmeric
- Salt and pepper
- 10 oz kale, chopped
- 1 garlic clove, minced
- 8 medium beets, cooked, peeled, and chopped
- 2 avocados, cubed
- 2 cups fresh blueberries
- ⅓ cup raw walnuts, chopped

Directions:

1. Preheat the oven to 425°F.
2. Cover a baking tray with foil and spray the foil with either coconut or olive oil.
3. Toss the cut cauliflower with 1 tbsp of olive oil and turmeric. Arrange it on the prepared baking tray. Season with salt and pepper and transfer the tray to the oven. Bake for about 30 minutes.
4. When the cauliflower is almost done, heat 1 tsp of olive oil in a large skillet. Add the kale and cook until it starts to wilt, then add the garlic.
5. When the cauliflower and kale are done, assemble the bowls. Start with kale, then top with cauliflower, beets, avocado, blueberries, and walnuts.
6. Serve, and enjoy!

Nutrition: Calories: 450, Fat: 27 g, Carbs: 49 g, Protein: 13 g, Sodium: 377 mg

108. Honey Ginger Shrimp Bowls

Preparation Time: 20 minutes

Cooking Time: 6 minutes

Servings: 2

Ingredients:

For the Shrimp:

- 2 tbsp honey
- 2 tbsp coconut aminos or soy sauce
- 1 tsp fresh ginger, minced
- 2 garlic cloves, minced
- 12 oz large uncooked shrimp, peeled and deveined
- 2 tsp avocado oil
- Lime, sea salt, and freshly ground pepper to taste

For the Salad:

- 4 cups greens of your choice
- ½ cup shredded carrots
- ½ cup shredded radishes
- 4 green onions, sliced
- ¼ cup cilantro, chopped
- 1 avocado, sliced

For the Dressing:

- 2 tbsp lime juice
- 2 tbsp extra-virgin olive oil
- 2 tsp coconut aminos
- 1 tbsp honey
- 1 garlic clove, minced
- ½ tsp ginger powder
- Sea salt and pepper to taste

Directions:

1. In a mixing bowl, whisk together the honey, coconut aminos (or soy sauce), ginger, and garlic as listed under the shrimp ingredients.

2. Put the shrimp in a resealable bag and pour the marinade mixture in. Manipulate the bag to make sure all the shrimp are covered. Refrigerate while you are preparing the salad and dressing.

3. In a large skillet, heat the avocado oil over medium-high heat. When hot, add the shrimp and the marinade and cook for about 3 minutes. Turn the shrimp and cook for another 3 minutes or until the shrimp is fully cooked and the sauce has thickened a bit. Season with lime juice, salt, and pepper.

4. Prepare the salad in a large bowl by mixing together all the ingredients.

5. Divide the salad into 2 servings, and top each with half the shrimp.

6. Prepare the dressing by whisking together all the ingredients.

7. Top the salad with dressing, and serve.

Nutrition: Calories: 516, Fat: 32 g, Carbs: 47 g, Protein: 12 g, Sodium: 636 mg

109. Bake Chicken Top-Up with Olives, Tomatoes, and Basil

Preparation Time: 10 minutes

Cooking Time: 40 minutes

Servings: 4

Ingredients:

- 8 chicken thighs
- Small Italian tomatoes
- 1 tbsp black pepper & salt
- 1 tbsp olive oil
- 15 Basil leaves (large)
- Small black olives
- 1 to 2 Fresh red chili flakes

Directions:

1. Marinate chicken pieces with all spices & olive oil and leave it for some time.

2. Assemble chicken pieces in a rimmed pan with a top-up of tomatoes, basil leaves, olives, and chili flakes.

3. Bake this chicken in an already preheated oven (at 220C) for 40 minutes.

4. Bake until the chicken is tender, tomatoes, basil, and olives are cooked.

5. Garnish it with fresh parsley and lemon zest.

Nutrition: Calories: 304, Carbs: 17 g, Fat: 7 g, Protein: 41 g

110. Ratatouille

Preparation Time: 10 minutes

Cooking Time: 30 minutes

Servings: 8

Ingredients:

- 1 zucchini, medium & diced
- 3 tbsp extra virgin olive oil
- 2 bell pepper, diced
- 1 yellow squash, medium & diced
- 1 onion, large & diced
- 28 oz whole tomatoes, peeled
- 1 eggplant, medium & diced with skin on
- Salt & pepper, as needed
- 4 thyme sprigs, fresh
- 5 garlic cloves, chopped

Directions:

1. To start with, heat a large sauté pan over medium-high heat.

2. Once hot, spoon in the oil, onion, and garlic to it.

3. Sauté the onion mixture for 3 to 5 minutes or until softened.

4. Next, stir the eggplant, pepper, thyme, and salt into the pan. Mix well.

5. Now, cook for further 5 minutes or until the eggplant becomes softened.

6. Then, add zucchini, bell peppers, and squash to the pan and continue cooking for another 5

minutes. Then, stir in the tomatoes and mix well.

7. Once everything is added, give a good stir until everything comes together. Allow it to simmer for 15 minutes.

8. Finally, check for seasoning and spoon in more salt and pepper if needed.

9. Garnish with parsley and ground black pepper.

Nutrition: Calories: 103, Protein: 2g, Carbs: 12g, Fat: 5g

111. Chicken Meatball Soup

Preparation Time: 10 minutes

Cooking Time: 30 minutes

Servings: 4

Ingredients:

- 2 lb chicken breast, skinless, boneless and minced
- 2 tbsp cilantro, chopped
- 2 eggs, whisked
- 1 garlic clove, minced
- ¼ cup green onions, chopped
- 1 yellow onion, chopped
- 1 carrot, sliced
- 1 tbsp olive oil
- 5 cups chicken stock
- 1 tbsp parsley, chopped
- A pinch of salt and black pepper

Directions:

1. In a bowl, combine the meat with the eggs and the other ingredients except for the oil, yellow onion, stock and the parsley, stir and shape medium meatballs out of this mix.

2. Heat up a pot with the oil over medium heat, add the yellow onion and the meatballs and brown for 5 minutes.

3. Add the remaining ingredients, toss, bring to a simmer and cook over medium heat for 25 minutes more.

4. Ladle the soup into bowls and serve.

Nutrition: Calories: 200, Fat: 2 g, Fiber: 2 g, Carbs: 14 g, Protein: 12 g

112. Cabbage Orange Salad with Citrusy Vinaigrette

Preparation Time: 10 minutes

Cooking Time: 0 minutes

Servings: 8

Ingredients:

- 1 tsp orange zest, grated
- 2 tbsp vegetable stock, reduced-sodium
- 1 tsp each cider vinegar
- 4 cups red cabbage, shredded
- 1 tsp lemon juice
- 1 fennel bulb, sliced thinly
- 1 tsp balsamic vinegar
- 1 tsp raspberry vinegar
- 2 tbsp fresh orange juice
- 2 oranges, peeled, cut into pieces
- 1 tbsp honey
- ¼ tsp salt
- Freshly ground pepper
- 4 tsp olive oil

Directions:

1. Put lemon juice, orange zest, cider vinegar, salt and pepper, broth, oil, honey, orange juice, balsamic vinegar, and raspberry in a bowl and whisk.

2. Extract the oranges, fennel, and cabbage. Toss to coat.

Nutrition: Calories: 70, Carbs: 14 g, Fat: 0 g, Protein: 1g

113. Green Soup

Preparation Time: 10 minutes

Cooking Time: 5 minutes

Servings: 2

Ingredients:

- 1 cup water
- 1 cup spinach, fresh & packed
- ½ lemon, peeled
- 1 zucchini, small & chopped
- 2 tbsp parsley, fresh & chopped
- 1 celery stalk, chopped
- Sea salt & black pepper, as needed
- 1 avocado, ripe
- ¼ cup basil
- 2 tbsp chia Seeds

- 1 garlic clove, minced

Directions:

1. To make this easy blended soup, place all the ingredients in a high-speed blender and blend for 3 minutes or until smooth.

2. Next, you can serve it cold, or you can warm it up on low heat for a few minutes.

Nutrition: Calories: 250, Protein: 6.9 g, Carbs: 18.4 g, Fat: 18.1 g

114. Pepperoni Pizza Loaf

Preparation Time: 20 minutes

Cooking Time: 40 minutes

Servings: 4

Ingredients:

- 1 portion (1 lb) solidified bread mixture, defrosted
- 2 enormous eggs, isolated
- 1 tbsp ground Parmesan cheddar
- 1 tbsp olive oil
- 1 tsp minced crisp parsley
- 1 tsp dried oregano
- ½ tsp garlic powder
- ¼ tsp pepper
- 8 oz cut pepperoni
- 2 cups destroyed part-skim mozzarella cheddar
- 1 can (4 oz) mushroom stems and pieces, depleted
- ¼ to ½ cup cured pepper rings
- 1 medium green pepper, diced
- 1 can (2¼ oz) cut ready olives
- 1 can (15 oz) pizza sauce

Directions:

1. Preheat stove to 350°. On a lubed preparing sheet, turn out batter into a 15x10-in. square shape. In a little bowl, consolidate the egg yolks, Parmesan cheddar, oil, parsley, oregano, garlic powder and pepper. Brush over the mixture.

2. Sprinkle with the pepperoni, mozzarella cheddar, mushrooms, pepper rings, green pepper and olives. Move up, jam move style, beginning with a long side; squeeze crease to seal and fold finishes under.

3. Position portion with crease side down; brush with egg whites. Try not to let rise. Prepare until brilliant dark colored and mixture is cooked

through, 35 to 40 minutes. Warm the pizza sauce; present with cut portion.

Nutrition: Calories: 387, Protein: 18.15 g, Fat: 33.14 g, Carbs: 2.79 g

115. Beets Gazpacho

Preparation Time: 10 minutes

Cooking Time: 0 minutes

Servings: 4

Ingredients:

- 1 (20 oz) can great northern beans, rinsed and drained
- ¼ tsp kosher salt
- 1 tbsp extra-virgin olive oil
- ½ tsp garlic, fresh and minced
- 1 6 oz pouch pink salmon flaked
- 2 tbsp lemon juice, freshly squeezed
- 4 green onions, sliced thinly
- ½ tsp ground black pepper
- ½ tsp lemon rind grated
- ¼ cup flat-leaf parsley, fresh and chopped

Directions:

1. First, place lemon rind, olive oil, lemon juice, black pepper, and garlic in a medium-sized mixing bowl and mix them with a whisker.

2. Combine beans, onions, salmon, and parsley in another medium-sized bowl and toss them well.

3. Then, spoon the lemon juice dressing over the bean's mixture. Mix well until the dressing coats the beans mixture.

4. Serve and enjoy.

Nutrition: Calories: 131, Protein: 1.9 g, Carbs: 14.7 g, Fat: 8.5 g

116. Baked Butternut Squash Rigatoni

Preparation Time: 10 minutes

Cooking Time: 1 hour 30 minutes

Servings: 4

Ingredients:

- 1 enormous butternut squash
- 3 garlic cloves
- 2 tbsp olive oil
- 1 lb rigatoni
- ½ cup substantial cream

- 3 cups fontina cheese
- 2 tbsp slashed crisp sage
- 1 tbsp salt
- 1 tsp naturally ground pepper
- 1 cup panko breadcrumbs

Directions:

1. Preheat the broiler to 425°F. In the meantime, in a huge bowl, hurl squash, garlic, and olive oil to cover. Spot on a huge, rimmed preparing sheet and dish until delicate, around 60 minutes. Move the container to a wire rack and let cool marginally for around 10 minutes. Decrease stove to 350°F.

2. In the meantime, heat a huge pot of salted water to the point of boiling and cook rigatoni as per bundle bearings. Channel and put it in a safe spot.

3. Utilizing a blender or nourishment processor, purée held squash with overwhelming cream until smooth.

4. In a huge bowl, hurl squash puree withheld rigatoni, 2 cups fontina, savvy, salt, and pepper. Brush the base and sides of a 9-by 13-inch preparing dish with olive oil. Move the rigatoni-squash blend to the dish.

5. In a little bowl, consolidate the remaining fontina and panko. Sprinkle over pasta and heat until brilliant darker, 20 to 25 minutes.

Nutrition: Calories: 654, Protein: 34.43 g, Fat: 47.92 g, Carbs: 23.17 g

117. Capellini Soup with Tofu and Shrimp

Preparation Time: 10 minutes

Cooking Time: 10 minutes

Servings: 8

Ingredients:

- 4 cups bok choy, sliced
- ¼ lb shrimp, peeled, deveined
- 1 block firm tofu, sliced into squares
- 1 can sliced water chestnuts, drained
- 1 bunch scallions, sliced
- 2 cups reduced-sodium chicken broth
- 2 tsp soy sauce, reduced-sodium
- 2 cups capellini
- 2 tsp sesame oil
- Freshly ground white pepper
- 1 tsp rice wine vinegar

Directions:

1. Pour the broth into a saucepan over medium-high heat. Bring to a boil. Add the shrimp, bok choy, oil, and sauce. Allow to boil and turn the heat to low. Simmer for 5 minutes.

2. Add the water chestnuts, pepper, vinegar, tofu, capellini, and scallions. Cook for 5 minutes or until the capellini is barely tender. Serve while hot.

Nutrition: Calories: 205, Carbs: 20g, Fat: 9g, Protein: 9g

118. Lemon Buttery Shrimp Rice

Preparation Time: 10 minutes

Cooking Time: 10 minutes

Servings: 3

Ingredients:

- ¼ cup cooked wild rice
- ½ tsp Butter divided
- ¼ tsp olive oil
- 1 cup raw shrimps, shelled, deveined, drained
- ¼ cup frozen peas, thawed, rinsed, drained
- 1 tbsp lemon juice, freshly squeezed
- 1 tbsp chives, minced
- Pinch of sea salt, to taste

Directions:

1. Pour ¼ tsp of butter and oil into a wok set over medium heat. Add in shrimps and peas. Sauté until shrimps are coral pink, about 5 to 7 minutes.

2. Add in wild rice and cook until well heated—season with salt and butter.

3. Transfer to a plate. Sprinkle chives and lemon juice on top. Serve.

Nutrition: Calories: 510, Carbs: 0g, Fat: 0g, Protein: 0g

119. Cauliflower Soup

Preparation Time: 10 minutes

Cooking Time: 10 minutes

Servings: 10

Ingredients:

- ¾ cup water
- 2 tsp olive oil
- 1 onion, diced
- 1 head cauliflower, only the florets

- 1 can full-fat coconut milk
- 1 tsp turmeric
- 1 tsp ginger
- 1 tsp raw honey

Directions:

1. Put all of the fixings into a large stockpot, and boil for about 10 minutes.

2. Use an immersion blender to blend and make the soup smooth. Serve.

Nutrition: Total Carbs: 7 g, Fiber: 2 g, Protein: 2 g, Total Fat: 11 g, Calories: 129

120. Apple and Tomato Dipping Sauce

Preparation Time: 10 minutes

Cooking Time: 34 minutes

Servings: 2 to 4

Ingredients:

- ¼ cup cider vinegar
- ¼ tsp freshly ground black pepper
- ½ tsp sea salt
- 1 garlic clove, finely chopped
- 1 large-sized shallot, diced
- 1 tbsp natural tomato paste
- 1 tbsp extra-virgin olive oil
- 1 tbsp maple syrup
- ⅛ tsp ground cloves
- 3 moderate-sized apples, roughly chopped
- 3 moderate-sized tomatoes, roughly chopped

Directions:

1. Put oil into a huge deep cooking pan and heat it up on moderate heat.

2. Put in shallot and cook until light brown for approximately 2 minutes.

3. Stir in the tomato paste, garlic, salt, pepper, and cloves for approximately half a minute. Then put in the apples, tomatoes, vinegar, and maple syrup.

4. Bring to its boiling point then decrease the heat to allow it to simmer for approximately 30 minutes. Allow cooling for 20 additional minutes before placing the mixture into your blender. Combine the mixture until the desired smoothness is achieved.

5. Keep in a mason jar or an airtight container; place in your fridge for a maximum of 5 days.

6. Serve it on a burger or with fries.

Nutrition: Calories: 142, Protein: 3 g, Fat: 3.46 g, Carbs: 26.93 g

121. Hot Tuna Steak

Preparation Time: 10 minutes

Cooking Time: 15 minutes

Servings: 6

Ingredients:

- ¼ cup whole black peppercorns
- 2 tbsp extra-virgin olive oil
- 2 tbsp fresh lemon juice
- 6 cut tuna steaks
- Pepper
- Roasted orange garlic mayonnaise
- Salt

Directions:

1. Bring the tuna in a container to fit. Place the oil, lemon juice, salt, and pepper. Turn the tuna to coat well in the marinade.

2. Rest for minimum 15 to 20 minutes, flipping over once.

3. Place the peppercorns in a twofold thickness of plastic bags. Tap the peppercorns with a heavy deep cooking pan or small mallet to crush them crudely. Put it on a big plate.

4. Once ready to cook the tuna, immerse the edges into the crushed peppercorns. Heat a nonstick frying pan on moderate heat. Sear the tuna steaks, in batches if required, for about 4 minutes per side for medium-rare fish, putting in 2 to 3 tbsp of the marinade to the frying pan if required, to stop sticking.

5. Serve dolloped with roasted orange garlic mayonnaise

Nutrition: Calories: 124, Fat: 0.4 g, Carbs: 0.6 g, Protein: 28 g, Sugar: 0 g, Sodium: 77 mg

122. Irish Style Clams

Preparation Time: 5 minutes

Cooking Time: 15 minutes

Servings: 4

Ingredients:

- 1 bottle infused cider
- 1 small green apple; chopped.

- 1 tbsp olive oil
- 2 garlic cloves; minced
- 2 lb clams; scrubbed
- 2 thyme springs; chopped.
- 3 oz pancetta
- 3 tbsp ghee
- Juice lemon
- Salt and black pepper to the taste.

Directions:

1. Heat a pan with the oil on moderate to high heat; put in pancetta, brown for about 3 minutes and decrease the temperature to moderate.

2. Put in ghee, garlic, salt, pepper, and shallot; stir and cook for about 3 minutes

3. Raise the heat again, put in cider; stir thoroughly and cook for a minute

4. Put in clams and thyme, cover the pan and simmer for 5 minutes

5. Discard unopened clams, put in lemon juice and apple pieces; stir and split into bowls. Serve hot.

Nutrition: Calories: 100, Fat: 2 g, Fiber: 1 g, Carbs: 1 g, Protein: 20 g

123. Italian Halibut Chowder

Preparation Time: 5 minutes

Cooking Time: 20 minutes

Servings: 8

Ingredients:

- ½ cup apple juice, organic and unsweetened
- ½ tsp dried basil
- 1 cup tomato juice
- 1 onion, chopped
- 1 red bell pepper, seeded and chopped
- ⅛ tsp dried thyme
- 2½ lb halibut steaks, cubed
- 2 tbsp olive oil
- 3 garlic cloves, minced
- 3 celery stalks, chopped
- Salt and pepper to taste

Directions:

1. Put a heavy-bottomed pot on moderate to high fire and heat the pot for a couple of minutes. Put in oil and heat for 1 minute.

2. Sauté the onion, celery, and garlic until aromatic.

3. Mix in the halibut steaks and bell pepper. Sauté for about 3 minutes.

4. Pour in the remaining ingredients and mix thoroughly.

5. Cover and bring to its boiling point. Once boiling, lower the fire to a simmer for about 10 minutes.

6. Tweak seasoning to taste.

7. Serve and enjoy.

Nutrition: Calories: 318, Fat: 23 g, Carbs: 6 g, Protein: 21 g, Fiber: 1 g

124. Keto Salmon Tandoori with Cucumber Sauce

Preparation Time: 15 minutes

Cooking Time: 20 minutes

Servings: 4

Ingredients:

- ½ shredded cucumber (squeeze out the water completely)
- ½ tsp salt (not necessary)
- 1¼ cup sour cream or mayonnaise
- 1 tbsp tandoori seasoning
- 1 yellow bell pepper (diced)
- 2 avocados (cubed)
- 2 minced garlic cloves
- 2 tbsp coconut oil
- 25 oz salmon (bite-sized pieces)
- 3½ oz lettuce (torn)
- 3 scallions (finely chopped)
- Lime juice

Directions:

1. Preheat your oven to 350°F. Combine the tandoori seasoning with oil in a small container and coat the salmon pieces with this mixture.

2. Coat the baking tray using parchment paper and spread the coated salmon pieces in it.

3. Bake for about 20 minutes until tender and the salmon flakes using a fork

4. Take another container and put the shredded cucumber in it. Put in the mayonnaise, minced garlic, and salt (if the mayonnaise doesn't have salt) to the shredded cucumber. Mix thoroughly. Squeeze the lime juice at the top and set the cucumber sauce aside.

5. Combine the lettuce, scallions, avocados, and bell pepper in a different container. Sprinkle the contents with the lime juice.

6. Move the veggie salad to a plate and put the baked salmon over it. Top the veggies and salmon with cucumber sauce.

7. Serve instantly and enjoy!

Nutrition: Calories: 847, Fat: 73 g, Protein: 35 g, Carbs: 6 g

125.   Keto Zoodles with White Clam Sauce

Preparation Time: 10 minutes

Cooking Time: 10 minutes

Servings: 4

Ingredients:

- ½ cup dry white wine
- 1 tbsp garlic (minced)
- 1 tsp kosher salt
- 1 tsp lemon zest (grated)
- ¼ cup butter
- ¼ cup fresh parsley (chopped)
- ¼ tsp black pepper (ground)
- 2 lb small clams
- 2 tbsp lemon juice
- 2 tbsp olive oil
- 8 cups zucchini noodles

Directions:

1. In a pan at moderate heat, put the olive oil, butter, pepper, and salt. Stir to melt the butter.

2. Put in the garlic. Sautee the garlic until aromatic for a minimum of 2 minutes

3. Set in the lemon juice and wine. Cook for a minimum of 2 minutes, until the liquid is slightly reduced

4. Put in the clams. Cook the clams until they are all opened (about 3 minutes). Discard any clam that does not open after 3 minutes.

5. Take away the pan from the heat. Put in the zucchini noodles. Toss the mixture to blend well. Allow the zoodles to rest for about 2 minutes to tenderize them.

6. Put in the lemon zest and parsley. Stir and serve.

Nutrition: Calories: 311, Carbs: 9 g, Fat: 19 g, Protein: 13 g, Fiber: 2 g

126.   Lemon-Caper Trout with Caramelized Shallots

Preparation Time: 10 minutes

Cooking Time: 20 minutes

Servings: 2

Ingredients:

For the Shallots:

- 1 tsp ghee
- 2 shallots, thinly cut
- Dash salt

For the Trout:

- ¼ cup freshly squeezed lemon juice
- ¼ tsp salt
- 1 lemon, thinly cut
- 1 tbsp plus 1 tsp ghee, divided
- 2 (4 oz) trout fillets
- 3 tbsp capers
- Dash freshly ground black pepper

Directions:

1. To make the Shallot: In a huge frying pan on moderate heat, cook the shallots, ghee, and salt for about 20 minutes, stirring every 5 minutes, until the shallots have fully wilted and caramelized.

2. To make the Trout: While the shallots cook, in another big frying pan on moderate heat, heat 1 tsp of ghee.

3. Put in the trout fillets. Cook for a minimum of 3 minutes on each side, or until the center is flaky. Move to a plate and save for later.

4. In the frying pan used for the trout, put in the lemon juice, capers, salt, and pepper. Heat it until it simmers. Whisk in the rest of the 1 tbsp of ghee. Ladle the sauce over the fish.

5. Decorate the fish with lemon slices and caramelized shallots before you serve.

Nutrition: Calories: 399, Total Fat: 22 g, Saturated Fat: 10 g, Cholesterol: 46 mg, Carbs: 17 g, Fiber: 2 g, Protein: 21 g

127. Lemony Mackerel

Preparation Time: 10 minutes

Cooking Time: 15 minutes

Servings: 4

Ingredients:

- 1 tbsp minced chives
- 2 tbsp olive oil
- 4 mackerels
- Juice of 1 lemon
- Pinch black pepper
- Pinch of sea salt
- Zest of 1 lemon

Directions:

1. Warm a pan with the oil on moderate to high heat put in the mackerel and cook for about 6 minutes on each side.
2. Put in the lemon zest, lemon juice, chives, salt, and pepper then cook for 2 more minutes on each side. Split everything between plates before you serve.
3. Enjoy!

Nutrition: Calories: 289, Fat: 20 g, Fiber: 0 g, Carbs: 1 g, Protein: 21 g

128. Lemony Trout

Preparation Time: 10 minutes

Cooking Time: 20 minutes

Servings: 2

Ingredients:

- 1 lemon
- 1 tsp rosemary
- 2 garlic cloves
- 2 tbsp capers
- 5 oz trout fillets
- 5 tbsp ghee butter
- Salt and pepper to taste

Directions:

1. Preheat your oven to 400°F
2. Peel the lemon, mince the garlic cloves and cut the capers
3. Flavor the trout fillets with salt, rosemary, and pepper

4. Grease a baking dish with the oil and put the fish onto it
5. Warm the butter in a frying pan on moderate heat
6. Put in the garlic and cook for 4 to 5 minutes until golden
7. Turn off the heat, put in the lemon zest and 2 tbsp of lemon juice, and stir thoroughly
8. Pour the lemon-butter sauce over the fish and top with the capers
9. Bake for 14 to 15 minutes. Serve hot

Nutrition: Carbs: 3.1 g, Fat: 25 g, Protein: 15.8 g, Calories: 302

129. Lime Cod Mix

Preparation Time: 10 minutes

Cooking Time: 15 minutes

Servings: 4

Ingredients:

- ½ cup chicken stock
- ½ tsp cumin, ground
- 1 tbsp olive oil
- 2 tbsp lime juice
- 2 tsp lime zest, grated
- 3 tbsp cilantro, chopped
- 4 cod fillets, boneless
- A pinch of salt and black pepper

Directions:

1. Set the instant pot on Sauté mode, put oil, heats it, put it in the cod and cook for a minute on each side.
2. Put in the rest of the ingredients, put the lid on, and cook on High for 13 minutes.
3. Release the pressure naturally for around 10 minutes, and split the mix between plates before you serve.

Nutrition: Calories: 187, Fat: 13.1 g, Fiber: 0.2 g, Carbs: 1.6 g, Protein: 16.1 g

130. Mackerel Bombs

Preparation Time: 15 minutes

Cooking Time: 10 minutes

Servings: 4

Ingredients:

- ¼ cup spinach, chopped
- ½ tsp thyme
- 1 egg, beaten
- 1 tsp chili flakes
- 1 tsp garlic, minced
- 1 tsp mustard
- 1 tsp salt
- 1 white onion, peeled and diced
- ⅓ cup almond flour
- 10 oz mackerel, chopped
- 4 tbsp coconut oil

Directions:

1. Put mackerel in a blender or food processor and pulse until the texture is smooth.

2. In a container, mix the onion with mackerel.

3. Put in garlic, flour, egg, thyme, salt, and mustard, stir thoroughly.

4. Put in chili flakes and mix up the mixture until getting a homogenous mass.

5. Put in spinach and stir.

6. Heat a pan at moderate heat then put in oil.

7. Shape fish mixture into bombs 1½ inch in diameter.

8. Put bombs on a pan and cook for 5 minutes on all sides.

9. Move to paper towels and drain grease and serve.

Nutrition: Calories: 328, Carbs: 3.35 g, Fat: 16.5 g, Protein: 20.1 g

Chapter 5
Dinner

---

131. Turmeric Rice Bowl with Garam Masala Root Vegetable and Chickpeas

Preparation Time: 25 minutes

Cooking Time: 30 minutes

Servings: 4

Ingredients:

For the Rice:

- 2½ cups water
- 1 cup brown basmati rice, cleaned and rinsed
- ½ cup raisins
- 2 tsp extra virgin olive oil
- 2 tsp onion powder
- 1 tsp ground turmeric
- ½ tsp ground cinnamon
- ½ tsp ground black pepper
- ¼ tsp kosher salt

For the Vegetables and Chickpeas:

- 4 tsp coconut oil
- 2 (15 oz) can chickpeas
- 2 tsp garam masala
- 2 cups roasted root vegetables
- 2 tsp honey
- ½ tsp kosher salt
- ½ tsp ground pepper
- 4 tsp lemon juice
- 4 tsp low-fat plain yogurt
- Chopped mint, parsley, and cilantro

Directions:

1. Combine all the rice ingredients in a saucepan and bring the rice to a boil.
2. Cook covered at a reduced heat for 20 minutes until all the water is absorbed.

3. Meanwhile, heat oil in a skillet over medium heat.
4. Stir the chickpeas into the skillet and cook for 5 minutes.
5. Stir in the garam masala to the chickpeas and cook for 1 minute.
6. Add the root vegetables, honey, salt, and pepper to the skillet and cook while stirring for 4 minutes.
7. Stir the lemon juice into the vegetable mixture and remove it from heat.
8. Allow the rice to stand covered for 10 minutes.
9. Serve the chickpeas over rice and top with yogurt.
10. Garnish the rice with mint, parsley, and cilantro.

Nutrition: Calories: 671, Total Fat: 13 g, Carbs: 107 g, Protein: 16 g

132. Roasted Root Veggies and Greens Over Spiced Lentil

Preparation Time: 25 minutes

Cooking Time: 30 minutes

Servings: 4

Ingredients:

For the Lentils:

- 3 cups water
- 1 cup French green lentil
- 2 tsp garlic powder
- 1 tsp ground coriander
- 1 tsp ground cumin
- ½ tsp ground allspice
- ½ tsp kosher salt
- 4 tsp lemon juice
- 2 tsp extra virgin olive oil

For the Vegetables:

- 2 tsp extra virgin olive oil
- 2 smashed garlic cloves
- 3 cups roasted root vegetables
- 4 cups chopped kales
- 2 tsp ground coriander
- ¼ tsp ground pepper
- Pinch of kosher salt
- 4 tsp tahini
- Fresh parsley

Directions:

1. Add all the lentil ingredients except the lime juice and oil to a pot and bring to a boil.
2. Cook the lentils covered at a reduced heat for 25 minutes.
3. Meanwhile, prepare the vegetables by heating oil in a skillet over medium heat.
4. Sauté the garlic for 1 minute until fragrant.
5. Stir the root vegetables into the skillet and cook for 4 minutes.
6. Add kale to the root vegetables and cook for about 3 minutes until they are wilted.
7. Stir in the coriander, pepper, and salt to the veggies and remove them from heat.
8. Uncover the lentil and allow the lentils to simmer for 5 minutes.
9. Drain excess water from the lentil and stir in the lemon juice and oil.
10. Serve the veggies over the lentils and top with tahini.
11. Garnish the lentils with parsley.

Nutrition: Calories: 453, Total Fat: 22 g, Carbs: 50 g, Protein: 17 g

133. Walnut Rosemary Crusted Salmon

Preparation Time: 10 minutes

Cooking Time: 15 minutes

Servings: 4

Ingredients:

- 2 tsp Dijon mustard
- 1 minced garlic clove
- ¼ tsp lemon zest
- 1 tsp lemon juice
- 1 tsp fresh rosemary, chopped

- ½ tsp honey
- ½ tsp kosher salt
- ¼ tsp crushed red pepper
- 3 tsp whole-wheat panko breadcrumbs
- 3 tsp walnuts, finely chopped
- 1 tsp extra virgin olive oil
- 1 lb salmon fillet, skinless
- Olive oil cooking spray
- Chopped fresh parsley
- Lemon wedges

Directions:

1. Preheat the oven to 420°F and line a rimmed baking sheet with parchment paper then set aside.
2. In a bowl mix the mustard, garlic, lemon zest, lemon juice, rosemary, honey, salt, and red pepper until well combined.
3. In another bowl mix the breadcrumbs, walnuts, and olive oil.
4. Place the salmon on the baking sheet and spread the mustard mixture over the fillet.
5. Sprinkle the salmon with the breadcrumbs mixture and press them over the salmon to adhere.
6. Coat the salmon with the cooking spray.
7. Bake the salmon for about 12 minutes.
8. Transfer the salmon to a serving platter and sprinkle the parsley.
9. Serve the salmon with lemon wedges.

Nutrition: Calories: 222, Total Fat: 12 g, Carbs: 4 g, Protein: 24 g

134. Roasted Salmon with Spicy Cranberry Relish

Preparation Time: 10 minutes

Cooking Time: 15 minutes

Servings: 8

Ingredients:

- 2½ lb salmon fillet, skin on
- 2 chopped garlic cloves
- 1½ tsp kosher salt
- ½ tsp whole black peppercorn, cracked
- 1 zested lemon cut into wedges
- 2 tsp extra virgin olive oil
- 2 tsp Dijon mustard

- 2 cups cranberries
- 1 minced shallot
- 1 serrano pepper, seeded
- 1 granny smith apple, peeled and diced
- 1 finely diced celery stalk
- 1 tsp apple cider vinegar
- 2 tsp fresh parsley, chopped

Directions:

1. Preheat the oven to 410°F and line a rimmed baking sheet with parchment paper.

2. Place the salmon on the baking sheet.

3. Using a mortar and pestle mash the garlic, 1 tbsp salt, peppercorns, and lemon zest into a paste.

4. Transfer the paste into a bowl and mix with 1 tbsp oil and mustard.

5. Spread the paste on the salmon and bake it for 15 minutes.

6. Meanwhile, place the cranberries, shallot, and serrano in a food processor and pulse until finely chopped.

7. Transfer the cranberry mixture to a bowl.

8. Stir in the apple, celery, vinegar, 1 tbsp parsley, remaining oil, and salt to the cranberry mixture.

9. Transfer the salmon to a serving platter and sprinkle it with the remaining parsley.

10. Serve the salmon with relish and lemon wedges.

Nutrition: Calories: 229, Total Fat: 9 g, Carbs: 7 g, Protein: 29 g

135. Roasted Cauliflower and Potato Curry Soup

Preparation Time: 20 minutes

Cooking Time: 50 minutes

Servings: 8

Ingredients:

- 2 tsp ground coriander
- 2 tsp ground cumin
- 1½ ground cinnamon
- 1½ ground turmeric
- 1¼ tsp salt
- ¾ tsp ground pepper
- ⅛ tsp cayenne pepper
- 1 cauliflower head, cut into florets
- 2 tsp extra virgin olive oil

- 1 chopped onion
- 1 cup diced carrot
- 3 minced garlic cloves
- 1½ tsp fresh ginger, grated
- 1 fresh jalapeno pepper, minced
- 4 cups low sodium vegetable broth
- 3 cups russet potatoes, peeled and diced
- 3 cups sweet potatoes, peeled and diced
- 2 tsp lime zest
- 2 tsp lime juice
- 1 (14 oz) can coconut milk
- Fresh cilantro, chopped

Directions:

1. Preheat the oven to 410°F.

2. In a bowl mix the coriander, cumin, cinnamon, turmeric, salt, pepper, and cayenne until well combined.

3. In a separate bowl toss the cauliflower with 1 tbsp olive oil.

4. Add 1 tbsp of the seasoning mixture to the cauliflower and toss again.

5. Spread the cauliflower on a rimmed baking sheet in a single layer.

6. Roast the cauliflower for 20 minutes until the edges are browned.

7. Meanwhile, pour the remaining oil into a skillet and heat it over medium heat.

8. Brown the onions and carrots for about 3 minutes.

9. Reduce the heat and cook the carrots for an additional 4 minutes.

10. Stir in garlic, ginger, jalapeno, and the remaining spice mixture to the carrots mixture and cook for 1 minute.

11. Add the broth, potatoes, sweet potatoes, lime zest, and lemon juice to the carrot mixture and bring it to a boil over high heat.

12. Cook the potatoes partially covered over medium heat for 20 minutes.

13. Stir in the milk and the roasted cauliflower to the potatoes curry and allow simmering for 1 minute.

14. Transfer the cauliflower to a serving platter and garnish it with cilantro.

15. This is a good dinner recipe.

Nutrition: Calories: 272, Total Fat: 15 g, Carbs: 33 g, Protein: 5 g

136. Dijon Salmon with Green Bean Pilaf

Preparation Time: 20 minutes

Cooking Time: 30 minutes

Servings: 4

Ingredients:

- 1¼ lb wild salmon, skinned and cut into pieces
- 3 tsp extra virgin olive oil
- 1 tsp garlic, minced
- ¾ tsp salt
- 2 tsp hummus
- 2 tsp wholegrain mustard
- ½ tsp ground pepper
- 12 oz thin green beans, pre-trimmed
- 1 lemon, zested, and cut into wedges
- 2 tsp pine nuts
- 1 (8 oz) package, precooked brown rice
- 2 tsp water
- Fresh parsley, chopped

Directions:

1. Preheat the oven to 425°F and line a baking sheet with parchment paper.
2. Brush the salmon with 1 tbsp of oil and place it on the baking sheet.
3. Using a mortar and a pestle mash the garlic and salt to form a paste.
4. Transfer 1 tbsp of the garlic paste to a bowl then add hummus, ¼ tbsp of pepper, and mix to combine.
5. Spread the seasoning mixture on top of the salmon.
6. Roast the salmon for about 8 minutes.
7. Meanwhile, heat the remaining oil in a skillet over medium-high heat.
8. Add the green beans, lemon zest, pine nuts, the remaining garlic paste, and pepper to the skillet.
9. Cook the green beans as you stir for about 4 minutes.
10. Reduce the heat to medium and add rice and water to the green beans.
11. Cook the rice for 3 minutes.
12. Transfer the salmon to a serving platter and sprinkle parsley.

13. Serve the salmon with green bean pilaf and lemon wedges.

Nutrition: Calories: 442, Total Fat: 25 g, Carbs: 22 g, Protein: 32 g

137. Vegan Coconut Chickpea Curry

Preparation Time: 5 minutes

Cooking Time: 15 minutes

Servings: 4

Ingredients:

- 2 tsp avocado oil
- 1 cup chopped onion
- 1 cup diced bell pepper
- 1 zucchini, halved and sliced
- 1 (15 oz) can chickpeas, drained and rinsed
- ½ cup vegetable broth
- 4 cups baby spinach
- 2 cups precooked brown rice

Directions:

1. Heat oil in a skillet over medium-high heat.
2. Sauté onion, pepper, and zucchini for about 6 minutes stirring often.
3. Add the chickpeas and broth to the onion mixture and bring to a simmer as you stir.
4. Reduce the heat to medium-low heat and allow the vegetables to simmer for 6 minutes.
5. Stir in the spinach to the chickpeas and remove from heat.
6. Serve the chickpeas over rice.

Nutrition: Calories: 471, Total Fat: 17 g, Carbs: 66 g, Protein: 11 g

138. Cauliflower Tikka Masala with Chickpeas

Preparation Time: 10 minutes

Cooking Time: 10 minutes

Servings: 4

Ingredients:

- 1 tsp olive oil
- 4 cups cauliflower florets
- ¼ tsp salt
- ¼ cup water
- 1 (15 oz) can chickpeas, drained and rinsed

- 1½ cups tikka masala sauce
- 2 tsp clarified butter
- Fresh cilantro

Directions:

1. Heat oil in a skillet over medium-high heat.

2. Add cauliflower and salt to a skillet and cook for 2 minutes stirring occasionally.

3. Add water to the cauliflower and cook covered for about 5 minutes until the cauliflower gets tender.

4. Add chickpeas and sauce to the cauliflower and cook for 2 minutes stirring often.

5. Remove the cauliflower from heat and stir in the butter.

6. Transfer the cauliflower and chickpeas to a serving platter and garnish with cilantro.

7. This is a healthy dinner recipe.

Nutrition: Calories: 268, Total Fat: 16 g, Carbs: 26 g, Protein: 7 g

139. Sheet-Pan Chicken and Vegetables with Romesco Sauce

Preparation Time: 25 minutes

Cooking Time: 25 minutes

Servings: 4

Ingredients:

- 2 Yukon gold potatoes, cubed
- 6 tbsp extra-virgin olive oil
- 1 tsp ground pepper
- ½ tsp salt
- 4 bone-in chicken thighs, skinless
- 4 cups broccoli florets
- 1 (7 oz) jar roasted red pepper
- ¼ cup slivered almonds
- 1 crushed garlic clove
- 1 tsp paprika
- ½ tsp ground cumin
- ¼ tsp crushed red pepper
- 2 tsp fresh cilantro, chopped

Directions:

1. Preheat the oven to 450°F.

2. Add the potatoes, 1 tbsp oil, ¼ tbsp pepper, and ⅛ tbsp salt to a bowl and toss to combine.

3. Move the potatoes to one side of a rimmed baking sheet.

4. Add the chicken, 1 tbsp oil, ¼ tsp pepper, and ⅛ tbsp salt into the same bowl and toss to coat.

5. Transfer the chicken to the other side of the baking sheet.

6. Roast the chicken and potatoes for 10 minutes.

7. Meanwhile add the broccoli, 2 tbsp oil, ¼ tbsp pepper, and ⅛ tbsp salt to a separate bowl and toss to mix.

8. Add the broccoli to the potato side of the baking sheet and stir to mix.

9. Roast the broccoli for 15 minutes.

10. Meanwhile add the roasted pepper, almonds, garlic, paprika, cumin, crushed red pepper, 2 tbsp oil, ⅛ tbsp salt, and ¼ tbsp pepper in a food processor and process until a smooth consistency is achieved.

11. Move the chicken and vegetables to a serving platter and sprinkle with the cilantro.

12. Serve with roasted pepper sauce.

Nutrition: Calories: 499, Total Fat: 27 g, Carbs: 30 g, Protein: 33 g

140. Gluten-Free Teriyaki Salmon

Preparation Time: 15 minutes

Cooking Time: 12 minutes

Servings: 4

Ingredients:

- 24 oz salmon steaks
- Sauce
- ¼ cup coconut aminos
- 1 tsp olive oil
- ½ cup lemon juice
- 1 tbsp honey
- 1 tbsp ginger, minced
- 1 tsp garlic, minced
- ½ cup onions, chopped
- ¼ tsp black pepper
- 1 stalk lemongrass, minced
- 1 tsp sesame seeds

Directions:

1. Preheat your oven to 350°F and line a baking sheet with wax paper.

2. Meanwhile, whisk the sauce ingredients in a mixing bowl until well mixed.

3. Place the salmon in a dish and pour over the sauce. Rub the salmon with the sauce until well covered.

4. Refrigerate for at least 20 minutes.

5. Transfer the salmon to the prepared baking sheet and bake for 12 minutes or until cooked through.

6. Serve the salmon with sautéed veggies or salad of choice.

Nutrition: Calories: 408, Total Fat: 24 g, Carbs: 8 g, Protein: 39 g

141. Gluten-Free Pineapple Burgers

Preparation Time: 10 minutes

Cooking Time: 10 minutes

Servings: 4

Ingredients:

- 2 lb lean meat, ground
- ½ cup gluten-free teriyaki sauce
- 8 oz pineapple slices, reserve the juice
- 4 lettuce leaves
- 4 slices fat-free cheese
- 4 slices tomato
- 4 buckwheat burger buns

Directions:

1. In a mixing bowl, mix meat, sauce and season with salt and pepper.

2. Divide the meat mixture into 4 patties.

3. Drizzle each patty with pineapple juice then place the pineapple slices on each patty.

4. Grill the patties over medium heat for 7 minutes or until cooked through.

5. Layer the burgers starting with the bottom bun, lettuce, pineapple, cheese, tomato, grilled patty, and the top bun.

Nutrition: Calories: 714, Total Fat: 23 g, Carbs: 39 g, Protein: 83 g

142. Vegan Mushrooms in Broth

Preparation Time: 15 minutes

Cooking Time: 20 minutes

Servings: 4

Ingredients:

- 1 tbsp extra-virgin olive oil
- 1 onion, sliced
- 3 garlic cloves, sliced
- 1 celery stalk, finely chopped
- 1 lb mushrooms, sliced
- A pinch of nutmeg
- 1 tsp salt
- ½ tsp black pepper
- 4 cups vegetable broth
- 1 cup cooked chicken
- 2 tbsp tarragon, freshly chopped

Directions:

1. Heat olive oil in a large pot over medium heat.

2. Sauté onions, garlic, and celery for 3 minutes or until the onions are fragrant.

3. Add mushrooms, nutmeg salt, and pepper. Sauté for an additional 10 minutes.

4. Add broth and bring the soup to a boil. Reduce heat and simmer for 5 minutes.

5. Stir in chicken and tarragon. Serve.

Nutrition: Calories: 111, Total Fat: 5 g, Carbs: 9 g, Protein: 9 g

143. Vegan and Mediterranean Mango and Bean Stew

Preparation Time: 10 minutes

Cooking Time: 10 minutes

Servings: 4

Ingredients:

- 2 tbsp coconut oil
- 1 onion, chopped
- 2 15 oz beans
- 1 tbsp chili powder
- 1 tsp salt
- ¼ tsp black pepper
- 1 cup water
- 2 ripe mangoes, thinly sliced
- ¼ cup cilantro, chopped

- ¼ cup scallions, sliced

Directions:

1. Heat coconut oil in a pot over medium heat.

2. Sauté onions in oil for 5 minutes then add beans, chili powder, salt, and pepper.

3. Add water and bring the mixture to a boil. Reduce heat and simmer for 5 minutes.

4. Remove the pot from heat and stir in mangoes.

5. Serve garnished with scallions and cilantro.

Nutrition: Calories: 431, Total Fat: 9 g, Carbs: 72 g, Protein: 20 g

144. Cod and Peas

Preparation Time: 10 minutes

Cooking Time: 15 minutes

Servings: 4

Ingredients:

- 10 oz peas, blanched
- 1 tbsp chopped parsley
- A drizzle olive oil
- 4 cod fillets, boneless
- 1 tsp dried oregano
- 2 oz veggie stock
- 2 garlic cloves, minced
- 1 tsp smoked paprika
- A pinch of sea salt and black pepper

Directions:

1. Put parsley, paprika, oregano, stock and garlic in your food processor and blend really well. Heat up a pan with the oil over low-high heat, add the cod, season with salt and pepper and cook for 4 minutes on each side. Add the peas and the parsley, mix and cook for 5 minutes more. Divide everything between plates and serve.

2. Enjoy!

Nutrition: Calories: 251, Fat: 4 g, Fiber: 6 g, Carbs: 14 g, Protein: 15 g

145. Roasted Vegetables and Sweet Potatoes with White Beans

Preparation Time: 15 minutes

Cooking Time: 25 minutes

Servings: 4

Ingredients:

- 2 small sweet potatoes, dice
- ½ red onion, cut into ¼-inch dice
- 1 medium carrot, peeled and thinly sliced
- 4 oz green beans, trimmed
- ¼ cup extra-virgin olive oil
- 1 tsp salt
- ¼ tsp freshly ground black pepper
- 1 (15½ oz) can white beans, drained and rinsed
- 1 tbsp minced or grated lemon zest
- 1 tbsp chopped fresh dill

Directions:

1. Preheat the oven to 400°F.

2. Combine the sweet potatoes, onion, carrot, green beans, oil, salt, and pepper on a large rimmed baking sheet and mix to combine well. Arrange in a single layer.

3. Roast until the vegetables are tender, 20 to 25 minutes.

4. Add the white beans, lemon zest, and dill, mix well and serve.

Nutrition: Calories: 315, Total Fat: 13 g, Total Carbs: 42 g, Sugar: 5 g, Fiber: 13 g, Protein: 10 g, Sodium: 632 mg

146. Roasted Tofu and Greens

Preparation Time: 10 minutes

Cooking Time: 20 minutes

Servings: 4

Ingredients:

- 3 cups baby spinach or kale
- 1 tbsp sesame oil
- 1 tbsp ginger, minced
- 1 garlic clove, minced
- 1 lb firm tofu, cut into 1-inch dice
- 1 tbsp gluten-free tamari or soy sauce
- ¼ tsp red pepper flakes (optional)
- 1 tsp rice vinegar
- 2 scallions, thinly sliced

Directions:

1. Preheat the oven to 400°F.

2. Combine the spinach, oil, ginger, and garlic on a large rimmed baking sheet.

3. Bake until the spinach has wilted, 3 to 5 minutes.

4. Add the tofu, tamari, and red pepper flakes (if using) and toss to combine well.

5. Bake until the tofu is beginning to brown, 10 to 15 minutes.

6. Top with the vinegar and scallions and serve.

Nutrition: Calories: 121, Total Fat: 7 g, Total Carbs: 4 g, Sugar: 1 g, Fiber: 2 g, Protein: 10 g, Sodium: 258 mg

147. Tofu and Italian-Seasoned Summer Vegetables

Preparation Time: 10 minutes

Cooking Time: 20 minutes

Servings: 4

Ingredients:

- 2 large zucchinis, cut into ¼-inch slices
- 2 large summer squash, cut into ¼-inch-thick slices
- 1 lb firm tofu, cut into 1-inch dice
- 1 cup vegetable broth or water
- 3 tbsp extra-virgin olive oil
- 2 garlic cloves, sliced
- 1 tsp salt
- 1 tsp Italian herb seasoning blend
- ¼ tsp freshly ground black pepper
- 1 tbsp thinly sliced fresh basil

Directions:

1. Preheat the oven to 400°F.

2. Combine the zucchini, squash, tofu, broth, oil, garlic, salt, Italian herb seasoning blend, and pepper on a large rimmed baking sheet, and mix well.

3. Roast within 20 minutes.

4. Sprinkle with the basil and serve.

Nutrition: Calories: 213, Total Fat: 16 g, Total Carbs: 9 g, Sugar: 4 g, Fiber: 3 g, Protein: 13 g, Sodium: 806 mg

148. Spiced Broccoli, Cauliflower with Tofu and Red Onion

Preparation Time: 10 minutes

Cooking Time: 25 minutes

Servings: 2

Ingredients:

- 2 cups broccoli florets
- 2 cups cauliflower florets
- 1 medium red onion, diced
- 3 tbsp extra-virgin olive oil
- 1 tsp salt
- ¼ tsp freshly ground black pepper
- 1 lb firm tofu, cut into 1-inch dice
- 1 garlic clove, minced
- 1 (¼-inch) piece fresh ginger, minced

Directions:

1. Preheat the oven to 400°F.

2. Combine the broccoli, cauliflower, onion, oil, salt, and pepper on a large rimmed baking sheet, and mix well.

3. Roast until the vegetables have softened, 10 to 15 minutes.

4. Add the tofu, garlic, and ginger. Roast within 10 minutes.

5. Gently mix the ingredients on the baking sheet to combine the tofu with the vegetables and serve.

Nutrition: Calories: 210, Total Fat: 15 g, Total Carbs: 11 g, Sugar: 4 g, Fiber: 4 g, Protein: 12 g, Sodium: 626 mg

149. Tempeh and Root Vegetable Bake

Preparation Time: 10 minutes

Cooking Time: 30 minutes

Servings: 4

Ingredients:

- 1 tbsp extra-virgin olive oil
- 1 large sweet potato, dice
- 2 carrots, thinly sliced
- 1 fennel bulb, trimmed and cut into ¼-inch dice
- 2 tsp minced fresh ginger
- 1 garlic clove, minced
- 12 oz tempeh, cut into ½-inch dice
- ½ cup vegetable broth
- 1 tbsp gluten-free tamari or soy sauce

- 2 scallions, thinly sliced

Directions:

1. Preheat the oven to 400°F. Grease a baking sheet with the oil.

2. Arrange the sweet potato, carrots, fennel, ginger, and garlic in a single layer on the baking sheet.

3. Bake until the vegetables have softened, about 15 minutes.

4. Add the tempeh, broth, and tamari.

5. Bake again until the tempeh is heated through and lightly browned for 10 to 15 minutes.

6. Add the scallions, mix well, and serve.

Nutrition: Calories: 276, Total Fat: 13 g, Total Carbs: 26 g, Sugar: 5 g, Fiber: 4 g, Protein: 19 g, Sodium: 397 mg

150. Garlicky Chicken and Vegetables

Preparation Time: 10 minutes

Cooking Time: 45 minutes

Servings: 4

Ingredients:

- 2 tsp extra-virgin olive oil
- 1 leek, white part only, thinly sliced
- 2 large zucchinis, cut into ¼-inch slices
- 4 bone-in, skin-on chicken breasts
- 3 garlic cloves, minced
- 1 tsp salt
- 1 tsp dried oregano
- ¼ tsp freshly ground black pepper
- ½ cup white wine
- Juice 1 lemon

Directions:

1. Preheat the oven to 400°F. Grease the baking sheet with the oil.

2. Place the leek and zucchini on the baking sheet.

3. Put the chicken, skin-side up, and sprinkle with the garlic, salt, oregano, and pepper. Add the wine.

4. Roast within 35 to 40 minutes. Remove and let rest for 5 minutes.

5. Add the lemon juice and serve.

Nutrition: Calories: 315, Total Fat: 7 g, Total Carbs: 12 g, Sugar: 4 g, Fiber: 2 g, Protein: 44 g, Sodium: 685 mg

151. Turmeric-Spiced Sweet Potatoes, Apple, and Onion with Chicken

Preparation Time: 15 minutes

Cooking Time: 45 minutes

Servings: 4

Ingredients:

- 2 tbsp unsalted butter, at room temperature
- 2 medium sweet potatoes
- 1 large Granny Smith apple
- 1 medium onion, thinly sliced
- 4 bone-in, skin-on chicken breasts
- 1 tsp salt
- 1 tsp turmeric
- 1 tsp dried sage
- ¼ tsp freshly ground black pepper
- 1 cup apple cider, white wine, or chicken broth

Directions:

1. Preheat the oven to 400°F. Grease the baking sheet with the butter.

2. Arrange the sweet potatoes, apple, and onion in a single layer on the baking sheet.

3. Put the chicken, skin-side up, and season with salt, turmeric, sage, and pepper. Add the cider.

4. Roast within 35 to 40 minutes. Remove, let it rest for 5 minutes and serve.

Nutrition: Calories: 386, Total Fat: 12 g, Total Carbs: 26 g, Sugar: 10 g, Fiber: 4 g, Protein: 44 g, Sodium: 932 mg

152. Honey-Roasted Chicken Thighs with Carrots

Preparation Time: 10 minutes

Cooking Time: 50 minutes

Servings: 4

Ingredients:

- 2 tbsp unsalted butter, at room temperature
- 3 large carrots, thinly sliced
- 2 garlic cloves, minced
- 4 bone-in, skin-on chicken thighs
- 1 tsp salt
- ½ tsp dried rosemary
- ¼ tsp freshly ground black pepper
- 2 tbsp honey
- 1 cup chicken broth or vegetable broth

- Lemon wedges, for serving

Directions:

1. Preheat the oven to 400°F. Grease the baking sheet with the butter.

2. Arrange the carrots and garlic in a single layer on the baking sheet.

3. Put the chicken, skin-side up, on top of the vegetables, and season with the salt, rosemary, and pepper.

4. Put the honey on top and add the broth.

5. Roast within 40 to 45 minutes. Remove, and then let it rest for 5 minutes, and serve with lemon wedges.

Nutrition: Calories: 428, Total Fat: 27 g, Total Carbs: 15 g, Sugar: 11 g, Fiber: 2 g, Protein: 30 g, Sodium: 732 mg

153. Sesame-Tamari Baked Chicken with Green Beans

Preparation Time: 10 minutes

Cooking Time: 45 minutes

Servings: 4

Ingredients:

- 1 lb green beans, trimmed
- 4 bone-in, skin-on chicken breasts
- 2 tbsp honey
- 1 tbsp sesame oil
- 1 tbsp gluten-free tamari or soy sauce
- 1 cup chicken or vegetable broth

Directions:

1. Preheat the oven to 400°F.

2. Arrange the green beans on a large rimmed baking sheet.

3. Put the chicken, skin-side up, on top of the beans.

4. Drizzle with honey, oil, and tamari. Add the broth.

5. Roast within 35 to 40 minutes. Remove, let it rest for 5 minutes and serve.

Nutrition: Calories: 378, Total Fat: 10 g, Total Carbs: 19 g, Sugar: 10 g, Fiber: 4 g, Protein: 54 g, Sodium: 336 mg

154. Sheet Pan Turkey Breast with Golden Vegetables

Preparation Time: 15 minutes

Cooking Time: 45 minutes

Servings: 4

Ingredients:

- 2 tbsp unsalted butter, at room temperature
- 1 medium acorn squash, seeded and thinly sliced
- 2 large golden beets, peeled and thinly sliced
- ½ medium yellow onion, thinly sliced
- ½ boneless, skin-on turkey breast (1 to 2 lb)
- 2 tbsp honey
- 1 tsp salt
- 1 tsp turmeric
- ¼ tsp freshly ground black pepper
- 1 cup chicken broth or vegetable broth

Directions:

1. Preheat the oven to 400°F. Grease the baking sheet with the butter.

2. Arrange the squash, beets, and onion in a single layer on the baking sheet. Put the turkey skin-side up. Drizzle with honey. Season with salt, turmeric, and pepper, and add the broth.

3. Roast until the turkey registers 165°F in the center with an instant-read thermometer, 35 to 45 minutes. Remove, and let rest for 5 minutes.

4. Slice, and serve.

Nutrition: Calories: 383, Total Fat: 15 g, Total Carbs: 25 g, Sugar: 13 g, Fiber: 3 g, Protein: 37 g, Sodium: 748 mg

155. Sheet Pan Steak and Brussels Sprouts with Red Wine

Preparation Time: 10 minutes

Cooking Time: 20 minutes

Servings: 4

Ingredients:

- 1 lb rib-eye steak
- 1 tsp salt
- ¼ tsp freshly ground black pepper
- 1 tbsp unsalted butter
- ½ red onion, minced
- 8 oz Brussels sprouts, trimmed and quartered
- 1 cup red wine
- Juice ½ lemon

Directions:

1. Preheat the broiler to high.

2. Massage the steak with salt and pepper on a large rimmed baking sheet. Broil until browned, 2 to 3 minutes per side.

3. Turn off and heat up the oven to 400°F.

4. Put the steak on one side of the baking sheet and add the butter, onion, Brussels sprouts, and wine to the other side.

5. Roast within 8 minutes. Remove, and let rest for 5 minutes.

6. Sprinkle with the lemon juice and serve.

Nutrition: Calories: 416, Total Fat: 27 g, Total Carbs: 7 g, Sugar: 2 g, Fiber: 3 g, Protein: 22 g, Sodium: 636 mg

156. Miso Salmon and Green Beans

Preparation Time: 10 minutes

Cooking Time: 25 minutes

Servings: 4

Ingredients:

- 1 tbsp sesame oil
- 1 lb green beans, trimmed
- 1 lb skin-on salmon fillets, cut into 4 steaks
- ¼ cup white miso
- 2 tsp gluten-free tamari or soy sauce
- 2 scallions, thinly sliced

Directions:

1. Preheat the oven to 400°F. Grease the baking sheet with the oil.

2. Put the green beans, then the salmon on top of the green beans, and brush each piece with the miso.

3. Roast within 20 to 25 minutes.

4. Drizzle with the tamari, sprinkle with the scallions and serve.

Nutrition: Calories: 213, Total Fat: 7 g, Total Carbs: 13 g, Sugar: 3 g, Fiber: 5 g, Protein: 27 g, Sodium: 989 mg

157. Tilapia with Asparagus and Acorn Squash

Preparation Time: 15 minutes

Cooking Time: 30 minutes

Servings: 4

Ingredients:

- 2 tbsp extra-virgin olive oil
- 1 medium acorn squash, seeded and thinly sliced or in wedges
- 1 lb asparagus, trimmed of woody ends and cut into 2-inch pieces
- 1 large shallot, thinly sliced
- 1 lb tilapia fillets
- ½ cup white wine
- 1 tbsp chopped fresh flat-leaf parsley
- 1 tsp salt
- ¼ tsp freshly ground black pepper

Directions:

1. Preheat the oven to 400°F. Grease the baking sheet with the oil.

2. Arrange the squash, asparagus, and shallot in a single layer on the baking sheet. Roast within 8 to 10 minutes.

3. Put the tilapia, and add the wine.

4. Sprinkle with parsley, salt, and pepper.

5. Roast within 15 minutes. Remove, then let rest for 5 minutes, and serve.

Nutrition: Calories: 246, Total Fat: 7 g, Total Carbs: 17 g, Sugar: 2 g, Fiber: 4 g, Protein: 25 g, Sodium: 639 mg

158. Shrimp-Lime Bake with Zucchini and Corn

Preparation Time: 10 minutes

Cooking Time: 20 minutes

Servings: 4

Ingredients:

- 1 tbsp extra-virgin olive oil
- 2 small zucchinis, cut into ¼-inch dice
- 1 cup frozen corn kernels
- 2 scallions, thinly sliced
- 1 tsp salt
- ½ tsp ground cumin
- ½ tsp chipotle chili powder

- 1 lb peeled shrimp, thawed if necessary
- 1 tbsp finely chopped fresh cilantro
- Zest and juice 1 lime

Directions:

1. Preheat the oven to 400°F. Grease the baking sheet with the oil.

2. On the baking sheet, combine the zucchini, corn, scallions, salt, cumin, and chili powder and mix well. Arrange in a single layer.

3. Add the shrimp on top. Roast within 15 to 20 minutes.

4. Put the cilantro and lime zest and juice, stir to combine, and serve.

Nutrition: Calories: 184, Total Fat: 5 g, Total Carbs: 11 g, Sugar: 3 g, Fiber: 2 g, Protein: 26 g, Sodium: 846 mg

159. Broccolini with Almonds

Preparation Time: 15 minutes

Cooking Time: 5 minutes

Servings: 6

Ingredients:

- 1 fresh red chili, deseeded and finely chopped
- 2 bunches broccolini, trimmed
- 1 tbsp extra-virgin olive oil
- 2 garlic cloves, thinly sliced
- ¼ cup natural almonds, coarsely chopped
- 2 tsp lemon rind, finely grated
- 4 anchovies in oil, chopped
- A squeeze of fresh lemon juice

Directions:

1. Preheat some oil in a pan. Add 2 tsp of lemon rind, drained anchovies, finely chopped chili, and thinly sliced gloves. Cook for about 30 seconds, with constant stirring.

2. Add ¼ cup coarsely chopped almonds and cook for a minute. Turn the heat off and add lemon juice on top.

3. Place the steamer basket over a pan with simmering water. Add broccolini to a basket and cover it.

4. Cook until tender-crisp, for about 3 to 4 minutes. Drain and then transfer to the serving platter.

5. Top with almond mixture and enjoy!

Nutrition: Calories: 414, Fat: 6.6 g, Carbs: 1.6 g, Protein: 5.4 g

160. Vegetable and Chicken Stir Fry

Preparation Time: 5 minutes

Cooking Time: 15 minutes

Servings: 6

Ingredients:

- 3 tbsp olive oil
- 3 chicken breasts
- 3 medium zucchini or yellow squash
- 2 onions
- 1 tsp garlic powder
- 1 broccoli
- 1 tsp basil
- 1 tsp pepper and salt

Directions:

1. Chop the vegetables and chicken.

2. Heat your skillet over medium temperature.

3. Pour olive oil and add the chicken. Cook while stirring.

4. Include the seasonings if you want.

5. Add the vegetables. Keep cooking until it gets slightly soft. Add the onions first and broccoli last.

Nutrition: Calories: 183, Carbs: 9 g, Cholesterol: 41 mg, Total Fat: 11 g, Protein: 12 g, Sugar: 4 g, Fiber: 3 g, Sodium: 468 mg

161. Baked Tilapia with Rosemary and Pecan

Preparation Time: 10 minutes

Cooking Time: 17 minutes

Servings: 4

Ingredients:

- ⅓ cup whole-wheat panko breadcrumbs
- ⅓ cup raw pecans, chopped
- ½ tsp agave nectar
- 2 tsp rosemary, chopped
- 1 pinch cayenne pepper
- 1½ tsp olive oil
- ¼ lb tilapia fillets, 4 pieces
- 1 egg white
- ⅛ tsp salt

Directions:

1. Preheat your oven to 350°F.

2. Stir together the breadcrumbs, pecans, agave, rosemary, cayenne pepper, and salt in a baking dish.

3. Pour the olive oil. Toss and coat the mixture. Bake for 7 minutes.

4. Now increase the temperature to 400°F.

5. Apply cooking spray to a glass baking dish. Whisk your egg white in a dish.

6. Dip the fish in the egg, and then into your pecan mix. One fish fillet at a time. Coat each side lightly.

7. Keep the fish fillets in your baking dish.

8. Keep the remaining pecan mix on the fillets. Bake for 10 minutes.

Nutrition: Calories: 244, Carbs: 7 g, Cholesterol: 55 mg, Total Fat: 12 g, Protein: 27 g, Sugar: 1 g, Fiber: 2 g, Sodium: 153 mg

162. Toasted Brown Rice with Thyme and Mushrooms

Preparation Time: 10 minutes

Cooking Time: 50 minutes

Servings: 3

Ingredients:

- ½ chopped yellow onion
- 1½ tsp olive oil
- 1 cup brown rice
- 2 garlic cloves, minced
- ½ lb cremini mushrooms, sliced
- 1 cup vegetable broth
- 3 tbsp parsley, minced
- 1 tbsp thyme, minced
- 1 cup water
- ¼ tsp ground pepper and salt

Directions:

1. Heat half a tsp of olive oil in your saucepan on medium heat.

2. Add the onion. Cook for 5 minutes. Add garlic. Cook for 1 minute.

3. Now include the rice. Cook for a minute while stirring.

4. Stir the vegetable broth in along with the water. Boil and then reduce the heat.

5. Cook for 35 minutes. The liquid should be absorbed.

6. Heat a tsp of oil in a nonstick skillet at medium temperature.

7. Include the mushrooms. Cook for 4 minutes.

8. Stir the thyme in. Cook for a minute.

9. Add the parsley, mushrooms, pepper, and salt to your rice. Combine well.

Nutrition: Calories: 62, Carbs: 9 g, Total Fat: 2 g, Protein: 2 g, Sugar: 1 g, Fiber: 1 g, Sodium: 202 mg

163. Italian Stuffed Peppers

Preparation Time: 10 minutes

Cooking Time: 50 minutes

Servings: 6

Ingredients:

- ½ onion, chopped
- 1 tbsp olive oil
- ½ tsp kosher salt
- 1 carrot, diced into ¼ inch thickness
- 1 tsp Italian seasoning
- 3 garlic cloves, minced
- 3 cups pumpkin, grated
- ½ tsp red pepper flakes
- 1¼ cup cooked quinoa
- 1 lb chickpeas, drained and rinsed
- 3 red bell pepper, cut, remove the seeds and membrane
- ¼ cup parsley, minced
- ¼ cup vegan Parmesan, grated

Directions:

1. Preheat your oven to 350°F.

2. Heat olive oil in your nonstick skillet over medium temperature.

3. Now add the carrots and onions.

4. Season with a little bit of salt. Cook for 5 minutes, stirring occasionally.

5. Stir the Italian seasoning, red pepper flakes, and garlic in. Cook for another minute.

6. Add the chickpeas, pumpkin, and the remaining salt. Boil and simmer for 8 minutes.

7. Remove from heat. Stir 3 tbsp of parsley and the cooked quinoa in.

8. Keep the pepper in your baking dish. The cut side should be up.

9. Now divide your chickpea mix between the peppers evenly.

10. Pour half of the water into your baking dish.

11. Use a foil to cover tightly for 30 minutes. The peppers should be tender.

12. Sprinkle the parmesan over each pepper.

13. Bake uncovered for 5 minutes.

14. Garnish with the remaining parsley.

Nutrition: Calories: 276, Carbs: 40 g, Cholesterol: 6 mg, Total Fat: 7 g, Protein: 11 g, Sugar: 6 g, Fiber: 7 g, Sodium: 612 mg

164. Chicken with Herb Parmesan Spaghetti Squash

Preparation Time: 15 minutes

Cooking Time: 20 minutes

Servings: 4

Ingredients:

- 1 lb chicken breast, skinless & boneless, cut into small pieces
- 3 lb spaghetti squash
- 2 tsp olive oil
- 3 tbsp shallots, minced
- 1 tbsp melted coconut oil
- ½ tsp rosemary, dried
- ½ tsp oregano, dried
- ½ tsp thyme, dried
- 3 garlic cloves, minced
- ¼ tsp ground pepper
- ¼ tsp kosher salt
- 2 tbsp parsley, minced
- ⅓ cup vegan Parmesan, grated
- ½ cup chicken broth
- Pepper and salt to taste

Directions:

1. Pierce your spaghetti squash with a knife in many places.

2. Keep it in a baking dish. Cook in your microwave for 12 minutes on high heat. Turn the spaghetti halfway through. Set aside.

3. Cut it in half along the length. Remove the fibers and seeds.

4. Twist the strands out with a fork. Keep in a bowl.

5. Heat your nonstick skillet over medium temperature.

6. Apply cooking spray lightly. Add the chicken.

7. Cook while stirring occasionally.

8. Transfer chicken to a bowl once done. Keep it aside.

9. Now bring down the heat to medium. Add the coconut oil and olive oil.

10. Include the shallots. Cook for 3 minutes.

11. Stir the rosemary, garlic, oregano, and thyme.

12. Cook for another minute, while stirring.

13. Now stir the chicken broth in.

14. Let your mixture simmer for a couple of minutes.

15. Include your cooked chicken and spaghetti squash in the skillet.

16. Toss with your sauce.

17. Add the parsley and Parmesan. Toss once more.

Nutrition: Calories: 295, Carbs: 12 g, Cholesterol: 80 mg Total Fat: 15 g, Protein: 27 g, Sugar: 5 g, Fiber: 3 g, Sodium: 557 mg

165. Chicken Curry with Tamarind & Pumpkins

Preparation Time: 10 minutes

Cooking Time: 45 minutes

Servings: 4

Ingredients:

- 1 tsp olive oil
- 8 chicken thighs, boneless & skinless, trimmed
- 1 onion, chopped
- ¾ tsp pepper, ground
- ½ tsp salt
- 2 cups pumpkins, diced
- 3 garlic cloves, minced
- ¼ lb tamarind, pulped
- 1½ tsp coriander, ground
- 1½ tsp curry powder
- 1½ tsp cumin, ground

- ¼ cup parsley, minced
- 1¼ cup chicken broth, fat-free
- Pepper and salt to taste

Directions:

1. Season your chicken thighs (both sides) with half of the pepper and salt.

2. Heat your nonstick skillet over medium temperature.

3. Apply cooking spray lightly.

4. Add the chicken. Cook each side for 2 minutes. Transfer to a plate.

5. Heat olive oil in a skillet. Add the garlic and onions. Cook for 3 minutes.

6. Stir together the curry powder, pumpkin, tamarind, cumin, coriander, chicken broth, ¼ tsp pepper, and ¼ tsp salt in your skillet.

7. Boil the mixture and reduce heat to medium.

8. Let it simmer for 12 minutes. Stir occasionally.

9. Include the chicken. Cook covered for 15 minutes.

10. Cook uncovered for 10 minutes.

11. Stir the parsley in.

Nutrition: Calories: 757, Carbs: 52 g, Cholesterol: 249 mg, Total Fat: 29 g, Protein: 86 g, Sugar: 40 g, Fiber: 7 g, Sodium: 750 mg

166. Zucchini and Lemon Herb Salmon

Preparation Time: 15 minutes

Cooking Time: 20 minutes

Servings: 4

Ingredients:

- 2 tbsp olive oil
- 4 chopped zucchinis
- 2 tbsp lemon juice
- 2 tbsp agave nectar
- 2 garlic cloves, minced
- 1 tbsp Dijon mustard
- ½ tsp oregano, dried
- ½ tsp dill, dried
- ¼ tsp rosemary, dried
- ¼ tsp thyme, dried
- 4 salmon fillets
- 2 tbsp parsley leaves, chopped
- Ground black pepper and kosher salt to taste

Directions:

1. Preheat your oven to 400°F.

2. Apply cooking spray on your baking sheet lightly.

3. Whisk together the lemon juice, brown sugar, dill, garlic, Dijon, rosemary, thyme, and oregano in a bowl.

4. Season with pepper and salt to taste. Set aside.

5. Keep the zucchini on your baking sheet in one single layer.

6. Drizzle some olive oil. Season with pepper and salt.

7. Add the fish in one layer. Brush each fillet with your herb mix.

8. Keep in the oven. Cook for 17 minutes.

9. Garnish with parsley and serve.

Nutrition: Calories: 355, Carbs: 15 g, Cholesterol: 78 mg Total Fat: 19 g, Protein: 31 g, Sugar: 12 g, Fiber: 2 g, Sodium: 132 mg

167. Parmesan and Lemon Fish

Preparation Time: 15 minutes

Cooking Time: 10 minutes

Servings: 2

Ingredients:

- 4 tilapia fillets
- ¼ cup cornflakes, crushed
- 2 tbsp vegan Parmesan, grated
- 2 tsp vegan dairy-free butter, melted
- ⅛ tsp black pepper, ground
- ½ tsp lemon peel, shredded
- Lemon wedges

Directions:

1. Heat your oven to 450°F.

2. Rinse and then dry the fish using paper towels.

3. Apply cooking spray to your baking pan.

4. Now roll up your fish fillets. Start from their short ends.

5. Keep in the baking pan.

6. Bring together the vegan butter, Parmesan, cornflakes, pepper and lemon peel in a bowl.

7. Sprinkle the crumb mix on your fish roll-ups.

8. Press the crumbs lightly into the fish.

9. Bake for 6 to 8 minutes. The fish should flake easily with your fork.

10. Serve with lemon wedges.

Nutrition: Calories: 191, Cholesterol: 71 mg, Carbs: 7 g, Fat: 7 g, Sugar: 1 g, Fiber: 0 g, Protein: 25 g

168. Chicken Lemon Piccata

Preparation Time: 10 minutes

Cooking Time: 30 minutes

Servings: 4

Ingredients:

- 2 chicken breasts, skinless & boneless
- 2 tbsp dairy-free margarine
- 1½ tbsp whole wheat flour
- ¼ tsp salt
- ¼ tsp white pepper
- ⅓ cup white wine, dry
- 2 tbsp olive oil
- ¼ cup lemon juice
- ⅓ cup chicken stock, low-sodium
- ¼ cup minced Italian parsley
- ¼ cup capers, drained
- Pepper and salt to taste

Directions:

1. Cut in half each chicken breast.

2. Spread your flour on a plate thinly. Season with pepper and salt.

3. Dredge the breast slices lightly in your seasoned flour. Set aside.

4. Heat your sauté pan over medium temperature.

5. Add the breast slices to your pan when you see the oil simmering.

6. Cook for 3 to 4 minutes.

7. Turn over the chicken slices.

8. Take out the slices. Set aside.

9. Add wine to the pan. Stir. Scrape up those browned bits from the bottom.

10. Now add the chicken stock and lemon juice.

11. Go to high heat. Boil till you have a thick sauce.

12. Bring down the heat. Stir the parsley and capers in.

13. Add back the breast slices to your pan. Rewarm.

Nutrition: Calories: 227, Cholesterol: 72 mg, Carbs: 3 g, Fat: 15 g, Fiber: 1 g, Sugar: 0 g, Protein: 20 g

169. Blackened Chicken Breast

Preparation Time: 10 minutes

Cooking Time: 15 minutes

Servings: 2

Ingredients:

- 2 chicken breast halves, skinless and boneless
- 1 tsp thyme, ground
- 2 tsp paprika
- 2 tsp olive oil
- ½ tsp onion powder

Directions:

1. Combine the thyme, paprika, onion powder, and salt together in your bowl.

2. Transfer the spice mix to a flat plate.

3. Rub olive oil on the chicken breast. Coat fully.

4. Roll the chicken pieces in the spice mixture. Press down, ensuring that all sides have the spice mix.

5. Keep aside for 5 minutes.

6. In the meantime, preheat your air fryer to 360°F.

7. Keep the chicken in the air fryer basket. Cook for 8 minutes.

8. Flip once and cook for another 7 minutes.

9. Transfer the breasts to a serving plate. Serve after 5 minutes.

Nutrition: Calories: 424, Carbs: 3 g, Cholesterol: 198 mg, Total Fat: 11 g, Protein: 79 g, Sugar: 1 g, Fiber: 2 g, Sodium: 516 mg

170. Chicken Marrakesh

Preparation Time: 25 minutes

Cooking Time: 4 hours

Servings: 8

Ingredients:

- 1 slice onion
- 2 garlic cloves, minced
- ½ lb pumpkins
- 2 carrots, diced & peeled
- 1 lb garbanzo beans, drained & rinsed

- ½ tsp cumin, ground
- 2 lb chicken breasts, skinless, halved, cut into small pieces
- ¼ tsp cinnamon, ground
- ½ tsp turmeric, ground
- ½ tsp black pepper, ground
- 1 tsp salt
- 1 tsp parsley, dried
- ½ lb tamarind, pulped

Directions:

1. Keep the garlic, onion, pumpkin, carrots, chicken breast and garbanzo beans in your slow cooker.

2. Mix turmeric, cumin, black pepper, cinnamon, salt and parsley in your bowl.

3. Sprinkle over the vegetables and chicken.

4. Add the tamarind. Combine well by stirring.

5. Keep your cooker covered. Set the heat to high.

6. Cook for 4 hours. The sauce should be thick.

Nutrition: Calories: 520, Carbs: 59 g, Cholesterol: 101 mg, Fat: 15 g, Fiber: 13 g, Sugar: 25 g, Protein: 45 g, Sodium: 424 mg

171. Shrimp and Vegetable Curry

Preparation Time: 5 minutes

Cooking Time: 10 minutes

Servings: 4

Ingredients:

- 1 sliced onion
- 3 tbsp olive oil
- 2 tsp curry powder
- 1 cup coconut milk
- 1 cauliflower
- 1 lb shrimp tails

Directions:

1. Add the onion to your oil.

2. Sauté to make it a bit soft.

3. Steam your vegetables in the meantime.

4. Add the curry seasoning, coconut milk, and spices if you want once the onion has become soft.

5. Cook for 2 minutes.

6. Include the shrimp. Cook for 5 minutes.

7. Serve with steamed vegetables.

Nutrition: Calories: 491, Carbs: 11 g, Cholesterol: 208 mg, Fat: 39 g, Protein: 24 g, Sugar: 3 g, Fiber: 5 g, Sodium: 309 mg

172. Banana and Peanut Butter Detox

Preparation Time: 10 minutes

Cooking Time: 0 minute

Servings: 1

Ingredients:

- ½ banana, frozen and fresh
- 2 tbsp almond butter
- ¼ cup dandelion green
- 1 cup beet greens
- ½ cup almond milk
- 6 ice cubes

Directions:

1. Add all ingredients to your blender

2. Blend it until you get a smooth and creamy mixture

3. Serve chilled and enjoy!

Nutrition: Calories: 366, Fat: 20 g, Carbs: 44 g, Protein: 10 g

173. Escarole, Pineapple, and Apple Smoothie

Preparation Time: 10 minutes

Cooking Time: 0 minute

Servings: 1

Ingredients:

- 2 cups pineapple, cubed
- 2 apples, cored
- 8 oz almond milk
- 1 head escarole lettuce
- 1 stalk celery

Directions:

1. Add all ingredients to your blender

2. Blend it until you get a smooth and creamy mixture

3. Serve chilled and enjoy!

Nutrition: Calories: 466, Fat: 7 g, Carbs: 103 g, Protein: 7 g

174. Green and Leafy Ginger-Apple Drink

Preparation Time: 10 minutes

Cooking Time: 0 minute

Servings: 1

Ingredients:

- 1 medium apple, cored
- 2 medium carrots, chopped
- 2 large handfuls baby spinach
- 1 tbsp ginger root, freshly grated
- 8 oz water, filtered

Directions:

1. Add all ingredients to your blender
2. Blend it until you get a smooth and creamy mixture
3. Serve chilled and enjoy!

Nutrition: Calories: 163, Fat: 0.1 g, Carbs: 40 g, Protein: 3 g

175. Nutty Pina Colada

Preparation Time: 10 minutes

Cooking Time: 0 minute

Servings: 1

Ingredients:

- ½ banana
- ½ cup fresh pineapple, diced
- ¼ tsp coconut extract
- ¼ cup quick-cooking oats
- 5 to 6 ice cubes
- 1 container (6 oz) Greek yogurt
- 1 cup almond milk
- 1 cup Swiss chard
- ¼ cup Dandelion greens

Directions:

1. Add all ingredients to your blender
2. Blend it until you get a smooth and creamy mixture
3. Serve chilled and enjoy!

Nutrition: Calories: 321, Fat: 6 g, Carbs: 16 g, Protein: 15 g

176. Chai Tea Drink

Preparation Time: 5 minutes

Cooking Time: 0 minute

Servings: 1

Ingredients:

- 1 cup almond milk
- 1 tbsp honey
- 1 cup boiling water
- ¼ tsp cacao powder
- 1 green tea bag

Directions:

1. Take a large mug, add a tea bag and hot water
2. Leave it for 5 minutes
3. Discard the tea bag and stir in cacao powder and honey
4. Mix them well
5. Stir in cold almond milk
6. Serve and enjoy!

Nutrition: Calories: 216, Fat: 7g, Carbs: 29g, Protein: 7g

177. Lemon-Mint Green Tea

Preparation Time: 10 minutes

Cooking Time: 0 minute

Servings: 1

Ingredients:

- 2 lemon slices
- 1 green tea bag
- 3 mint leaves
- 1 tbsp honey
- 2 cups boiling water

Directions:

1. Take a large mug, add lemon slices, a tea bag, and hot water
2. Leave it for 10 minutes
3. Discard the tea bag and stir in lemon slices and honey
4. Mix them well
5. Stir in mint leaves
6. Serve and enjoy!

Nutrition: Calories: 87, Fat: 0.2 g, Carbs: 24 g, Protein: 0.7 g

178. Spicy Chicken Vegetable Soup

Preparation Time: 10 minutes

Cooking Time: 25 minutes

Servings: 4

Ingredients:

- 1 lb chicken, skinless
- 1 tsp basil, dried
- 1 small onion, diced
- 1 can tomatoes, diced
- 2 cups vegetable, frozen
- 3 bay leaves
- 1 garlic clove, minced
- 1½ cups sweet potatoes, cubed
- ½ tsp red chili pepper flakes
- 1 jar spicy tomato sauce
- ½ tsp sea salt
- 2 cups chicken broth

Directions:

1. Add all ingredients to your Dutch oven, mix them well
2. Season with salt and pepper
3. Simmer for 15 minutes
4. Then cook for 10 minutes
5. Serve warm and enjoy!

Nutrition: Calories: 279, Fat: 11 g, Carbs: 17 g, Protein: 27 g

179. Lemon and Garlic Scallops

Preparation Time: 10 minutes

Cooking Time: 5 minutes

Servings: 4

Ingredients:

- 1 tbsp olive oil
- 1¼ lb dried scallops
- 2 tbsp all-purpose flour
- ¼ tsp sunflower seeds
- 4 to 5 garlic cloves, minced
- 1 scallion, chopped
- A pinch of ground sage
- Lemon juice
- 2 tbsp parsley, chopped

Directions:

1. Take a non-stick skillet and place it over medium-high heat
2. Add oil and allow the oil to heat up
3. Take a medium-sized bowl and add scallops alongside sunflower seeds and flour
4. Place the scallops in the skillet and add scallions, garlic, and sage
5. Sauté for 3 to 4 minutes until they show an opaque texture
6. Stir in lemon juice and parsley
7. Remove heat and serve hot!

Nutrition: Calories: 151, Fat: 4 g, Carbs: 10 g, Protein: 17 g

180. Walnut Encrusted Salmon

Preparation Time: 10 minutes

Cooking Time: 14 minutes

Servings: 34

Ingredients:

- ½ cup walnuts
- 2 tbsp stevia
- ½ tbsp Dijon mustard
- ¼ tsp dill
- 2 salmon fillets (3 oz each)
- 1 tbsp olive oil
- Sunflower seeds and pepper to taste

Directions:

1. Preheat your oven to 350°F
2. Add walnuts, mustard, and stevia to a food processor and process until your desired consistency is achieved
3. Take a frying pan and place it over medium heat
4. Add oil and let it heat up
5. Add salmon and sear for 3 minutes
6. Add walnut mix and coat well
7. Transfer coated salmon to the baking sheet, bake in the oven for 8 minutes
8. Serve and enjoy!

Nutrition: Calories: 373, Fat: 43 g, Carbs: 4 g, Protein: 20 g

181.   Broccoli and Tilapia

Preparation Time: 4 minutes

Cooking Time: 14 minutes

Servings: 2

Ingredients:

- 6 oz tilapia, frozen
- 1 tbsp almond butter
- 1 tbsp garlic, minced
- 1 tsp lemon pepper seasoning
- 1 cup broccoli florets, fresh

Directions:

1. Preheat your oven to 350°F.
2. Add fish in aluminum foil packets.
3. Arrange broccoli around fish.
4. Sprinkle lemon pepper on top.
5. Close the packets and seal them.
6. Bake for 14 minutes.
7. Take a bowl and add garlic and almond butter, mix well and keep the mixture on the side.
8. Remove the packets from the oven and transfer them to a platter.
9. Place almond butter on top of the fish and broccoli, serve and enjoy!

Nutrition: Calories: 362, Fat: 25 g, Net Carbs: 2 g, Protein: 29 g

182.   Especial Glazed Salmon

Preparation Time: 45 minutes

Cooking Time: 15 minutes

Servings: 4

Ingredients:

- 4 pieces salmon fillets, 5 oz each
- 4 tbsp coconut aminos
- 4 tsp olive oil
- 2 tsp ginger, minced
- 4 tsp garlic, minced
- 2 tbsp sugar-free ketchup
- 4 tbsp dry white wine
- 2 tbsp red boat fish sauce, low sodium

Directions:

1. Take a bowl and mix in coconut aminos, garlic, ginger, fish sauce, and mix

2. Add salmon and let it marinate for 15 to 20 minutes
3. Take a skillet/pan and place it over medium heat
4. Add oil and let it heat up
5. Add salmon fillets and cook on high for 3 to 4 minutes per side
6. Remove dish once crispy
7. Add sauce and wine
8. Simmer for 5 minutes on low heat
9. Return salmon to the glaze and flip until both sides are glazed
10. Serve and enjoy!

Nutrition: Calories: 372, Fat: 24 g, Carbs: 3 g, Protein: 35 g

183.   Generous Stuffed Salmon Avocado

Preparation Time: 10 minutes

Cooking Time: 0 minutes

Servings: 2

Ingredients:

- 1 ripe organic avocado
- 2 oz wild-caught smoked salmon
- 1 oz cashew cheese
- 2 tbsp extra virgin olive oil
- Sunflower seeds as needed

Directions:

1. Cut avocado in half and deseed
2. Add rest of the ingredients to a food processor and process until coarsely chopped
3. Place mixture into avocado
4. Serve and enjoy!

Nutrition: Calories: 525, Fat: 47 g, Carbs: 4 g, Protein: 19 g

184.   Cajun Jambalaya Soup

Preparation Time: 15 minutes

Cooking Time: 40 minutes

Servings: 6

Ingredients:

- 1 lb large shrimp, raw and deveined
- 4 oz chicken, diced

- ¼ cup Frank's red-hot sauce
- 2 cups okra
- 3 tbsp Cajun seasoning
- 2 bay leaves
- ½ head cauliflower
- 1 large can organic, diced
- 1 large onion, chopped
- 2 garlic cloves, diced
- 5 cups chicken stock
- 4 pepper

Directions:

1. Take a heavy-bottomed pot and add all ingredients except cauliflower
2. Place it over on high heat
3. Mix them well and bring them to boil
4. Once boiled lower the heat to simmer
5. Simmer for 30 minutes
6. Rice the cauliflower in your blender
7. Stir into the pot and simmer for another 5 minutes
8. Serve and enjoy!

Nutrition: Calories: 143, Fat: 3 g, Carbs: 14 g, Protein: 17 g

185. Anti-Inflammatory Turmeric Gummies

Preparation Time: 4 hours

Cooking Time: 10 minutes

Servings: 6

Ingredients:

- 1 tsp turmeric, grounded
- 8 tbsp gelatin powder, unflavored
- 6 tbsp maple syrup
- 3½ cups water

Directions:

1. Take a pot and combine maple syrup, turmeric, and water
2. Bring it to boil for 5 minutes
3. Remove from the heat and sprinkle with gelatin powder
4. Mix to hydrate the gelatin
5. Then turn on the heat again and bring to a boil till the gelatin dissolve properly

6. Take a dish and pour the mixture
7. Let it chill for 4 hours in your refrigerator
8. Once ready, slice and serve
9. Enjoy!

Nutrition: Calories: 68, Fat: 0.03 g, Carbs: 17 g, Protein: 0.2 g

186. Spicy Tuna Rolls

Preparation Time: 10 minutes

Cooking Time: 0 minute

Servings: 6

Ingredients:

- 1 can yellowfin tuna, wild-caught
- 1 medium cucumber
- 2 slices avocado, diced
- ⅛ tsp salt
- ⅛ tsp pepper

Directions:

1. Take a cucumber and use a mandolin to thinly slice it lengthwise
2. Take a mixing bowl and add avocado and tuna
3. Season with salt and pepper to taste
4. Spoon the tuna and avocado mixture
5. Spread it consistently on cucumber slices
6. Roll the cucumber slices
7. Use a toothpick to secure the ends
8. Serve chilled and enjoy!

Nutrition: Calories: 135, Fat: 10g, Carbs: 6g, Protein: 7g

187. Ginger Date Bars

Preparation Time: 10 minutes

Cooking Time: 20 minutes

Servings: 8

Ingredients:

- ¾ cup dates pitted
- 1½ cups almond, soaked in overnight water
- ¼ cup almond milk
- 1 tsp ginger, grounded

Directions:

1. Preheat your oven to 350°F

2. Place the almond in a food processor

3. Pulse it until you get a thick dough form

4. Press the dough in a baking dish lined with parchment paper

5. Set it aside

6. Make the date mix by combining the rest of the ingredients in your food processor

7. Pour the date mixture onto the almond crust

8. Bake for 20 minutes

9. Allow it to cool before you slice them

10. Serve and enjoy!

Nutrition: Calories: 45, Fat: 0.3 g, Carbs: 11 g, Protein: 0.5 g

188.   **Tasty Roasted Broccoli**

Preparation Time: 5 minutes

Cooking Time: 20 minutes

Servings: 4

Ingredients:

- 4 cups broccoli florets
- 1 tbsp olive oil
- Sunflower seeds and pepper to taste

Directions:

1. Preheat your oven to 400°F

2. Add broccoli in a zip bag alongside oil and shake until coated

3. Add seasoning and shake again

4. Spread broccoli out on the baking sheet, bake for 20 minutes

5. Let it cool and serve

6. Enjoy!

Nutrition: Calories: 62, Fat: 4 g, Carbs: 4 g, Protein: 4 g

189.   **The Almond Breaded Chicken Goodness**

Preparation Time: 15 minutes

Cooking Time: 15 minutes

Servings: 3

Ingredients:

- 2 large chicken breasts, boneless and skinless

- ⅓ cup lemon juice
- 1½ cups seasoned almond meal
- 2 tbsp coconut oil
- Lemon pepper, to taste
- Parsley for decoration

Directions:

1. Halve the chicken breasts and pound each half to a thickness of 14 inches.

2. Place a pan over medium heat, add the oil, and heat it up.

3. Allow each chicken breast slice to soak in lemon juice for 2 minutes.

4. Turn over and set aside for 2 minutes on the other side.

5. Coat both sides of the chicken in almond meal.

6. Add the coated chicken to the hot oil and cook for 4 minutes per side, making careful to liberally sprinkle with lemon pepper.

7. Repeat with a paper-lined sheet until all of the chicken is fried.

8. Enjoy! Garnish with parsley and serve!

Nutrition: Calories: 315, Fat: 22 g, Carbs: 3 g, Protein: 16 g

190.   **Vanilla Turmeric Orange Juice**

Preparation Time: 2 hours

Cooking Time: 0 minute

Servings: 2

Ingredients:

- 3 oranges, peeled and quartered
- 1 tsp vanilla extract
- 1 cup almond milk, unsweetened
- ½ tsp cinnamon
- ¼ tsp turmeric
- A pinch of pepper

Directions:

1. Add all ingredients into your blender

2. Pulse until smooth

3. Serve chilled and enjoy!

Nutrition: Calories: 188, Fat: 5g, Carbs: 33g, Protein: 5g

191. Hibiscus Ginger Gelatin

Preparation Time: 2 hours

Cooking Time: 20 minutes

Servings: 5

Ingredients:

- 3 tbsp hibiscus flower, dried
- 2 tbsp gelatin powder
- 1 tsp ginger juice
- 1½ tbsp honey
- 1 cup water

Directions:

1. Bring water to boil
2. Once boiled, remove from the heat
3. Add hibiscus flowers to boiled water
4. Allow infusing for 5 minutes
5. Remove the flowers and discard
6. Heat the liquid and add honey, ginger, and gelatin
7. Dissolve the gelatin
8. Take a baking sheet and pour the mixture
9. Place in the fridge and allow to set
10. Slice the gelatin and serve. Enjoy!

Nutrition: Calories: 27, Fat: 0.06 g, Carbs: 7 g, Protein: 0.2 g

192. Lemony Mussels

Preparation Time: 5 minutes

Cooking Time: 5 minutes

Servings: 4

Ingredients:

- 1 tbsp extra virgin olive oil
- 2 minced garlic cloves
- 2 lb scrubbed mussels
- Juice 1 lemon

Directions:

1. Put some water in a pot, add mussels, bring to a boil over medium heat, cook for 5 minutes, discard unopened mussels and transfer them to a bowl.

2. In another bowl, mix the oil with garlic and freshly squeezed lemon juice, whisk well, and add over the mussels, toss and serve.

3. Enjoy!

Nutrition: Calories: 140, Fat: 4 g, Carbs: 8 g, Protein: 8 g, Sugar: 4 g, Sodium: 600 mg

193. Tropical Fruit Parfait

Preparation Time: 10 minutes

Cooking Time: 0 minutes

Servings: 1

Ingredients:

- 1 tbsp toasted sliced almonds
- ¼ cup plain soy yogurt
- ½ cup fruit combination cut into ½-inch cubes (pineapple, mango and kiwi)

Directions:

1. Prepare fresh fruit by peeling and slicing into ½-inch cubes.

2. Place cubed fruit in a bowl and top with a dollop of soy yogurt.

3. Garnish with sliced almonds and if desired, refrigerate for an hour before.

Nutrition: Calories: 119, Fat: 21 g, Carbs: 25 g, Protein: 9 g, Sugar: 23 g, Fiber: 7 g

194. Zucchini Pasta with Avocado Sauce

Preparation Time: 10 minutes

Cooking Time: 5 minutes

Servings: 1

Ingredients:

- A squeeze lemon juice
- Salt and pepper to taste
- 1 tbsp coconut milk
- ½ ripe avocado
- 1 medium zucchini cut into noodles
- 2 tbsp olive oil

Directions:

1. Heat the oil in a skillet over medium heat and add the zucchini noodles. Sauté for 3 minutes or until the noodles have softened.

2. While the zucchini is cooking, mash the avocado together with the coconut milk, lemon juice and salt and pepper.

3. Add the sauce to the zucchini noodles and sauté. Serve warm.

Nutrition: Calories: 471, Fat: 41 g, Carbs: 23 g, Protein: 6 g, Sugar: 23 g, Fiber: 7 g

195.   Cherries and Quinoa

Preparation Time: 5 minutes

Cooking Time: 15 minutes

Servings: 1

Ingredients:

- 1 tsp honey – optional
- ¼ tsp ground cinnamon
- ½ tsp vanilla extract
- ½ cup dried unsweetened cherries
- ½ cup dry quinoa
- 1 cup water

Directions:

1. Wash quinoa in a bowl, by rubbing it vigorously between your hands. Discard water and repeat rinsing 2 more times.
2. On medium-high fire, place a medium nonstick skillet.
3. Add cinnamon, vanilla extract, cherries and quinoa.
4. Bring to a boil and stir occasionally.
5. Once boiling, slow fire to a simmer, cover skillet and cook until all water is absorbed and quinoa is tender around 15 minutes.
6. Turn off the fire and let it stand covered for 10 minutes more.
7. Transfer to a serving bowl and if using honey, pour and mix.
8. Serve and enjoy.

Nutrition: Calories: 386, Fat: 5.3 g, Carbs: 72.12 g, Protein: 13.0 g, Fiber: 7.7 g

196.   Fruit Bowl with Yogurt Topping

Preparation Time: 15 minutes

Cooking Time: 0 minutes

Servings: 6

Ingredients:

- ¼ cup golden brown sugar
- ⅔ cup minced fresh ginger
- 1 16-oz Greek yogurt
- ¼ tsp ground cinnamon
- 2 tbsp honey
- ½ cup dried cranberries
- 3 navel oranges
- 2 large tangerines
- 1 pink grapefruit, peeled

Directions:

1. Into sections, break tangerines and grapefruit.
2. Slice tangerine sections in half and grapefruit sections into thirds. Place all sliced fruits and their juices in a large bowl.
3. Peel oranges, remove the pith, slice into ¼-inch thick rounds and then cut into quarters. Transfer to the bowl of fruit along with juices.
4. In the bowl, add cinnamon, honey and ¼ cup of cranberries. Place in the ref for an hour.
5. In a medium bowl mix ginger and yogurt. Place on top of the fruit bowl, and drizzle with remaining cranberries and brown sugar.
6. Serve and enjoy.

Nutrition: Calories: 171, Fat: 1 g, Carbs: 35 g, Protein: 9 g, Sugar: 23 g, Fiber: 7 g

197.   Broiled White Sea Bass

Preparation Time: 5 minutes

Cooking Time: 10 minutes

Servings: 2

Ingredients:

- 1 tsp minced garlic
- Ground black pepper
- 1 tbsp lemon juice
- 8 oz white sea bass fillets
- ¼ tsp salt-free herbed seasoning blend

Directions:

1. Preheat the broiler and position the rack 4 inches from the heat source.
2. Lightly spray a baking pan with cooking spray. Place the fillets in the pan. Sprinkle the lemon juice, garlic, herbed seasoning and pepper over the fillets.
3. Broil until the fish is opaque throughout when tested with a tip of a knife, about 8 to 10 minutes.

4. Serve immediately.

Nutrition: Calories: 114, Fat: 2 g, Carbs: 2 g, Protein: 21 g, Sugar: 0.5 g, Sodium: 78 mg

198. Celery Root Hash Browns

Preparation Time: 10 minutes

Cooking Time: 10 minutes

Servings: 4

Ingredients:

- 4 tbsp coconut oil
- ½ tsp sea salt
- 2 to 3 medium celery roots

Directions:

1. Scrub the celery root clean and peel it using a vegetable peeler.
2. Grate the celery root in a food processor or a manual grater.
3. In a skillet, add oil and heat it over medium heat.
4. Place the grated celery root on the skillet and sprinkle with salt.
5. Let it cook for 10 minutes on each side or until the grated celery turns brown.
6. Serve warm.

Nutrition: Calories: 161, Fat: 3 g, Carbs: 35 g, Protein: 1.9 g, Sugar: 0 g, Fiber: 3 g

199. Braised Kale

Preparation Time: 10 minutes

Cooking Time: 5 minutes

Servings: 3

Ingredients:

- 2 to 3 tbsp water
- 1 tbsp coconut oil
- ½ sliced red pepper
- 2 stalk celery (sliced to ¼-inch thick
- 5 cups chopped kale

Directions:

1. Heat a pan over medium heat.
2. Add coconut oil and sauté the celery for at least 5 minutes.
3. Add the kale and red pepper.
4. Add a tbsp of water.

5. Let the vegetables wilt for a few minutes. Add a tbsp of water if the kale starts to stick to the pan.
6. Serve warm.

Nutrition: Calories: 61, Fat: 5 g, Carbs: 3 g, Protein: 1 g, Sugar: 1 g, Fiber: 1 g

200. Tender Salmon in Mustard Sauce

Preparation Time: 10 minutes

Cooking Time: 20 minutes

Servings: 2

Ingredients:

- 5 tbsp Minced dill
- ⅔ cup sour cream
- Pepper
- 2 tbsp Dijon mustard
- 1 tsp garlic powder
- 5 oz salmon fillets
- 2 to 3 tbsp Lemon juice

Directions:

1. Mix sour cream, mustard, lemon juice and dill.
2. Season the fillets with pepper and garlic powder.
3. Arrange the salmon on a baking sheet skin side down and cover with the prepared mustard sauce.
4. Bake for 20 minutes at 390°F.

Nutrition: Calories: 318, Fat: 12 g, Carbs: 8 g, Protein: 40.9 g, Sugar: 909.4 g, Sodium: 1.4 mg

201. Braised Leeks, Cauliflower and Artichoke Hearts

Preparation Time: 10 minutes

Cooking Time: 10 minutes

Servings: 4

Ingredients:

- 2 tbsp coconut oil
- 2 garlic cloves, chopped
- 1½ cups artichoke hearts
- 1½ cups chopped leeks
- 1½ cups cauliflower flowerets

Directions:

1. Heat oil in a skillet over medium-high heat.

2. Add the garlic and sauté for 1 minute. Add the vegetables and stir constantly until the vegetables are cooked.

3. Serve with roasted chicken, fish or pork.

Nutrition: Calories: 111, Fat: 1 g, Carbs: 1 3 g, Protein: 3 g, Sugar: 2 g, Fiber: 4 g

202. Scallops Stew

Preparation Time: 10 minutes

Cooking Time: 20 minutes

Servings: 4

Ingredients:

- 2 leeks, chopped
- 2 tbsp olive oil
- 1 tsp chopped jalapeno
- 2 tsp chopped garlic
- A pinch of salt and black pepper
- ¼ tsp ground cinnamon
- 1 carrot, chopped
- 1 tsp ground cumin
- 1½ cups chopped tomatoes
- 1 cup veggie stock
- 1 lb shrimp, peeled and deveined
- 1 lb sea scallops
- 2 tbsp chopped cilantro

Directions:

1. Heat up a pot with the oil over medium heat, add garlic and leeks, stir and cook for 7 minutes. Add jalapeno, salt, pepper, cayenne, carrots, cinnamon and cumin, stir and cook for 5 more minutes.

2. Add tomatoes, stock, shrimp and scallops, stir, cook for 6 more minutes then divide into bowls, sprinkle cilantro on top and serve.

3. Enjoy!

Nutrition: Calories: 251, Fat: 4 g, Fiber: 4 g, Carbs: 11 g, Protein: 17 g

203. Spicy Baked Fish

Preparation Time: 5 minutes

Cooking Time: 15 minutes

Servings: 5

Ingredients:

- 1 tbsp olive oil
- 1 tsp spice salt-free seasoning
- 1 lb salmon fillet

Directions:

1. Preheat the oven to 350°F.

2. Sprinkle the fish with olive oil and the seasoning.

3. Bake for 15 minutes uncovered.

4. Slice and serve.

Nutrition: Calories: 192, Fat: 11 g, Carbs: 14.9 g, Protein: 33.1 g, Sugar: 0.3 g, Sodium: 505.6 mg

Chapter 6
Fish and Seafood

204. Shrimp Scampi

Preparation Time: 10 minutes

Cooking Time: 15 minutes

Servings: 4

Ingredients:

- ¼ cup extra olive oil
- 1 onion, finely chopped
- 1 red bell pepper, chopped
- 1½ pound shrimp, peeled and tails removed
- 6 garlic cloves, minced
- 2 lemon juices
- 2 lemon zest
- ½ tsp sea salt
- ⅛ tsp freshly ground black pepper

Directions:

1. In a huge nonstick skillet on medium-high heat, warm the olive oil until it shimmers.
2. Add the onion and red bell pepper. Cook for about 6 minutes, occasionally stirring, until soft.
3. Add the shrimp and cook for about 5 minutes until pink.
4. Add the garlic. Cook for 30 seconds, stirring constantly.
5. Add the lemon juice and zest, salt, and pepper. Simmer for 3 minutes.

Nutrition: Calories: 345, Total Fat: 16, Total Carbs: 10 g, Sugar: 3 g, Fiber: 1 g, Protein: 40 g, Sodium: 424 mg

205. Shrimp with Spicy Spinach

Preparation Time: 10 minutes

Cooking Time: 15 minutes

Servings: 4

Ingredients:

- ¼ cup extra olive oil, divided
- 1½ pound peeled shrimp
- 1 tsp sea salt, divided
- 4 cups baby fresh spinach
- 6 garlic cloves, minced
- ½ cup freshly squeezed orange juice
- 1 tbsp sriracha sauce
- ⅛ tsp freshly ground black pepper

Directions:

1. In a huge nonstick skillet on medium-high heat, heat 2 tbsp of the olive oil until it shimmers.
2. Add the shrimp and ½ tsp salt. Cook for at least 4 minutes, occasionally stirring, until the shrimp are pink. Transfer the shrimp to a plate, tent with aluminum foil to keep warm, and set aside.
3. Put back the skillet to the heat and heat the remaining 2 tbsp of olive oil until it shimmers.
4. Add the spinach. Cook for 3 minutes, stirring.
5. Add the garlic. Cook for 30 seconds, stirring constantly.
6. In a small bowl, put and mix together the orange juice, Sriracha, the remaining ½ tsp of salt, and pepper. Add this to the spinach and cook for 3 minutes. Serve the shrimp with spinach on the side.

Nutrition: Calories: 317, Total Fat: 16, Total Carbs: 7 g, Sugar: 3 g, Fiber: 1 g, Protein: 37 g, Sodium: 911 mg

206. Shrimp with Cinnamon Sauce

Preparation Time: 10 minutes

Cooking Time: 10 minutes

Servings: 4

Ingredients:

- 2 tbsp extra virgin olive oil
- 1½ pound peeled shrimp
- 2 tbsp Dijon mustard
- 1 cup no salt added chicken broth
- 1 tsp ground cinnamon
- 1 tsp onion powder
- ½ tsp sea salt
- ¼ tsp freshly ground black pepper

Directions:

1. In a huge nonstick skillet at medium-high heat, heat the olive oil until it shimmers.

2. Add the shrimp. Cook for at least 4 minutes, occasionally stirring, until the shrimp is opaque.

3. Whisk the mustard, chicken broth, cinnamon, onion powder, salt, and pepper in a small bowl. Pour this into the skillet and continue to cook for 3 minutes, stirring occasionally.

Nutrition: Calories: 270, Total Fat: 11 g, Total Carbs: 4 g, Sugar: 1 g, Fiber: 1 g, Protein: 39 g, Sodium: 664 mg

207. Pan-Seared Scallops with Lemon-Ginger Vinaigrette

Preparation Time: 10 minutes

Cooking Time: 7 minutes

Servings: 4

Ingredients:

- 2 tbsp extra virgin olive oil
- 1½ pound sea scallop
- ½ tsp sea salt
- ⅛ tsp freshly ground black pepper
- ¼ cup lemon ginger vinaigrette

Directions:

1. In a huge nonstick skillet at medium-high heat, heat the olive oil until it shimmers.

2. Season the scallops with pepper and salt and add them to the skillet. Cook for at least 3 minutes per side until just opaque.

3. Serve with the vinaigrette spooned over the top.

Nutrition: Calories: 280, Total Fat: 16 g, Total Carbs: 5 g, Sugar: 1 g, Fiber: 0 g, Protein: 29 g, Sodium: 508 mg

208. Manhattan-Style Salmon Chowder

Preparation Time: 10 minutes

Cooking Time: 15 minutes

Servings: 4

Ingredients:

- ¼ cup extra virgin olive oil
- 1 red bell pepper, chopped
- 1 pound skinless salmon. Pin bones removed, chopped into ½ inch
- 2 (28 oz) cans crushed tomatoes, 1 drained, 1 undrained
- 6 cups no salt added chicken broth
- 2 cups diced (½ inch) sweet potato
- 1 tsp onion powder
- ½ tsp sea salt
- ¼ tsp freshly ground black pepper

Directions:

1. Add the red bell pepper and salmon. Cook for at least 5 minutes, occasionally stirring, until the fish is opaque and the bell pepper is soft.

2. Stir in the tomatoes, chicken broth, sweet potatoes, onion powder, salt, and pepper. Place to a simmer, then lower the heat to medium. Cook for at least 10 minutes, occasionally stirring, until the sweet potatoes are soft.

Nutrition: Calories: 570, Total Fat: 42 g, Total Carbs: 55 g, Sugar: 24g, Fiber: 16g, Protein: 41g, Sodium: 1,249mg

209. Roasted Salmon and Asparagus

Preparation Time: 5 minutes

Cooking Time: 15 minutes

Servings: 4

Ingredients:

- 1 lb asparagus spears, trimmed
- 2 tbsp extra virgin olive oil
- 1 tsp sea salt, divided
- 1½ lb salmon, cut into 4 fillets
- ⅛ tsp freshly ground cracked black pepper
- 1 lemon, zest, and slice

Directions:

1. Preheat the oven to 425°F.

2. Stir the asparagus with olive oil, then put ½ tsp of the salt. Place in a single layer at the bottom of a roasting pan.

3. Season the salmon with the pepper and the remaining ½ tsp of salt. Put the skin-side down on top of the asparagus.

4. Sprinkle the salmon and asparagus with the lemon zest and place the lemon slices over the fish.

5. Roast in the oven for at least 12 to 15 minutes until the flesh is opaque.

Nutrition: Calories: 308, Total Fat: 17 g, Total Carbs: 5 g, Sugar: 2 g, Fiber: 2 g, Protein: 36 g, Sodium: 545 mg

210. Citrus Salmon on a Bed of Greens

Preparation Time: 10 minutes

Cooking Time: 19 minutes

Servings: 4

Ingredients:

- ¼ cup extra virgin olive oil, divided
- 1½ lb salmon
- 1 tsp sea salt, divided
- ½ tsp freshly ground black pepper, divided
- 1 lemon zest
- 6 cups swiss chard, stemmed and chopped
- 3 garlic cloves, chopped
- 2 lemon Juice

Directions:

1. In a huge nonstick skillet at medium-high heat, heat 2 tbsp of the olive oil until it shimmers.

2. Season the salmon with ½ tsp of salt, ¼ tsp of pepper, and lemon zest. Put the salmon in the skillet, skin-side up, and cook for about 7 minutes until the flesh is opaque. Flip the salmon and cook for at least 3 to 4 minutes to crisp the skin. Set aside on a plate, and cover using aluminum foil.

3. Put back the skillet to the heat, add the remaining 2 tbsp of olive oil, and heat it until it shimmers.

4. Add the Swiss chard. Cook for about 7 minutes, occasionally stirring, until soft.

5. Add the garlic. Cook for 30 seconds, stirring constantly.

6. Sprinkle in the lemon juice, the remaining ½ tsp of salt, and the remaining ¼ tsp of pepper. Cook for 2 minutes.

7. Serve the salmon on the Swiss chard.

Nutrition: Calories: 363, Total Fat: 25 g, Total Carbs: 3 g, Sugar: 1 g, Fiber: 1 g, Protein: 34 g, Sodium: 662 mg

211. Orange and Maple-Glazed Salmon

Preparation Time: 15 minutes

Cooking Time: 15 minutes

Servings: 4

Ingredients:

- 2 orange juice
- 1 orange zest
- ¼ cup pure maple syrup
- 2 tbsp low sodium soy sauce
- 1 tsp garlic powder
- 4 4 to 6 oz salmon fillet, pin bones removed

Directions:

1. Preheat the oven to 400°F.

2. Whisk the orange juice and zest, maple syrup, soy sauce, and garlic powder in a small, shallow dish.

3. Put the salmon pieces, flesh-side down, into the dish. Let it marinate for 10 minutes.

4. Transfer the salmon, skin-side up, to a rimmed baking sheet and bake for about 15 minutes until the flesh is opaque.

Nutrition: Calories: 297, Total Fat: 11 g, Total Carbs: 17 g, Sugar: 15 g, Fiber: 1 g, Protein: 34, Sodium: 528 mg

212. Salmon Ceviche

Preparation Time: 10 minutes + 20 resting time

Cooking Time: 0 minutes

Servings: 4

Ingredients:

- 1 lb salmon, skinless & boneless, cut into bite-size pieces
- ½ cup freshly squeezed lime juice
- 2 tomatoes, diced
- ¼ cup fresh cilantro leaves, chopped
- 1 jalapeno pepper, seeded and diced
- 2 tbsp extra virgin olive oil
- ½ tsp sea salt

Directions:

1. In a medium bowl, put and stir together the salmon and lime juice. Let it marinate for 20 minutes.

2. Stir in the tomatoes, cilantro, jalapeño, olive oil, and salt.

Nutrition: Calories: 222, Total Fat: 14 g, Total Carbs: 3 g, Sugar: 2 g, Fiber: 1 g, Protein: 23 g, Sodium: 288 mg

213. Cod with Ginger

Preparation Time: 10 minutes

Cooking Time: 15 minutes

Servings: 4

Ingredients:

- 2 tbsp extra virgin olive oil
- 4 (6 oz) cod fillets
- 1 tbsp grated fresh ginger
- 1 tsp sea salt, divided
- ¼ tsp freshly ground black pepper
- 5 garlic cloves, minced
- ¼ cup fresh cilantro leaves, chopped

Directions:

1. In a huge nonstick skillet at medium-high heat, heat the olive oil until it shimmers.

2. Season the cod with ginger, ½ tsp of salt, and pepper. Put it in the hot oil, then cook for at least 4 minutes per side until the fish is opaque. Take off the cod from the pan and set it aside on a platter tented with aluminum foil.

3. Put back the skillet to the heat and add the garlic. Cook for 30 seconds, stirring constantly.

4. Cook for 5 minutes, stirring occasionally.

5. Stir in the cilantro over the cod.

Nutrition: Calories: 41, Total Fat: 2 g, Total Carbs: 33 g, Sugar: 1 g, Fiber: 8 g, Protein: 50 g, Sodium: 605 mg

214. Rosemary-Lemon Cod

Preparation Time: 5 minutes

Cooking Time: 10 minutes

Servings: 4

Ingredients:

- 2 tbsp extra virgin olive oil
- 1½ lb cod, skin and bone removed, cut into 4 fillets

- 1 tbsp fresh rosemary leaves, chopped
- ½ tsp ground black pepper, or more to taste
- ½ tsp sea Salt
- 1 lemon juice

Directions:

1. In a huge nonstick skillet at medium-high heat, heat the olive oil until it shimmers.

2. Season the cod with rosemary, pepper, and salt. Put the fish in the skillet and cook for 3 to 5 minutes per side until opaque.

3. Pour the lemon juice over the cod fillets and cook for 1 minute.

Nutrition: Calories: 24, Total Fat: 9 g, Total Carbs: 1 g, Sugar: 1 g, Fiber: 1 g, Protein: 39 g, Sodium: 370 mg

215. Halibut Curry

Preparation Time: 10 minutes

Cooking Time: 10 minutes

Servings: 4

Ingredients:

- 2 tbsp extra virgin olive oil
- 2 tsp ground turmeric
- 2 tsp curry powder
- 1½ lb halibut, skin, and bones removed, cut into 1-inch pieces
- 4 cups no-salt-added chicken broth
- 1 (14 oz) can lite coconut milk
- ½ tsp sea salt
- ¼ tsp freshly ground black pepper

Directions:

1. In a huge nonstick skillet at medium-high, heat the olive oil until it shimmers.

2. Add the turmeric and curry powder. Cook for 2 minutes, constantly stirring, to bloom the spices.

3. Add the halibut, chicken broth, coconut milk, salt, and pepper. Place to a simmer, then lower the heat to medium. Simmer for 6 to 7 minutes, occasionally stirring, until the fish is opaque.

Nutrition: Calories: 429, Total Fat: 47 g, Total Carbs: 5 g, Sugar: 1 g, Fiber: 1 g, Protein: 27 g, Sodium: 507 mg

216. Marinated Fish Steaks

Preparation Time: 10 minutes

Cooking Time: 15 minutes

Servings: 4

Ingredients:

- 4 lime wedges
- 2 tbsp lime juice
- 2 minced garlic cloves
- 2 tsp olive oil
- 1 tbsp snipped fresh oregano
- 1 lb fresh swordfish
- 1 tsp lemon-pepper seasoning

Directions:

1. Rinse fish steaks; pat dry using paper towels. Cut into 4 serving-size pieces, if necessary.

2. Put and combine lime juice, oregano, oil, lemon-pepper seasoning, and garlic in a shallow dish. Add fish; turn to coat with marinade.

3. Cover and marinate in the refrigerator for 30 minutes to 1½ hours, turning steaks occasionally. Drain fish, reserving marinade.

4. Put the fish on the greased, unheated rack of a broiler pan.

5. Broil 4 inches from the heat for at least 8 to 12 minutes or until fish starts to flake when tested with a fork, turning once and brushing with reserved marinade halfway through cooking.

6. Take off any remaining marinade.

7. Before serving, squeeze the lime juice on each steak.

Nutrition: Calories: 240, Fat: 6 g, Carbs: 19 g, Protein: 12 g, Sugar: 3.27 g, Sodium: 325 mg

217. Baked Tomato Hake

Preparation Time: 10 minutes

Cooking Time: 20 to 25 minutes

Servings: 4

Ingredients:

- ½ cup tomato sauce
- 1 tbsp olive oil
- Parsley
- 2 sliced tomatoes
- ½ cup grated cheese
- 4 lb deboned and sliced hake fish
- Salt.

Directions:

1. Preheat the oven to 400°F.

2. Season the fish with salt.

3. In a skillet or saucepan, stir-fry the fish in the olive oil until half-done.

4. Take 4 foil papers to cover the fish.

5. Shape the foil to resemble containers; add the tomato sauce into each foil container.

6. Add the fish, tomato slices, and top with grated cheese.

7. Bake until you get a golden crust, for approximately 20 to 25 minutes.

8. Open the packs and top with parsley.

Nutrition: Calories: 265, Fat: 15 g, Carbs: 18 g, Protein: 22 g, Sugar: 0.5 g, Sodium: 94.6 mg

218. Cheesy Tuna Pasta

Preparation Time: 10 minutes

Cooking Time: 20 minutes

Servings: 2 to 4

Ingredients:

- 2 cups arugula
- ¼ cup chopped green onions
- 1 tbsp red vinegar
- 5 oz drained canned tuna
- ¼ tsp black pepper
- 2 oz cooked whole-wheat pasta
- 1 tbsp olive oil
- 1 tbsp grated low-fat parmesan

Directions:

1. Cook the pasta in unsalted water until ready. Drain and set aside.

2. Thoroughly mix the tuna, green onions, vinegar, oil, arugula, pasta, and black pepper in a large-sized bowl.

3. Toss well and top with the cheese.

4. Serve and enjoy.

Nutrition: Calories: 566.3, Fat: 42.4 g, Carbs: 18.6 g, Protein: 29.8 g, Sugar: 0.4 g, Sodium: 688.6 mg

219. Salmon and Roasted Peppers

Preparation Time: 5 minutes

Cooking Time: 25 minutes

Servings: 4

Ingredients:

- 1 cup red peppers, cut into strips
- 4 salmon fillets, boneless
- ¼ cup chicken stock
- 2 tbsp olive oil
- 1 yellow onion, chopped
- 1 tbsp cilantro, chopped
- Pinch of sea salt
- Pinch black pepper

Directions:

1. Warm a pan with the oil on medium-high heat; add the onion and sauté for 5 minutes.
2. Put the fish and cook for at least 5 minutes on each side.
3. Add the rest of the ingredients, introduce the pan to the oven, and cook at 390°F for 10 minutes.
4. Divide the mix between plates and serve.

Nutrition: Calories: 265, Fat: 7g, Carbs: 1g, Protein: 16g

220. Shrimp and Beets

Preparation Time: 10 minutes

Cooking Time: 10 minutes

Servings: 4

Ingredients:

- 1 lb shrimp, peeled and deveined
- 2 tbsp avocado oil
- 2 spring onions, chopped
- 2 garlic cloves, minced
- 1 beet, peeled and cubed
- 1 tbsp lemon juice
- Pinch of sea salt
- Pinch of black pepper
- 1 tsp coconut aminos

Directions:

1. Warm a pan with the oil on medium-high heat, add the spring onions and the garlic and sauté for 2 minutes.

2. Add the shrimp and the other ingredients, toss, cook the mix for 8 minutes, divide into bowls and serve.

Nutrition: Calories: 281, Fat: 6 g, Fiber: 7, Carbs: 11 g, Protein: 8 g

221. Shrimp and Corn

Preparation Time: 5 minutes

Cooking Time: 10 minutes

Servings: 4

Ingredients:

- 1 lb shrimp, peeled and deveined
- 2 garlic cloves, minced
- 1 cup corn
- ½ cup veggie stock
- 1 bunch parsley, chopped
- Juice 1 lime
- 2 tbsp olive oil
- Pinch of sea salt
- Pinch of black pepper

Directions:

1. Warm a pan with the oil on medium-high heat, then put the garlic and the corn and sauté for 2 minutes.
2. Add the shrimp and the other ingredients, toss, cook everything for 8 minutes more, divide between plates and serve.

Nutrition: Calories: 343, Protein: 29.12 g, Fat: 10.97 g, Carbs: 34.25 g

222. Chili Shrimp and Pineapple

Preparation Time: 10 minutes

Cooking Time: 10 minutes

Servings: 4

Ingredients:

- 1 lb shrimp, peeled and deveined
- 2 tbsp chili paste
- Pinch of sea salt
- Pinch of black pepper
- 1 tbsp olive oil
- 1 cup pineapple, peeled and cubed
- ½ tsp ginger, grated
- 2 tsp almonds, chopped
- 2 tbsp cilantro, chopped

Directions:

1. Warm a pan with the oil on medium-high heat, add the ginger and the chili paste, stir and cook for 2 minutes.

2. Add the shrimp and the other ingredients, toss, cook the mix for 8 minutes more, divide into bowls, and serve.

Nutrition: Calories: 261, Fat: 4 g, Fiber: 7 g, Carbs: 15 g, Protein: 8 g

223. Balsamic Scallops

Preparation Time: 5 minutes

Cooking Time: 10 minutes

Servings: 4

Ingredients:

- 1 lb sea scallops
- 4 scallions, chopped
- 2 tbsp olive oil
- 1 tbsp balsamic vinegar
- 1 tbsp cilantro, chopped
- A pinch of salt and black pepper

Directions:

1. Warm a pan with the oil on medium-high heat, add the scallops, the scallions, and the other ingredients, toss, cook for 10 minutes, divide into bowls and serve.

Nutrition: Calories: 300, Fat: 4 g, Fiber: 4 g, Carbs: 14 g, Protein: 17 g

224. Whitefish Curry

Preparation Time: 10 minutes

Cooking Time: 15 minutes

Servings: 6

Ingredients:

- 1 chopped onion
- 1 lb firm white fish fillets
- ¼ cup chopped fresh cilantro
- 1 cup vegetable broth
- 2 minced garlic cloves
- 1 tbsp minced fresh ginger
- 1 tsp salt
- ¼ tsp ground black pepper
- Lemon wedges
- 1 bruised lemongrass
- 2 cups cubed butternut squash

- 2 tsp curry powder
- 2 tbsp coconut oil
- 2 cups chopped broccoli
- 1 oz coconut milk
- 1 thinly sliced scallion

Directions:

1. In a pot, add coconut oil and melt.

2. Add onion, curry powder, ginger, garlic, and seasonings, then sauté for 5 minutes

3. Add broccoli, lemongrass and butternut squash and sauté for 2 more minutes

4. Stir in broth and coconut milk and bring to a boil. Lower the heat to simmer and add the fish.

5. Cover the pot, then simmer for 5 minutes, then discard the lemongrass.

6. Spoon the curry into a medium serving bowl.

7. Add scallion and cilantro to garnish before serving with lemon wedges.

8. Enjoy.

Nutrition: Calories: 218, Protein: 18.1 g, Fat: 8.57 g, Carbs: 18.2 g

225. Swordfish with Pineapple and Cilantro

Preparation Time: 10 minutes

Cooking Time: 20 minutes

Servings: 4

Ingredients:

- 1 cup fresh pineapple chunks
- 1 tbsp coconut oil
- 2 lb sliced swordfish
- 2 tbsp chopped fresh parsley
- ¼ tsp ground black pepper.
- 2 minced garlic cloves
- ¼ cup chopped fresh cilantro
- 1 tbsp coconut aminos
- 1 tsp Salt.

Directions:

1. Preheat the oven to 400°F.

2. Grease a baking tray with coconut oil

3. Add cilantro, swordfish, coconut aminos, pepper, salt, garlic, parsley, and pineapple to the dish, then mix well.

4. Put the dish in an already preheated oven and bake for 20 minutes.

5. Serve and enjoy.

Nutrition: Calories: 444, Protein: 47.53 g, Fat: 20.32 g, Carbs: 16.44 g

226. Sesame-Tuna Skewers

Preparation Time: 10 minutes

Cooking Time: 15 minutes

Servings: 6

Ingredients:

- 6 oz cubed thick tuna steaks
- Cooking spray
- ¼ tsp ground black pepper
- ¾ cup sesame seeds
- 1 tsp salt
- ½ tsp ground ginger
- 2 tbsp toasted sesame oil

Directions:

1. Preheat the oven to about 400°F.

2. Coat a rimmed baking tray with cooking spray.

3. Soak 12 wooden skewers in water

4. In a small mixing bowl, combine pepper, ground ginger, salt, and sesame seeds.

5. In another bowl, toss the tuna with sesame oil.

6. Press the oiled cubes into a sesame seed mixture and put the cubes on each skewer.

7. Put the skewers on a readily prepared baking tray and put the tray into the preheated oven.

8. Bake for 12 minutes and turn once.

9. Serve and enjoy.

Nutrition: Calories: 196, Protein: 14.47 g, Fat: 15.01 g, Carbs: 2.48 g

227. Trout with Chard

Preparation Time: 10 minutes

Cooking Time: 15 minutes

Servings: 4

Ingredients:

- ½ cup vegetable broth
- 2 bunches sliced chard
- 4 boneless trout fillets
- Salt
- 1 tbsp extra-virgin olive oil
- 2 minced garlic cloves
- ¼ cup golden raisins
- Ground black pepper
- 1 chopped onion
- 1 tbsp apple cider vinegar

Directions:

1. Preheat the oven to about 375°F.

2. Add seasonings to the trout

3. Add olive oil to a pan, then heat.

4. Add garlic and onion, then sauté for 3 minutes.

5. Add chard to sauté for 2 more minutes.

6. Add broth, raisins, and cedar vinegar to the pan.

7. Layer a topping of trout fillets

8. Cover the pan and put it in the preheated oven for 10 minutes.

9. Serve and enjoy.

Nutrition: Calories: 284, Protein: 2.07 g, Fat: 30.32 g, Carbs: 3.49 g

228. Sole with Vegetables

Preparation Time: 10 minutes

Cooking Time: 15 minutes

Servings: 4

Ingredients:

- 4 tsp divided extra virgin olive oil
- 1 thinly sliced and divided carrot
- Salt
- Lemon wedges
- ½ cup divided vegetable broth
- 5 oz sole fillets
- 2 sliced and thinly divided shallots
- Ground black pepper
- 2 tbsp divided snipped fresh chives
- 1 thinly sliced and divided zucchini

Directions:

1. Preheat the oven to about 425°F.

2. Separate the aluminum foil into medium-sized pieces

3. Put a fillet on one half of the aluminum foil piece and add seasonings

4. Add shallots, zucchini, and ¼ each of the carrots on top of the fillet. Sprinkle with 1½ tsp of chives

5. Drizzle 2 tbsp of broth and a tbsp of olive oil over the fish and vegetables

6. Seal to make a packet and put the packet on a large baking tray.

7. Repeat for the rest of the ingredients and make more packets

8. Put the sheet in a preheated oven and bake the packets for 15 minutes

9. Peel back the foil and put the contents with the liquid onto a serving plate.

10. Garnish with lemon wedges before serving.

11. Enjoy.

Nutrition: Calories: 130, Protein: 9.94 g, Fat: 7.96 g, Carbs: 4.92 g

229. Poached Halibut and Mushrooms

Preparation Time: 5 minutes

Cooking Time: 30 minutes

Servings: 8

Ingredients:

- ⅛ tsp sesame oil
- 2 lb halibut, cut into bite-sized pieces
- 1 tsp fresh lemon juice
- ½ tsp soy sauce
- 4 cups mushrooms, sliced ¼ cup water
- Salt and pepper to taste ¾ cup green onions

Directions:

1. Place a heavy-bottomed pot on the medium-high fire.

2. Add all ingredients and mix well.

3. Cover and bring to a boil. Once boiling, lower fire to a simmer. Cook for 25 minutes.

4. Adjust seasoning to taste.

5. Serve and enjoy.

Nutrition: Calories: 217, Fat: 15.8 g, Carbs: 1.1 g, Protein: 16.5 g, Fiber: 0.4 g

230. Halibut Stir Fry

Preparation Time: 5 minutes

Cooking Time: 20 minutes

Servings: 6

Ingredients:

- 2 lb halibut fillets
- 2 tbsp olive oil
- ½ cup fresh parsley
- 1 onion, sliced 2 celery stalks, chopped
- 2 tbsp capers
- 4 garlic cloves minced
- Salt and pepper to taste

Directions:

1. Place a heavy-bottomed pot on high fire and heat for 2 minutes. Add oil and heat for 2 more minutes.

2. Stir in garlic and onions. Sauté for 5 minutes. Add remaining ingredients except for the parsley and stir fry for 10 minutes or until fish is cooked.

3. Adjust seasoning to taste and serve with a sprinkle of parsley.

Nutrition: Calories: 331, Fat: 26 g, Carbs: 2 g, Protein: 22 g, Fiber: 0.5 g

231. Steamed Garlic-Dill Halibut

Preparation Time: 5 minutes

Cooking Time: 25 minutes

Servings: 4

Ingredients:

- 1 lb halibut fillet
- 1 lemon, freshly squeezed
- Salt and pepper to taste
- 1 tsp garlic powder
- 1 tbsp dill weed, chopped

Directions:

1. Place a large pot on medium fire and fill up to 1.5-inches of water. Place a trivet inside the pot.

2. In a baking dish that fits inside your large pot, add all ingredients and mix well. Cover the dish with foil. Place the dish on top of the trivet inside the pot.

3. Cover pot and steam fish for 15 minutes.

4. Let the fish rest for at least 10 minutes before removing it from the pot.

5. Serve and enjoy.

Nutrition: Calories: 270, Fat: 6.5 g, Carbs: 3.9 g, Protein: 47.8 g, Fiber: 2.1 g

232. Honey Crusted Salmon with Pecans

Preparation Time: 20 minutes

Cooking Time: 20 minutes

Servings: 6

Ingredients:

- 3 tbsp olive oil
- 3 tbsp mustard
- 5 tsp raw honey
- ½ cup chopped pecans
- 6 salmon fillets, boneless
- 3 tsp chopped parsley
- Salt and black pepper to the taste

Directions:

1. In a bowl, whisk the mustard with honey and oil. In another bowl, mix the pecans with parsley and stir.

2. Season salmon fillets with salt and pepper, place them on a baking sheet, brush with mustard mixture, top with the pecans mix, and place them in the oven at 400°F to bake for 20 minutes. Divide into plates and serve with a side salad.

3. Enjoy!

Nutrition: Calories: 200, Fat: 10 g, Fiber: 5 g, Carbs: 12 g, Protein: 16 g

Chapter 7

Meat

233. Pork with Balsamic Onion Sauce

Preparation Time: 10 minutes

Cooking Time: 35 minutes

Servings: 4

Ingredients:

- 1 yellow onion, chopped
- 4 scallions, chopped
- 2 tbsp avocado oil
- 1 tbsp rosemary, chopped
- 1 tbsp lemon zest, grated
- 2 lb pork roast, sliced
- 2 tbsp balsamic vinegar
- ½ cup vegetable stock
- Pinch of sea salt
- Pinch black pepper

Directions:

1. Warm a pan with the oil on medium heat, add the onion, and the scallions and sauté for 5 minutes.

2. Add the rest of the ingredients except the meat, stir, and simmer for 5 minutes. Add the meat, toss gently, cook over medium heat for 25 minutes, divide between plates and serve.

Nutrition: Calories: 217, Protein: 14 g, Carbs: 10 g, Fat: 11 g

234. Pork with Olives

Preparation Time: 10 minutes

Cooking Time: 40 minutes

Servings: 4

Ingredients:

- 1 yellow onion, chopped
- 4 pork chops
- 2 tbsp olive oil
- 1 tbsp sweet paprika
- 2 tbsp balsamic vinegar
- ¼ cup kalamata olives, pitted and chopped
- 1 tbsp cilantro, chopped
- Pinch of sea salt
- Pinch black pepper

Directions:

1. Warm a pan with the oil on medium heat; add the onion and sauté for 5 minutes. Add the meat and brown for a further 5 minutes.

2. Put the rest of the ingredients, toss, cook over medium heat for 30 minutes, divide between plates and serve.

Nutrition: Calories: 280, Protein: 21 g, Carbs: 10 g, Fat: 11 g

235. Pork with Tomato Salsa

Preparation Time: 10 minutes

Cooking Time: 15 minutes

Servings: 4

Ingredients:

- 4 pork chops
- 1 tbsp olive oil
- 4 scallions, chopped
- 1 tsp cumin, ground
- ½ tbsp hot paprika
- 1 tsp garlic powder
- Pinch of sea salt
- Pinch of black pepper
- 1 small red onion, chopped
- 2 tomatoes, cubed
- 2 tbsp lime juice
- 1 jalapeno, chopped
- ¼ cup cilantro, chopped
- 1 tbsp lime juice

Directions:

1. Warm a pan with the oil on medium heat, add the scallions and sauté for 5 minutes.

2. Add the meat, cumin paprika, garlic powder, salt, and pepper, toss, cook for 5 minutes on each side, and divide between plates.

3. In a bowl, combine the tomatoes with the remaining ingredients, toss, divide next to the pork chops and serve.

Nutrition: Calories: 220, Protein: 33g, Carbs: 4g, Fat: 7g

236. Beef with Carrot & Broccoli

Preparation Time: 15 minutes

Cooking Time: 14 minutes

Servings: 4

Ingredients:

- 2 tbsp coconut oil, divided
- 2 medium garlic cloves, minced
- 1 lb beef sirloin steak, sliced into thin strips
- Salt, to taste
- ¼ cup chicken broth
- 2 tsp fresh ginger, grated
- 1 tbsp ground flax seeds
- ½ tsp Red pepper flakes, crushed
- ¼ tsp freshly ground black pepper
- 1 large carrot, peeled and sliced thinly
- 2 cups broccoli florets
- 1 medium scallion, sliced thinly

Directions:

1. In a skillet, warm 1 tbsp of oil on medium-high heat.

2. Put garlic and sauté for approximately 1 minute.

3. Add beef and salt and cook for at least 4 to 5 minutes or till browned.

4. Using a slotted spoon, transfer the beef to a bowl.

5. Take off the liquid from the skillet.

6. Put together broth, ginger, flax seeds, red pepper flakes, and black pepper, then mix in a bowl.

7. In the same skillet, warm the remaining oil on medium heat.

8. Put the carrot, broccoli, and ginger mixture, then cook for at least 3 to 4 minutes or till the desired doneness.

9. Mix in beef and scallion, then cook for around 3 to 4 minutes.

Nutrition: Calories: 41, Fat: 13 g, Carbs: 27 g, Fiber: 9 g, Protein: 35 g

237. Beef with Mushroom & Broccoli

Preparation Time: 15 minutes

Cooking Time: 12 minutes

Servings: 4

Ingredients:

For the Beef Marinade:

- 1 garlic clove, minced
- 1 (2-inch piece fresh ginger, minced
- Salt, to taste
- Freshly ground black pepper, to taste
- ¾ cup beef broth
- 1 lb flank steak, trimmed and sliced into thin strips

For the Vegetables:

- 2 tbsp coconut oil, divided
- 2 minced garlic cloves
- 3 cups broccoli rabe, chopped
- 4 oz shiitake mushrooms halved
- 8 oz cremini mushrooms, sliced

Directions:

1. For marinade in a bowl, put together all ingredients except beef, then mix.

2. Add beef and coat with marinade. Bring in the fridge to marinate for at least 15 minutes.

3. In the skillet, warm the oil on medium-high heat. Take off beef from the bowl, reserving the marinade.

4. Put beef and garlic and cook for about 3 to 4 minutes or till browned.

5. Using a slotted spoon, transfer the beef to a bowl.

6. Put the reserved marinade, broccoli, and mushrooms in the same skillet and cook for at least 3 to 4 minutes.

7. Stir in beef and cook for at least 3 to 4 minutes.

Nutrition: Calories: 417, Fat: 10 g, Carbs: 23 g, Fiber: 11 g, Protein: 33 g

238. Citrus Beef with Bok Choy

Preparation Time: 15 minutes

Cooking Time: 11 minutes

Servings: 4

Ingredients:

For the Marinade:

- 2 minced garlic cloves
- 1 (1-inch piece fresh ginger, grated
- ⅓ cup fresh orange juice
- ½ cup coconut aminos
- 2 tsp fish sauce
- 2 tsp Sriracha
- 1¼ lb sirloin steak, sliced thinly

For the Veggies:

- 2 tbsp coconut oil, divided
- 3 to 4 wide strips fresh orange zest
- 1 jalapeño pepper, sliced thinly
- 1 tbsp arrowroot powder
- ½ lb Bok choy, chopped
- 2 tsp sesame seeds

Directions:

1. In a big bowl, put together garlic, ginger, orange juice, coconut aminos, fish sauce, and Sriracha for the marinade, then mix.
2. Put the beef and coat with marinade.
3. Place in the fridge to marinate for around a couple of hours.
4. In a skillet, warm oil on medium-high heat.
5. Add orange zest and sauté for approximately 2 minutes.
6. Take off the beef from a bowl, reserving the marinade.
7. In the skillet, add beef and increase the heat to high.
8. Stir fry for at least 2 to 3 minutes or till browned.
9. With a slotted spoon, transfer the beef and orange strips right into a bowl.
10. With a paper towel, wipe out the skillet.
11. In a similar skillet, heat the remaining oil on medium-high heat.
12. Add jalapeño pepper and stir fry for about 3 to 4 minutes.
13. Meanwhile, add arrowroot powder to reserved marinade and stir to mix.
14. In the skillet, add the marinade mixture, beef, and Bok choy and cook for about 1 to 2 minutes.
15. Serve hot with garnishing of sesame seeds.

Nutrition: Calories: 39, Fat: 11 g, Carbs: 20 g, Fiber: 6 g, Protein: 34 g

239. Beef with Zucchini Noodles

Preparation Time: 15 minutes

Cooking Time: 9 minutes

Servings: 4

Ingredients:

- 1 tsp fresh ginger, grated
- 2 medium garlic cloves, minced
- ¼ cup coconut aminos
- 2 tbsp fresh lime juice
- 1½ lb NY strip steak, trimmed and sliced thinly
- 2 medium zucchinis, spiralized with Blade C
- Salt, to taste
- 3 tbsp essential olive oil
- 2 medium scallions, sliced
- 1 tsp red pepper flakes, crushed
- 2 tbsp fresh cilantro, chopped

Directions:

1. In a big bowl, mix ginger, garlic, coconut aminos, and lime juice.
2. Add beef and coat with marinade generously.
3. Refrigerate to marinate for approximately 10 minutes.
4. Place zucchini noodles over a large paper towel and sprinkle with salt. Keep aside for around 10 minutes.
5. In a big skillet, heat oil on medium-high heat.
6. Add scallion and red pepper flakes and sauté for about 1 minute.
7. Add beef with marinade and stir fry for around 3 to 4 minutes or till browned.
8. Add zucchini and cook for approximately 3 to 4 minutes.
9. Serve hot with all the topping of cilantro.

Nutrition: Calories: 434, Fat: 17 g, Carbs: 23 g, Fiber: 12 g, Protein: 29 g

240. Beef with Asparagus & Bell Pepper

Preparation Time: 15 minutes

Cooking Time: 13 minutes

Servings: 4 to 5

Ingredients:

- 4 garlic cloves, minced
- 3 tbsp coconut aminos
- ⅛ tsp red pepper flakes, crushed
- ⅛ tsp ground ginger
- Freshly ground black pepper, to taste
- 1 bunch asparagus, trimmed and halved
- 2 tbsp olive oil, divided
- 1 lb flank steak, trimmed and sliced thinly
- 1 red bell pepper, seeded and sliced
- 3 tbsp water
- 2 tsp arrowroot powder

Directions:

1. Mix garlic, coconut aminos, red pepper flakes, crushed, ground ginger, and black pepper in a bowl. Keep aside.

2. In a pan of boiling water, cook asparagus for about 2 minutes.

3. Drain and rinse under cold water.

4. In a substantial skillet, heat 1 tbsp of oil on medium-high heat.

5. Add beef and stir fry for around 3 to 4 minutes.

6. With a slotted spoon, transfer the beef to a bowl.

7. In a similar skillet, heat the remaining oil on medium heat.

8. Add asparagus and bell pepper and stir fry for approximately 2 to 3 minutes.

9. Meanwhile, in the bowl, mix water and arrowroot powder.

10. Stir in beef, garlic, and arrowroot mixture, and cook for around 3 to 4 minutes or desired thickness.

Nutrition: Calories: 399, Fat: 17 g, Carbs: 27 g, Fiber: 7 g, Protein: 35 g

241. Spiced Ground Beef

Preparation Time: 10 minutes

Cooking Time: 25 minutes

Servings: 5

Ingredients:

- 2 tbsp coconut oil
- 2 whole cloves
- 2 whole cardamoms
- 1 (2-inch piece cinnamon stick
- 2 bay leaves
- 1 tsp cumin seeds
- 2 onions, chopped
- Salt, to taste
- ½ tbsp garlic paste
- ½ tbsp fresh ginger paste
- 1 lb lean ground beef
- 1½ tsp fennel seeds powder
- 1 tsp ground cumin
- 1½ tsp red chili powder
- ⅛ tsp ground turmeric
- Freshly ground black pepper, to taste
- 1 cup coconut milk
- ¼ cup water
- ¼ cup fresh cilantro, chopped

Directions:

1. In a sizable pan, heat oil on medium heat.

2. Add cloves, cardamoms, cinnamon sticks, bay leaves, and cumin seeds and sauté for about 20 seconds.

3. Add onion and 2 pinches of salt and sauté for about 3 to 4 minutes.

4. Add garlic-ginger paste and sauté for about 2 minutes.

5. Add beef and cook for about 4 to 5 minutes, entering pieces using the spoon.

6. Cover and cook for approximately 5 minutes.

7. Stir in spices and cook, stirring for approximately 2 to 2½ minutes.

8. Stir in coconut milk and water and cook for about 7 to 8 minutes.

9. Season with salt and take away from heat.

10. Serve hot using the garnishing of cilantro.

Nutrition: Calories: 444, Fat: 15 g, Carbs: 29 g, Fiber: 11 g, Protein: 39 g

242. Ground Beef with Cabbage

Preparation Time: 10 minutes

Cooking Time: 20 minutes

Servings: 6

Ingredients:

- 1 tbsp olive oil
- 1 onion, sliced thinly
- 2 tsp fresh ginger, minced
- 4 garlic cloves, minced
- 1 lb lean ground beef
- 1½ tbsp fish sauce
- 2 tbsp fresh lime juice
- 1 small head purple cabbage, shredded
- 2 tbsp peanut butter
- ½ cup fresh cilantro, chopped

Directions:

1. In a huge skillet, warm oil on medium heat.
2. Add onion, ginger, and garlic and sauté for about 4 to 5 minutes.
3. Add beef and cook for approximately 7 to 8 minutes, getting into pieces using the spoon.
4. Drain off the extra liquid in the skillet.
5. Stir in fish sauce and lime juice and cook for approximately 1 minute.
6. Add cabbage and cook around 4 to 5 minutes or till the desired doneness.
7. Stir in peanut butter and cilantro and cook for about 1 minute.
8. Serve hot.

Nutrition: Calories: 402, Fat: 13 g, Carbs: 21 g, Fiber: 10 g, Protein: 33 g

243. Ground Beef with Veggies

Preparation Time: 15 minutes

Cooking Time: 20 minutes

Servings: 2 to 4

Ingredients:

- 1 to 2 tbsp coconut oil
- 1 red onion, sliced
- 2 red jalapeño peppers, seeded and sliced
- 2 minced garlic cloves
- 1 lb lean ground beef
- 1 small head broccoli, chopped
- ½ head cauliflower, chopped
- 3 carrots, peeled and sliced
- 3 celery ribs, sliced
- Chopped fresh thyme to taste
- Dried sage to taste
- Ground turmeric, to taste
- Salt, to taste
- Freshly ground black pepper, to taste

Directions:

1. In a huge skillet, melt coconut oil on medium heat.
2. Add onion, jalapeño peppers, and garlic and sauté for about 5 minutes.
3. Add beef and cook for around 4 to 5 minutes, entering pieces using the spoon.
4. Add remaining ingredients and cook, occasionally stirring for about 8 to 10 min.
5. Serve hot.

Nutrition: Calories: 453, Fat: 17 g, Carbs: 26 g, Fiber: 7 g, Protein: 35 g

244. Ground Beef with Cashews & Veggies

Preparation Time: 15 minutes

Cooking Time: 15 minutes

Servings: 4

Ingredients:

- 1½ lb lean ground beef
- 1 tbsp garlic, minced
- 2 tbsp fresh ginger, minced
- ¼ cup coconut aminos
- Salt, to taste
- Freshly ground black pepper, to taste
- 1 medium onion, sliced
- 1 can water chestnuts, drained and sliced
- 1 large green bell pepper, sliced
- ½ cup raw cashews, toasted

Directions:

1. Heat a nonstick skillet on medium-high heat.
2. Add beef and cook for about 6 to 8 minutes, breaking into pieces with all the spoons.
3. Add garlic, ginger, coconut aminos, salt, and black pepper and cook for approximately 2 minutes.

4. Put the vegetables and cook for approximately 5 minutes or till the desired doneness.

5. Stir in cashews and immediately remove from heat.

6. Serve hot.

Nutrition: Calories: 452, Fat: 20 g, Carbs: 26 g, Fiber: 9 g, Protein: 36 g

245. Ground Beef with Greens & Tomatoes

Preparation Time: 15 minutes

Cooking Time: 15 minutes

Servings: 4

Ingredients:

- 1 tbsp organic olive oil
- ½ white onion, chopped
- 2 garlic cloves, chopped finely
- 1 jalapeño pepper, chopped finely
- 1 lb lean ground beef
- 1 tsp ground coriander
- 1 tsp ground cumin
- ½ tsp ground turmeric
- ½ tsp ground ginger
- ½ tsp ground cinnamon
- ½ tsp ground fennel seeds
- Salt, to taste
- Freshly ground black pepper, to taste
- 8 fresh cherry tomatoes, quartered
- 8 collard greens leave, stemmed, and chopped
- 1 tsp fresh lemon juice

Directions:

1. In a huge skillet, warm oil on medium heat. Put onion and sauté for approximately 4 minutes.

2. Add garlic and jalapeño pepper and sauté for approximately 1 minute.

3. Add beef and spices and cook for approximately 6 minutes, breaking into pieces while using a spoon.

4. Stir in tomatoes and greens and cook, stirring gently for about 4 minutes.

5. Stir in lemon juice and take away from heat.

Nutrition: Calories: 432, Fat: 16 g, Carbs: 27 g, Fiber: 12 g, Protein: 39 g

246. Beef & Veggies Chili

Preparation Time: 15 minutes

Cooking Time: 1 hour

Servings: 6 to 8

Ingredients:

- 2 lb lean ground beef
- ½ head cauliflower, chopped into large pieces
- 1 onion, chopped
- 6 garlic cloves, minced
- 2 cups pumpkin puree
- 1 tsp dried oregano, crushed
- 1 tsp dried thyme, crushed
- 1 tsp ground cumin
- 1 tsp ground turmeric
- 1 to 2 tsp chili powder
- 1 tsp paprika
- 1 tsp cayenne pepper
- ¼ tsp red pepper flakes, crushed
- Salt, to taste
- Freshly ground black pepper, to taste
- 1 (26 oz) can tomatoes, drained
- ½ cup water
- 1 cup beef broth

Directions:

1. Heat a substantial pan on medium-high heat.

2. Add beef and stir fry for around 5 minutes.

3. Add cauliflower, onion, and garlic and stir fry for approximately 5 minutes.

4. Add spices and herbs and stir to mix well.

5. Stir in the remaining ingredients and provide to a boil.

6. Reduce heat to low and simmer, covered for approximately 30 to 45 minutes.

7. Serve hot.

Nutrition: Calories: 453, Fat: 10 g, Carbs: 20 g, Fiber: 7 g, Protein: 33 g

247. Ground Beef & Veggies Curry

Preparation Time: 15 minutes

Cooking Time: 36 minutes

Servings: 6 to 8

Ingredients:

- 2 to 3 tbsp coconut oil

- 1 cup onion, chopped
- 1 garlic clove, minced
- 1 lb lean ground beef
- 1½ tbsp curry powder
- ⅛ tsp ground ginger
- ⅛ tsp ground cinnamon
- ⅛ tsp ground turmeric
- Salt, to taste
- 2½-3 cups tomatoes, chopped finely
- 2½-3 cups fresh peas shelled
- 2 sweet potatoes, peeled and chopped

Directions:

1. In a sizable pan, melt coconut oil on medium heat.

2. Add onion and garlic and sauté for around 4 to 5 minutes.

3. Add beef and cook for about 4 to 5 minutes.

4. Add curry powder and spices and cook for about 1 minute.

5. Stir in tomatoes, peas, and sweet potato and bring to your gentle simmer.

6. Simmer covered approximately 25 minutes.

Nutrition: Calorie: 432, Fat: 16 g, Carbs: 21 g, Fiber: 11 g, Protein: 36 g

248. Spicy & Creamy Ground Beef Curry

Preparation Time: 15 minutes

Cooking Time: 32 minutes

Servings: 4

Ingredients:

- 1 to 2 tbsp coconut oil
- 1 tsp black mustard seeds
- 2 sprigs curry leaves
- 1 serrano pepper, minced
- 1 large red onion, chopped finely
- 1 (1-inch) fresh ginger, minced
- 4 garlic cloves, minced
- 1 tsp ground coriander
- 1 tsp ground cumin
- ½ tsp ground turmeric
- ¼ tsp red chili powder
- Salt, to taste
- 1 lb lean ground beef
- 1 potato, peeled and chopped
- 3 medium carrots, peeled and chopped

- ¼ cup water
- 1 (14 oz) can coconut milk
- Salt, to taste
- Freshly ground black pepper, to taste
- Chopped fresh cilantro for garnishing

Directions:

1. In a big pan, melt coconut oil on medium heat.

2. Add mustard seeds and sauté for about 30 seconds.

3. Add curry leaves and Serrano pepper and sauté for approximately half a minute.

4. Add onion, ginger, and garlic and sauté for about 4 to 5 minutes.

5. Add spices and cook for about 1 minute.

6. Add beef and cook for about 4 to 5 minutes.

7. Stir in potato, carrot, and water and provide with a gentle simmer.

8. Simmer, covered for around 5 minutes.

9. Stir in coconut milk and simmer for around 15 minutes.

10. Stir in salt and black pepper and remove from heat.

11. Serve hot while using garnishing of cilantro.

Nutrition: Calories: 432, Fat: 14 g, Carbs: 22 g, Fiber: 8, Protein: 39 g

249. Curried Beef Meatballs

Preparation Time: 20 minutes

Cooking Time: 22 minutes

Servings: 6

Ingredients:

For the Meatballs:

- 1 lb lean ground beef
- 2 organic eggs, beaten
- 3 tbsp red onion, minced
- ¼ cup fresh basil leaves, chopped
- 1 (1-inch fresh ginger piece, chopped finely
- 4 garlic cloves, chopped finely
- 3 Thai bird's eye chilies, minced
- 1 tsp coconut sugar
- 1 tbsp red curry paste
- Salt, to taste
- 1 tbsp fish sauce
- 2 tbsp coconut oil

For the Curry:

- 1 red onion, chopped
- Salt, to taste
- 4 garlic cloves, minced
- 1 (1-inch) fresh ginger piece, minced
- 2 Thai bird's eye chilies, minced
- 2 tbsp red curry paste
- 1 (14 oz) coconut milk
- Salt, to taste
- Freshly ground black pepper, to taste
- Lime wedges, for

Directions:

1. For meatballs in a huge bowl, put all together with the ingredients except oil and mix till well combined.

2. Make small balls from the mixture.

3. In a huge skillet, melt coconut oil on medium heat.

4. Add meatballs and cook for about 3 to 5 minutes or till golden brown all sides.

5. Transfer the meatballs right into a bowl.

6. In the same skillet, add onion and a pinch of salt and sauté for around 5 minutes.

7. Add garlic, ginger, and chilies, and sauté for about 1 minute.

8. Add curry paste and sauté for around 1 minute.

9. Add coconut milk and meatballs and convey to some gentle simmer.

10. Reduce the warmth to low and simmer, covered for around 10 minutes.

11. Serve using the topping of lime wedges.

Nutrition: Calories: 44, Fat: 15 g, Carbs: 20 g, Fiber: 2 g, Protein: 37 g

250. Beef Meatballs in Tomato Gravy

Preparation Time: 20 minutes

Cooking Time: 37 minutes

Servings: 4

Ingredients:

For the Meatballs:

- 1 lb lean ground beef
- 1 organic egg, beaten
- 1 tbsp fresh ginger, minced
- 1 garlic oil, minced

- 2 tbsp fresh cilantro, chopped finely
- 2 tbsp tomato paste
- ⅓ cup almond meal
- 1 tbsp ground cumin
- Pinch of ground cinnamon
- Salt, to taste
- Freshly ground black pepper, to taste
- ¼ cup coconut oil

For the Tomato Gravy:

- 2 tbsp coconut oil
- ½ small onion, chopped
- 2 garlic cloves, chopped
- 1 tsp fresh lemon zest, grated finely
- 2 cups tomatoes, chopped finely
- Pinch of ground cinnamon
- 1 tsp red pepper flakes, crushed
- ¾ cup chicken broth
- Salt, to taste
- Freshly ground black pepper, to taste
- ¼ cup fresh parsley, chopped

Directions:

1. For meatballs in a sizable bowl, add all ingredients except oil and mix till well combined.

2. Make about 1-inch-sized balls from the mixture.

3. In a substantial skillet, melt coconut oil on medium heat.

4. Add meatballs and cook for approximately 3 to 5 minutes or till golden brown on all sides.

5. Transfer the meatballs into a bowl.

6. For gravy in a big pan, melt coconut oil on medium heat.

7. Add onion and garlic and sauté for approximately 4 minutes.

8. Add lemon zest and sauté for approximately 1 minute.

9. Add tomatoes, cinnamon, red pepper flakes, and broth and simmer for approximately 7 minutes.

10. Stir in salt, black pepper, and meatballs and reduce the warmth to medium-low.

11. Simmer for approximately 20 minutes.

12. Serve hot with all the garnishing of parsley.

Nutrition: Calories: 40, Fat: 11 g, Carbs: 27 g, Fiber: 4 g, Protein: 37 g

251.   Pork with Lemongrass

Preparation Time: 10 minutes

Cooking Time: 30 minutes

Servings: 4

Ingredients:

- 4 pork chops
- 2 tbsp olive oil
- 2 spring onions, chopped
- A pinch of salt and black pepper
- ½ cup vegetable stock
- 1 stalk lemongrass, chopped
- 2 tbsp coconut aminos
- 2 tbsp cilantro, chopped

Directions:

1. Warm a pan with the oil on medium-high heat, add the spring onions and the meat, and brown for 5 minutes.

2. Add the rest of the ingredients, toss, and cook everything over medium heat for 25 minutes.

3. Divide the mix between plates and serve.

Nutrition: Calories: 290, Fiber: 6 g, Carbs: 8 g, Protein: 14 g

252.   Pork Chops with Tomato Salsa

Preparation Time: 10 minutes

Cooking Time: 15 minutes

Servings: 4

Ingredients:

- 4 pork chops
- 1 tbsp olive oil
- 4 scallions, chopped
- 1 tsp cumin, ground
- ½ tbsp hot paprika
- 1 tsp garlic powder
- Pinch of sea salt
- Pinch of black pepper
- 1 small red onion, chopped
- 2 tomatoes, cubed
- 2 tbsp lime juice
- 1 jalapeno, chopped
- ¼ cup cilantro, chopped
- 1 tbsp lime juice

Directions:

1. Warm a pan with the oil on medium heat, add the scallions and sauté for 5 minutes.

2. Add the meat, cumin paprika, garlic powder, salt, and pepper, toss, cook for 5 minutes on each side, and divide between plates.

3. Combine the tomatoes with the remaining ingredients in a bowl, toss, divide next to the pork chops, and serve.

Nutrition: Calories: 313, Fat: 23.7 g, Fiber: 1 g, Carbs: 5 g, Protein: 19.2 g

Chapter 8
Poultry

253. Turkey Sloppy Joes

Preparation Time: 15 minutes

Cooking Time: 4 to 6 hours

Servings: 4

Ingredients:

- 1 tbsp extra-virgin olive oil
- 1 lb ground turkey
- 1 celery stalk, minced
- 1 carrot, minced
- ½ medium sweet onion, diced
- ½ red bell pepper, finely chopped
- 6 tbsp tomato paste
- 2 tbsp apple cider vinegar
- 1 tbsp maple syrup
- 1 tsp Dijon mustard
- 1 tsp chili powder
- ½ tsp garlic powder
- ½ tsp sea salt
- ½ tsp dried oregano

Directions:

1. Incorporate the olive oil, turkey, celery, carrot, onion, red bell pepper, tomato paste, vinegar, maple syrup, mustard, chili powder, garlic powder, salt, and oregano in the slow cooker and stir to combine. As the turkey combines with the other ingredients, break it up into smaller chunks using a large spoon.

2. Set the cooker to low and cover it. Cook for 4 to 6 hours, stirring frequently, before serving.

Nutrition: Calories: 241, Total Fat: 14 g, Total Carbs: 12 g, Sugar: 7 g, Fiber: 4 g, Protein: 24 g, Sodium: 690 mg

254. Hidden Valley Chicken Dummies

Preparation Time: 15 minutes

Cooking Time: 30 minutes

Servings: 4

Ingredients:

- 2 tbsp hot sauce
- ½ cup melted butter
- Celery sticks
- 2 packages hidden valley dressing dry mix
- 3 tbsp vinegar
- 12 chicken drumsticks
- Paprika

Directions:

1. Preheat the oven to 350°F.

2. Rinse and pat dry the chicken.

3. In a bowl, blend the dry dressing, melted butter, vinegar, and hot sauce. Stir until combined.

4. Place the drumsticks in a large plastic baggie, and pour the sauce over the drumsticks. Massage the sauce until the drumsticks are coated.

5. Place the chicken in a single layer on a baking dish. Sprinkle with paprika.

6. Bake for 30 minutes, flipping halfway.

7. Serve with crudités or salad.

Nutrition: Calories: 155, Fat: 18 g, Carbs: 96 g, Protein: 15 g, Sugar: 0.7 g, Sodium: 340 mg

255. Chicken Divan

Preparation Time: 15 minutes

Cooking Time: 30 minutes

Servings: 4

Ingredients:

- 1 cup croutons
- 1 cup cooked and diced broccoli pieces
- ½ cup water
- 1 cup grated extra-sharp cheddar cheese
- ½ lb de-boned and skinless cooked chicken pieces
- 1 can mushroom soup

Directions:

1. Preheat the oven to 350°F
2. In a large pot, heat the soup and water. Add the chicken, broccoli, and cheese. Combine thoroughly.
3. Pour into a greased baking dish.
4. Place the croutons over the mixture.
5. Bake for 30 minutes or until the casserole is bubbling and the croutons are golden brown.

Nutrition: Calories: 38, Fat: 22 g, Carbs: 10 g, Protein: 25 g, Sugar: 2 g, Sodium: 475 mg

256. Apricot Chicken Wings

Preparation Time: 15 minutes

Cooking Time: 45 to 60 minutes

Servings: 3 to 4

Ingredients:

- 1 medium jar apricot preserve
- 1 package Lipton onion dry soup mix
- 1 medium bottle Russian dressing
- 2 lb chicken wings

Directions:

1. Preheat the oven to 350°F.
2. Rinse and pat dry the chicken wings.
3. Bring the chicken wings on a baking pan, single layer.
4. Bake for 45 to 60 minutes, turning halfway.
5. In a medium bowl, combine the Lipton soup mix, apricot preserve, and Russian dressing.

6. Once the wings are cooked, toss with the sauce until the pieces are coated.
7. Serve immediately with a side dish.

Nutrition: Calories: 162, Fat: 17 g, Carbs: 76 g, Protein: 13 g, Sugar: 24 g, Sodium: 700 mg

257. Champion Chicken Pockets

Preparation Time: 5 minutes

Cooking Time: 0 minutes

Servings: 4

Ingredients:

- ½ cup chopped broccoli
- 2 halved whole wheat pita bread rounds
- ¼ cup bottled reduced-fat ranch salad dressing
- ¼ cup chopped pecans or walnuts
- 1½ cups chopped cooked chicken
- ¼ cup plain low-fat yogurt
- ¼ cup shredded carrot

Directions:

1. In a bowl, put together yogurt and ranch salad dressing, then mix.
2. In a medium bowl, put then combine chicken, broccoli, carrot, and, if desired, nuts. Pour yogurt mixture over chicken; toss to coat.
3. Spoon chicken mixture into pita halves.

Nutrition: Calories: 384, Fat: 11.4 g, Carbs: 7.4 g, Protein: 59.3 g, Sugar: 1.3 g, Sodium: 368.7 mg

258. Chicken-Bell Pepper Sauté

Preparation Time: 10 minutes

Cooking Time: 35 minutes

Servings: 6

Ingredients:

- 1 tbsp olive oil
- 1 sliced large yellow bell pepper
- 1 sliced large red bell pepper
- 3 cups onion sliced crosswise
- 6 4-oz skinless, boneless chicken breast halves
- Cooking spray
- 20 Kalamata olives
- ¼ tsp Freshly ground black pepper
- ½ tsp salt
- 2 tbsp finely chopped fresh flat-leaf parsley
- 2⅓ cups coarsely chopped tomato

- 1 tsp chopped fresh oregano

Directions:

1. Adjust your heat to medium-high and set non-stick frying in place. Heat the oil. Sauté the onions for 8 minutes once the oil is hot.

2. Add bell pepper and sauté for 10 more minutes. Add tomato, salt, and black pepper to cook for about 7 minutes until the tomato juice has evaporated.

3. Add parsley, oregano, and olives to cooking for 2 minutes until heated. Set into a bowl and keep warm.

4. Using a paper towel, wipe the pam and grease with cooking spray. Set back to heat and add chicken breasts. Cook for 3 more minutes on each of the sides. You can opt to cook the chicken in batches

5. When cooking the last batch, add back the previous batch of chicken and onion-bell pepper mixture, then cook for a minute as you toss.

6. Serve warm and enjoy.

Nutrition: Calories: 223, Protein: 28.13 g, Fat: 7.82 g, Carbs: 9.5 g

259. Honey Chicken Tagine

Preparation Time: 60 minutes

Cooking Time: 25 minutes

Servings: 12

Ingredients:

- 1 tbsp extra virgin olive oil
- 1 tsp ground coriander
- 1 tbsp minced fresh ginger
- ½ tsp ground pepper
- 2 thinly sliced onions
- 12 oz seeded and roughly chopped kumquats
- 14 oz vegetable broth
- ⅛ tsp ground cloves
- ½ tsp salt
- 1½ tbsp honey
- 1 tsp ground cumin
- 2 lb boneless, skinless chicken thighs
- 4 slivered garlic cloves
- 15 oz rinsed chickpeas
- ¾ tsp ground cinnamon

Directions:

1. Preheat the oven to about 375°F.

2. Put a heatproof casserole on medium heat and heat the oil.

3. Add onions to sauté for 4 minutes Add garlic and ginger to sauté for 1 minute

4. Add coriander, cumin, cloves, salt, pepper, and cloves seasonings. Sauté for a minute.

5. Add kumquats, broth, chickpeas, and honey, then bring to a boil before turning off the heat.

6. Set the casserole in the oven while covered. Bake for 15 minutes as you stir at a 15-minute interval. Serve and enjoy

Nutrition: Calories: 586, Protein: 15.5 g, Fat: 40.82 g, Carbs: 43.56 g

260. Roasted Chicken

Preparation Time: 60 minutes

Cooking Time: 60 minutes

Servings: 8

Ingredients:

- ½ tsp thyme
- 3 lb whole chicken
- 1 bay leaf
- 3 garlic cloves
- 4 tbsp coarsely chopped orange peel
- ½ tsp black pepper
- ½ tbsp salt

Directions:

1. Put the chicken under room temperature for about 1 hour.

2. Pat dries the inside and outside of the chicken using paper towels.

3. Preheat the oven to 450°F as soon as you start preparing the chicken seasoning.

4. Combine thyme, salt, and pepper in a small bowl.

5. Wipe inside using ⅓ of the seasoning. Inside the chicken, put the garlic, citrus peel, and bay leaf.

6. Tuck the tips of the wing and tie the legs together. Spread the rest of the seasoning all over the chicken and put it on a roasting pan.

7. Put in the oven to bake for 60 minutes at 160°F.

8. Set aside to rest for 15 minutes.

9. Cut up the roasted chicken and serve.

10. Enjoy.

Nutrition: Calories: 201, Protein: 35.48 g, Fat: 5.36 g, Carbs: 0.5 g

261. Chicken in Pita Bread

Preparation Time: 10 minutes

Cooking Time: 10 minutes

Servings: 4

Ingredients:

- 1 tbsp Greek seasoning blend
- 2 lightly beaten large egg whites
- ½ cup chopped green onions
- ½ cup diced tomato
- 2 cups shredded lettuce
- 4 pieces 6-inch halved pitas
- 2 tsp Divided grated lemon rind
- ½ cup plain low-fat yogurt
- 1 tbsp olive oil
- 1½ tbsp chopped fresh oregano
- 1 lb ground chicken
- ½ tsp coarsely ground black pepper

Directions:

1. Combine egg whites, Greek seasoning, a tbsp of lemon rind, green onions, and black pepper. Separate into 8 parts and mold each into ¼ inch thick patty.

2. Adjust your heat to medium-high. Set a non-stick skillet in place and fry patties until browned.

3. Lower the heat to medium. Then, cover the skillet to cook for 4 more minutes.

4. Set up a small bowl and combine yogurt, oregano, and a tbsp of lemon rind.

5. Spread the mixture on the pita and add ¼ cup lettuce and a tbsp of tomato.

Nutrition: Calories: 421, Protein: 29.72 g, Fat: 23.37 g, Carbs: 23.26 g

262. Skillet Chicken with Brussels Sprouts Mix

Preparation Time: 10 minutes

Cooking Time: 17 minutes

Servings: 4

Ingredients:

- 1½ lb chicken thighs, skinless and boneless
- 1 tbsp olive oil
- 2 tsp chopped thyme
- A pinch of salt and black pepper
- 12 oz Brussels sprouts, shredded
- 1 apple, cored and sliced
- ½ red onion, sliced
- 1 garlic clove, minced
- 2 tbsp balsamic vinegar
- ¼ cup walnuts, chopped

Directions:

1. Warm a pan with the oil over medium-high heat, then add the chicken thighs, and season with salt, pepper, and thyme. Cook for 5 minutes on each side and transfer to a bowl.

2. Heat the pan again over medium heat, add the onion, apple, sprouts, and garlic. Toss the mix and cook for 5 minutes. Add vinegar to the pan and return the chicken as well. Add the walnuts, toss, cook for 1 to 2 minutes more, then divide between plates and serve.

3. Enjoy!

Nutrition: Calories: 211, Fat: 4 g, Fiber: 7 g, Carbs: 13 g, Protein: 8 g

263. Spicy Chipotle Chicken

Preparation Time: 10 minutes

Cooking Time: 12 minutes

Servings: 4

Ingredients:

- 1 lb chicken breasts, skinless, boneless and cut into strips
- 1 tsp chili powder
- 1 tsp ground cumin
- A pinch of salt and black pepper
- 1 tbsp olive oil
- 1 red bell pepper, sliced
- 1 cup halved mushrooms
- 1 yellow onion, chopped

- 3 garlic cloves, minced
- 1 tbsp chopped chipotles in adobo
- 1½ tbsp lime juice

Directions:

1. Warm a pan with the oil on medium-high heat and add the chicken.

2. Mix and cook for 3 to 4 minutes. Add the chili powder, cumin, salt, pepper, bell pepper, mushrooms, onion, garlic, chipotles, and lime juice. Mix and cook for 7 minutes more, divide into bowls and serve.

3. Enjoy!

Nutrition: Calories: 241, Fat: 4 g, Fiber: 7 g, Carbs: 14 g, Protein: 7 g

264.   Chicken with Fennel

Preparation Time: 10 minutes

Cooking Time: 8 minutes

Servings: 4

Ingredients:

- 1¼ lb chicken cutlets
- 1½ tsp smoked paprika
- A pinch of salt and black pepper
- 3 tbsp olive oil
- 1 fennel bulb, sliced
- ¾ cup fennel fronds
- ⅓ cup red onion, sliced
- 1 avocado, peeled, pitted, and sliced
- 2 tbsp lemon juice

Directions:

1. Warm a pan with 1 tbsp of olive oil on medium-high heat temperature, then add the chicken, season with salt, pepper, and smoked paprika, and cook for 4 minutes on each side.

2. In a bowl, mix the rest of the oil with the fennel, fennel fronds, onion, avocado, and lemon juice. Toss the salad and place it next to the chicken, then serve. Divide between plates.

3. Enjoy!

Nutrition: Calories: 288, Fat: 4 g, Fiber: 6 g, Carbs: 12 g, Protein: 7 g

265.   Adobo Lime Chicken Mix

Preparation Time: 10 minutes

Cooking Time: 40 minutes

Servings: 6

Ingredients:

- 6 chicken thighs
- Salt and black pepper to the taste
- 1 tbsp olive oil
- Zest 1 lime
- 1½ tsp chipotle peppers in adobo sauce
- 1 cup sliced peach
- 1 tbsp lime juice

Directions:

1. Warm a pan with the oil on medium-high heat and add the chicken thighs. Season with salt and pepper, then brown for 4 minutes on each side and bake in the oven at 375°F for 20 minutes.

2. In your food processor, mix the peaches with the chipotle, lime zest, and lime juice, then blend and pour over the chicken. Bake for 10 minutes more, divide everything between plates and serve.

3. Enjoy!

Nutrition: Calories: 309 g, Fat: 6 g, Fiber: 4 g, Carbs: 16 g, Protein: 15 g

266.   Cajun Chicken & Prawn

Preparation Time: 5 minutes

Cooking Time: 40 minutes

Servings: 2

Ingredients:

- 2 free-range skinless chicken breasts, chopped
- 1 onion, chopped
- 1 red pepper, chopped
- 2 Garlic cloves, crushed
- 10 fresh or frozen prawns
- 1 tsp cayenne powder
- 1 tsp chili powder
- 1 tsp paprika
- ¼ tsp chili powder
- 1 tsp dried oregano
- 1 tsp dried thyme
- 1 cup brown or wholegrain rice
- 1 tbsp extra virgin olive oil
- 1 can tomatoes, chopped

- 2 cups homemade chicken stock

Directions:

1. Put all the spices and herbs in a bowl, then mix to form your Cajun spice mix.

2. Grab a large pan and add the olive oil, heating on medium heat.

3. Add the chicken and brown each side for around 4 to 5 minutes. Then place to one side.

4. Add the onion to the pan and fry until soft.

5. Add the garlic, prawns, Cajun seasoning, and red pepper to the pan and cook for around 5 minutes or until prawns become opaque.

6. Add the brown rice along with the chopped tomatoes, chicken, and chicken stock to the pan.

7. Cover the pan and allow to simmer for around 25 minutes or until the rice is soft.

8. Serve and enjoy!

Nutrition: Calories: 557, Protein: 18.96 g, Fat: 12.34 g, Carbs: 93.28 g

267. Healthy Turkey Gumbo

Preparation Time: 5 minutes

Cooking Time: 2 hours

Servings: 1

Ingredients:

- 1 whole turkey
- 1 onion, quartered
- Celery stalk, chopped
- 3 garlic cloves, chopped
- ½ cup okra
- 1 can chopped tomatoes
- 1 tbsp extra virgin olive oil
- 1 to 2 bay leaves
- Black pepper to taste

Directions:

1. Take the first 4 ingredients and add 2 cups of water to a stockpot, heating on high heat until boiling.

2. Lower the heat and simmer for 45 to 50 minutes or until the turkey is cooked through.

3. Remove the turkey and strain the broth.

4. Grab a skillet, heat the oil on medium heat, and brown the rest of the vegetables for 5 to 10 minutes.

5. Stir until tender, and then add to the broth.

6. Add the tomatoes and turkey meat to the broth and stir.

7. Add the bay leaves and continue to cook for an hour or until the sauce has thickened.

8. Season with black pepper and enjoy.

Nutrition: Calories: 261, Protein: 11.72 g, Fat: 12.91 g, Carbs: 28.33 g

268. Chinese-Orange Spiced Duck Breasts

Preparation Time: 4 minutes

Cooking Time: 20 minutes

Servings: 2

Ingredients:

- 1 tsp extra virgin olive oil
- 2 duck breasts, skin removed
- 1 white onion, sliced
- 3 garlic cloves, minced
- 2 tsp ginger, grated
- 1 tsp cinnamon
- 1 tsp cloves
- 1 orange zest and juice (reserved the wedges)
- 2 bok or Pak Choy, plant leaves separated

Directions:

1. Slice the duck breasts into strips and add to a dry, hot pan, cooking for 5 to 7 minutes on each side or until cooked through to your liking.

2. Remove to one side.

3. Add olive oil to a clean pan and sauté the onions with the ginger, garlic, and the rest of the spices for 1 minute.

4. Put the juice and zest of the orange and continue to sauté for 3 to 5 minutes.

5. Add the duck and bok choi and heat through until wilted and the duck is piping hot.

6. Serve and garnish with the orange segments.

Nutrition: Calories: 267, Protein: 36.58 g, Fat: 11.1 g, Carbs: 3.31 g

269. Super Sesame Chicken Noodles

Preparation Time: 10 minutes

Cooking Time: 20 minutes

Servings: 2

Ingredients:

- 2 free-range skinless chicken breasts, chopped
- 1 cup rice/buckwheat noodles such as Japanese udo
- 1 carrot, chopped
- ½ orange juiced
- 1 tsp sesame seed
- 2 tsp coconut oil
- 1 thumb-size piece ginger, minced
- ½ cup sugar snap peas

Directions:

1. Warm 1 tsp oil on medium heat in a skillet.

2. Sauté the chopped chicken breast for about 10 to 15 minutes or until cooked through.

3. While cooking the chicken, place the noodles, carrots, and peas in a pot of boiling water for about 5 minutes. Drain.

4. In a bowl, mix the ginger, sesame seeds, 1 tsp oil, and orange juice to make your dressing.

5. Once the chicken is cooked and the noodles are cooked and drained, add the chicken, noodles, carrots, and peas to the dressing and toss.

6. Serve warm or chilled.

Nutrition: Calories: 168, Protein: 5.31 g, Fat: 8.66 g, Carbs: 19.34 g

270. Lebanese Chicken Kebabs and Hummus

Preparation Time: 10 minutes + 1 hour marinate

Cooking Time: 25 minutes

Servings: 4

Ingredients:

For the Chicken:

- 1 cup lemon juice
- 8 garlic cloves, minced
- 1 tbsp thyme, finely chopped
- 1 tbsp paprika
- 2 tsp ground cumin
- 1 tsp cayenne pepper
- 4 free-range skinless chicken breasts, cubed
- 4 metal kebabs skewers
- Lemon wedges to garnish

For the Hummus:

- 1 can chickpeas/1 cup dried (soaked overnight)
- 2 tbsp tahini paste
- 1 lemon juice
- 1 tsp turmeric
- 1 tsp black pepper
- 2 tbsp olive oil

Directions:

1. Whisk the lemon juice, garlic, thyme, paprika, cumin, and cayenne pepper in a bowl.

2. Skewer the chicken cubes using kebab sticks (metal).

3. Baste the chicken per side with the marinade, covering for as long as possible in the fridge (the lemon juice will tenderize the meat and means it will be more suitable for the anti-inflammatory diet).

4. When ready to cook, set the oven to 400°F/200°C/Gas Mark 6 and bake for 20 to 25 minutes or until the chicken is thoroughly cooked through.

5. Prepare the hummus by putting the ingredients into a blender and whizzing up until smooth. If it is a little thick and chunky, add a little water to loosen the mix.

6. Serve the chicken kebabs garnished with lemon wedges and the hummus on the side.

Nutrition: Calories: 576, Protein: 61.66 g, Fat: 18.55 g, Carbs: 42.07 g

271. Nutty Pesto Chicken Supreme

Preparation Time: 10 minutes

Cooking Time: 30 minutes

Servings: 2

Ingredients:

- 2 Free ranges skinless chicken/turkey breasts
- 1 bunch fresh basil
- ½ cup raw spinach
- 1 cup Crashed macadamias/almonds/walnuts or a combination
- 2 tbsp Extra virgin olive oil
- ½ cup low-fat hard cheese (optional)

Directions:

1. Set the oven to 350°F.

2. Get the chicken breasts and use a meat pounder to 'thin' each breast into a 1 cm thick escalope.

3. Reserve a handful of the nuts before adding the rest of the ingredients and a little black pepper to a blender or pestle and mortar and blend until smooth (you can leave this a little chunky for a rustic feel if you wish).

4. Add a little water if the pesto needs loosening.

5. Coat the chicken in the pesto.

6. Bake for at least 30 minutes in the oven or until the chicken is completely cooked through.

7. Top each chicken escalope with the remaining nuts and place under the broiler for 5 minutes for a crispy topping to complete.

Nutrition: Calories: 2539, Protein: 444.61 g, Fat: 71.66 g, Carbs: 5.99 g

272. **Delicious Roasted Duck**

Preparation Time: 10 minutes

Cooking Time: 4 hours 50 minutes

Servings: 4

Ingredients:

- 1 medium duck
- 1 celery stalk, chopped
- 2 yellow onions, chopped
- 2 tsp thyme, dried
- 8 garlic cloves, minced
- 2 bay leaves
- ¼ cup parsley, chopped
- A pinch of salt and black pepper
- 1 tsp herbs de Provence

For the Sauce:

- 1 tbsp tomato paste
- 1 yellow onion, chopped
- ½ tsp sugar
- 3 cups water
- 1 cup chicken stock
- 1½ cups black olives, pitted and chopped
- ¼ tsp herbs de Provence

Directions:

1. In a baking dish, arrange thyme, parsley, garlic, and 2 onions.

2. Add duck, season with salt, 1 tsp herbs de Provence and pepper.

3. Place in the oven at 475°F and roast for 10 minutes.

4. Cover the dish, reduce heat to 275°F, and roast the duck for 3 hours and 30 minutes.

5. Meanwhile, heat a pan over medium heat, add 1 yellow onion, stir and cook for 10 minutes.

6. Add tomato paste, stock, sugar, ¼ tsp herbs de Provence, olives, and water, cover, reduce heat to low, and cook for 1 hour.

7. Transfer duck to a work surface, carve, discard bones, and divide between plates.

8. Drizzle the sauce all over and serve right away.

Nutrition: Calories: 254, Fat: 3 g, Fiber: 3 g, Carbs: 8 g, Protein: 13 g

273. **Duck Breast with Apricot Sauce**

Preparation Time: 10 minutes

Cooking Time: 10 minutes

Servings: 4

Ingredients:

- 4 duck breasts, boneless
- Salt and black pepper to taste
- ¼ tsp cinnamon, ground
- ¼ tsp coriander, ground
- 5 tbsp apricot preserving
- 3 tbsp chives, chopped
- 2 tbsp parsley, chopped
- A drizzle of olive oil
- 3 tbsp apple cider vinegar
- 2 tbsp red onions, chopped
- 1 cup apricots, chopped
- ¾ cup blackberries

Directions:

1. Season duck breasts with salt, pepper, coriander, and cinnamon, place them on a preheated grill pan over medium-high heat, cook for 2 minutes, flip them and cook for 3 minutes more.

2. Flip duck breasts again, add 3 tbsp apricot preserving, cook for 1 minute, transfer them to a cutting board, leave aside for 2 to 3 minutes, and slice.

3. Heat a pan over medium heat, add vinegar, onion, 2 tbsp apricot preserving, apricots,

blackberries, and chives, stir and cook for 3 minutes.

4. Divide sliced duck breasts between plates and serve with apricot sauce drizzled on top.

Nutrition: Calories: 275, Fat: 4 g, Fiber: 4 g, Carbs: 7 g, Protein: 12 g

274. Duck Breast Salad

Preparation Time: 10 minutes

Cooking Time: 20 minutes

Servings: 4

Ingredients:

- 2 tbsp sugar
- 2 oranges, peeled and cut into segments
- 1 tsp orange zest, grated
- 1 tbsp lemon juice
- 1 tsp lemon zest, grated
- 3 tbsp shallot, minced
- 1 tbsp canola oil
- Salt and black pepper to taste
- 2 duck breasts, boneless but the skin on, cut into 4 pieces
- 1 head fries, torn
- 2 small lettuce heads washed, torn into small pieces
- 2 tbsp chives, chopped

Directions:

1. Warm a small saucepan on medium-high heat, add vinegar and sugar, stir and boil for 5 minutes and take off the heat.

2. Add orange zest, lemon zest and lemon juice, stir and leave aside for a few minutes.

3. Add shallot, salt, and pepper to taste and the oil, whisk well and leave aside.

4. Pat dry duck pieces' score skin, trim, and season with salt and pepper.

5. Warm a pan on medium-high heat for 1 minute, arrange duck breast pieces skin side down, brown for 7 minutes, reduce heat to medium, and cook for 4 more minutes.

6. Flip pieces, cook for 3 minutes, transfer to a cutting board and cover them with foil.

7. Put fries and lettuce in a bowl, stir and divide between plates.

8. Slice duck, arrange on top, add orange segments, sprinkle chives, and drizzle the vinaigrette.

Nutrition: Calories: 320, Fat: 4 g, Fiber: 4 g, Carbs: 6 g, Protein: 14 g

275. Duck Breast and Blackberries Mix

Preparation Time: 10 minutes

Cooking Time: 28 minutes

Servings: 4

Ingredients:

- 4 duck breasts
- 2 tbsp balsamic vinegar
- 3 tbsp sugar
- Salt and black pepper to taste
- 1½ cups water
- 4 oz blackberries
- ¼ cup chicken stock
- 1 tbsp butter
- 2 tsp cornflour

Directions:

1. Pat dry duck breasts with paper towels score the skin, season with salt and pepper to taste and set aside for 30 minutes.

2. Put breasts skin side down in a pan, heat over medium heat, and cook for 8 minutes.

3. Flip breasts and cook for 30 more seconds.

4. Transfer duck breasts to a baking dish skin side up, place in the oven at 425°F and bake for 15 minutes.

5. Pull out the meat from the oven and leave it aside to cool down for 10 minutes before you cut them.

6. Meanwhile, put sugar in a pan, heat over medium heat, and melt it, stirring all the time.

7. Take the pan off the heat, add the water, stock, balsamic vinegar, and blackberries.

8. Heat this mix to medium temperature and cook until the sauce is reduced to half.

9. Transfer sauce to another pan, add cornflour mixed with water, heat again, and cook for 4 minutes until it thickens.

10. Add salt and pepper, the butter, and whisk well. Slice the duck breasts, divide between plates and serve with the berries sauce on top.

Nutrition: Calories: 320, Fat: 15 g, Fiber: 15 g, Carbs: 16 g, Protein: 11 g

276. Chicken Piccata

Preparation Time: 15 minutes

Cooking Time: 30 minutes

Servings: 4

Ingredients:

- 4 boneless, skinless chicken breast
- 1 cup ground almond meal
- ¼ cup grated Parmesan cheese
- ½ tsp Dijon mustard
- 1 yellow onion, chopped
- 1 tsp sea salt
- ½ tsp ground black pepper
- 4 tbsp olive oil
- 4 tbsp organic unsalted butter
- ½ cup organic, gluten-free chicken broth
- 3 tbsp lemon juice
- 2 tbsp capers
- 3 tbsp organic butter
- ¼ cup fresh parsley, chopped

Directions:

1. Combine the almond meal, cheese, mustard, salt, and pepper and spread the mixture on a shallow dish.

2. Wash the pounded chicken breasts in water and shake off the excess. Dredge the chicken in the flour mixture.

3. Add tbsp of butter to a large saucepan over high heat; add the olive oil.

4. Cook chicken in butter and oil for approximately 3 to 4 minutes on each side until golden brown.

5. Place the cooked chicken on a serving dish and cover to keep warm.

6. Stir in the chicken broth, lemon juice, and capers, scraping up any brown bits in the pan.

7. Add the chicken broth, lemon juice, and capers to the skillet, stirring and scraping up any brown bits in the skillet. Simmer until the sauce is reduced and reaches a light syrup consistency. Reduce heat to low and stir in remaining butter.

8. Ladle the sauce over the chicken breasts and top with chopped parsley. Serve with lemon slices or wedges.

Nutrition: Calories: 357, Protein: 4.51 g, Fat: 35.73 g, Carbs: 6.16 g

277. Honey-Mustard Lemon Marinated Chicken

Preparation Time: 10 minutes

Cooking Time: 20 minutes

Servings: 4

Ingredients:

- 1 lb lean chicken breast
- ¼ cup Dijon mustard
- 1 tbsp olive oil
- ¼ cup rosemary leaves, chopped
- 1 lemon, zested and juiced
- 1 tbsp cayenne pepper
- ½ tsp ground black pepper
- ½ tsp sea salt

Directions:

1. Place chicken breasts in a 7 x 11-inch baking dish.

2. Mix all ingredients except the chicken in a medium bowl.

3. Pour prepared marinade over chicken; turn sides to coat. Cover, place in the fridge and marinate for 1 hour or overnight for the best flavor.

4. Bake at 350°F for 20 minutes.

5. Use the extra sauce over the top and serve.

Nutrition: Calories: 265, Protein: 26.12 g, Fat: 16.27 g, Carbs: 3.08 g

278. Spicy Almond Chicken Strips with Garlic Lime Tartar Sauce

Preparation Time: 10 minutes

Cooking Time: 10 minutes

Servings: 4

Ingredients:

Chicken Sticks:

- 1½ lb chicken breast, cut into 1x5-inch pieces
- 2 organic free-range eggs, whisked
- ½ cup blanched almond flour
- ½ tsp ground cayenne pepper
- ¼ cup dried basil

- 3 garlic cloves, finely chopped
- 1 tsp salt
- ¼ tsp freshly ground black pepper
- ½ cup coconut oil

Garlic Lime Tartar Sauce:

- 1 cup mayonnaise
- 1 tsp garlic powder
- 2 tbsp lime juice
- 1½ tbsp dill pickle relish
- 1 tbsp dried onion flakes
- ½ tsp salt

Directions:

1. Whisk together all the ingredients for the tartar sauce until well combined. Chill for at least 30 minutes until serving.

2. Whisk eggs in a medium bowl. Combine almond flour, cayenne pepper, basil, garlic, salt, and pepper in another bowl.

3. Dip chicken strips in egg, then flour mixture; coat well and place sticks on a plate.

4. Heat some coconut oil in a saucepan over medium-high heat. Add half of the chicken strips and cook for 2 to 3 minutes on each side until well-browned. Leave enough room around chicken strips so that they aren't overcrowded.

5. Drain sticks on paper towels on a plate. Heat another ¼ cup coconut oil and cook the remaining half of the chicken strips. Serve with the prepared Garlic Lime Tartar Sauce.

Nutrition: Calories: 1092, Protein: 94.15 g, Fat: 75.01 g, Carbs: 7.5 g

279. Chicken Scarpariello with Spicy Sausage

Preparation Time: 10 minutes

Cooking Time: 45 minutes

Servings: 6

Ingredients:

- 1 lb boneless chicken thighs
- Sea salt, for seasoning
- Freshly ground black pepper for seasoning
- 3 tbsp good-quality olive oil, divided
- ½ lb Italian sausage (sweet or hot)
- 1 tbsp minced garlic
- 1 pimiento, chopped
- 1 cup chicken stock

- 2 tbsp chopped fresh parsley

Directions:

1. Preheat the oven. Set the oven temperature to 425°F.

2. Brown the chicken and sausage. Pat the chicken thighs to dry using paper towels and season them lightly with salt and pepper. In a large oven-safe skillet over medium-high heat, warm 2 tbsp of olive oil. Add the chicken thighs and sausage to the skillet and brown them on all sides, turning them carefully, for about 10 minutes.

3. Bake the chicken and sausage. Bring the skillet into the oven and bake for 25 minutes or until the chicken is cooked through. Take the skillet out of the oven, transfer the chicken and sausage to a plate, and put the skillet over medium heat on the stovetop.

4. Make the sauce. Warm the remaining 1 tbsp of olive oil, add the garlic and pimiento, and sauté for 3 minutes. Deglaze the skillet by using a spoon to scrape up any browned bits from the bottom of the skillet. Pour in the chicken stock, bring it to a boil, then reduce the heat to low and simmer until the sauce reduces by about half, about 6 minutes.

5. Finish and serve. Put back the chicken and sausage to the skillet, toss it to coat it with the sauce, and serve it topped with the parsley.

Nutrition: Calories: 370, Total Fat: 30 g, Total Carbs: 3 g, Fiber: 0 g, Net Carbs: 3 g, Sodium: 314 mg, Protein: 19 g

280. Almond Chicken Cutlets

Preparation Time: 10 minutes

Cooking Time: 15 minutes

Servings: 4

Ingredients:

- 2 eggs
- ½ tsp garlic powder
- 1 cup almond flour
- 1 tbsp chopped fresh oregano
- 4 (4 oz) boneless skinless chicken breasts, pounded to about ¼ inch thick
- ¼ cup good-quality olive oil
- 2 tbsp grass-fed butter

Directions:

1. Bread the chicken. Whisk together the eggs, and garlic powder in a medium bowl, and set it aside. Stir together the almond flour and oregano on a plate and set the plate next to the egg mixture. Pat the chicken breasts to dry using paper towels and dip them into the egg mixture. Remove excess egg, then roll the chicken in the almond flour until they are coated.

2. Fry the chicken. In a large skillet over medium-high heat, warm the olive oil and butter. Add the breaded chicken breasts and fry them, turning them once until they are cooked through, crispy, golden brown, and 14 to 16 minutes in total.

3. Serve. Place 1 cutlet on each of the 4 plates and serve them immediately.

Nutrition: Calories: 328, Total Fat: 23 g, Total Carbs: 0 g, Fiber: 0 g, Net Carbs: 0 g, Sodium: 75m, Protein: 27 g

281. Cheesy Chicken Sun-Dried Tomato Packets

Preparation Time: 15 minutes

Cooking Time: 40 minutes

Servings: 4

Ingredients:

- 1 cup goat cheese
- ½ cup chopped oil-packed sun-dried tomatoes
- 1 tsp minced garlic
- ½ tsp dried basil
- ½ tsp dried oregano
- 4 (4 oz) boneless chicken breasts
- Sea salt, for seasoning
- Freshly ground black pepper, for seasoning
- 3 tbsp olive oil

Directions:

1. Preheat the oven. Set the oven temperature to 375°F.

2. Prepare the filling. Put the goat cheese, sun-dried tomatoes, garlic, basil, and oregano in a medium bowl, then mix until everything is well blended.

3. Stuff the chicken. Make a horizontal slice in the middle of each chicken breast to make a pocket, making sure not to cut through the sides or ends. Spoon ¼ of the filling into each breast, folding the skin and chicken meat over the slit

to form packets. Secure the packets with a toothpick. Lightly season the breasts with salt and pepper.

4. Brown the chicken. In a large oven-safe skillet over medium heat, warm the olive oil. Add the breasts and sear them, turning them once, until they are golden, about 8 minutes in total.

5. Bake the chicken. Bring the skillet into the oven and bake the chicken for 30 minutes or until it's cooked through.

6. Serve. Remove the toothpicks. Divide the chicken into 4 plates and serve them immediately.

Nutrition: Calories: 388, Total Fat: 29 g, Total Carbs: 4 g, Fiber: 1 g, Net Carbs: 3 g, Sodium: 210 mg, Protein: 27 g

282. Tuscan Chicken Saute

Preparation Time: 10 minutes

Cooking Time: 35 minutes

Servings: 4

Ingredients:

- 1 lb boneless chicken breasts, each cut into 3 pieces
- Sea salt for seasoning
- Freshly ground black pepper for seasoning
- 3 tbsp olive oil
- 1 tbsp minced garlic
- ¾ cup chicken stock
- 1 tsp dried oregano
- ½ tsp dried basil
- ½ cup heavy (whipping) cream
- ½ cup shredded Asiago cheese
- 1 cup fresh spinach
- ¼ cup sliced Kalamata olives

Directions:

1. Prepare the chicken. Pat the chicken, breasts dry, and lightly season them with salt and pepper.

2. Sauté the chicken. In a large skillet over medium-high heat, warm the olive oil. Add the chicken and sauté until it is golden brown and just cooked through, about 15 minutes in total. Transfer the chicken to a plate and set it aside.

3. Make the sauce. Put the garlic into the skillet, then sauté until it's softened for about 2 minutes. Stir in the chicken stock, oregano, and

basil, scraping up any browned bits in the skillet. Bring to a boil, then reduce the heat to low and simmer until the sauce is reduced by about one-quarter, about 10 minutes.

4. Finish the dish. Stir in the cream, Asiago, and simmer, stirring the sauce frequently, until it has thickened about 5 minutes. Put back the chicken into the skillet along with any accumulated juices. Stir in the spinach and olives and simmer until the spinach is wilted for about 2 minutes.

5. Serve. Divide the chicken and sauce between 4 plates and serve it immediately.

Nutrition: Calories: 483, Total Fat: 37 g, Total Carbs: 5 g, Fiber: 1 g, Net Carbs: 3 g, Sodium: 332 mg, Protein: 31 g

283. Turkey Ham and Mozzarella Pate

Preparation Time: 10 minutes

Cooking Time: 0 minutes

Servings: 6

Ingredients:

- 4 oz turkey ham, chopped
- 2 tbsp fresh parsley, roughly chopped
- 2 tbsp flaxseed meal
- 4 oz mozzarella cheese, crumbled
- 2 tbsp sunflower seeds

Directions:

1. Thoroughly combine the ingredients, except for the sunflower seeds, in your food processor.

2. Spoon the mixture into a serving bowl and scatter the sunflower seeds over the top.

Nutrition: Calories: 212, Fat: 18.7 g, Carbs: 2 g, Protein: 10.6 g, Fiber: 1.6 g

284. Avocado-Orange Grilled Chicken

Preparation Time: 10 minutes

Cooking Time: 12 minutes

Servings: 4

Ingredients:

- ¼ cup fresh lime juice
- ¼ cup minced red onion
- 1 cup low-fat yogurt
- 1 deseeded avocado, peeled and chopped
- 1 tbsp honey

- 1 thinly cut small red onion
- 2 peeled and sectioned oranges
- 2 tbsp chopped cilantro
- 4 pieces 4 to 6 oz boneless, skinless chicken breasts
- Pepper
- Salt

Directions:

1. Set up a big mixing container and mix yogurt, minced red onion, cilantro and honey

2. Put in chicken into the mixture and marinate for half an hour

3. Grease the grate and preheat the grill to moderate-high heat.

4. Position the chicken aside and put in seasonings

5. Grill for about 6 minutes on each side

6. Set the avocado in a container.

7. Put in lime juice and toss avocado to coat well.

8. Put in oranges, thinly cut onions, and cilantro into the container with avocado and mix well.

9. Serve avocado dressing alongside grilled chicken.

Nutrition: Calories: 206, Protein: 8.73 g, Fat: 12.48 g, Carbs: 21.86 g

285. Bacon-Wrapped Chicken with Cheddar Cheese

Preparation Time: 10 minutes

Cooking Time: 4 hours 5 minutes

Servings: 6

Ingredients:

- ½ cup cheddar cheese, grated
- 1 tbsp olive oil
- 2 big chicken breasts, each cut into 6 pieces
- 4 garlic cloves, crushed
- 6 slices streaky bacon, each cut in half widthwise
- Freshly ground black pepper, to taste
- Salt, to taste

Directions:

1. Grease the insert of the slow cooker with olive oil.

2. Cover each piece of chicken breast with each half of the bacon slice, and place them in the

slow cooker. Drizzle with garlic, salt, and black pepper.

3. Place the lid and then cook on low for 4 hours.

4. Set the oven to 350°F (180°C).

5. Move the cooked bacon-wrapped chicken to a baking dish, then sprinkle with cheese.

6. Cook in the preheated oven for 5 minutes or until the cheese melts.

7. Take it off from the oven and serve warm.

Nutrition: Calories: 318, Total Fat: 21.7 g, Total Carbs: 3.9 g, Fiber: 0 g, Net Carbs: 2.7 g, Protein: 26.1 g

286. Baked Chicken Meatballs - Habanero & Green Chili

Preparation Time: 10 minutes

Cooking Time: 25 minutes

Servings: 15

Ingredients:

- ½ cup cilantro
- 1 habanero pepper
- 1 jalapeno pepper
- 1 poblano pepper
- 1 lb ground chicken
- 1 tbsp olive oil
- 1 tbsp vinegar
- Salt to taste

Directions:

1. Preheat broiler to 400°F.

2. In an enormous blending container, join chicken, minced peppers, cilantro, salt, and vinegar with your hands. Structure 1-inch meatballs with the blend

3. Coat every meatball with olive oil, at that point, place on a rimmed heating sheet or meal dish.

4. Heat for about 25 minutes

Nutrition: Calories: 54, Fat: 3 g, Carbs: 5 g, Protein: 5 g

287. Balsamic-Glazed Turkey Wings

Preparation Time: 15 minutes

Cooking Time: 7 to 8 hours

Servings: 4

Ingredients:

- 1 tsp garlic powder
- 1¼ cup balsamic vinegar
- 2 lb turkey wings
- 2 tbsp raw honey

Directions:

1. In a container, put together the vinegar, honey, and garlic powder then mix.

2. Place the wings on the bottom of the slow cooker, and pour the vinegar sauce on top.

3. Secure the lid of your cooker and set it to low. Cook for about 8 hours.

4. Baste the wings with the sauce from the bottom of the slow cooker before you serve.

Nutrition: Calories: 511, Total Fat: 22 g, Sugar: 9 g, Fiber: 0 g, Protein: 47 g, Sodium: 162 mg

288. Basic "Rotisserie" Chicken

Preparation Time: 15 minutes

Cooking Time: 6 to 8 hours

Servings: 6

Ingredients:

- ½ medium onion, cut
- 1 (4 to 5 lb) whole chicken, neck and giblets removed
- 1 tsp chili powder
- 1 tsp dried thyme leaves
- 1 tsp garlic powder
- 1 tsp paprika
- 1 tsp sea salt
- Freshly ground black pepper
- Pinch cayenne pepper

Directions:

1. In a small container, mix together the garlic powder, chili powder, paprika, thyme, salt, and cayenne. Flavor it with black pepper, and stir again to blend. Rub the spice mix all over the exterior of the chicken.

2. Put the chicken in the cooker with the cut onion sprinkled around it.

3. Secure the lid of your cooker and set it to low. Cook for a minimum of 6 to 8 hours, or until the internal temperature reaches 165°F on a meat thermometer and the juices run clear before you serve.

Nutrition: Calories: 862, Total Fat: 59 g, Total Carbs: 7 g, Sugar: 6 g, Fiber: 0 g, Protein: 86 g, Sodium: 1,200 mg

289.   Basil Chicken Sauté

Preparation Time: 10 minutes

Cooking Time: 15 minutes

Servings: 2

Ingredients:

- 1 chicken breast, minced or chopped minuscule
- 1 chili pepper, diced (not necessary)
- 1 cup basil leaves, finely chopped
- 1 tbsp tamari sauce
- 2 garlic cloves, minced
- 2 tbsp avocado or coconut oil to cook in
- Salt, to taste

Directions:

1. Put in oil into a frying pan and sauté the garlic and pepper.
2. Then put in the minced chicken and sauté until the chicken is cooked.
3. Put in the tamari sauce and salt to taste. Put in the basil leaves and mix them in.

Nutrition: Calories: 320, Fat: 24 g, Net Carbs: 2 g, Protein: 24 g

290.   Bbq Chicken Zucchini Boats

Preparation Time: 10 minutes

Cooking Time: 15 to 20 minutes

Servings: 4

Ingredients:

- ¼ cup diced green onions
- ⅓ cup shredded Mexican cheese
- ½ cup bbq sauce
- ½ cup halved cherry tomatoes
- 1 avocado, cut
- 1 lb cooked chicken breast
- 3 tbsp keto-friendly ranch dressing
- 3 zucchini halved
- Also needed: 9x13 casserole dish

Directions:

1. Set the oven to reach 350°F.
2. Using a knife, chop the zucchini in half. Discard the seeds. Make the boat by carving out of the center. Put the zucchini flesh side up into the casserole dish.
3. Discard and chop the skin and bones from the chicken. Shred and put the chicken in with the barbeque sauce. Toss to coat all the chicken fully.
4. Fill the zucchini boats with the mixture using about ¼ to ⅓ cup each.
5. Drizzle with Mexican cheese on top.
6. Bake for roughly 15 minutes. (If you would like it tenderer; bake for another 5 to 10 minutes to reach the desired tenderness.)
7. Take out of the oven. Top it off with avocado, green onion, tomatoes, and a sprinkle of dressing and serve.

Nutrition: Calories: 212, Net Carbs: 9 g, Total Fat: 11 g, Protein: 19 g

291.   Blue Cheese Buffalo Chicken Balls

Preparation Time: 10 minutes

Cooking Time: 18 minutes

Servings: 4 to 6

Ingredients:

- ¼ cup chopped celery
- ½ cup crumbled organic blue cheese
- ½ tsp freshly ground black pepper
- ½ tsp sea salt
- 1 big free-range egg, lightly beaten
- 1 cup shredded organic mozzarella cheese
- 1 lb free-range ground chicken
- 1 recipe Buffalo Sauce
- 1 tsp onion powder
- 2 tbsp water

Directions:

1. Preheat your oven to 450°F.
2. Coat a baking pan using parchment paper.
3. In a big container, put and mix the chicken, egg, mozzarella, blue cheeses, celery, water, onion powder, salt, and pepper. Use your hands to combine the ingredients thoroughly.

4. Make 20 meatballs into a mixture then put them in the baking pan as you do.

5. Bake until the internal temperature reaches 165°F, approximately 18 minutes.

6. On the other hand, warm the buffalo sauce in a moderate-sized deep cooking pan using low heat.

7. When the meatballs are done, toss them in the warm sauce before you serve.

Nutrition: Calories: 340, Total Fat: 17 g, Saturated Fat: 6 g, Protein: 44 g, Cholesterol: 157 mg, Carbs: 2 g, Fiber: 0 g, Net Carbs: 2 g

1. Heat oil in the skillet and sauté onion and garlic. Put in leftover pepper and Italian seasoning. Cook till veggies are browned and pour on top of chicken in cooker.

2. Put tomato paste and wine into the skillet and bring to a boil. Then pour on top of chicken and onions.

3. Put in peppers and set on high. Cook for 3½ hours, covered.

4. Remove cover and add in okra and cook for 30 additional minutes.

5. Put the chicken into the bowl and stir veggies together and spoon the mixture into the bowl. Garnish with parsley.

Nutrition: Calories: 252, Fat: 15.5 g, Saturated Fat: 4.5 g, Carbs: 10 g, Protein: 1.6 g

Chapter 9
Soup

292. Vegetable Soup

Preparation Time: 30 minutes

Cooking Time: 65 minutes

Servings: 4

Ingredients:

- 4 cups black and white beans
- 2 tbsp olive oil
- 1 medium onion
- 2 garlic cloves
- 5 cups vegetable stock
- 8 cups water
- 1 cup brown rice
- 2 cups carrots
- Salt and Pepper
- 1 tbsp rosemary

Directions:

1. Soak beans for 30 minutes in water.
2. Take the saucepan and put it on medium heat.
3. Add olive oil, garlic, and chopped onions into the saucepan and stir for 5 minutes, until the onions turn golden brown.
4. Add the other ingredients into the saucepan and boil on lower heat for 50 to 60 minutes.
5. Add some salt and pepper and serve hot.

Nutrition: Calories: 385, Carbs: 53 g, Protein: 20 g, Fat: 7 g, Sugar: 1 g, Fiber: 15 g, Sodium: 327 mg

293. Lentil Soup

Preparation Time: 10 minutes

Cooking Time: 35 minutes

Servings: 4

Ingredients:

- 2 tbsp olive oil

- 1 small onion
- 2 garlic cloves
- 5 cups vegetable stock
- 5 cups water
- 1 tbsp sesame seeds
- 4 cups lentil
- ½ cup lemon juice (optional)
- ½ cup parsley
- ⅓ cup mustard
- Sea salt
- Pepper

Directions:

1. Put a saucepan on medium heat and add olive oil, chopped onions, and garlic. Stir for about 5 minutes until the onions turn golden brown.
2. Add vegetable stock, water, sesame seeds, and lentil, stir it and let boil for 30 minutes.
3. Add the mustard, salt, pepper, and parsley.
4. Add lemon juice for some sour taste.

Nutrition: Calories: 333, Carbs: 53 g, Protein: 21 g, Fat: 6 g, Sugar: 2 g, Fiber: 19 g, Sodium: 468 mg

294. Pea Soup

Preparation Time: 10 minutes

Cooking Time: 45 minutes

Servings: 2

Ingredients:

- 2 tbsp olive oil
- 5 cups vegetable stock
- 4 cups green peas
- 1 cup carrots
- 1½ cup brown rice
- Sea salt
- Pepper
- ¼ cup onions, finely chopped

Directions:

1. Put some olive oil into a saucepan on medium heat and add olive oil.

2. Add onions and stir for 5 minutes.

3. Add vegetable stock, green peas, carrots, and brown rice and let it boil. It should take around 35 to 40 minutes for the brown rice gets cooked.

4. Add the salt and pepper.

5. Serve hot.

Nutrition: Calories: 321, Carbs: 56 g, Protein: 17 g, Fat: 6 g, Sugar: 0.5 g, Fiber: 19 g, Sodium: 349 mg

295. Cabbage Soup

Preparation Time: 10 minutes

Cooking Time: 45 minutes

Servings: 4

Ingredients:

- 8 cups green cabbage
- 3 carrots
- 1 medium onion
- 2 cups mushrooms
- 4 cups vegetable stock
- 4 cups water
- 1 tbsp thyme
- 1 tbsp rosemary
- Sea salt
- Pepper

Directions:

1. Slice all of the vegetables and put them in a pot with the vegetable stock.

2. Add water and put it on medium heat for 15 to 20 minutes. Let it boil then lower the heat and add the thyme and rosemary and cook for 25 minutes more.

3. Season the soup with salt and pepper

4. Serve hot.

Nutrition: Calories: 90, Carbs: 20 g, Protein: 5 g, Fat: 1 g, Sugar: 0 g, Fiber: 5 g, Sodium: 521 mg

296. German Cream-Soup

Preparation Time: 10 minutes

Cooking Time: 45 minutes

Servings: 4

Ingredients:

- 1 medium butternut squash
- 1 medium onion
- 1 tbsp mixed herbs
- 1 tsp cinnamon
- 7 cups vegetable stock
- 1 cup Greek yogurt

Directions:

1. Pour the vegetable stock into a pan and heat it on medium heat until it boils (It will take about 15 minutes).

2. Add all the ingredients and cook for 25 to 30 minutes.

3. Let it cool down for 5 to 10 minutes and pour the soup into the blender. You are going to have a smooth consistency.

4. Serve with yogurt on the side and parsley on top.

Nutrition: Calories: 72, Carbs: 10 g, Protein: 3.3 g, Fat: 2.9 g, Sugar: 5 g, Fiber: 2.1 g, Sodium: 361 mg

297. Asian Soup

Preparation Time: 5 minutes

Cooking Time: 23 minutes

Servings:

Ingredients:

- 1 tbsp olive oil
- 2 garlic cloves
- 1 tbsp ginger powder
- 2 cups mushrooms
- 5 cups water
- 2 cups rice noodles
- Nori seaweed (optional)
- 1 cup green onions
- 1½ tbsp miso paste

Directions:

1. In a saucepan add the olive oil, garlic and ginger powder. Put it on medium heat and stir for 1 minute.

2. Add mushrooms and stir for another 5 minutes.

3. Add water and rice noodles into the pan and let it cook on low heat for 10 to 15 minutes, till it boils.

4. Finally add the seaweed, and green onions and boil for 2 minutes.

5. Add miso paste and serve hot.

Nutrition: Calories: 280, Carbs: 45 g, Protein: 13 g, Fat: 5 g, Sugar: 1 g, Fiber: 4 g, Sodium: 343 mg

298.   Chicken Soup

Preparation Time: 10 minutes

Cooking Time: 43 minutes

Servings: 4

Ingredients:

- 2 tbsp olive oil
- 1 small onion
- 2 garlic cloves
- 2 large green onion heads
- 4 cups vegetable stock
- 2 cups water
- 2 carrots
- 1 cup brown rice
- 1½ cups chicken breast
- Parsley
- Sea salt
- Pepper

Directions:

1. In a pan add the olive oil, chopped onions, and garlic and stir for 3 minutes, till the onions turn golden brown.

2. After adding water to the pot and let it boil on high heat for 10 minutes.

3. Add the vegetable stock, rice, chopped carrots, and cooked chicken breast into the soup.

4. Lower the heat and let it cook for 30 minutes.

5. Add the salt, pepper, and parsley.

6. Serve hot.

Nutrition: Calories: 214, Carbs: 21 g, Protein: 23 g, Fat: 7 g, Sugar: 2 g, Fiber: 3 g, Sodium: 321 mg

299.   Arigato Soup

Preparation Time: 10 minutes

Cooking Time: 23 minutes

Servings: 4

Ingredients:

- 5 cups water
- 1 cup mushroom
- 2 cups tofu
- ½ cup kale
- Nori seaweed
- 2 radishes
- ½ cup green onion
- 2½ tbsp miso paste

Directions:

1. Add the water to a pan and boil it on medium heat for about 5 to 7 minutes.

2. Add mushrooms, cubed tofu, kale, a piece of Nori and chopped radish into the pan. Lower the heat and let it cook for 15 minutes.

3. Turn the heat off and add the green onions into the soup.

4. Put it on the heat for another 1 minute and add the miso paste.

5. Serve hot.

Nutrition: Calories: 113, Carbs: 21 g, Protein: 14 g, Fat: 6 g, Sugar: 1 g, Fiber: 2.5 g, Sodium: 236 mg

300.   Anti-Inflammatory Spring Pea Soup

Preparation Time: 5 minutes

Cooking Time: 15 minutes

Servings: 6

Ingredients:

- ½ tsp black pepper powder
- ½ tsp ground cumin
- 1 L vegetable stock
- 1 medium chopped onion
- 2 tbsp coconut oil
- 2 tsp Celtic sea salt
- 700 g fresh peas
- Chopped flat-leaf parsley
- Chopped mint leaves
- Fresh lemon juice
- Grated nutmeg
- Toasted sunflower seeds

Directions:

1. Warm the coconut oil in a pan set on moderate heat.

2. Mix in onions and stir fry for approximately 5 minutes.

3. Put in the stock and raise the heat. Throw in fresh peas and cook for 5 minutes. If you're using frozen peas, it should take half the time.

4. Pour in the lemon juice, salt, pepper, herbs, and spices. Stirring continuously

5. Remove the heat and allow it to cool before running it through a food processor to whatever consistency you prefer.

6. Serve with sunflower seed sprinkles and mint or parsley leaves.

7. Enjoy!

Nutrition: Calories: 115, Protein: 5 g, Fat: 5.91 g, Carbs: 11.8 g

301. Anti-Inflammatory Sweet Potato Soup

Preparation Time: 20 minutes

Cooking Time: 30 minutes

Servings: 8

Ingredients:

- 1 (13.66 oz) can lite coconut milk
- 1 big zucchini, cut width-wise
- 1 garlic clove
- 1 liter low-sodium vegetable stock
- 1 tbsp sweet yellow curry powder
- 1 tsp black pepper
- 1 tsp cayenne pepper
- 1 tsp turmeric
- 1 white onion
- 2 moderate-sized white potatoes
- 3 moderate-sized sweet potatoes
- ¾ tbsp salt
- 4 cups hot water
- 4 tbsp olive oil
- A pinch of cinnamon
- A pinch of cloves

Directions:

1. Cut, clean, and cube all of your vegetables before serving. Place in a secure location.

2. 4 tbsp extra virgin olive oil, added to a big pot. Allow it to quickly heat up before adding your

white onion. Allow for a minimum of 5 minutes of sweating on low heat.

3. Add all of your seasonings and garlic. Give it a good stir; at this point, add the potatoes.

4. Allow for a 5-minute cook time on low heat to achieve a pleasing deeper shade. Continue blending if you don't want to eat anything.

5. Place your stalk and water in a pot, bring to a boil, and then simmer for 20 to 25 minutes. Include your zucchini in the stewing process halfway through.

6. Include your coconut milk after 20 to 25 minutes. Do a fork content before pouring the soup into the blender to ensure your potatoes are cooked.

7. Purée the soup in your blender. Lemon juice, dark pepper, herbs, and tastes of your choice can be added to the dish.

Nutrition: Calories: 281, Protein: 4.1 g, Fat: 20.22 g, Carbs: 23.8 g

302. Bacon & Cheese Soup

Preparation Time: 15 minutes

Cooking Time: 40 minutes

Servings: 6

Ingredients:

- ½ cup sour cream, for serving
- ½ tsp cumin
- ½ tsp onion powder
- ½ tsp paprika
- 1 cup heavy cream
- 1 cup shredded cheddar cheese
- 1 lb lean ground beef
- 1 tbsp coconut oil, for cooking
- 1 tsp garlic powder
- 1 yellow onion, chopped
- 6 cups beef broth
- 6 slices uncured bacon

Directions:

1. Put the coconut oil into a frying pan and cook the bacon until crunchy. Allow the bacon to cool and cut into little pieces. Set aside.

2. Once cooked, put the lean ground beef in the same frying pan with the bacon fat and cook until browned.

3. Put in the onions and cook for an extra 2 to 3 minutes.

4. Put in all the ingredients minus the bacon, heavy cream, sour cream and cheese to a stockpot and stir. Cook for about 25 minutes.

5. Warm the heavy cream, and then put in the warmed cream and cheese and serve with the bacon and a spoonful of sour cream.

Nutrition: Calories: 498, Carbs: 5 g, Fiber: 1 g, Net Carbs: 4 g, Fat: 34 g, Protein: 41 g

303. Beef and Veggie Soup

Preparation Time: 10 minutes

Cooking Time: 20 minutes

Servings: 8

Ingredients:

- ½ cup heavy whipping cream
- ½ cup onion, chopped
- 1 (8 oz/227 g) package cream cheese, softened
- 1 lb (454 g) ground beef
- 1 tbsp ground cumin
- 1 tsp chili powder
- 2 (10 oz/284 g) cans diced tomatoes and green chiles
- 2 (14.5 oz/411 g) cans of beef broth
- 2 garlic cloves, minced
- 2 tsp salt, or to taste

Directions:

1. Position the ground beef, chopped onion, and garlic in a pot, and stir until blended well. Cook on moderate to high heat for 5 minutes or until the beef is thoroughly browned. Stir continuously.

2. Discard the grease extract from the beef, then put in chili powder and cumin, and cook for an extra 2 minutes. Stir continuously.

3. Put the cream cheese into the pot and cook for 3 to 5 minutes more, then fold in the tomatoes and green chiles, beef broth, heavy whipping cream, and salt, and cook for about 10 minutes to cook through. Keep stirring during the cooking.

4. Serve the soup in a big serving container. Allow standing for a couple of minutes before you serve.

Nutrition: Calories: 278, Total Fat: 24 g, Carbs: 5.4 g, Protein: 13.4 g, Cholesterol: 85 mg, Sodium: 1310 mg

304. Broccoli Cheddar & Bacon Soup

Preparation Time: 10 minutes

Cooking Time: 5 minutes

Servings: 6

Ingredients:

- ¼ tsp black pepper
- ½ tsp salt
- ½ white onion, chopped
- 1 cup broccoli florets finely chopped
- 1 cup heavy cream
- 1 cup shredded cheddar cheese
- 2 garlic cloves, chopped
- 2 cups chicken broth
- 3 slices cooked bacon, crumbled for serving

Directions:

1. Put in all the ingredients minus the heavy cream, cheddar cheese and bacon to a stockpot on moderate heat.

2. Heat to a simmer and cook for 5 minutes.

3. Warm the cream, and then put in the warm cream and cheddar cheese. Whisk until the desired smoothness is achieved.

4. Serve with crumbled bacon.

Nutrition: Calories: 220, Carbs: 4 g, Fiber: 1 g, Net Carbs: 3 g, Fat: 17 g, Protein: 11 g

305. Broccoli Soup with Gorgonzola Cheese

Preparation Time: 10 minutes

Cooking Time: 30 minutes

Servings: 4

Ingredients:

- ½ cup 18% cream
- 1 big broccoli, divided into little roses
- 1 flat tsp of sweet pepper
- 1 onion, diced
- 1 tbsp chopped fresh basil
- 1 tbsp chopped parsley
- 1 tbsp oil
- 150 g Gorgonzola cheese, diced
- 2 potatoes, peeled and diced
- 4 tbsp almond flakes roasted in a dry pan
- 5 garlic cloves, chopped
- 750 ml broth

- A pinch sugar
- Pumpkin oil (not necessary)
- Salt and pepper

Directions:

1. In a big deep cooking pan, warm the oil on moderate heat, put the onion and garlic, and fry it until the vitrified glass onion.

2. Then put the broccoli with potatoes, pour the broth and cook for approximately 15 to 20 minutes until the vegetables become tender. Put in basil, parsley, sugar, pepper, and pepper to taste.

3. Put in cheese and cream, and when the cheese dissolves, blend with a blender until the desired smoothness is achieved. Sprinkle with salt and pepper if required.

4. Serve the soup sprinkled with almond flakes and sprinkled with pumpkin oil.

Nutrition: Calories: 372, Protein: 13.06 g, Fat: 17.93 g, Carbs: 41.65 g

306. Brown Rice with Shitake Miso Soup and Scallion

Preparation Time: 10 minutes

Cooking Time: 45 minutes

Servings: 4

Ingredients:

- ½ tsp salt
- 1 (1½-inch) piece fresh ginger, peeled and cut
- 1 cup medium-grain brown rice
- 1 cup thinly cut shiitake mushroom caps
- 1 garlic clove, minced
- 1 tbsp white miso
- 2 scallions, thinly cut
- 2 tbsp finely chopped fresh cilantro
- 2 tbsp sesame oil

Directions:

1. In a large pot, heat the oil on moderate to high heat.

2. Put in the mushrooms, garlic, and ginger and sauté until the mushrooms start to tenderize approximately 5 minutes.

3. Place the rice and stir to uniformly coat with the oil.

4. Put in 2 cups of water and salt and place it to its boiling point.

5. Reduce the heat then cook until the rice is soft, 30 to 40 minutes.

6. Use a little of the soup broth to tenderize the miso, then mix it into the pot until well mixed.

7. Stir in the scallions and cilantro, then serve.

Nutrition: Calories: 265, Total Fat: 7 g, Total Carbs: 33 g, Sugar: 2 g, Fiber: 3 g, Protein: 5 g, Sodium: 446 mg

307. Buffalo Sauce and Turkey Soup

Preparation Time: 5 minutes

Cooking Time: 10 minutes

Servings: 4

Ingredients:

- ⅓ cup buffalo sauce
- 2 cups turkey, cooked, shredded
- 3 tbsp butter, melted
- 4 cups chicken broth
- 4 oz (113 g) cream cheese
- 4 tbsp cilantro, chopped
- Salt and freshly ground black pepper, to taste

Directions:

1. Place the buffalo sauce, cream cheese, and melted butter in a blender, and process until the desired smoothness is achieved.

2. Pour the buffalo sauce mixture into a deep cooking pan, and put in the chicken broth. Heat the soup using high heat until hot and nearly boil-off but not boiling. Keep stirring during the heating.

3. Put in the shredded turkey, and drizzle with salt and black pepper. Cook for 5 minutes or until the desired smoothness is achieved. Stir continuously.

4. Ladle the soup into a big container and top with chopped cilantro before you serve.

Nutrition: Calories: 419, Total Fat: 29.7 g, Net Carbs: 9.2 g, Protein: 26.4 g

308. Butternut Squash Soup with Shrimp

Preparation Time: 10 minutes

Cooking Time: 20 minutes

Servings: 4

Ingredients:

- ¼ cup slivered almonds (not necessary)
- ¼ tsp freshly ground black pepper
- 1 cup unsweetened almond milk
- 1 garlic clove, cut
- 1 lb cooked peeled shrimp, thawed if required
- 1 small red onion, finely chopped
- 1 tsp salt
- 1 tsp turmeric
- 2 cups peeled butternut squash cut into ¼-inch dice
- 2 tbsp finely chopped fresh flat-leaf parsley
- 2 tsp grated or minced lemon zest
- 3 cups vegetable broth
- 3 tbsp unsalted butter

Directions:

1. In a large pot, melt the butter on high heat.
2. Put in the onion, garlic, turmeric, salt, and pepper and sauté until the vegetables are tender and translucent for 5 minutes.
3. Put in the broth and squash and bring it to its boiling point.
4. Reduce the heat and cook until the squash has tenderized approximately 5 minutes.
5. Put in the shrimp and almond milk and cook until thoroughly heated, approximately 2 minutes.
6. Drizzle with the almonds (if using), parsley, and lemon zest before you serve.

Nutrition: Calories: 265, Total Fat: 12 g, Total Carbs: 12 g, Sugar: 3 g, Fiber: 2 g: Protein: 30 g, Sodium: 1765 mg

309. Cannellini Bean Soup

Preparation Time: 25 minutes

Cooking Time: 30 minutes

Servings: 6

Ingredients:

- 1 bunch red Swiss chard
- 1 cannellini beans
- 1 garlic clove (minced)
- 1 onion (chopped)
- 1 tbsp extra-virgin olive oil
- ¼ tsp nutmeg (grated)
- ⅛ tsp red pepper flakes (crushed)
- 2 oz Parmesan cheese rind
- 2 slices smoked bacon (chopped)
- 2 tbsp chopped sun-dried tomatoes
- 5 big sage leaves (minced)
- 5 leaves basil (chopped)
- 6 cups chicken broth

Directions:

1. Cook the bacon with garlic, onion, nutmeg, and red pepper flakes for 5 minutes.
2. Pour in beans, chicken broth, sun-dried tomatoes, and Parmesan cheese rind, simmering for about 10 minutes.
3. Put the cut chard and chard leaves into the soup.
4. Simmer and then put into bowls with a sprinkle of oil and Parmesan cheese.

Nutrition: Calories: 215, Carbs: 23 g, Fat: 10 g, Protein: 9.7 g

310. Carrot Broccoli Stew

Preparation Time: 10 minutes

Cooking Time: 40 minutes

Servings: 3

Ingredients:

- 1 cup broccoli, florets
- 1 cup carrots, cut
- 1 cup heavy cream
- 3 cups chicken broth
- Salt and black pepper to taste

Directions:

1. Put in florets, cream, carrots, salt, and chicken broth; toss thoroughly. Secure the lid and cook on Meat/Stew mode for 40 minutes on High. When ready, do a quick pressure release.
2. Move into serving bowls and drizzle black pepper on top.

Nutrition: Calories: 145, Protein: 1.5 g, Carbs: 1.2 g

311. Carrot, Ginger & Turmeric Soup

Preparation Time: 15 minutes

Cooking Time: 40 minutes

Servings: 8

Ingredients:

- ¼ cup full-fat unsweetened coconut milk
- ¾ lb carrots, peeled and chopped
- 1 sweet yellow onion, chopped
- 1 tsp ground turmeric
- 2 garlic cloves, chopped
- 2 tsp grated ginger
- 6 cups vegetable broth
- Pinch of sea salt & pepper, to taste

Directions:

1. Put in all the ingredients minus the coconut milk to a stockpot on moderate heat and bring to its boiling point. Reduce to a simmer and cook for 40 minutes or until the carrots are soft.

2. Use an immersion blender and blend the soup until the desired smoothness is achieved. Mix in the coconut milk.

3. Enjoy immediately and freeze any remaining.

Nutrition: Calories: 73, Carbs: 7 g, Fiber: 2 g, Net Carbs: 5 g, Fat: 3 g, Protein: 4 g

312. Cauliflower and Clam Chowder

Preparation Time: 10 minutes

Cooking Time: 10 minutes

Servings: 6

Ingredients:

- ½ tsp dried thyme
- 1 small yellow onion
- 1½ cup heavy whipping cream
- 3 (6.5 oz/184-g) cans chopped clams
- 3 tbsp butter
- 4 cups chopped cauliflower
- From the cupboard:
- Salt and freshly ground black pepper, to taste

Directions:

1. Split the clams and clam juice into 2 bowls. Thin the clam juice with water to make 2 cups of juice.

2. Place the onion and butter in an instant pot and press the Sauté bottom, then sauté for a couple of minutes or until the onion is translucent.

3. Put the clam juice and cauliflower into the instant pot. Place the lid on and press the Manual button, and set the temperature to 375°F (190°C), then cook for 5 minutes.

4. Quick Release the pressure, then open the lid and mix in the heavy cream and clams.

5. Push the Sauté bottom and cook for about 3 minutes or until the clams are opaque and firm, then drizzle with thyme, salt, and black pepper. Stir to mix thoroughly.

6. Ladle the chowder in a big container and serve warm.

Nutrition: Calories: 242, Total Fat: 17.3 g, Total Carbs: 8.9 g, Fiber: 2.1 g, Net Carbs: 6.7 g, Protein: 17.1 g

313. Cauliflower, Coconut Milk, and Shrimp Soup

Preparation Time: 5 minutes

Cooking Time: 2 hours 15 minutes

Servings: 4

Ingredients:

- 1 (13.5 oz/383 g) can unsweetened full-fat coconut milk
- 1 cup shrimp, peeled, deveined, tail off, and cooked
- 1 cup water
- 2 cups riced cauliflower
- 2 tbsp chopped fresh cilantro leaves, divided
- 2 tbsp red curry paste
- Salt and freshly ground black pepper, to taste

Directions:

1. Put in the riced cauliflower, red curry paste, coconut milk, 1 tbsp cilantro, and water, then drizzle with salt and black pepper. Combine the mixture to blend well.

2. Place the slow cooker lid on and cook on high for about 2 hours.

3. Place the shrimp on a clean working surface, then drizzle salt and black pepper to season.

4. Place the shrimp in the slow cooker and cook for 15 minutes more.

5. Move the soup into a big container and top with the rest of the cilantro leaves before you serve.

Nutrition: Calories: 268, Total Fat: 31.3 g, Total Carbs: 7.7 g, Fiber: 3.2 g, Net Carbs: 4.6 g, Protein: 16.1 g

314. Celery Soup

Preparation Time: 10 minutes

Cooking Time: 25 minutes

Servings: 4

Ingredients:

- ½ cup brown onion, chopped
- ½ cup full-fat milk
- ½ lb with sausage links, casing removed and cut
- ½ tsp dried chili flakes
- ½ tsp ground black pepper
- 1 carrot, chopped
- 1 garlic clove, pressed
- 2 tsp coconut oil
- 3 cups celery, chopped
- 3 cups roasted vegetable broth
- Kosher salt, to taste

Directions:

1. Simply throw all of the above ingredients into your Instant Pot; gently stir until blended.

2. Secure the lid. Choose "Soup/Broth" mode and High pressure; cook for about 25 minutes. Once cooking is complete, use a quick pressure release; cautiously remove the lid.

3. Ladle into 4 soup bowls and serve hot. Enjoy!

Nutrition: Calories: 140, Fat: 5.9 g, Total Carbs: 4.9 g, Protein: 16.4 g, Sugar: 4.1 g

315. Greek Spring Soup

Preparation Time: 10 minutes

Cooking Time: 25 minutes

Servings: 4

Ingredients:

- 1½ cups chicken, cooked and diced
- 1½ cups dill, fresh, chopped
- 6 cups vegetable broth
- 1 tsp black pepper
- ⅓ cup brown rice
- Chives, fresh minced for garnish
- 1 bay leaf
- 1 onion, small diced
- 1½ tsp salt
- 1 cup carrots, diced

- 1 cup asparagus, chopped
- 2 tbsp lemon juice
- 1 egg
- 2 tbsp olive oil

Directions:

1. Use a large pot for cooking the onions for 5 minutes. Pour in 1½ of the dill, the bay leaf, and the chicken broth and bring to a boil. Mix in the rice and lower the heat; simmer for 10 minutes.

2. Put in the carrots and asparagus and simmer for 10 more minutes. Continue simmering while adding the chicken, stir well. In a bowl, blend 2 tbsp of water with the lemon juice and the egg.

3. Pour a half cup of the hot soup into the egg mixture while you are stirring well, and then pour the egg mixture into the soup, stirring it constantly until it is well mixed. Remove the bay leaf when the soup has thickened.

4. Garnish with the fresh dill and the chives.

Nutrition: Calories: 341, Carbs: 30 g, Fiber: 4 g, Protein: 31 g, Fat: 9.7 g

316. Moroccan Lentil Soup

Preparation Time: 20 minutes

Cooking Time: 45 minutes

Servings: 6

Ingredients:

- 1 cup red lentils, dry, rinsed
- 28 oz whole tomatoes, canned, mashed with juice
- 1 (15 oz) can chickpeas, drain and rinse
- 1 tsp salt
- 1 tsp black pepper
- 8 cups vegetable broth, low salt
- 2 celery stalks, fine chop
- 1 onion, yellow, fine chop
- 2 tsp paprika
- 1 tsp cinnamon
- 1 tsp turmeric
- 2 tbsp ginger, minced
- ½ cup cilantro, chopped
- ½ cup parsley, chopped
- 2 tbsp olive oil

Directions:

1. Cook garlic, celery, ginger, carrots, and onion in hot oil for 10 minutes, stirring often.

2. Stir in the paprika, cinnamon, salt, pepper, and turmeric, cooking for 5 minutes to mix well.

3. Pour in the broth and tomatoes and mix well. Lower the heat to simmer and stir in the cilantro, chickpeas, parsley, and lentils. Simmer the soup for 30 minutes.

Nutrition: Calories: 238, Fat: 7.3 g, Fiber: 6.2 g, Carbs: 32 g, Protein: 14 g

317. Zucchini Soup

Preparation Time: 15 minutes

Cooking Time: 20 minutes

Servings: 8

Ingredients:

- 2½ lb zucchini, sliced
- 4 cups vegetable broth
- ⅓ cup basil, fresh
- 1½ tsp salt
- 1 medium onion, diced
- 1 tsp black pepper
- 2 tbsp olive oil
- 1 tsp rosemary
- 2 tbsp garlic, minced
- 1 tsp tarragon

Directions:

1. Cook zucchini, onion, and garlic for 5 minutes in hot oil stirring often.

2. Pour in broth and let the soup simmer for 15 minutes.

3. Mix in tarragon, rosemary, salt, and pepper and then blend the soup until it is creamy. Return to the stove just until warm.

Nutrition: Calories: 79, Carbs: 8.8 g, Fiber: 2.4 g, Protein: 1.6 g, Fat: 4.9 g

318. Roasted Cauliflower and Cheddar Soup

Preparation Time: 5 minutes

Cooking Time: 40 minutes

Servings: 8

Ingredients:

- 1 cauliflower head, chopped
- 2½ cups cheddar cheese, shredded
- 5 cups vegetable broth
- 1 tsp salt
- 1 tsp black pepper
- 2 tbsp olive oil
- 3 tbsp garlic, minced
- ½ medium onion, chopped
- 1 tsp garlic powder

Directions:

1. Heat oven to 425°F. Mix the chopped cauliflower with 1 tbsp of olive oil and the garlic powder, salt, and pepper to coat well. Bake the chopped cauliflower on a cookie sheet for 30 minutes.

2. Use the rest of the olive oil for cooking the onion in a large pot for 5 minutes. Place the cooked cauliflower and the broth in the pot and stir for 5 minutes while it starts to boil, then cook on low for 30 minutes.

3. Puree the soup in a blender, and then return it to the pot and stir in the cheese, mixing well.

Nutrition: Calories: 243, Protein: 13.7 g, Fiber: 2.3 g, Carbs: 8.3 g, Fat: 17 g

319. White Bean Soup

Preparation Time: 15 minutes

Cooking Time: 8 hours

Servings: 6

Ingredients:

- 2 cups Navy beans, dry
- 1½ tsp sage, dried
- 1 medium onion, chopped
- 1 cup celery, chopped
- 1 cup carrots, chopped
- 6 cups vegetable broth
- 1 tsp salt
- 1½ tsp basil, dried
- 1 tsp thyme, dried
- 1½ tsp rosemary, dried
- 2 tbsp garlic, minced

Directions:

1. Cook the soup at a low temperature in a crockpot for 8 hours.

Nutrition: Calories: 183, Fiber: 3.7 g, Protein: 4.5 g, Fat: 9.3 g, Carbs: 21.8 g

320. Halibut Chowder

Preparation Time: 20 minutes

Cooking Time: 1 hour 5 minutes

Servings: 8

Ingredients:

- 3 lb halibut steaks, cubed
- 2 tbsp garlic, minced
- 3 celery stalks, chopped
- 1 medium onion, peel and chop
- 1 red bell pepper, clean and chop
- 1½ tsp black pepper
- ¼ cup olive oil
- ¼ tsp thyme, dried
- 1 cup tomato juice
- 1½ tsp basil, dried
- 1½ cup apple juice
- 1 tsp salt
- 2 tbsp parsley, fresh, chopped
- 2 (16 oz) cans whole peeled tomatoes, mashed with juice

Directions:

1. Cook onion, garlic, celery, and peppers in hot oil in a large pot for 5 minutes. Mix in the herbs, apple juice, mashed tomatoes, and tomato juice and stir well.

2. Simmer this mixture for 30 minutes. Drop the pieces of halibut into the soup while stirring. Add in the salt and pepper and simmer for 30 minutes.

Nutrition: Calories: 262, Fat: 10.3 g, Carbs: 10.7 g, Protein: 31.2 g, Fiber: 2.1 g

321. Beef Barley Soup

Preparation Time: 10 minutes

Cooking Time: 5 hours

Servings: 6

Ingredients:

- 1 tbsp parsley, chopped
- 2 lb beef chuck roast, cubed
- 1 tsp rosemary
- 2 tbsp beef bouillon, granulated
- 1 tsp black pepper
- 1 cup pearl barley, uncooked
- 5 cups water
- 1½ tsp salt

- 1 (8 oz) can tomato sauce
- 1½ onion, chopped

Directions:

1. Use a crockpot to cook the barley, tomato sauce, onion, salt, pepper, bouillon, water, and beef for 5 hours on low.

Nutrition: Calories: 512, Fat: 27.8 g, Carbs: 35.4 g, Fiber: 5 g, Protein: 29.7 g

322. Cabbage and Smoked Sausage Soup

Preparation Time: 20 minutes

Cooking Time: 1 hour 5 minutes

Servings: 8

Ingredients:

- 1 lb smoked sausage, sliced thinly
- 1 cabbage head, remove the core and chop fine
- 1 onion, chopped
- 3 celery stalks sliced
- 3 carrots sliced
- 1½ tsp thyme, crushed
- 1 bay leaf
- 1½ tsp salt
- 2 chicken bouillon cubes
- 1 (28 oz) can crushed tomatoes
- 1 (8 oz) can tomato sauce
- 1 (15 oz) can red beans, with liquid
- 1½ cup brown rice, uncooked
- 3 cups water
- 1 tbsp olive oil

Directions:

1. Cook the onion in a large skillet in olive oil for 5 minutes. Stir in the water and sausage. Add in tomato sauce, crushed tomatoes, rice, beans, carrots, celery, and cabbage and mix well.

2. Mix in the bay leaf, thyme, salt, and bouillon. Boil for 1 minute, then lower the heat and let it simmer for 1 hour.

Nutrition: Calories: 404, Fat: 20.6 g, Carbs: 37.4 g, Fiber: 9.8 g, Protein: 20.3 g

323. Eggplant Chickpea Stew

Preparation Time: 30 minutes

Cooking Time: 20 minutes

Servings: 2

Ingredients:

- 1 eggplant, peeled and cubed
- 1 tsp black pepper
- 1 (14 oz) can chickpeas, drain and rinse
- 1 (14 oz) can tomatoes, drained
- 1½ tsp salt
- 1 tbsp hot sauce, any brand
- 1 tsp rosemary
- 1½ tsp thyme
- 3 tbsp olive oil
- 2 tbsp garlic powder
- 1 tbsp cilantro
- 1 onion, diced fine

Directions:

1. Fry the salt, onion, eggplant, garlic, and pepper in the olive oil for 5 minutes.
2. Pour in the chickpeas, tomatoes, and hot sauce; mix well and simmer for 15 minutes.

Nutrition: Calories: 350, Protein: 12 g, Fat: 10 g, Carbs: 16 g

324. Red Pepper and Tomato Soup

Preparation Time: 15 minutes

Cooking Time: 45 minutes

Servings: 4

Ingredients:

- 2 red bell peppers, seeded and diced
- 2 tbsp tomato paste
- 3 tomatoes, clean and diced
- 1½ tsp paprika, ground
- ¼ cup parsley, fresh, chopped
- 1 tsp black pepper
- 2 cups vegetable broth
- 2 tbsp garlic, minced
- ¼ tsp cayenne pepper
- 1½ tsp Italian seasoning
- 3 tbsp olive oil
- 1 medium onion, cut into quarters
- 1½ tsp salt

Directions:

1. Heat oven to 425°F. Use a large mixing bowl to mix the red pepper, garlic, tomatoes, and onion, with the pepper, salt, and olive oil. Spread the veggies on a lined baking pan and bake uncovered for 45 minutes.
2. Pour the vegetable broth into a pot and heat it to boiling, and then turn the heat down and add in the roasted veggies. Stir this mixture well and simmer for 5 minutes and serve.

Nutrition: Calories: 150, Carbs: 14g, Protein: 4g, Fat: 4g

325. Tuscany Vegetable Soup

Preparation Time: 15 minutes

Cooking Time: 30 minutes

Servings: 8

Ingredients:

- 2 large tomatoes, diced small
- 1 medium zucchini, peeled and chopped
- 1½ cup celery, chopped
- 1½ cup carrot, chopped
- 1 medium yellow onion, diced
- Parsley, fresh and chopped for garnish
- 3 tbsp olive oil
- 1½ tsp salt
- 2 tbsp garlic, minced
- 1 tsp black pepper
- 6 cups vegetable broth
- 1 tbsp basil, chopped
- 2 cups kale, chopped
- 2 tbsp tomato paste

Directions:

1. Fry the garlic and the onion in the heated olive oil in a large pan. Then add in the zucchini, celery, and carrots and cook for 10 minutes, stirring frequently. Mix in the salt, pepper, and tomatoes, and cook for 2 more minutes.
2. Pour in the vegetable broth and the tomato paste and boil. Turn lower the heat and let the mixture simmer for 15 minutes.
3. Put in the basil and the parsley, then remove the pot from the heat and let the soup sit for 10 minutes. Top soup with fresh parsley and serve.

Nutrition: Calories: 225, Fat: 6 g, Protein: 17 g, Carbs: 12 g

326.   Cheesy Cauliflower Soup

Preparation Time: 10 minutes

Cooking Time: 15 minutes

Servings: 6

Ingredients:

- 8 oz cheddar cheese, grated
- 1 shallot
- 2 cups heavy cream
- 1½ tsp salt
- 2 cups vegetable stock
- 2 tbsp garlic, minced
- 1 tsp black pepper
- 1 tbsp olive oil
- 1 large head cauliflower, grated

Directions:

1. Cook the garlic and the shallot in a large pot with olive oil. Place the cauliflower in the pot and mix well with the olive oil and cook for 5 minutes. Add in the vegetable stock and the heavy cream and boil.

2. Cook low for 5 minutes. Blend in the pepper, salt, and cheese, stirring gently for a minute and serve.

Nutrition: Calories: 227, Carbs: 9 g, Protein: 10 g, Fat: 16 g

327.   Creole Chicken Gumbo

Preparation Time: 20 minutes

Cooking Time: 25 minutes

Servings: 6

Ingredients:

- 1 cup cooked chicken, diced
- 4 cups chicken broth
- 4 regular cans tomatoes, stewed
- 3 tbsp olive oil
- 1½ cup green bell pepper, chopped
- 1 cup okra, fresh, chunked
- 1 tsp salt
- 1 tsp black pepper
- 2 tbsp parsley, chopped

Directions:

1. Cook the okra, onion, and green pepper for 10 minutes in the olive oil. Add the tomatoes and

broth and boil for 15 minutes. Add chicken and parsley, stir well and serve.

Nutrition: Calories: 227, Carbs: 19g, Fat: 3g, Protein: 6g

328.   Quinoa Chili

Preparation Time: 10 minutes

Cooking Time: 30 minutes

Servings:

Ingredients:

- 1 cup quinoa, cooked
- 1 can kidney beans, rinsed
- 1 tbsp oil
- 1 can black beans, rinsed
- 3 tbsp cilantro, fresh chopped
- 1 avocado, peeled and thinly sliced
- 1 tsp black pepper,
- 3 garlic cloves minced
- 1 small onion, diced
- 1 tsp salt
- 1 can tomatoes, diced
- 1 (15 oz) can tomato sauce
- 5 oz green chilies, canned
- 1 tbsp chili powder
- 2 tsp cumin, ground
- 1 tsp paprika
- 1½ tsp cayenne pepper
- 1 package corn, thawed

Directions:

1. Cook onion and garlic in oil for 3 minutes. Add quinoa, paprika, cayenne pepper, chili powder, cumin, tomato sauce, green chilies, tomatoes, and 2 cups of water.

2. Season with pepper and salt and simmer for 30 minutes. Add corn, cilantro, and beans and heat for 5 minutes.

Nutrition: Calories: 337, Carbs: 64 g, Fiber: 12 g, Protein: 17 g, Fat: 3 g

329.   Tomato Basil Chicken Stew

Preparation Time: 15 minutes

Cooking Time: 30 minutes

Servings: 4

Ingredients:

- 3 cups chicken, diced and cooked
- ¼ tsp red pepper flakes, crushed

- ¼ cup basil, fresh chopped
- 2 (28 oz) cans whole tomatoes, with juice
- 1 tsp black pepper,
- 1 can white beans, rinsed
- 1 tsp salt
- 1 tbsp olive oil
- 1 small onion, chopped
- 2 carrots, peeled and diced
- 2 celery stalks, diced
- 4 garlic cloves, minced
- 2 cups baby spinach

Directions:

1. Warm oil in a large pot and add carrots, celery, and onion and cook for 10 minutes. Add in the garlic and cook for 2 minutes.

2. Add the rest of the ingredients and stir well. Boil the mixture, and then simmer for 15 minutes and serve.

Nutrition: Calories: 330, Carbs: 24 g, Fiber: 7 g, Protein: 28 g, Fat: 15 g

330.   Minestrone

Preparation Time: 20 minutes

Cooking Time: 1 hour

Servings: 8

Ingredients:

- ¼ cup cheese, Parmesan or Romano, shredded
- 1 tsp black pepper
- 4 cups baby spinach, fresh
- 1½ tsp basil
- 1 medium yellow squash, thinly sliced
- 1 medium zucchini, thinly sliced
- ½ cup carrots, diced
- 4 tbsp garlic, minced
- 1 small white onion, minced
- 1 cup pasta shells, whole wheat
- 2 tsp oregano
- 2 cups water
- 4 cups vegetable broth
- 3 tbsp olive oil
- ½ cup celery, thinly sliced
- ¼ tsp thyme
- 2 tbsp parsley, fresh minced
- 1 (15 oz) can tomatoes, diced, fire-roasted
- 1 tsp salt
- 2 (15 oz) cans red kidney beans, rinse and drain
- 2 (15 oz) cans cannellini beans, rinse and drain

Directions:

1. Cook parsley, celery, zucchini, squash, garlic, carrots, and onion in hot olive oil in a large pot for 5 minutes, stirring often.

2. Pour in water, diced tomatoes, kidney beans, herbs, salt, pepper, cannellini beans, and broth and stir well to blend flavors.

3. Boil the mix, then lower the heat and simmer for 30 minutes. Drop in the pasta and spinach and simmer for 30 more minutes. Mix in the grated cheese and serve immediately.

Nutrition: Calories: 110, Carbs: 17 g, Fiber: 4 g, Protein: 5 g, Fat: 1 g

331.   Pasta Faggioli

Preparation Time: 10 minutes

Cooking Time: 1 hour 10 minutes

Servings: 8

Ingredients:

- 1 lb Ditalini pasta, cooks by package directions
- ⅓ cup Parmesan cheese, grated
- 2 tbsp garlic, minced
- 1 onion, peeled and chunked
- 3 tbsp olive oil
- 1 (15 oz) can navy beans, drain and rinse
- 1 (15 oz) can cannellini beans, drain and rinse
- 1 tsp salt
- 1½ tsp oregano, dried
- 1½ tsp basil, dried
- 1 tbsp parsley
- 6 cups water
- 1 (29 oz) can tomato sauce

Directions:

1. Cook the garlic and onion in a large pot in olive oil for 5 minutes.

2. Lower the heat and add water, navy beans, cannellini beans, parmesan cheese, parsley, salt, oregano, basil, and tomato sauce, stir well and simmer for 1 hour. Mix in cooked pasta and simmer for 5 more minutes.

Nutrition: Calories: 403, Carbs: 68 g, Fiber: 8.4 g, Protein: 16.3 g, Fat: 7.6 g

Chapter 10

Vegetable

332. Beets and Carrots Bowls

Preparation Time: 10 minutes

Cooking Time: 7 hours

Servings: 8

Ingredients:

- 2 tbsp stevia
- ¾ cup pomegranate juice
- 2 tsp ginger, grated
- 2½ lb beets, peeled and cut into wedges
- 12 oz carrots, cut into medium wedges

Directions:

1. In your Slow cooker, mix beets with carrots, ginger, stevia, and pomegranate juice, toss, cover, and cook on Low for 7 hours.

2. Divide between plates and serve as a side dish.

Nutrition: Calories: 95, Protein: 2.7 g, Carbs: 22.1 g, Fat: 0.3 g, Fiber: 4 g, Cholesterol: 0 mg, Sodium: 140 mg, Potassium: 631 mg

333. Italian Style Vegetable Mix

Preparation Time: 10 minutes

Cooking Time: 6 hours

Servings: 8

Ingredients:

- 38 oz canned cannellini beans, drained
- 1 yellow onion, chopped
- ¼ cup basil pesto
- 19 oz fava beans, drained
- 4 garlic cloves, minced
- 1½ tsp Italian seasoning, dried and crushed
- 1 tomato, chopped
- 2 cups spinach
- 1 cup radicchio, torn

Directions:

1. In your slow cooker, mix cannellini beans with fava beans, basil pesto, onion, garlic, Italian seasoning, tomato, spinach, and radicchio, toss, cover, and cook on Low for 6 hours.

2. Divide between plates and serve as a side dish.

Nutrition: Calories: 690, Protein: 50 g, Carbs: 122.7 g, Fat: 2.2 g, Fiber: 51 g, Cholesterol: 0 mg, Sodium: 49 mg, Potassium: 2712 mg

334. Wild Rice Pilaf

Preparation Time: 10 minutes

Cooking Time: 7 hours

Servings: 12

Ingredients:

- ½ cup wild rice
- ½ cup barley
- ⅔ cup wheat berries
- 27 oz vegetable stock
- 2 cups baby lima beans
- 1 red bell pepper, chopped
- 1 yellow onion, chopped
- 1 tbsp olive oil
- 1 tsp sage, dried and crushed
- 4 garlic cloves, minced

Directions:

1. In your slow cooker, mix rice with barley, wheat berries, stock, lima beans, bell pepper, onion, oil, sage, and garlic, stir, cover, and cook on Low for 7 hours.

2. Stir one more time, divide between plates and serve as a side dish.

Nutrition: Calories: 115, Protein: 4.7 g, Carbs: 21 g, Fat: 1.7 g, Fiber: 3.7 g, Cholesterol: 0 mg, Sodium: 37 mg, Potassium: 231 mg

335. Apples Mix

Preparation Time: 10 minutes

Cooking Time: 7 hours

Servings: 10

Ingredients:

- 2 green apples, cored and cut into wedges
- 3 lb sweet potatoes, peeled and cut into medium wedges
- 1 cup coconut cream
- 1 cup apple butter
- 1½ tsp pumpkin pie spice

Directions:

1. In your slow cooker, mix sweet potatoes with green apples, cream, apple butter, and spice, toss, cover, and cook on Low for 7 hours.
2. Toss, divide between plates and serve as a side dish.

Nutrition: Calories: 288, Protein: 2.9 g, Carbs: 57.4 g, Fat: 6.1 g, Fiber: 7.6 g, Cholesterol: 0 mg, Sodium: 20 mg, Potassium: 1247 mg

336. Asparagus Mix

Preparation Time: 10 minutes

Cooking Time: 5 hours

Servings: 4

Ingredients:

- 2 lb asparagus spears, cut into medium pieces
- 1 cup mushrooms, sliced
- A drizzle olive oil
- 2 cups coconut milk
- 5 eggs, whisked

Directions:

1. Grease your Slow cooker with the oil and spread asparagus and mushrooms on the bottom.
2. In a bowl, mix the eggs with milk, and whisk, pour into the slow cooker, toss everything, and cover and cook on Low for 6 hours.
3. Divide between plates and serve as a side dish.

Nutrition: Calories: 404, Protein: 15.2 g, Carbs: 65.5 g, Fat: 34.4 g, Fiber: 7.6 g, Cholesterol: 205 mg, Sodium: 101 mg, Potassium: 903 mg

337. Asparagus and Eggs Mix

Preparation Time: 10 minutes

Cooking Time: 6 hours

Servings: 4

Ingredients:

- 10 oz cream celery
- 12 oz asparagus, chopped
- 2 eggs, hard-boiled, peeled and sliced
- 5 oz tofu, crumbled
- 1 tsp olive oil

Directions:

1. Grease your Slow cooker with the oil, add cream of celery and tofu to the slow cooker and stir.
2. Add asparagus and eggs, cover, and cook on Low for 6 hours.
3. Divide between plates and serve as a side dish.

Nutrition: Calories: 134, Protein: 8.5 g, Carbs: 9.1 g, Fat: 8.1 g, Fiber: 2.5 g, Cholesterol: 0 mg, Sodium: 573 mg, Potassium: 323 mg

338. Classic Vegetable Meals

Preparation Time: 10 minutes

Cooking Time: 3 hours

Servings: 4

Ingredients:

- 1½ cups red onion, cut into medium chunks
- 1 cup cherry tomatoes, halved
- 2½ cups zucchini, sliced
- 2 cups yellow bell pepper, chopped
- 1 cup mushrooms, sliced
- 2 tbsp basil, chopped
- 1 tbsp thyme, chopped
- ½ cup olive oil
- ½ cup balsamic vinegar

Directions:

1. In your slow cooker, mix onion pieces with tomatoes, zucchini, bell pepper, mushrooms, basil, thyme, oil, and vinegar, toss to coat everything, cover, and cook on High for 3 hours.
2. Divide between plates and serve as a side dish.

Nutrition: Calories: 295, Protein: 3.7 g, Carbs: 16.3 g, Fat: 25.7 g, Fiber: 4.3 g, Cholesterol: 0 mg, Sodium: 22 mg, Potassium: 739 mg

339. Okra and Mushrooms Side Dish

Preparation Time: 10 minutes

Cooking Time: 3 hours

Servings: 4

Ingredients:

- 2 cups okra, sliced
- 1½ cups red onion, roughly chopped
- 1 cup cherry tomatoes, halved
- 2½ cups zucchini, sliced
- 2 cups bell peppers, sliced
- 1 cup white mushrooms, sliced
- ½ cup olive oil
- ½ cup balsamic vinegar
- 2 tbsp basil, chopped
- 1 tbsp thyme, chopped

Directions:

1. In your slow cooker, mix okra with onion, tomatoes, zucchini, bell peppers, mushrooms, basil, and thyme.
2. In a bowl mix oil with vinegar, whisk well, add to the slow cooker, cover and cook on High for 3 hours.
3. Divide between plates and serve as a side dish.

Nutrition: Calories: 304, Protein: 3.9 g, Carbs: 17.7 g, Fat: 25.7 g, Fiber: 5.1 g, Cholesterol: 0 mg, Sodium: 19 mg, Potassium: 703 mg

340. Okra and Tomato Sauce Mix

Preparation Time: 10 minutes

Cooking Time: 8 hours

Servings: 4

Ingredients:

- 2 garlic cloves, minced
- 1 yellow onion, chopped
- 14 oz tomato sauce
- 1 tsp sweet paprika
- 2 cups okra, sliced

Directions:

1. In your Slow cooker, mix garlic with the onion, tomato sauce, paprika, and okra, cover and cook on Low for 8 hours.
2. Divide between plates and serve as a side dish.

Nutrition: Calories: 59, Protein: 2.7 g, Carbs: 12.3 g, Fat: 0.4 g, Fiber: 3.9 g, Cholesterol: 0 mg, Sodium: 525 mg, Potassium: 537 mg

341. Stewed Okra with Cayenne Pepper

Preparation Time: 10 minutes

Cooking Time: 3 hours

Servings: 4

Ingredients:

- 2 cups okra, sliced
- 2 garlic cloves, minced
- 6 oz tomato sauce
- 1 red onion, chopped
- A pinch of cayenne peppers

Directions:

1. In your Slow cooker, mix okra with garlic, onion, cayenne, and tomato sauce, cover and cook on Low for 3 hours.
2. Divide between plates and serve as a side dish.

Nutrition: Calories: 43, Protein: 1.9 g, Carbs: 9.1 g, Fat: 0.2 g, Fiber: 2.9 g, Cholesterol: 0 mg, Sodium: 228 mg, Potassium: 336 mg

342. Okra and Corn Bowls

Preparation Time: 10 minutes

Cooking Time: 8 hours

Servings: 4

Ingredients:

- 3 garlic cloves, minced
- 1 small green bell pepper, chopped
- 1 small yellow onion, chopped
- 1 cup water
- 16 oz okra, sliced
- 2 cups corn kernels
- 1½ tsp smoked paprika
- 28 oz canned tomatoes, crushed
- 1 tsp oregano, dried
- 1 tsp thyme, dried
- 1 tsp marjoram, dried

- A pinch of cayenne pepper

Directions:

1. In your slow cooker, mix garlic with bell pepper, onion, water, okra, corn, paprika, tomatoes, oregano, thyme, marjoram, and pepper, cover, and cook on Low for 8 hours, divide between plates and serve as a side dish.

Nutrition: Calories: 171, Protein: 7.3 g, Carbs: 36.3 g, Fat: 1.7 g, Fiber: 9.6 g, Cholesterol: 0 mg, Sodium: 33 mg, Potassium: 1138 mg

343. Roasted Beets with Olive Oil

Preparation Time: 10 minutes

Cooking Time: 4 hours

Servings: 5

Ingredients:

- 10 small beets
- 5 tsp olive oil

Directions:

1. Divide each beet on a tin foil piece, drizzle oil, wrap beets in the foil, place them in your slow cooker, and cover and cook on High for 4 hours.

2. Unwrap beets, cool them down a bit, peel, and slice and serve them as a side dish.

Nutrition: Calories: 128, Protein: 3.4 g, Carbs: 19.9 g, Fat: 5 g, Fiber: 4 g, Cholesterol: 0 mg, Sodium: 154 mg, Potassium: 610 mg

344. Thyme Beets with Garlic

Preparation Time: 10 minutes

Cooking Time: 6 hours

Servings: 8

Ingredients:

- 12 small beets, peeled and sliced
- ¼ cup water
- 4 garlic cloves, minced
- 2 tbsp olive oil
- 1 tsp thyme, dried
- 1 tbsp fresh thyme, chopped

Directions:

1. In your Slow cooker, mix beets with water, garlic, oil, and dried thyme, cover, and cook on Low for 6 hours.

2. Divide beets on plates, sprinkle fresh thyme all over and serve as a side dish.

Nutrition: Calories: 99, Protein: 2.6 g, Carbs: 15.5 g, Fat: 3.7 g, Fiber: 3.1 g, Cholesterol: 0 mg, Sodium: 116 mg, Potassium: 465 mg

345. Beets and Honey Side Salad

Preparation Time: 10 minutes

Cooking Time: 7 hours

Servings: 12

Ingredients:

- 5 beets, peeled and sliced
- ¼ cup balsamic vinegar
- ⅓ cup honey
- 1 tbsp rosemary, chopped
- 2 tbsp olive oil
- 2 garlic cloves, minced

Directions:

1. In your Slow cooker, mix beets with vinegar, honey, oil, rosemary, and garlic, cover, and cook on Low for 7 hours.

2. Divide between plates and serve as a side dish.

Nutrition: Calories: 70, Protein: 0.7 g, Carbs: 12.3 g, Fat: 2.5 g, Fiber: 1 g, Cholesterol: 0 mg, Sodium: 33 mg, Potassium: 140 mg

346. Lemony Beets with White Vinegar

Preparation Time: 10 minutes

Cooking Time: 8 hours

Servings: 6

Ingredients:

- 6 beets, peeled and cut into medium wedges
- 2 tbsp honey
- 2 tbsp olive oil
- 2 tbsp lemon juice
- 1 tbsp white vinegar
- ½ tsp lemon peel, grated

Directions:

1. In your Slow cooker, mix beets with honey, oil, lemon juice, vinegar, and lemon peel, cover, and cook on Low for 8 hours.

2. Divide between plates and serve as a side dish.

Nutrition: Calories: 107, Protein: 1.7 g, Carbs: 15.9 g, Fat: 4.9 g, Fiber: 2 g, Cholesterol: 0 mg, Sodium: 78 mg, Potassium: 317 mg

347. Carrot Side Salad

Preparation Time: 10 minutes

Cooking Time: 7 hours

Servings: 6

Ingredients:

- ½ cup walnuts, chopped
- ¼ cup lemon juice
- ½ cup olive oil
- 1 shallot, chopped
- 1 tsp Dijon mustard
- 1 tbsp honey
- 2 beets, peeled and cut into wedges
- 2 carrots, peeled and sliced
- 1 cup parsley
- 5 oz arugula

Directions:

1. In your Slow cooker, mix beets with carrots, honey, mustard, shallot, oil, lemon juice, and walnuts, cover, and cook on Low for 7 hours.

2. Transfer everything to a bowl, add parsley and arugula, toss, divide between plates and serve as a side dish.

Nutrition: Calories: 256, Protein: 4.3 g, Carbs: 11.3 g, Fat: 23.4 g, Fiber: 2.7 g, Cholesterol: 0 mg, Sodium: 64 mg, Potassium: 385 mg

348. Cauliflower Gratin

Preparation Time: 10 minutes

Cooking Time: 7 hours

Servings: 12

Ingredients:

- 16 oz baby carrots
- 6 tbsp pumpkin puree
- 1 cauliflower head, florets separated
- 1 yellow onion, chopped
- 1 tsp mustard powder
- 1½ cups coconut milk
- 6 oz tofu, crumbled

Directions:

1. Put the pumpkin puree in your Slow cooker, add carrots, cauliflower, onion, mustard powder, and coconut milk, and toss.

2. Sprinkle tofu all over, cover, and cook on Low for 7 hours.

3. Divide between plates and serve as a side dish.

Nutrition: Calories: 105, Protein: 2.7 g, Carbs: 7.7 g, Fat: 7.9 g, Fiber: 2.9 g, Cholesterol: 0 mg, Sodium: 43 mg, Potassium: 287 mg

349. Tarragon Beets

Preparation Time: 10 minutes

Cooking Time: 7 hours

Servings: 4

Ingredients:

- 6 medium assorted-color beets, peeled and cut into wedges
- 2 tbsp balsamic vinegar
- 2 tbsp olive oil
- 2 tbsp chives, chopped
- 1 tbsp tarragon, chopped
- 1 tsp orange peel, grated

Directions:

1. In your Slow cooker, mix beets with vinegar, oil, chives, tarragon, and orange peel, cover and cook on Low for 7 hours.

2. Divide between plates and serve as a side dish.

Nutrition: Calories: 130, Protein: 2.7 g, Carbs: 15.4 g, Fat: 7.3 g, Fiber: 3.1 g, Cholesterol: 0 mg, Sodium: 116 mg, Potassium: 482 mg

350. Summer Mix

Preparation Time: 10 minutes

Cooking Time: 2 hours

Servings: 4

Ingredients:

- ¼ cup olive oil
- 2 tbsp basil, chopped
- 2 tbsp balsamic vinegar
- 2 garlic cloves, minced
- 2 tsp mustard
- 3 summer squash, sliced
- 2 zucchinis, sliced

Directions:

1. In your Slow cooker, mix squash with zucchinis, mustard, garlic, vinegar, basil, and oil, toss a bit, cover, and cook on High for 2 hours.

2. Divide between plates and serve as a side dish.

Nutrition: Calories: 154, Protein: 2.7 g, Carbs: 8.2 g, Fat: 13.5 g, Fiber: 2.4 g, Cholesterol: 0 mg, Sodium: 13 mg, Potassium: 495 mg

351. Instant Pot Collard Greens

Preparation Time: 5 minutes

Cooking Time: 60 minutes

Servings: 6

Ingredients:

- 2 lb collard greens, shredded
- 1 organic turkey bone
- 6 cups water
- ¼ tsp red pepper flakes
- Salt and pepper to taste

Directions:

1. Place all ingredients in the Instant Pot.

2. Give a good stir.

3. Close the lid and make sure that the steam release valve is set to "Sealing."

4. Press the Manual button and adjust the cooking time to 60 minutes.

5. Do manual pressure release.

Nutrition: Calories: 71, Carbs: 5 g, Protein: 7 g, Fat: 2 g, Sugar: 0 g, Sodium: 57 mg, Fiber: 3 g

352. Braised Kale and Carrots

Preparation Time: 5 minutes

Cooking Time: 12 minutes

Servings: 6

Ingredients:

- 1 tbsp olive oil
- 3 onions, chopped
- 5 garlic cloves, minced
- 1 carrot, peeled and julienned
- 3 cups kale, chopped
- ½ cup water
- Salt and pepper to taste
- ¼ tsp red pepper flakes

Directions:

1. Press the Sauté button on the Instant Pot and heat the oil.

2. Stir in the onions and garlic. Stir for 2 minutes until fragrant.

3. Add the rest of the ingredients.

4. Close the lid and make sure that the steam release valve is set to "Sealing."

5. Press the Manual button and adjust the cooking time to 10 minutes.

6. Do quick pressure release.

Nutrition: Calories: 107, Carbs: 8.5 g, Protein: 1.4 g, Fat: 2.4 g, Sugar: 0 g, Sodium: 14 mg, Fiber: 5.3 g

353. Instant Pot Saag Aloo

Preparation Time: 5 minutes

Cooking Time: 18 minutes

Servings: 6

Ingredients:

- 1 tbsp olive oil
- 1 tsp cumin seeds, whole
- 1 tbsp coriander powder
- ½ tsp turmeric powder
- ½ tsp red chili flakes
- 1 red onion, chopped
- 1 thumb-size ginger
- 1 package frozen kale, torn
- 1½ cups water
- Salt and pepper to taste

Directions:

1. Press the Sauté button on the Instant Pot.

2. Heat the oil and stir in the cumin seeds, coriander, turmeric, and red chili flakes. Keep stirring until a little bit toasted.

3. Stir in the onion and ginger and continue stirring for another minute.

4. Add the rest of the ingredients.

5. Close the lid and make sure that the steam release valve is set to "Sealing."

6. Press the Manual button and adjust the cooking time to 15 minutes or until the kale leaves are very soft.

Nutrition: Calories: 39, Carbs: 3.4 g, Protein: 1.5 g, Fat: 2.6 g, Sugar: 0 g, Sodium: 18 mg, Fiber: 2.1 g

354. 3-Minute Instant Pot Kale

Preparation Time: 5 minutes

Cooking Time: 3 minutes

Servings: 3

Ingredients:

- 2 tbsp extra virgin olive oil
- 2 large heads kale, chopped
- ¾ tsp salt
- ⅛ tsp red pepper flakes, crushed
- ⅓ cup water
- 1 tbsp lemon juice, freshly squeezed

Directions:

1. Place all ingredients in the Instant Pot.

2. Close the lid and make sure that the steam release valve is set to "Sealing."

3. Press the Manual button and adjust the cooking time to 3 minutes.

4. Do manual pressure release.

Nutrition: Calories: 60, Carbs: 4.4 g, Protein: 2.1 g, Fat: 4.4 g, Sugar: 0 g, Sodium: 129 mg, Fiber: 3.1 g

355. Instant Pot Turnip Greens

Preparation Time: 5 minutes

Cooking Time: 10 minutes

Servings: 3

Ingredients:

- 1 bag turnip greens, chopped
- ¼ cup diced onions
- ½ cup organic chicken broth
- Salt and pepper to taste

Directions:

1. Place all ingredients in the Instant Pot.

2. Give a good stir.

3. Close the lid and make sure that the steam release valve is set to "Sealing."

4. Press the Manual button and adjust the cooking time to 10 minutes.

Nutrition: Calories: 18, Carbs: 3.7 g, Protein: 0.9 g, Fat: 0.2 g, Sugar: 0 g, Sodium: 163 mg, Fiber: 1.9 g

356. Sarson Ka Saag (Spiced Mustard Greens)

Preparation Time: 5 minutes

Cooking Time: 12 minutes

Servings: 4

Ingredients:

- 2 tsp olive oil
- 1 tsp cumin seeds
- 2 tbsp grated ginger
- 1 onion, chopped
- ½ tsp turmeric powder
- 2 tsp coriander powder
- 1 tsp garam masala
- 1 bunch mustard greens, chopped
- 1 bunch spinach leaves, chopped
- 2 green chilies, chopped
- ¾ cup water

Directions:

1. Press the Sauté button on the Instant Pot.

2. Heat the oil and sauté the cumin seeds, ginger, onion, turmeric powder, coriander powder, and garam masala for 2 minutes or until fragrant.

3. Stir in the mustard greens, spinach, and chilies.

4. Pour in water.

5. Close the lid and set the steam release valve to "Sealing."

6. Press the Manual button and adjust the cooking time to 10 minutes.

7. Do quick pressure releases.

Nutrition: Calories: 40, Carbs: 4.2 g, Protein: 0.9 g, Fat: 2.5 g, Sugar: 0 g, Sodium: 6 mg, Fiber: 2.1 g

357. Spicy Turnip Greens

Preparation Time: 5 minutes

Cooking Time: 11 minutes

Servings: 6

Ingredients:

- 1 tbsp olive oil
- 1 onion, cut into wedges
- 1 lb turnip greens
- ¼ cup water
- ⅛ tsp red pepper flakes
- Salt and pepper to taste

Directions:

1. Press the Sauté button on the Instant Pot and heat the oil.

2. Sauté the onion for 1 minute until fragrant.

3. Stir in the rest of the ingredients.

4. Close the lid and make sure that the steam release valve is set to "Sealing."

5. Press the Manual button and adjust the cooking time to 10 minutes.

Nutrition: Calories: 57, Carbs: 6.2 g, Protein: 2.6 g, Fat: 2.7 g, Sugar: 0 g, Sodium: 16 mg, Fiber: 4.3 g

358. Sautéed Swiss Chard with Garlic and Lemon

Preparation Time: 5 minutes

Cooking Time: 11 minutes

Servings: 4

Ingredients:

- 2 tbsp olive oil
- 4 garlic cloves, sliced
- 1 tsp red pepper flakes, crushed
- 2 large bunches Swiss chard, torn
- Salt and pepper to taste
- 2 tbsp lemon juice, freshly squeezed

Directions:

1. Press the Sauté button on the Instant Pot and heat the oil.

2. Sauté the garlic for 1 minute until fragrant.

3. Stir in the red pepper flakes and Swiss chard. Season with salt and pepper to taste

4. Close the lid and make sure that the steam release valve is set to "Sealing."

5. Press the Manual button and adjust the cooking time to 10 minutes.

6. Do quick pressure release.

7. Drizzle with lemon juice before serving.

Nutrition: Calories: 82, Carbs: 5 g, Protein: 1.3 g, Fat: 6.9 g, Sugar: 0 g, Sodium: 79 mg, Fiber: 3.2 g

359. Dandelion Greens with Currants and Pine Nuts

Preparation Time: 5 minutes

Cooking Time: 11 minutes

Servings: 6

Ingredients:

- 2 tbsp extra virgin olive oil
- 1 garlic clove, minced
- 1 lb dandelion greens, trimmed and chopped
- Salt and pepper to taste
- 3 tbsp dried currants
- 2 tbsp toasted pine nuts
- Lemon wedges for garnish

Directions:

1. Press the Sauté button on the Instant Pot and heat the oil.

2. Sauté the garlic for 1 minute until fragrant.

3. Stir in dandelion greens and season with salt and pepper to taste

4. Add the dried currants.

5. Close the lid and make sure that the steam release valve is set to "Sealing."

6. Press the Manual button and adjust the cooking time to 10 minutes.

7. Do quick pressure release.

8. Garnish with toasted pine nuts and lemon wedges before serving.

Nutrition: Calories: 113, Carbs: 11 g, Protein: 7.9 g, Fat: 2.7 g, Sugar: 1.3 g, Sodium: 96 mg, Fiber: 3.9 g

360. Radicchio and Onions

Preparation Time: 5 minutes

Cooking Time: 15 minutes

Servings: 3

Ingredients:

- 1 tbsp olive oil
- 1 large onion, sliced
- 1 head radicchio, cut into wedges
- Salt and pepper to taste
- ½ cup pine nuts
- ¼ cup chopped parsley
- Balsamic vinegar to taste

Directions:

1. Press the Sauté button on the Instant Pot and heat the oil.

2. Sauté the onion for 5 minutes until fragrant and slightly caramelized.

3. Stir in the radicchio and season with salt and pepper to taste

4. Close the lid and make sure that the steam release valve is set to "Sealing."

5. Press the Manual button and adjust the cooking time to 10 minutes.

6. Do quick pressure release.

7. Toss pine nuts, parsley, and balsamic vinegar before serving.

Nutrition: Calories: 229, Carbs: 11.4 g, Protein: 4.6 g, Fat: 20.1 g, Sugar: 0 g, Sodium: 111 mg, Fiber: 6.4 g

361. Escarole and Bean Soup

Preparation Time: 5 minutes

Cooking Time: 50 minutes

Servings: 4

Ingredients:

- 2 tbsp olive oil
- 2 garlic cloves, minced
- 1 cup cannellini beans, soaked overnight
- 5 cups water
- Salt and pepper to taste
- 1 lb escarole, chopped
- A dash of hot pepper flakes

Directions:

1. Press the Sauté button and heat the olive oil.

2. Sauté the garlic for a minute until fragrant.

3. Stir in the beans and add water.

4. Close the lid and make sure that the steam release valve is set to "Sealing."

5. Press the Bean/Chili button and adjust the cooking time to 45 minutes.

6. Do natural pressure release.

7. Once the lid is open, press the Sauté button to allow the beans to simmer.

8. Add the escarole and simmer for 5 minutes.

9. Serve with a dash of hot pepper flakes.

Nutrition: Calories: 146, Carbs: 9.6 g, Protein: 2.9 g, Fat: 11.7 g, Sugar: 0 g, Sodium: 671 mg, Fiber: 5.2 g

362. Miso Soup with Shitake and Bok Choy

Preparation Time: 5 minutes

Cooking Time: 10 minutes

Servings: 3

Ingredients:

- 1 tsp red miso paste
- 2½ cups water
- 2 tsp soy sauce
- 2 thin slices ginger
- 1 garlic clove
- 3 large shitake mushrooms, sliced
- 1 small head baby bok choy, sliced

Directions:

1. Place all ingredients in the Instant Pot.

2. Give a good stir.

3. Close the lid and make sure that the steam release valve is set to "Sealing."

4. Press the Soup button and adjust the cooking time to 10 minutes.

5. Do quick pressure release.

Nutrition: Calories: 56, Carbs: 9.9 g, Protein: 3.5 g, Fat: 1.1 g, Sugar: 0 g, Sodium: 155 mg, Fiber: 6.3 g

363. Lentils with Tomatoes and Turmeric

Preparation Time: 10 minutes

Cooking Time: 10 minutes

Servings: 4

Ingredients:

- 2 tbsp extra virgin olive oil, plus extra for garnish
- 1 onion, finely chopped
- 1 tbsp ground turmeric
- 1 tsp garlic powder
- 1 (14 oz) can lentils, drained
- 1 (14 oz) can chopped tomatoes, drained
- ½ tsp sea salt
- ¼ tsp freshly ground black pepper

Directions:

1. In a huge pot on medium-high heat, warm the olive oil until it shimmers.

2. Add the onion and turmeric, and cook for about 5 minutes, occasionally stirring, until soft.

3. Add the garlic powder, lentils, tomatoes, salt, and pepper. Cook for 5 minutes, stirring occasionally. Serve garnished with additional olive oil, if desired.

Nutrition: Calories: 24, Total Fat: 7 g, Total Carbs: 34 g, Sugar: 5 g, Fiber: 15 g, Protein: 12 g, Sodium: 243 mg

364. Whole-Wheat Pasta with Tomato-Basil Sauce

Preparation Time: 15 minutes

Cooking Time: 11 minutes

Servings: 4

Ingredients:

- 2 tbsp extra virgin olive oil
- 1 onion, minced
- 6 garlic cloves, minced
- 2 (28 oz) can crushed tomatoes, undrained
- ½ tsp sea salt
- ¼ tsp ground black pepper
- ¼ cup basil leaves, chopped
- 1 (8 oz) package whole-wheat pasta

Directions:

1. In a huge pot on medium-high heat, warm the olive oil until it shimmers.

2. Add the onion. Cook for about 5 minutes, occasionally stirring, until soft.

3. Add the garlic. Cook for 30 seconds, stirring constantly.

4. Stir in the tomatoes, salt, and pepper. Bring it to a simmer. Reduce the heat to medium and cook for 5 minutes, stirring occasionally.

5. Pull it out from the heat then stir in the basil. Toss with the pasta.

Nutrition: Calories: 330, Total Fat: 7 g, Total Carbs: 56 g, Sugar: 24 g

365. Fried Rice with Kale

Preparation Time: 10 minutes

Cooking Time: 12 minutes

Servings: 4

Ingredients:

- 2 tbsp extra virgin olive oil
- 8 oz tofu, chopped
- 6 scallion, white and green parts, thinly sliced
- 2 cups kale, stemmed and chopped
- 3 cups cooked brown rice
- ¼ cup stir-fry sauce

Directions:

1. In a huge skillet on medium-high heat, warm the olive oil until it shimmers.

2. Add the tofu, scallions, and kale. Cook for 5 to 7 minutes, frequently stirring, until the vegetables are soft.

3. Add the brown rice and stir-fry sauce. Cook for 3 to 5 minutes, occasionally stirring, until heated through.

Nutrition: Calories: 301, Total Fat: 11 g, Total Carbs: 36 g, Sugar: 1 g

366. Nutty and Fruity Garden Salad

Preparation Time: 10 minutes

Cooking Time: 0 minutes

Servings: 2

Ingredients:

- 6 cups baby spinach
- ½ cup chopped walnuts, toasted
- 1 ripe red pear, sliced
- 1 ripe persimmon, sliced
- 1 tsp garlic minced
- 1 shallot, minced
- 1 tbsp extra-virgin olive oil
- 2 tbsp fresh lemon juice
- 1 tsp wholegrain mustard

Directions:

1. Mix well garlic, shallot, oil, lemon juice, and mustard in a large salad bowl.

2. Add spinach, pear, and persimmon. Toss to coat well.

3. To serve, garnish with chopped walnuts.

Nutrition: Calories: 332, Total Fat: 21 g, Saturated Fat: 2 g, Total Carbs: 37 g, Net Carbs: 27 g, Protein: 7 g

367. Stir-Fried Brussels Sprouts and Carrots

Preparation Time: 10 minutes

Cooking Time: 15 minutes

Servings: 6

Ingredients:

- 1 tbsp cider vinegar
- ⅓ cup water
- 1 lb Brussels sprouts halved lengthwise
- 1 lb carrots cut diagonally into ½-inch thick lengths
- 3 tbsp olive oil, divided
- 2 tbsp chopped shallot
- ½ tsp pepper
- ¾ tsp salt

Directions:

1. On medium-high fire, place a nonstick medium fry pan and heat 2 tbsp oil.
2. Ass shallots and cook until softened, around 1 to 2 minutes while occasionally stirring.
3. Add pepper salt, Brussels sprouts, and carrots. Stir fry until vegetables start to brown on the edges, around 3 to 4 minutes.
4. Add water, cook, and cover.
5. After 5 to 8 minutes, or when veggies are already soft, add the remaining butter.
6. If needed, season with more pepper and salt to taste.
7. Turn off fire, transfer to a platter, serve and enjoy.

Nutrition: Calories: 9, Total Fat: 4, Saturated Fat: 2, Total Carbs: 14 g, Net Carbs: 9 g, Protein: 3 g

368. Curried Veggies and Poached Eggs

Preparation Time: 10 minutes

Cooking Time: 40 minutes

Servings: 4

Ingredients:

- 4 large eggs
- ½ tsp white vinegar
- ⅛ tsp crushed red pepper – optional
- 1 cup water
- 1 (14 oz) can chickpeas, drained
- 2 medium zucchinis, diced
- ½ lb sliced button mushrooms
- 1 tbsp yellow curry powder
- 2 garlic cloves, minced
- 1 large onion, chopped
- 2 tsp extra virgin olive oil

Directions:

1. On medium-high fire, place a large saucepan and heat oil.
2. Sauté onions until tender, around 4 to 5 minutes.
3. Put the garlic and continue sautéing for another half minute.
4. Add curry powder, stir and cook until fragrant, around 1 to 2 minutes.
5. Add mushrooms, mix, cover, and cook for 5 to 8 minutes or until mushrooms are tender and have released their liquid.
6. Add red pepper if using water, chickpeas, and zucchini. Mix well to combine and bring to a boil.
7. Once boiling, reduce fire to a simmer, cover, and cook until zucchini is tender, around 15 to 20 minutes of simmering.
8. Meanwhile, in a small pot filled with 3-inches deep water, bring to a boil on a high fire.
9. When boiling, lower the heat temperature to a simmer and add vinegar.
10. Slowly add 1 egg, slipping it gently into the water. Allow simmering until egg is cooked, around 3 to 5 minutes.
11. Please take off the egg using a slotted spoon and transfer it to a plate: 1 plate, 1 egg.
12. Repeat the process with the remaining eggs.
13. Once the veggies are done cooking, divide evenly into 4 servings and place 1 serving per plate of the egg.
14. Serve and enjoy.

Nutrition: Calories: 254, Total Fat: 9 g, Saturated Fat: 2, Total Carbs: 30 g, Net Carbs: 21 g, Protein: 16 g

369. Braised Carrots and Kale

Preparation Time: 10 minutes

Cooking Time: 10 minutes

Servings: 2

Ingredients:

- 1 tbsp coconut oil
- 1 onion, sliced thinly
- 5 garlic cloves, minced
- 3 medium carrots, sliced thinly
- 10 oz kale, chopped
- ½ cup water
- Salt and pepper to taste
- A dash of red pepper flakes

Directions:

1. Warm oil in a skillet over medium flame and sauté the onion and garlic until fragrant.
2. Toss in the carrots and stir for 1 minute. Add the kale and water. Season with salt and pepper to taste.
3. Close the lid and allow to simmer for 5 minutes.
4. Sprinkle with red pepper flakes.
5. Serve and enjoy.

Nutrition: Calories: 161, Total Fat: 7 g, Saturated Fat: 1 g, Total Carbs: 20 g, Net Carbs: 14 g, Protein: 7 g

370. Stir-Fried Gingery Veggies

Preparation Time: 10 minutes

Cooking Time: 10 minutes

Servings: 4

Ingredients:

- 1 tbsp oil
- 3 garlic cloves, minced
- 1 onion, chopped
- 1 thumb-size ginger, sliced
- 1 tbsp water
- 1 large carrot, peeled and julienned and seedless
- 1 large green bell pepper, julienned and seedless
- 1 large yellow bell pepper, julienned and seedless
- 1 large red bell pepper, julienned and seedless
- 1 zucchini, julienned
- Salt and pepper to taste

Directions:

1. Heat oil in a nonstick saucepan over a high flame and sauté the garlic, onion, and ginger until fragrant.
2. Stir in the rest of the ingredients.
3. Keep on stirring for at least 5 minutes until the vegetables are tender.
4. Serve and enjoy.

Nutrition: Calories: 70, Total Fat: 4 g, Saturated Fat: 1 g, Total Carbs: 9 g, Net Carbs: 7 g,

Protein: 1 g

371. Cauliflower Fritters

Preparation Time: 10 minutes

Cooking Time: 15 minutes

Servings: 6

Ingredients:

- 1 large cauliflower head, cut into florets
- 2 eggs, beaten
- ½ tsp turmeric
- ½ tsp salt
- ¼ tsp black pepper
- 1 tbsp coconut oil

Directions:

1. Put the cauliflower florets in a pot with water and bring them to a boil. Cook until tender, around 5 minutes of boiling. Drain well.
2. Place the cauliflower, eggs, turmeric, salt, and pepper into the food processor.
3. Pulse until the mixture becomes coarse.
4. Transfer into a bowl. Using your hands, form 6 small flattened balls and place them in the fridge for at least 1 hour until the mixture hardens.
5. Warm the oil in a nonstick pan and fry the cauliflower patties for 3 minutes on each side.
6. Serve and enjoy.

Nutrition: Calories: 53, Total Fat: 6 g, Saturated Fat: 2 g, Net Carbs: 1 g, Protein: 3 g

372. Stir-Fried Squash

Preparation Time: 10 minutes

Cooking Time: 10 minutes

Servings: 4

Ingredients:

- 1 tbsp olive oil
- 3 garlic cloves, minced
- 1 butternut squash, seeded and sliced
- 1 tbsp coconut aminos
- 1 tbsp lemon juice
- 1 tbsp water
- Salt and pepper to taste

Directions:

1. Heat oil over medium flame and sauté the garlic until fragrant.

2. Stir in the squash for another 3 minutes before adding the rest of the ingredients.

3. Close the lid and allow to simmer for 5 more minutes or until the squash is soft.

4. Serve and enjoy.

Nutrition: Calories: 83, Total Fat: 3 g, Saturated Fat: 0.5, Total Carbs: 14 g, Net Carbs: 12 g, Protein: 2 g

373. Cauliflower Hash Brown

Preparation Time: 10 minutes

Cooking Time: 20 minutes

Servings: 6

Ingredients:

- 4 eggs, beaten
- ½ cup coconut milk
- ½ tsp dry mustard
- Salt and pepper to taste
- 1 large head cauliflower, shredded

Directions:

1. Place all together ingredients in a mixing bowl and mix until well combined.

2. Place a nonstick fry pan and heat over medium flame.

3. Add a large dollop of cauliflower mixture to the skillet.

4. Fry one side for 3 minutes, flip and cook the other side for a minute, like a pancake. Repeat the process to the remaining ingredients.

5. Serve and enjoy.

Nutrition: Calories: 102, Total Fat: 7 g, Saturated Fat: 1 g, Total Carbs: 4 g, Net Carbs: 3 g

374. Sweet Potato Puree

Preparation Time: 10 minutes

Cooking Time: 15 minutes

Servings: 5

Ingredients:

- 2 lb sweet potatoes, peeled
- 1½ cups water
- 5 Medjool dates, pitted and chopped

Directions:

1. Place water and potatoes in a pot.

2. Close the lid and boil for at least 15 minutes until the potatoes are soft.

3. Drain the potatoes and place them in a food processor together with the dates.

4. Pulse until smooth.

5. Serve and enjoy.

Nutrition: Calories: 112, Total Fat: 7 g, Saturated Fat: 1 g, Total Carbs: 4 g, Net Carbs: 3 g

375. Curried Okra

Preparation Time: 10 minutes

Cooking Time: 12 minutes

Servings: 4

Ingredients:

- 1 lb small to medium okra pods, trimmed
- ¼ tsp curry powder
- ½ tsp kosher salt
- 1 tsp finely chopped serrano chile
- 1 tsp ground coriander
- 1 tbsp canola oil
- ¾ tsp brown mustard seeds

Directions:

1. Place a large and heavy skillet on medium-high fire and cook mustard seeds until fragrant, around 30 seconds.

2. Add canola oil. Add okra, curry powder, salt, chile, and coriander. Sauté for a minute while stirring every once in a while.

3. Cover and cook low fire for at least 8 minutes. Stir occasionally.

4. Uncover, increase the fire to medium-high and cook until okra is lightly browned, around 2 minutes more.

5. Serve and enjoy.

Nutrition: Calories: 102, Total Fat: 7 g, Saturated Fat: 1 g, Total Carbs: 4 g, Net Carbs: 3 g

376. Vegetable Potpie

Preparation Time: 10 minutes

Cooking Time: 40 minutes

Servings: 8

Ingredients:

- 1 recipe pastry for double-crust pie
- 2 tbsp cornstarch
- 1 tsp ground black pepper
- 1 tsp kosher salt
- 3 cups vegetable broth
- 2 cups cauliflower florets
- 2 celery stalks, sliced ¼ inch wide
- 2 potatoes, peeled and diced
- 2 large carrots, diced
- 1 garlic clove, minced
- 8 oz mushroom
- 1 onion, chopped
- 2 tbsp olive oil

Directions:

1. In a large saucepan, sauté garlic in oil until lightly browned, add onions and continue sautéing until soft and translucent.

2. Add celery, potatoes, and carrots, and sauté for 3 minutes.

3. Add vegetable broth and cauliflower and bring to a boil. Slow fire and simmer until vegetables are slightly tender. Season with pepper and salt.

4. Mix ¼ cup of water and cornstarch in a small bowl. Stir until the mixture is smooth and has no lumps. Then pour into the vegetable pot while mixing constantly.

5. Continue mixing until soup thickens, around 3 minutes. Remove from fire.

6. Meanwhile, roll out pastry dough and place it on an oven-safe 11x7 baking dish. Pour the vegetable filling and then cover with another pastry dough. Seal and flute the edges of the dough and prick the top dough with a fork in several places.

7. Bake the dish in a preheated oven of 425°F for 30 minutes or until the crust has turned a golden brown.

Nutrition: Calories: 202, Total Fat: 10 g, Saturated Fat: 2 g, Total Carbs: 26 g, Net Carbs: 23 g, Protein: 4 g

377. Grilled Eggplant Roll-Ups

Preparation Time: 5 minutes

Cooking Time: 3 minutes

Servings: 8

Ingredients:

- 1 tomato
- 2 tbsp chopped fresh basil
- 2 tbsp olive oil
- 4 oz mozzarella cheese
- 1 eggplant, sliced

Directions:

1. Thinly slice the tomato and mozzarella and reserve.

2. Rub the eggplant slices with olive oil and grill them in a skillet for 3 minutes per side.

3. Lay a slice of cheese and tomato on top of each zucchini.

4. Sprinkle basil and black pepper and grill for 3 minutes to soften the cheese.

5. Remove the slices and set them on a plate.

6. Roll each of the slices before serving.

7. Enjoy.

Nutrition: Calories: 50, Protein: 6.12 g, Fat: 0.92 g, Carbs: 5.14 g

Chapter 11
Vegan

378. Eggplant Gratin

Preparation Time: 10 minutes

Cooking Time: 40 minutes

Servings: 6

Ingredients:

- ¾ cup Gruyere cheese
- ½ tsp black pepper
- 1 cup heavy cream
- 2 sliced eggplant
- 3 tbsp Olive oil
- ½ cup tomato sauce
- ½ tsp salt
- 3 oz crumbled feta cheese
- 1 tsp Chopped thyme
- ¼ cup chopped fresh basil
- 1 tbsp chopped chives

Directions:

1. Heat the oven to about 375°F.

2. Cover the slices of eggplant with salt, pepper, and olive oil and bake them for 20 minutes on a baking pan.

3. Meanwhile, put feta cheese and heavy cream in a pot and boil them.

4. Remove the pot from heat and add chives and thyme, then stir before setting aside.

5. Spread the tomato sauce on a medium-sized pan and lay the eggplant slices over it.

6. Cover eggplant slices with basil and Gruyere cheese.

7. Add another layer of the remaining eggplant and cover it with the heavy cream mixture.

8. Bake for about 20 minutes and serve.

Nutrition: Calories: 217, Protein: 8.37 g, Fat: 15.47 g, Carbs: 13.66 g

379. Veggie Stuffed Peppers

Preparation Time: 5 minutes

Cooking Time: 0 minutes

Servings: 6

Ingredients:

- 1 cup quartered cherry tomatoes
- 1 tsp black pepper
- 3 tbsp Dijon mustard
- ¼ cup chopped fresh parsley
- 3 halved green bell peppers
- ½ peeled and sliced cucumber
- 1 bunch sliced scallions
- ½ tsp Salt
- ½ cup Greek yogurt
- 4 diced celery stalks

Directions:

1. In a medium bowl, combine salt, pepper, yogurt, and mustard.

2. Add cucumbers, celery, tomatoes, and scallions and combine well.

3. Stuff the mix into the pepper halves.

4. Add the chopped parsley to garnish.

5. Serve immediately and enjoy

Nutrition: Calories: 41, Protein: 2.49 g, Fat: 1.78 g, Carbs: 4.3 g

380. Cheesy Gratin Zucchini

Preparation Time: 15 minutes

Cooking Time: 45 minutes

Servings: 9

Ingredients:

- Spray oil
- ½ cup heavy cream
- 1 tsp rosemary
- 1 tsp turmeric
- 1 tsp black pepper
- 2 tbsp olive oil
- 1 peeled and sliced small white onion
- 4 cups sliced raw zucchini
- 1 tbsp garlic powder
- 2 cups shredded pepper jack cheese
- ½ tsp salt

Directions:

1. Heat the oven to about 375°F.

2. Grease the baking tray with cooking oil

3. Add a third of the zucchini and onion slices to the pan and sprinkle seasonings and half of the pepper jack cheese.

4. Add one more layer of zucchini slices, and onion then season with pepper, salt, and the remaining pepper jack cheese.

5. Lay on the remaining zucchini slices and onions.

6. Microwave garlic powder, butter, and heavy cream for a minute to melt the butter and mix well.

7. Pour the mixture over the top layer of slices

8. Bake uncovered for 45 minutes

9. Serve and enjoy

Nutrition: Calories: 151, Protein: 8.49 g, Fat: 12.08 g, Carbs: 2.49 g

381. Korean Barbecue Tofu

Preparation Time: 10 minutes

Cooking Time: 15 minutes

Servings: 3

Ingredients:

- 1 tbsp olive oil
- 2 tsp onion powder
- 4 garlic cloves, minced
- 2 tsp dry mustard
- 3 tbsp brown sugar
- ½ cup soy sauce
- 1½ lb firm tofu, sliced into ¼-inch cubes

Directions:

1. In a re-sealable bag, mix all ingredients except for tofu and oil. Mix well until sugar is dissolved.

2. Add sliced tofu and slowly turn the bag to mix. Seal bag and place flatly inside the ref for an hour.

3. After an hour, turn the bag to the other side and marinate for another hour.

4. To cook, in a nonstick fry pan, heat oil on medium-high fire. Add tofu and stir fry until sides are browned.

5. Serve and enjoy.

Nutrition: Calories: 437, Fat: 25 g, Carbs: 23 g, Protein: 40 g, Fiber: 6 g

382. Collard Green Wrap

Preparation Time: 10 minutes

Cooking Time: 0 minutes

Servings: 4

Ingredients:

- ½ block feta, cut into 4 (1-inch thick) strips (4-oz)
- ½ cup purple onion, diced
- ½ medium red bell pepper, julienned
- 1 medium cucumber, julienned
- 4 large cherry tomatoes, halved
- 4 large collard green leaves, washed
- 8 whole kalamata olives, halved

For the Sauce:

- 1 cup low-fat plain Greek yogurt
- 1 tbsp white vinegar

- 1 tsp garlic powder
- 2 tbsp minced fresh dill
- 2 tbsp olive oil
- 2 oz cucumber, seeded and grated (¼-whole)
- Salt and pepper to taste

Directions:

1. Make the sauce first: make sure to squeeze out all the excess liquid from the cucumber after grating. In a small bowl, put all together with the sauce ingredients and mix thoroughly, then refrigerate.

2. Prepare and slice all wrap ingredients.

3. On a flat surface, spread 1 collard green leaf. Spread 2 tbsp of Tzatziki sauce in the middle of the leaf.

4. Layer ¼ of each of the tomatoes, feta, olives, onion, pepper, and cucumber. Place them in the center of the leaf, piling them high instead of spreading them.

5. Fold the leaf like you would like a burrito. Repeat the process for the remaining ingredients.

6. Serve and enjoy.

Nutrition: Calories: 463, Fat: 31 g, Carbs: 31 g, Protein: 20 g, Fiber: 7 g

383. Zucchini Garlic Fries

Preparation Time: 10 minutes

Cooking Time: 20 minutes

Servings: 6

Ingredients:

- ¼ tsp garlic powder
- ½ cup almond flour
- 2 large egg whites, beaten
- 3 medium zucchinis, sliced into fry sticks
- Salt and pepper to taste

Directions:

1. Set the oven to 400°F.

2. Mix the ingredients in a bowl until the zucchini fries are well coated.

3. Place fries on the cookie sheet and spread evenly.

4. Put in the oven and cook for 20 minutes.

5. Halfway through cooking time, stir-fries.

Nutrition: Calories: 11, Fat: 0.1 g, Carbs: 1 g, Protein1.5 g, Fiber: 0.5 g

384. Stir-Fried Eggplant

Preparation Time: 10 minutes

Cooking Time: 10 minutes

Servings: 2

Ingredients:

- 1 tbsp coconut oil
- 2 eggplants, sliced into 3-inch in length
- 4 garlic cloves, minced
- 1 onion, chopped
- 1 tsp ginger, grated
- 1 tsp lemon juice, freshly squeezed
- ½ tsp salt
- ½ tsp pepper

Directions:

1. Heat oil in a nonstick saucepan.

2. Pan-fry the eggplants for 2 minutes on all sides.

3. Add the garlic and onions until fragrant, around 3 minutes.

4. Stir in the ginger, salt, pepper, and lemon juice.

5. Add a ½ cup of water and bring to a simmer. Cook until eggplant is tender.

Nutrition: Calories: 232, Fat: 7 g, Carbs: 41 g, Protein: 7 g, Fiber: 17 g

385. Sautéed Garlic Mushrooms

Preparation Time: 10 minutes

Cooking Time: 10 minutes

Servings: 4

Ingredients:

- 1 tbsp olive oil
- 3 garlic cloves, minced
- 16 oz fresh brown mushrooms, sliced
- 7 oz fresh shiitake mushrooms, sliced
- ½ tsp salt
- ½ tsp pepper or more to taste

Directions:

1. Place a nonstick saucepan on medium-high fire and heat the pan for a minute.

2. Add oil and heat for 2 minutes.

3. Stir in garlic and sauté for a minute.

4. Add remaining ingredients and stir fry until soft and tender, around 5 minutes.

5. Turn off the fire, and let the mushrooms rest while the pan is covered for 5 minutes.

6. Serve and enjoy.

Nutrition: Calories: 95, Fat: 4 g, Carbs: 14 g, Protein: 3 g, Fiber: 4 g

386. Stir-Fried Asparagus and Bell Pepper

Preparation Time: 10 minutes

Cooking Time: 10 minutes

Servings: 6

Ingredients:

- 1 tbsp olive oil
- 4 garlic cloves, minced
- 1 lb fresh asparagus spears, trimmed
- 2 large red bell peppers, seeded and julienned
- ½ tsp thyme
- 5 tbsp water
- ½ tsp salt
- ½ tsp pepper or more to taste

Directions:

1. Place a nonstick saucepan on high fire and heat the pan for a minute.

2. Add oil and heat for 2 minutes.

3. Stir in garlic and sauté for a minute.

4. Add remaining ingredients and stir fry until soft and tender, around 6 minutes.

5. Turn off the fire, and let veggies rest while the pan is covered for 5 minutes.

Nutrition: Calories: 45, Fat: 2 g, Carbs: 5 g, Net Protein: 2 g, Fiber: 2 g

387. Wild Rice with Spicy Chickpeas

Preparation Time: 15 minutes

Cooking Time: 1 hour 10 minutes

Servings: 6 to 7

Ingredients:

- 1 cup basmati rice
- 1 cup wild rice
- Salt & pepper to taste
- 4 tbsp olive oil
- 1 tbsp garlic powder
- 2 tsp cumin powder
- ¼ cup sunflower oil
- 3 cups chickpeas
- 1 tsp flour
- 1 tsp curry powder
- 3 tsp paprika powder
- 1 tsp dill
- 3 tbsp parsley (chopped)
- 1 medium onion (thinly sliced)
- 2 cups currants

Directions:

1. For cooking wild rice, fill the half pot with water and bring it to a boil. Put the rice and let it simmer for at least 40 minutes.

2. Take olive in the pot and heat it on medium flame. Now add cumin powder, salt, and water and bring it to a boil. Then add basmati rice and cook for 20 minutes.

3. Leave rice for cooking and prepare spicy chickpeas. Heat 2 tbsp of olive oil in the pan and toss chickpeas, garlic powder, salt & pepper, cumin, and paprika powder in it.

4. In another pan, cook onion with sunflower oil until it is golden brown and add flour.

5. Mix flour and onion with your hands.

6. For serving, place both types of rice in a bowl with spicy chickpeas and fry the onion. Garnish it with parsley and herbs.

Nutrition: Calories: 647, Protein: 25.43 g, Fat: 25.72 g, Carbs: 88.3 g

388. Cashew Pesto & Parsley with Veggies

Preparation Time: 15 minutes

Cooking Time: 10 minutes

Servings: 3 to 4

Ingredients:

- 3 zucchini (sliced)
- 8 soaked bamboo skewers
- 2 red capsicums
- ¼ cup olive oil
- 750 g eggplant
- 4 lemon cheeks

For Serving:

- Couscous salad

For Preparing Cashew Pesto:

- ½ Cup cashew (roasted)
- ½ Cup parsley
- 2 cup grated parmesan
- 2 tbsp Lime juice
- ¼ Cup olive oil

Directions:

1. Toss capsicum, eggplant, and zucchini with oil and salt and thread them onto skewers.
2. Cook bamboo sticks for 6 to 8 minutes on a barbecue grill pan on medium heat.
3. Also, grill lemon cheeks from both sides.
4. For preparing cashew pesto, combine all ingredients in the food processor and blend.
5. Place grill skewers on a plate with grilled lemon slices and drizzle some cashew pesto over it for serving.

Nutrition: Calories: 666, Protein: 23.96 g, Fat: 48.04 g, Carbs: 41.4 g

389. Spicy Chickpeas with Roasted Vegetables

Preparation Time: 10 minutes

Cooking Time: 25 minutes

Servings: 2 to 3

Ingredients:

- 1 large carrot (peeled)
- 2 tbsp sunflower oil
- 1 cauliflower head
- 1 tbsp ground cumin
- ½ red onions (diced)
- 1 red pepper (deseeded)
- 400 g can chickpeas

Directions:

1. Line a large baking tin in the preheated oven (at 460°F).
2. Cut all the vegetables and toss with salt, pepper, and onion.
3. In a bowl, whisk olive oil, pepper, and cumin powder.
4. Add all veggies to the bowl and toss.
5. Transfer vegetables to a baking tin and bake them almost for 15 minutes.

6. Now add chickpeas and stir.
7. Return to the oven and bake it for the next 10 minutes.
8. Serve it with toast bread.

Nutrition: Calories: 348, Protein: 14.29 g, Fat: 15.88 g, Carbs: 40.65 g

390. Special Vegetable Kitchree

Preparation Time: 10 minutes

Cooking Time: 46 minutes

Servings: 5 to 6

Ingredients:

- ½ cup brown grain rice
- 1 cup dry lentil or split peas
- 1 tsp Sea salt, cumin powder, ground turmeric, ground fenugreek, and ground coriander
- 3 tbsp coconut oil
- 1 tbsp ginger
- 5 cups vegetable stock
- 1 cup baby spinach
- 1 medium zucchini (roughly chopped)
- 1 small crown broccoli (chopped)
- Greek yogurt (for serving)

Directions:

1. In a saucepan, warm the coconut oil on medium flame and add ginger, cumin, coriander, fennel seeds, fenugreek, and turmeric and cook it for 1 minute.
2. Now add lentils and brown rice to the spices and stir. Pour the vegetable stock into it and simmer for 40 minutes.
3. Add broccoli to the tender rice and lentils and cook for another 5 minutes. Now add other vegetables and stir for 10 minutes.
4. For serving, pour some Greek yogurt over vegetable kitcheree and serve hot.

Nutrition: Calories: 1728, Protein: 4.13 g, Fat: 190.35 g, Carbs: 17.31 g

391. Mashed Sweet Potato Burritos

Preparation Time: 15 minutes

Cooking Time: 60 minutes

Servings: 4

Ingredients:

- 4 tortillas
- 1 avocado
- 1 tsp capsicum, paprika powder, and oregano
- Salt & pepper as needed
- ½ cup sour cream
- 1 can diced tomato
- 2 sweet potatoes (mashed)
- 2 garlic cloves (minced)
- 1 tbsp cumin powder
- Fresh cilantro or parsley

Directions:

1. Before mashing, roast sweet potatoes for 45 minutes in an already preheated (at 320°F) oven.

2. Cook onion in a frying pan with oil on medium heat. Add garlic cloves and cook for 1 minute.

3. Add 1 tin of tomatoes and leave it to simmer for 10 minutes. Halfway through, add salt & pepper, paprika, and cumin powder.

4. After 5 minutes, add avocado to it.

5. Now make burritos, mix one scoop of mashed potatoes with avocado filling.

6. Wrap your tortilla and grill it in the oven at 400°F for 30 seconds.

7. Serve it with sour cream and hot sauce.

Nutrition: Calories: 442, Protein: 12.05 g, Fat: 15.43 g, Carbs: 66.85 g

Chapter 12

Snack

392. Homemade Guacamole

Preparation Time: 10 minutes

Cooking Time: 0 minutes

Servings: 4

Ingredients:

- 2 ripe avocados, peeled, pitted, and cubed
- 2 garlic cloves, finely minced
- Juice 1 lime
- ½ red onion, minced
- 2 tbsp chopped fresh cilantro leaves
- ½ tsp sea salt

Directions:

1. Place the avocados, garlic, lime juice, red onion, cilantro, and sea salt in a medium bowl. Mash them lightly with the back of a fork until a uniform consistency is achieved.

2. Serve chilled.

Nutrition: Calories: 214, Fat: 19.9 g, Protein: 2.1 g, Carbs: 10.7 g, Fiber: 7.3 g, Sugar: 1.0 g, Sodium: 242 mg

393. Lemony Berry Gummies

Preparation Time: 5 minutes

Cooking Time: 10 minutes

Servings: 24 gummies

Ingredients:

- 1 cup fresh or frozen berries of choice
- ½ cup freshly squeezed lemon juice
- 3 tbsp raw honey
- ¼ cup filtered water
- ¼ cup gelatin powder

Directions:

3. Purée the berries, lemon juice, honey, and water in a blender.

4. Transfer the purée to a small saucepan and heat over medium heat until it warms.

5. Add the gelatin powder and continue whisking for 5 minutes until well combined.

6. Pour the mixture into a mini muffin tin and freeze until the mixture gels, about 15 minutes.

7. Serve immediately or refrigerate for up to 1 week.

Nutrition: Calories: 67, Fat: 0 g, Protein: 4.1 g, Carbs: 13.2 g, Fiber: 1.0 g, Sugar: 16.9 g, Sodium: 2 mg

394. Carrot and Pumpkin Seed Crackers

Preparation Time: 10 minutes

Cooking Time: 15 minutes

Servings: 4

Ingredients:

- 1⅓ cups pumpkin seeds
- ½ cup packed shredded carrot (about 1 carrot)
- 3 tbsp chopped fresh dill
- ¼ tsp sea salt
- 2 tbsp extra-virgin olive oil

Directions:

1. Preheat the oven to 350°F (180°C). Line a baking sheet with parchment paper.

2. Ground the pumpkin seeds in a food processor, then add the carrot, dill, salt, and olive oil to the food processor and pulse to combine well.

3. Pour them into the prepared baking sheet, and then shape the mixture into a rectangle with a spatula.

4. Line a sheet of parchment paper over the rectangle, and then flatten the rectangle to about ⅛ inch thick with a rolling pin.

5. Remove the parchment paper-lined over the rectangle, then score it into 40 small rectangles with a sharp knife.

6. Arrange the baking sheet in the preheated oven and bake for 15 minutes or until golden browned and crispy.

7. Transfer the crackers to a large plate and allow them to cool for a few minutes before serving.

Nutrition: Calories: 130, Fat: 11.9 g, Protein: 5.1 g, Carbs: 3.7 g, Fiber: 1.0 g, Sugar: 0 g, Sodium: 66 mg

395. Zucchini Chips

Preparation Time: 15 minutes

Cooking Time: 2 hours

Servings: 6

Ingredients:

- 2 medium zucchini, sliced thin with a mandoline or sharp knife
- 2 tbsp extra-virgin olive oil
- 1½ tsp dried rosemary
- 1½ tsp dried oregano
- 1½ tsp dried basil
- ½ tsp sea salt

Directions:

1. Preheat the oven to 200°F (93°C). Line a baking sheet with parchment paper.

2. Combine the zucchini slices with olive oil in a large bowl, then toss to coat well.

3. Combine the remaining ingredients in a separate bowl. Stir to mix well.

4. Pour the mixture into the bowl of zucchini, then toss to coat well.

5. Arrange the zucchini slices in a single layer on the prepared baking sheet.

6. Bake in the preheated oven for 2 hours or until golden brown and crispy.

7. Transfer the zucchini chips to a cooling rack and allow them to cool for a few minutes. Serve warm.

Nutrition: Calories: 52, Fat: 5.1 g, Protein: 1.0 g, Carbs: 2.7 g, Fiber: 1.1 g, Sugar: 1.2 g, Sodium: 202 mg

396. Butternut Squash Fries

Preparation Time: 20 minutes

Cooking Time: 40 minutes

Servings: 4

Ingredients:

- 1 large butternut squash, peeled, deseeded, and cut into fry-size pieces, about 3 inches long and ½-inch thick
- 2 tbsp coconut oil
- ¾ tsp sea salt
- 3 fresh rosemary sprigs, stemmed and chopped (about 1½ tbsp)

Directions:

1. Preheat the oven to 375°F (190°C). Line a baking sheet with parchment paper.

2. Put the butternut squash in a large bowl, then drizzle with coconut oil and sprinkle with salt. Toss to coat well.

3. Arrange the butternut squash pieces in a single layer on the prepared baking sheet.

4. Bake in the preheated oven for 40 minutes or until golden brown and crunchy. Flip the zucchini fries at least 3 times during the cooking and top the fries with rosemary sprigs halfway through.

5. Transfer the fries to a cooling rack and allow them to cool for a few minutes. Serve warm.

Nutrition: Calories: 191, Fat: 6.7 g, Protein: 3.0 g, Carbs: 34.1 g, Fiber: 7.2 g, Sugar: 5.9 g, Sodium: 451 mg

397. White Fish Ceviche with Avocado

Preparation Time: 20 minutes

Cooking Time: 0 minutes

Servings: 6

Ingredients:

- Juice 5 limes
- Juice 8 lemons
- 1 lb (454 g) fresh wild white fish, cut into ½-inch cubes
- 1 tsp minced fresh ginger
- 3 garlic cloves, minced
- 1 cup minced red onions
- ½ cup minced fresh cilantro
- 1 tsp Himalayan salt
- 1 tsp ground black pepper

- ½ medium Hass avocado, peeled, pitted, and diced

Directions:

1. Combine the lime juice and lemon juice in a large bowl, then dunk the fish cubes in the mixture, and press so the fish is submerged in the juice.

2. Cover the bowl in plastic and refrigerate for at least 40 minutes.

3. Meanwhile, combine the ginger, garlic, onions, cilantro, salt, and ground black pepper in a small bowl. Stir to mix well.

4. Remove the fish bowl from the refrigerator, then sprinkle with the powder mixture. Toss to coat well.

5. Spread the diced avocado over the ceviche and serve immediately.

Nutrition: Calories: 159, Fat: 4.9 g, Protein: 19.0 g, Carbs: 11.6 g, Fiber: 2.0 g, Sugar: 3.2 g, Sodium: 677 mg

398. Massaged Kale Chips

Preparation Time: 5 minutes

Cooking Time: 20 minutes

Servings: 2

Ingredients:

- 4 cups kale, stemmed, rinsed, drained, torn into 2-inch pieces
- 2 tbsp extra-virgin olive oil
- 1 tsp sea salt
- 2 tbsp apple cider vinegar

Directions:

1. Preheat the oven to 350°F (180°C).

2. Combine all the ingredients in a large bowl. Stir to mix well.

3. Gently massage the kale leaves in the bowl for 5 minutes or until wilted and bright.

4. Place the kale on a baking sheet. Bake in the preheated oven for 20 minutes or until crispy. Toss the kale halfway through.

5. Remove the kale from the oven and serve immediately.

Nutrition: Calories: 138, Fat: 13.7 g, Protein: 1.4 g, Carbs: 2.9 g, Fiber: 1.2 g, Sugar: 0.7 g, Sodium: 1176 mg

399. Almond Yogurt, Berry, and Walnut Parfait

Preparation Time: 10 minutes

Cooking Time: 0 minutes

Servings: 2

Ingredients:

- 2 cups plain unsweetened almond yogurt
- 2 tbsp honey
- 1 cup fresh raspberries
- 1 cup fresh blueberries
- ½ cup walnut pieces

Directions:

1. Combine the yogurt and honey in a bowl. Stir to mix well, then pour half of the honey yogurt into a large glass.

2. Top the honey yogurt with berries, then top the berries with the remaining honey yogurt.

3. Spread the walnut pieces on top and serve immediately.

Nutrition: Calories: 504, Fat: 22.1 g, Protein: 22.9 g, Carbs: 56.0 g, Fiber: 8.1 g, Sugar: 45.2 g, Sodium: 175mg

400. Buckwheat Waffles

Preparation Time: 15 minutes

Cooking Time: 12 minutes

Servings: 4

Ingredients:

- 1½ cups buckwheat flour
- ½ cup brown rice flour
- 1 tsp baking soda
- 2 tsp baking powder
- ½ tsp sea salt
- 1 egg
- 2 tsp vanilla extract
- 1 tbsp pure maple syrup
- 1½ cups almond milk
- 1 cup water
- Coconut oil, for greasing the waffle iron

Directions:

1. Combine the flours, baking soda, baking powder, and salt in a bowl. Stir to mix well.

2. Whisk together the egg, vanilla, maple syrup, almond milk, and water in a separate bowl.

3. Pour the egg mixture into the flour mixture and keep stirring until a smooth batter forms. Let the batter stand for 10 minutes.

4. Preheat the waffle iron and grease with coconut oil.

5. Pour the batter into the waffle iron to cover ¾ of the bottom. Cook for 10 to 12 minutes or until golden brown and crispy. Flip the waffle halfway through the cooking time. The cooking time will vary depending on the waffle iron you use.

6. Serve the waffles immediately.

Nutrition: Calories: 281, Fat: 3.6 g, Protein: 9.3 g, Carbs: 54.9 g, Fiber: 6.1 g, Sugar: 7.1 g, Sodium: 691 mg

401. Simple Coconut Pancakes

Preparation Time: 10 minutes

Cooking Time: 5 minutes

Servings: 8

Ingredients:

- 4 eggs
- 1 cup coconut milk, plus additional as needed
- 1 tbsp pure maple syrup
- 1 tsp vanilla extract
- 1 tbsp melted coconut oil, plus additional for greasing the pan
- ½ cup coconut flour
- 1 tsp baking soda
- ½ tsp sea salt

Directions:

1. Whisk together the eggs, coconut milk, maple syrup, vanilla, and coconut oil in a large bowl. Stir to mix well.

2. Combine the coconut flour, baking soda, and salt in a separate bowl. Stir to mix well.

3. Make a well in the middle of the coconut flour mixture, then pour the egg mixture into the well. Stir to mix well until smooth and no lump.

4. Grease a nonstick skillet with coconut oil, then heat over medium-high heat until shimmering.

5. Divide the batter and pour ½ cup of batter into the skillet and cook for 5 minutes or until lightly browned. Flip halfway through the cooking time. Repeat with the remaining batter.

6. Transfer the pancakes to 4 plates and serve immediately.

Nutrition: Calories: 192, Fat: 10.6 g, Protein: 9.1 g, Carbs: 14.9 g, Fiber: 6.5 g, Sugar: 5.7 g, Sodium: 736 mg

402. Coconut Rice with Dates, Almonds, and Blueberries

Preparation Time: 10 minutes

Cooking Time: 30 minutes

Servings: 4

Ingredients:

- 1 cup brown basmati rice
- 2 dates, pitted and chopped
- 1 cup coconut milk
- 1 tsp sea salt
- 1 cup water
- ¼ cup toasted slivered almonds, divided
- ½ cup shaved coconut, divided
- 1 cup fresh blueberries, divided

Directions:

1. Combine the basmati rice, dates, coconut milk, salt, and water in a saucepan. Stir to mix well. Bring to a boil.

2. Reduce the heat to low, then simmer for 30 minutes or until the rice is soft.

3. Divide them into 4 bowls and serve with almonds, coconut, and blueberries on top.

Nutrition: Calories: 280, Fat: 8.1 g, Protein: 6.3 g, Carbs: 48.9 g, Fiber: 5.0 g, Sugar: 7.2 g, Sodium: 621 mg

403. Mandarin Cottage Cheese

Preparation Time: 5 minutes

Cooking Time: 0 minutes

Servings: 1

Ingredients:

- ½ cup low-fat cottage cheese
- ½ cup canned mandarin oranges
- 1½ tbsp slivered almonds

Directions:

1. Place the cottage cheese in a bowl.

2. Drain the mandarin oranges, place them atop the cottage cheese, and sprinkle with almonds.

Nutrition: Calories: 360, Protein: 26.24 g, Fat: 21.37 g, Carbs: 15.22 g

404. Candied Dates

Preparation Time: 5 minutes

Cooking Time: 0 minutes

Servings: 2

Ingredients:

- 4 pitted Medjool dates
- 2 tbsp peanut butter
- 2 tbsp dark cocoa nibs

Directions:

1. Slice the pitted dates in half, and spread half a tbsp of peanut butter on each date.

2. Top each date with half a tbsp of dark cocoa nibs.

3. Divide the candied dates between 2 plates, and enjoy!

Nutrition: Total Carbs: 20 g, Fiber: 3 g, Protein: 5 g, Total Fat: 12 g, Calories: 187

405. Berry Delight

Preparation Time: 15 minutes

Cooking Time: 0 minutes

Servings: 6

Ingredients:

- 1 cup fresh organic blueberries
- 1 cup fresh organic raspberries
- 1 cup fresh organic blackberries
- ¼ cup raw honey
- 1 tbsp cinnamon

Directions:

1. Mix all the berries in a large bowl, add in the honey, and gently stir.

2. Sprinkle with cinnamon.

Nutrition: Total Carbs: 20 g, Fiber: 3 g, Protein: 1 g, Total Fat: 0 g, Calories: 78

406. Blueberry & Chia Flax Seed Pudding

Preparation Time: 10 minutes

Cooking Time: 5 minutes

Servings: 4

Ingredients:

- 2 cups almond milk
- 3 tbsp chia seeds
- 3 tbsp ground flaxseed
- ¼ cup blueberries

Directions:

1. Warm a pan on medium heat, then put all the ingredients except the blueberries.

2. Stir all the ingredients until the pudding is thick; this will take around 3 minutes.

3. Put the pudding into a bowl, then top with blueberries.

Nutrition: Total Carbs: 23 g, Fiber: 12 g, Protein: 7 g, Total Fat: 15 g, Calories: 243

407. Spicy Roasted Chickpeas

Preparation Time: 10 minutes

Cooking Time: 40 minutes

Servings: 6

Ingredients:

- 2 (15 oz) cans chickpeas, drained and rinsed
- 1 tsp paprika
- 1 tsp turmeric
- ¼ tsp cayenne pepper
- 2 tsp coconut oil, melted

Directions:

1. Set the oven to 425°F.

2. Line a baking sheet using a paper towel, then place the chickpeas on them and use more paper towels to take off the excess water in the chickpeas. Remove all of the paper towels.

3. Put the oil and spices into the chickpeas and mix well.

4. Roast your chickpeas for 40 minutes, stirring every 10 minutes.

5. Once the chickpeas are done, take them off the oven and let them completely cool.

Nutrition: Total Carbs: 19 g, Fiber: 3 g, Protein: 5 g, Total Fat: 12 g, Calories: 177

408. Berry Energy Bites

Preparation Time: 10 minutes

Cooking Time: 0 minutes

Servings: 6

Ingredients:

- ½ cup coconut flour
- 1 tsp cinnamon
- 1 tbsp coconut sugar
- ¼ cup dried blueberries
- 1 cup almond milk

Directions:

1. Put together the coconut flour, cinnamon, coconut sugar, and blueberries in a huge mixing bowl, and mix well.
2. Add the almond milk slowly until a firm dough is formed.
3. Form into bite-sized balls and refrigerate for 30 minutes so they can harden up.
4. Store leftovers in the refrigerator.

Nutrition: Total Carbs: 17 g, Fiber: 1 g, Protein: 5 g, Total Fat: 12 g, Calories: 87

409. Roasted Beets

Preparation Time: 10 minutes

Cooking Time: 35 to 45 minutes

Servings: 6

Ingredients:

- 2½ lb beets, peeled and diced
- 1 tbsp coconut oil, melted
- 1 tsp salt

Directions:

1. Preheat the oven to 400°F.
2. Spread the beets onto a baking sheet and drizzle with melted coconut oil.
3. Add salt and mix well.
4. Roast the beets in the oven for 35 to 45 minutes until the beets are soft.

Nutrition: Total Carbs: 7 g, Fiber: 2 g, Protein: 5 g, Total Fat: 12 g, Calories: 57

410. Bruschetta

Preparation Time: 60 minutes

Cooking Time: 0 minutes

Servings: 4

Ingredients:

- 4 medium tomatoes, diced
- 1 red onion, diced
- ¼ cup extra virgin olive oil
- 2 tbsp balsamic vinegar
- 2 garlic cloves, minced
- 1 tsp sea salt
- ¼ tsp ground black pepper

Directions:

1. Place the ingredients into a large bowl, and stir gently.
2. Refrigerate for 1 hour before serving on gluten-free toast (toast is not included in nutritional information)

Nutrition: Total Carbs: 7 g, Fiber: 2 g, Protein: 5 g, Total Fat: 12 g, Calories: 185

411. Cashew Cheese

Preparation Time: 2 hours

Cooking Time: 0 minutes

Servings: 6

Ingredients:

- 1 cup raw cashews
- Juice ½ lemon
- 1 tbsp nutritional yeast
- Salt and pepper to taste
- ¼ cup fresh basil

Directions:

1. In a cup of water, soak the cashew for at least 2 hours. Drain.
2. Place the cashews, lemon juice, nutritional yeast, and fresh basil into a food processor and blend until smooth. Put in 1 tbsp of water at a time to make it creamy but not runny.
3. Season with pepper and salt, then spread it on gluten-free bread or toast.
4. Store in an airtight jar in the refrigerator.

Nutrition: Total Carbs: 10 g, Fiber: 1 g, Protein: 5 g, Total Fat: 12 g, Calories: 127

412. Low Cholesterol-Low Calorie Blueberry Muffin

Preparation Time: 10 minutes

Cooking Time: 25 minutes

Servings: 12

Ingredients:

- 1 cup blueberries, fresh
- 2 tbsp melted margarine
- 2 tsp baking powder
- 1½ cups flour, all-purpose
- 1 egg white
- ½ cup skim milk or non-fat milk
- 1 tbsp coconut oil
- ½ cup white sugar
- Pinch of salt

Directions:

1. Set the oven to 205C.

2. Grease a 12-cup muffin pan using oil.

3. In a small bowl, place the blueberries. Add ¼ cup of the flour and mix it. Set aside.

4. In another bowl, whisk the egg white and the coconut oil. Add the melted margarine.

5. In a separate bowl, mix the dry ingredients and sift. Sift again over the egg white mixture. Mix to moisten the flour. The flour should look lumpy, so do not overmix.

6. Fold in the blueberries. Separate the blueberries so that each scoop will have blueberries. Scoop the mixture into the muffin pans. Fill only up to ⅔ of the pan.

7. Bake for 25 minutes or until the muffin turns golden brown.

Nutrition: Calories: 114, Protein: 2.66 g, Fat: 5.34 g, Carbs: 14.25 g

413. Carrot Sticks with Avocado Dip

Preparation Time: 10 minutes

Cooking Time: 0 minutes

Servings: 6

Ingredients:

- 1 large avocado, pitted
- 6 oz shelled edamame
- ½ cup cilantro, tightly packed
- ½ onion
- Juice 1 lemon
- 2 tbsp olive oil
- 1 tbsp chili-garlic sauce or chili sauce
- Salt and pepper

Directions:

1. Place the edamame, cilantro, onion, and chili sauce in a blender or food processor. Pulse it to chop and mix the ingredients. Add the avocado and lemon juice. Gradually add the olive oil as you blend. Transfer to a jar.

2. Scoop 2 spoons and serve with carrot sticks.

Nutrition: Calories: 154, Protein: 5.16 g, Fat: 11.96 g, Carbs: 8.44 g

414. Boiled Okra and Squash

Preparation Time: 5 minutes

Cooking Time: 5 minutes

Servings: 1

Ingredients:

- ½ cup okra, cut into 1-inch cubes
- ½ cup squash, cut into 1-inch cubes
- 1 garlic clove, minced
- ⅔ cup Vegetable stock or fish stock, plain water may be used as well
- Salt to taste

Directions:

1. Boil the liquid in high heat.

2. Add the okra and squash. Bring to a boil. Add the garlic. Reduce the heat and simmer for at least 5 minutes or until the squash is tender.

3. Add salt to taste and serve hot.

Nutrition: Calories: 117, Protein: 8.2 g, Fat: 6.25 g, Carbs: 7.82 g

415. Oven Crisp Sweet Potato

Preparation Time: 10 minutes

Cooking Time: 20 minutes

Servings: 2

Ingredients:

- 1 medium-sized sweet potato, raw
- 1 tsp sugar
- 1 tsp coconut oil

Directions:

1. Preheat the oven to 160°C.

2. Using a mandolin slicer or a peeler, slice the sweet potato into thin chips or strips. Wash and pat dry.

3. Drizzle the coconut oil over the potatoes. Toss until all chips are coated.

4. Arrange in an oven baking sheet. Bake for 10 minutes. Check the crispiness. If it is not that crispy enough, bake for another 5 or 1o minutes or until the chips attain the crispiness desired.

5. Take out the crispy sweet potatoes. Sprinkle with sugar and serve.

Nutrition: Calories: 123, Protein: 4.23 g, Fat: 5.39 g, Carbs: 14.63 g

416. Olive and Tomato Balls

Preparation Time: 10 minutes

Cooking Time: 0 minutes

Servings: 5

Ingredients:

- 5 tbsp parmesan cheese, grated
- ¼ tsp salt
- Black pepper (as desired)
- 2 garlic cloves, crushed
- 4 kalamata olives, pitted
- 4 sun-dried tomatoes, drained
- 2 tbsp oregano, chopped
- 2 tbsp thyme, chopped
- 2 tbsp basil, chopped
- ¼ cup coconut oil
- ½ cup cream cheese

Directions:

1. Add the coconut oil to a small mixing bowl with the cream cheese, and leave them to soften for about 30 minutes. Mix well to combine.

2. Add in the Kalamata olives and sun-dried tomatoes and mix well before adding in the herbs and seasonings. Combine thoroughly before placing the mixing bowl in the refrigerator to allow the results to solidify.

3. Once it has solidified, form the mixture into a total of 5 balls using an ice cream scoop. Roll each of the finished balls into the parmesan cheese before plating.

4. Stored the extras in the fridge in an air-tight container for up to 7 days.

Nutrition: Calories: 212, Protein: 4.77 g, Fat: 20.75 g, Carbs: 3.13 g

417. Mini Pepper Nachos

Preparation Time: 5 minutes

Cooking Time: 10 minutes

Servings: 8

Ingredients:

- ½ cup tomato, chopped
- 1 tbsp chili powder
- 1 cup cheddar cheese, shredded
- 1 tsp cumin, ground
- 16 oz mini peppers, seeded, halved
- 1 tsp garlic powder
- 16 oz ground beef
- 1 tsp paprika
- ¼ tsp red pepper flakes
- ½ tsp salt
- ½ tsp oregano
- ½ tsp pepper

Directions:

1. Mix seasonings together in a bowl.

2. On medium heat, brown the meat, and be sure all the clumps are broken up.

3. Mix in the spices and continue to sauté until the seasoning has gone through all of the meat.

4. Heat the oven to 400°F.

5. Place the peppers in a single line. They can touch.

6. Coat with the beef mix.

7. Sprinkle with cheese.

8. Bake for at least 10 minutes or until cheese has melted.

9. Pull out of the oven and top with the toppings.

Nutrition: Calories: 240, Protein: 11.01 g, Fat: 18.2 g, Carbs: 9.49 g

418. Avocado Hummus

Preparation Time: 15 minutes

Cooking Time: 0 minutes

Servings: 4

Ingredients:

- ¼ tsp pepper
- ½ tsp salt
- ½ tsp cumin
- 1 clove pressed garlic
- ½ lemon juice
- ¼ cup tahini
- ¼ cup sunflower seeds
- ½ cup coconut oil
- ½ cup cilantro
- 3 avocados

Directions:

1. Halve the avocados, take off the pits, and then spoon out the flesh.

2. Put all together ingredients in a blender and mix until completely smooth.

3. Add water, lemon juice, or oil if you need to loosen the mixture bit.

Nutrition: Calories: 651, Protein: 9.62 g, Fat: 64.05 g, Carbs: 19.95 g

419. Flavorsome Almonds

Preparation Time: 10 minutes

Cooking Time: 15 minutes

Servings: 8

Ingredients:

- 2 cups whole almonds
- 3 tbsp raw honey
- 1 tsp extra-virgin olive oil
- 1 tbsp filtered water
- ½ tsp chili powder
- ½ tsp ground cinnamon
- ¼ tsp ground cumin
- ¼ tsp cayenne pepper
- Salt, to taste

Directions:

1. Preheat the oven to 350°F.

2. Arrange the almonds onto a large rimmed baking sheet in a single layer.

3. Roast for about 10 minutes.

4. Meanwhile, in a microwave-safe bowl, add honey and microwave on Hugh for about 30 seconds.

5. Remove from microwave and stir in oil and water.

6. In a small bowl, mix all spices.

7. Remove the almonds from the oven, add them to the bowl of honey mixture, and stir to combine well.

8. Transfer the almond mixture onto the baking sheet in a single layer.

9. Sprinkle with spice mixture evenly.

10. Roast for about 3 to 4 minutes.

11. Take off from the oven and keep aside to cool completely before serving.

12. You can preserve these roasted almonds in an airtight jar.

Nutrition: Calories: 168, Fat: 12.5 g, Carbs: 11.7 g, Protein: 5.1 g, Fiber: 3.1 g

420. Chewy Blackberry Leather

Preparation Time: 15 minutes

Cooking Time: 5 to 6 hours

Servings: 8

Ingredients:

- 2 cups fresh blackberries
- 1 tbsp fresh mint leaves
- 1 tsp ground cinnamon
- ⅛ tsp fresh lemon juice
- ¼ cup raw honey

Directions:

1. Set the oven to 170°F. Line baking sheet with parchment paper.

2. In a food processor, put all ingredients and pulse till smooth.

3. Take the mixture onto the prepared baking sheet and smooth the top with the back of a spoon.

4. Bake for about 5 to 6 hours.

5. Cut the leather into equal-sized strips.

6. Now, roll each rectangle to make fruit rolls.

Nutrition: Calories: 48, Fat: 12.5 g, Carbs: 11.7 g, Protein: 5.1 g, Fiber: 2.1 g

421. Party-Time Chicken Nuggets

Preparation Time: 10 minutes

Cooking Time: 12 minutes

Servings: 6

Ingredients:

- 2 (6 oz) grass-fed skinless, boneless chicken breasts
- 2 large organic eggs
- 1½ cups blanched almond flour
- ½ cup tapioca flour
- ½ tsp paprika
- ½ tsp onion powder
- ½ tsp garlic powder
- Salt, to taste
- Freshly ground black pepper, to taste

Directions:

1. Set the oven to 400°F, then grease a large baking sheet.
2. With a rolling pin, roll the chicken breasts to an even thickness.
3. Cut each breast into bite-sized pieces.
4. In a shallow dish, crack the eggs and beat well.
5. In another shallow dish, mix flours and spices.
6. Dip the chicken nuggets in beaten eggs.
7. Then roll in the flour mixture completely.
8. Arrange the nuggets onto the prepared baking sheet in a single layer.
9. Bake for about 10 to 12 minutes, flipping once after 5 minutes.

Nutrition: Calories: 238, Fat: 12.5 g, Carbs: 11.7 g, Protein: 4.1 g, Fiber: 2.1 g

422. Protein-Packed Croquettes

Preparation Time: 10 minutes

Cooking Time: 8 minutes

Servings: 12

Ingredients:

- ¼ cup plus 1 tbsp olive oil, divided
- ½ cup thawed frozen peas
- 2 minced garlic cloves
- 1 cup cooked quinoa
- 2 large peeled and mashed boiled potatoes
- ¼ cup chopped fresh cilantro leaves
- 2 tsp ground cumin
- ½ tsp paprika
- ¼ tsp ground turmeric
- Salt, to taste
- Freshly ground black pepper, to taste

Directions:

1. In a frying pan, heat 1 tbsp of oil on medium heat.
2. Add peas and garlic and sauté for about 1 minute.
3. Transfer the pea mixture into a large bowl.
4. Put remaining ingredients, then mix till well combined.
5. Make equal-sized oblong-shaped patties from the mixture.
6. In a huge skillet, warm the remaining oil on medium-high heat.
7. Add croquettes in batches and fry for about 4 minutes per side.

Nutrition: Calories: 165, Fat: 12.5 g, Carbs: 10.7 g, Protein: 5.1 g, Fiber: 3.1 g

423. Energy Dates Balls

Preparation Time: 10 minutes

Cooking Time: 0 minutes

Servings: 7

Ingredients:

- 1 cup toasted almonds
- 1 cup pitted and chopped dates
- ¼ cup fresh lemon juice
- ½ cup shredded sweetened coconut

Directions:

1. Line a large baking sheet using parchment paper. Keep aside.
2. In a food processor, add almonds and pulse till chopped coarsely.
3. Add dates and lemon juice and pulse till a soft dough forms.
4. Make equal-sized balls from the mixture.
5. In a shallow, dish place shredded coconut.

6. Roll the balls in shredded coconut evenly.

7. Put the balls onto the baking sheet in a single layer.

8. Refrigerate to set completely before serving.

Nutrition: Calories: 148, Fat: 14.5 g, Carbs: 11.7 g, Protein: 5.1 g, Fiber: 2.1 g

424.   Energetic Oat Bars

Preparation Time: 10 minutes

Cooking Time: 25 minutes

Servings: 6

Ingredients:

- ½ cup gluten-free rolled oats
- 2 tbsp flax seeds
- 1 tbsp sunflower seeds
- 1 tbsp chopped walnuts
- 2 tbsp raisins
- ¾ cup fresh blueberries
- 1 peeled and mashed banana
- 2 tbsp pitted and chopped finely dates
- 1 tbsp fresh pomegranate juice

Directions:

1. Set the oven to 350°F. Lightly oil an 8-inch baking dish.

2. In a huge mixing bowl, put all ingredients and mix till well combined.

3. Place the mixture into the prepared baking dish evenly.

4. Bake for about 25 minutes. Take off from the oven, then cool.

5. Using a knife, divide the bars into the size of your desired pieces, then serve.

Nutrition: Calories: 88, Fat: 12.5 g, Carbs: 11.7 g, Protein: 5.1 g, Fiber: 2.7 g

425.   Bell Pepper Veggie Wraps

Preparation Time: 10 minutes

Cooking Time: 6 hours

Servings: 4

Ingredients:

- 6 cups chopped red bell pepper
- 4 cups chopped tomatoes
- 2 tsp salt

- 1 small avocado
- ½ cup flaxseed, ground

Directions:

1. Blend peppers, tomatoes, and salt.

2. Add avocado and continue blending.

3. Add flaxseed.

4. Spread over parchment paper on a dehydrator tray into a thin layer.

5. Shape as tortillas.

6. Dehydrate at 109°F for 5 to 6 hrs.

7. Then flip over for 4 hours.

8. Wraps should be dry but still very pliable.

Nutrition: Calories: 524, Protein: 15.05 g, Fat: 33.86 g, Carbs: 48.94 g

426.   Vegetable Nuggets

Preparation Time: 10 minutes

Cooking Time: 25 minutes

Servings: 24

Ingredients:

- ¼ tsp black pepper
- 2 cups cauliflower florets
- 1 egg, large & pastured
- 2 cups broccoli florets
- ½ cup almond meal
- 1 cup carrots, chopped coarsely
- ¼ tsp salt
- 1 tsp garlic, minced
- ½ tsp turmeric, grounded

Directions:

1. To make these tasty nuggets, you first need to preheat the oven to 400°F.

2. Next, place broccoli, turmeric, cauliflower, black pepper, carrots, sea salt, and turmeric in a food processor.

3. Pulse them for a minute or until you get a finely ground mixture.

4. Then, stir in the almond meal and egg into it and pulse them again until mixed.

5. Now, transfer the veggie-almond mixture to a large mixing bowl.

6. Scoop out the mixture with a tbsp and make circular discs with your hands.

7. After that, place the discs on the parchment paper-lined baking sheet.

8. Finally, bake them for 20 to 25 minutes while flipping them once.

9. Tip: Serve it along with homemade ranch sauce.

Nutrition: Calories: 220, Protein: 1.1 g, Carbs: 2.1 g, Fat: 1.2 g

427. Turmeric Muffins

Preparation Time: 10 minutes

Cooking Time: 25 minutes

Servings: 8 Muffins

Ingredients:

- ¾ cup + 2 tbsp coconut flour
- 6 eggs, large & preferably pastured
- ½ tsp ginger powder
- ½ cup coconut milk, unsweetened
- Dash of salt & pepper
- ⅓ cup maple syrup
- ½ tsp baking soda
- 1 tsp vanilla extract
- 2 tsp turmeric

Directions:

1. Preheat the oven to 350°F.

2. After that, mix eggs, vanilla extract, milk, maple syrup, and milk in a large mixing bowl until combined well.

3. In another bowl, combine turmeric, coconut flour, ginger powder, baking soda, pepper, and salt.

4. Now, stir in the coconut flour mixture gradually to the milk mixture until you get a smooth batter.

5. Then, pour the smooth mixture into a paper-lined muffin pan while distributing it evenly.

6. Finally, bake them for 20 to 25 minutes or until slightly browned at the edges.

7. Allow the muffins to cool completely.

Tip: They are freezer friendly and stay good for 1 month.

Nutrition: Calories: 220, Protein: 1.1 g, Carbs: 2.1 g, Fat: 1.2 g

428. Quinoa Tortillas

Preparation Time: 10 minutes

Cooking Time: 20 minutes

Servings: 4

Ingredients:

- 2 medium potatoes, unpeeled
- 1 cup arrowroot powder, plus more for rolling
- 1 cup sprouted quinoa flour
- 1½ tsp flaxseed, ground
- 1½ tsp guar gum
- 1 tsp unrefined salt

Directions:

1. Place whole potatoes into a steamer basket and saucepan with approximately 1 inch of water at the bottom of the saucepan. Cover the saucepan.

2. Bring water to a boil and then lower heat to simmer until tender, about 20 minutes.

3. Drain fluid and remove potatoes from the saucepan.

4. Cut potatoes so that they fill a measuring cup and measure 1½ cup to use for the recipe.

5. Place potatoes in a food processor with the remaining ingredients and process until a dough is formed. The dough should not be sticky; add quinoa flour until the dough is soft, pliable, and does not stick to your hands.

6. When the dough is well blended, spoon it into your hand and form into small balls, approximately 2 inches in diameter

7. Use a tortilla press (lined with waxed paper or plastic) to press the dough ball into a flat tortilla. If no tortilla press is available, roll the dough into thin circles, dusting lightly with arrowroot flour to prevent sticking.

8. Place the tortillas in heated cast iron or ceramic skillet for about 1 minute, turn over with a spatula and toast until lightly golden brown on both sides.

9. Use them as you would use a tortilla or taco.

Nutrition: Calories: 650, Protein: 22.47 g, Fat: 6.69 g, Carbs: 127.77 g

429. Steamed Cauliflower

Preparation Time: 5 minutes

Cooking Time: 2 minutes

Servings: 6

Ingredients:

- 1 large head cauliflower, cored and cut into large florets

Directions:

1. Put 2 cups of water into the inner pot. Place a steam rack inside.

2. Place the cauliflower inside a steamer basket and place the basket on the steam rack, steam within 2 minutes.

3. Carefully remove the steamer basket and serve.

Nutrition: Calories: 34, Fat: 0 g, Protein: 3 g, Sodium: 41 mg, Fiber: 3 g, Carbs: 7 g, Sugar: 3 g

430. Saucy Brussels Sprouts and Carrots

Preparation Time: 15 minutes

Cooking Time: 12 minutes

Servings: 4

Ingredients:

- 1 tbsp coconut oil
- 12 oz Brussels sprouts, tough ends removed and cut in half
- 12 oz carrots (about 4 medium), peeled, ends removed, and cut into 1" chunks
- ¼ cup fresh lime juice
- ¼ cup apple cider vinegar
- ½ cup coconut amino
- ¼ cup almond butter

Directions:

1. Sauté the Brussels sprouts and carrots and sauté until browned, about 5 to 7 minutes.

2. While the vegetables are browning, make the sauce. Mix the lime juice, vinegar, coconut amino, and almond butter in a small bowl.

3. Pour the sauce over the vegetables—Cook within 6 minutes. Serve.

Nutrition: Calories: 216, Fat: 11 g, Protein: 6 g, Sodium: 738 mg Fiber: 6 g, Carbs: 22 g, Sugar: 5 g

431. Steamed Purple Sweet Potatoes

Preparation Time: 5 minutes

Cooking Time: 40 minutes

Servings: 4

Ingredients:

- 4 purple sweet potatoes, whole and unpeeled

Directions:

1. Place in a steamer basket and steam until thoroughly cooked, approximately 40 minutes.

Nutrition: Calories: 762, Protein: 45.18 g, Fat: 9.25 g, Carbs: 160.03 g

432. Mexican Veggie Meat

Preparation Time: 10 minutes

Cooking Time: 5 hours

Servings: 4

Ingredients:

- 2 cups sunflower seeds, soaked for 8 hours and rinsed
- 5 cups zucchini, shredded
- ½ cup onion, minced
- 1 cup celery, minced
- ½ cup homemade chili powder
- ¼ cup lemon juice
- 1 tsp unrefined salt
- 2 garlic cloves, crushed

Directions:

1. Use a food processor to process sunflower seeds into flour.

2. In a large bowl, combine with other ingredients.

3. Spread the mixture onto 2 dehydrator sheets lined with parchment paper.

4. Dehydrate at 109°F for 5 hours (or until it reaches your desired consistency).

Nutrition: Calories: 2132, Protein: 80.1 g, Fat: 163.49 g, Carbs: 153.89 g

433. Flaxseed Crackers

Preparation Time: 10 minutes

Cooking Time: 18 hours

Servings: 3

Ingredients:

- 2 cups flax seeds (soaked for 1 to 2 hours in 2 cups water)
- ⅓ cup red bell pepper, chopped finely
- ⅔ cup sun-dried tomatoes
- ⅓ cup fresh cilantro or basil, chopped finely
- 1¼ cups tomatoes, diced
- 1 garlic clove, minced
- Pinch cayenne
- 1 tsp unrefined salt

Directions:

1. Place bell pepper, cilantro, sun-dried tomatoes, tomatoes, cayenne, garlic, and salt into a food processor and process until pureed.

2. Transfer contents into a large bowl and mix in the flax seeds.

3. Spread mixture onto a dehydrator sheet and dehydrate at 109°F for about 18 hours.

Nutrition: Calories: 1774, Protein: 65.67 g, Fat: 145.63 g, Carbs: 86.04 g

434. Buckwheat Crackers

Preparation Time: 10 minutes

Cooking Time: 18 hours

Servings: 4

Ingredients:

- 1½ cup raw buckwheat groats, sprouted 2 days and rinsed
- 1 small bell pepper
- ½ zucchini
- 1 cup young coconut meat. (This requires 1 to 2 young coconuts)
- ½ tsp unrefined salt.
- 1 tsp dried basil (optional)
- ¼ tsp dried oregano (optional)

Directions:

1. Pulse buckwheat groats in the food processor. The groats should be coarsely chopped and not overly processed.

2. Place the processed groats into a large bowl.

3. Quarter the bell pepper and cut zucchini into smaller pieces before placing them into the processor.

4. In the food processor, pulse the bell pepper and zucchini into finely chopped pieces (doing your best not to puree the mixture) and add them to the bowl when done.

5. Process coconut meat very thoroughly and add it to the bowl.

6. Mix all ingredients well.

7. Spread onto dehydrator trays lined with parchment paper.

8. Dehydrate at 109°F for about 18 hours. Crackers should be very dry without a hint of moisture or softness.

9. Use in place of bread for lunch.

10. Top with avocado slices and a pinch of salt.

Nutrition: Calories: 268, Protein: 6.21 g, Fat: 14.25 g, Carbs: 33.7 g

435. Zucchini Slices

Preparation Time: 10 minutes

Cooking Time: 15 minutes

Servings: 4

Ingredients:

- ¼ cup tomato sauce
- 1 zucchini, sliced
- Salt and black pepper to the taste
- ½ tsp ground cumin
- Cooking spray

Directions:

1. Spray a baking sheet with cooking spray and spread the zucchini slices on the tray evenly. Pour the tomato sauce over the zucchini. Sprinkle with cumin, salt and pepper, introduce in the oven at 350°F, bake for 15 minutes, arrange on a platter and serve.

2. Enjoy!

Nutrition: Calories: 140, Fat: 4 g, Fiber: 2 g, Carbs: 6 g, Protein: 4 g

436.   Easy Zucchini Snack

Preparation Time: 10 minutes

Cooking Time: 3 hours

Servings: 8

Ingredients:

- 3 zucchinis, thinly sliced
- Salt and black pepper to the taste
- 2 tbsp avocado oil
- 2 tbsp balsamic vinegar

Directions:

1. In a bowl, whisk the oil with vinegar, salt and pepper. Add zucchini slices to the bowl and toss to coat well.

2. Spread the zucchini on a lined baking sheet and place the tray in the oven at 200°F and bake for 3 hours. Leave chips to cool down and serve them. Enjoy!

Nutrition: Calories: 100, Fat: 3 g, Fiber: 7 g, Carbs: 3 g, Protein: 7 g

437.   Cumin Zucchini Spread

Preparation Time: 10 minutes

Cooking Time: 0 minutes

Servings: 5

Ingredients:

- 4 cups chopped zucchini
- ¼ cup olive oil
- Salt and black pepper to the taste
- 4 garlic cloves, minced
- ¾ cup tahini
- ½ cup lemon juice
- 1 tbsp ground cumin

Directions:

1. In your blender, mix zucchini with salt, pepper, oil, lemon juice, garlic, tahini and cumin. Pulse until smooth then divide into small bowls and serve.

2. Enjoy!

Nutrition: Calories: 110, Fat: 5 g, Fiber: 3 g, Carbs: 6 g, Protein: 7 g

438.   Celery Spread

Preparation Time: 10 minutes

Cooking Time: 0 minutes

Servings: 2

Ingredients:

- 6 celery stacks, chopped
- 3 tbsp tomato sauce
- ¼ cup avocado mayonnaise
- Salt and black pepper to the taste
- ½ tsp garlic powder

Directions:

1. In a bowl, mix the celery with mayo, tomato sauce, black pepper, salt and garlic powder. Stir well and divide into bowls and serve.

2. Enjoy!

Nutrition: Calories: 100, Fat: 12 g, Fiber: 3 g, Carbs: 1 g, Protein: 6 g

439.   Stuffed Mushrooms

Preparation Time: 10 minutes

Cooking Time: 20 minutes

Servings: 5

Ingredients:

- ¼ cup avocado mayonnaise
- 1 tsp garlic powder
- 1 small yellow onion, chopped
- 24 oz white mushroom caps
- Salt and black pepper to the taste
- 1 tsp curry powder
- ¼ cup coconut cream
- 1 cup shrimp, cooked, peeled, deveined and chopped

Directions:

1. In a bowl, whisk together the mayo with garlic powder, onion, salt, pepper, curry powder, coconut cream and shrimp. Stuff the mushrooms with this mix and arrange them on a baking sheet. Cook in the oven at 350°F for 20 minutes.

2. Arrange on a platter and serve. Enjoy!

Nutrition: Calories: 204, Fat: 10 g, Fiber: 3 g, Carbs: 7 g, Protein: 11 g

440.   Simple Mango Salsa

Preparation Time: 10 minutes

Cooking Time: 0 minutes

Servings: 4

Ingredients:

- 1 avocado, pitted, peeled and cubed
- 2 cups cubed mango
- ¼ cup chopped cilantro
- ½ cup chopped red onion
- 2 tbsp olive oil
- Salt and black pepper to the taste
- Juice 1 lime
- A pinch of red pepper flakes

Directions:

1. In a bowl, mix avocado with mango, onion and cilantro.
2. Add olive oil, salt, pepper, lime juice and pepper flakes then toss to coat and serve as a snack. Enjoy!

Nutrition: Calories: 100, Fat: 3 g, Fiber: 4 g, Carbs: 8 g, Protein: 9 g

441.   Spicy Kale Chips

Preparation Time: 10 minutes

Cooking Time: 1 hour 30 minutes

Servings: 10

Ingredients:

- 2 cups cashews, soaked and drained
- 1 bunch kale, trimmed and leaves separated
- Salt and black pepper to the taste
- 3 tbsp avocado oil
- Juice 1 lemon
- ⅔ cup jarred roasted peppers
- 1 tsp Italian seasoning
- ¼ tsp chili powder
- ½ tsp garlic powder

Directions:

1. In your food processor, mix cashews with peppers, oil, lemon juice, Italian seasoning, chili powder, garlic powder, salt and pepper and blend very well. In a bowl, mix kale leaves with cashews mix and massage well.
2. Spread them on a lined baking sheet and bake in the oven at 400°F for 1 hour. Flip and cook

Spicy Kale Chips for 30 minutes more, then allow to cool. Serve the chips cold. Enjoy!

Nutrition: Calories: 126, Fat: 7 g, Fiber: 2 g, Carbs: 9 g, Protein: 7 g

442.   Green Bean Snack

Preparation Time: 10 minutes

Cooking Time: 8 hours

Servings: 8

Ingredients:

- ⅓ cup coconut oil, melted
- 5 lb green beans
- Salt to the taste
- 1 tsp garlic powder
- 1 tsp onion powder

Directions:

1. In a bowl, mix green beans with coconut oil, salt, garlic and onion powder.
2. Put them in your dehydrator and dry them for 8 hours at 135°F. Serve cold as a snack. Enjoy!

Nutrition: Calories: 100, Fat: 12 g, Fiber: 4 g, Carbs: 8 g, Protein: 5 g

443.   Avocado and Pepper Hummus

Preparation Time: 10 minutes

Cooking Time: 0 minutes

Servings: 6

Ingredients:

- 2 avocados, peeled, pitted, chopped
- Salt and black pepper to the taste
- 1 tbsp coconut oil
- 4 garlic cloves, chopped
- ½ cup tahini
- 2 tbsp lemon juice
- 4 oz roasted peppers, chopped

Directions:

1. In a blender, mix the avocados with salt, pepper, oil, garlic, tahini, lemon juice and peppers.
2. Pulse until smooth then divide into bowls and serve as a snack. Enjoy!

Nutrition: Calories: 140, Fat: 6 g, Fiber: 2 g, Carbs: 9 g, Protein: 8 g

444. Easy Veggie Stuffed Mushrooms

Preparation Time: 10 minutes

Cooking Time: 30 minutes

Servings: 12

Ingredients:

- 1 tbsp olive oil
- 2 small red bell peppers, chopped
- 1 small yellow onion, chopped
- 2 lb button mushrooms, stems reserved
- 3 garlic cloves, minced
- 2 cups chopped spinach
- Salt and black pepper to the taste
- ¼ cup chopped parsley

Directions:

1. Heat up a pan with the oil over medium heat and add the mushroom stems. Stir and cook for 2 minutes. Add bell peppers, garlic, parsley, spinach, salt, pepper and onion. Stir, cook for 6 minutes then remove from heat. Stuff each mushroom with this mix and arrange them all on a lined baking sheet. Cook in the oven at 350°F for 20 minutes and serve as an appetizer.

2. Enjoy!

Nutrition: Calories: 120, Fat: 8 g, Fiber: 5 g, Carbs: 10 g, Protein: 9 g

445. Sesame Spread

Preparation Time: 10 minutes

Cooking Time: 0 minutes

Servings: 6

Ingredients:

- 1 cup tahini sesame seed paste
- Salt and black pepper to the taste
- 1 cup veggie stock
- ½ cup lemon juice
- 1 tbsp chopped cilantro
- ½ tsp ground cumin
- 3 garlic cloves, chopped

Directions:

1. Place the sesame seed paste with salt, pepper, lemon juice, stock, cilantro, cumin and garlic into a food processor.

2. Pulse well, divide into bowls and serve as a party spread. Enjoy!

Nutrition: Calories: 120, Fat: 12 g, Fiber: 2 g, Carbs: 11 g, Protein: 5 g

446. Easy Eggplant Spread

Preparation Time: 10 minutes

Cooking Time: 0 minutes

Servings: 6

Ingredients:

- 2 lb eggplant, baked, peeled and chopped
- A pinch of salt and black pepper
- 4 tbsp olive oil
- 4 garlic cloves, chopped
- Juice 1 lemon
- ¼ cup black olives, pitted
- 1 tbsp sesame paste

Directions:

1. In a blender, mix the eggplant with salt, pepper, oil, garlic, lemon juice, olives and sesame paste.

2. Blend until smooth then divide into bowls and serve. Enjoy!

Nutrition: Calories: 165, Fat: 11 g, Fiber: 4 g, Carbs: 8 g, Protein: 5 g

447. Creamy Artichoke Spread

Preparation Time: 10 minutes

Cooking Time: 35 minutes

Servings: 6

Ingredients:

- 2 garlic cloves, minced
- Juice ½ lemon
- 1 cup veggie stock
- 1 lb baby artichokes, trimmed and stems cut off
- 1 cup coconut cream
- A pinch of salt and black pepper

Directions:

1. In a small pot, mix the artichokes with the stock, salt and pepper.

2. Stir and bring to a simmer over medium heat. Simmer for 35 minutes then transfer to a blender, add the garlic, lemon juice and cream and pulse well. Divide into bowls and serve. Enjoy!

Nutrition: Calories: 150, Fat: 2 g, Fiber: 3 g, Carbs: 8 g, Protein: 5 g

448. Balsamic Onion Snack

Preparation Time: 10 minutes

Cooking Time: 10 minutes

Servings: 4

Ingredients:

- 1 lb pearl onions, peeled
- A pinch of salt and black pepper
- ½ cup water
- 4 tbsp balsamic vinegar
- 1 tbsp coconut flour

Directions:

1. In a small pot, whisk the water with vinegar and coconut flour. Bring to a simmer over medium heat.

2. Add the pearl onions, toss, cook for 10 minutes, drain the liquid, divide into bowls and serve as a snack. Enjoy!

Nutrition: Calories: 100, Fat: 9 g, Fiber: 4 g, Carbs: 11 g, Protein: 6 g

449. Lentil and Mushrooms Cakes

Preparation Time: 10 minutes

Cooking Time: 10 minutes

Servings: 8

Ingredients:

- 2 tsp fresh grated ginger
- 1 cup chopped yellow onion
- 1 cup minced mushrooms
- 1 cup canned red lentils, drained and rinsed
- 1 sweet potato, grated
- ¼ cup chopped parsley
- 1 tbsp curry powder
- ¼ cup chopped cilantro
- 2 tbsp coconut flour
- 1 tbsp olive oil

Directions:

1. Put the lentils in a bowl and mash them well using a potato masher. Add the onion, ginger, mushrooms, potato, curry powder, parsley, cilantro and flour to the bowl with the lentils. Stir well and shape medium cakes out of this mix.

2. Heat up a pan with the oil over medium-high heat, add the cakes and cook them for about 5 minutes on each side. Serve as an appetizer while warm. Enjoy!

Nutrition: Calories: 142, Fat: 4 g, Fiber: 3 g, Carbs: 8 g, Protein: 8 g

Chapter 13
Dessert

450. After's Apple Cinnamon Chips

Preparation Time: 20 minutes

Cooking Time: 2 hours

Servings: 3

Ingredients:

- 3 large apples, cored, rinsed, and drained
- ¾ tsp cinnamon, ground

Directions:

1. Preheat your oven to 200°F. Line 2 baking pans with parchment paper.

2. By using a very sharp knife, or preferably, a mandolin, slice the apples horizontally into ⅛-inch thick rounds. Assemble the slices in a single layer on the baking pans. Sprinkle over with the cinnamon.

3. Place the pans in the upper and lower racks of the oven and then bake for 1 hour. Switch positions of the pans on the upper and lower racks. Bake further for another hour, or until a single chip becomes crispy when set at room temperature for 3 minutes.

4. Switch off the oven and allow the chips to sit in the oven for an hour while they cool down for further crispiness.

Nutrition: Calories: 65, Fat: 2.1 g, Protein: 3.2 g, Sodium: 2 mg, Total Carbs: 13.2 g, Fiber: 5 g, Net Carbs: 8.2 g

451. Avocado Choco Cake

Preparation Time: 10 minutes

Cooking Time: 25 minutes

Servings: 8

Ingredients:

- 1 large avocado
- 1 tsp vanilla extract
- ½ cup maple syrup
- ½ cup applesauce, unsweetened
- 3 large eggs
- 1 tsp baking soda
- ½ cup cocoa powder, unsweetened and Dutch-processed
- ½ cup coconut flour
- ¼ tsp sea salt

Directions:

1. Preheat the oven to 350°F. Coconut oil should be used to grease a baking pan.

2. In a food processor, combine the avocado, vanilla, syrup, and applesauce. Blend until everything is well incorporated.

3. Fill a large mixing bowl halfway with the mixture. Incorporate the eggs into the mixture. Combine the baking soda, cocoa powder, coconut flour, and salt in a mixing bowl. In a large mixing bowl, blend all of the ingredients until they are completely incorporated.

4. In the baking pan, pour the batter. Preheat the oven to 350°F. Place the pan in the oven. Preheat the oven to 350°F and bake for 25 minutes.

5. Allow the cake to cool for 20 minutes before cutting it into 16 squares.

Nutrition: Calories: 253, Fat: 8.4 g, Protein: 12.6 g, Sodium: 245 mg, Total Carbs: 43.9 g, Fiber: 12.3 g, Net Carbs: 31.6 g

452. Sweet Strawberry Sorbet

Preparation Time: 5 minutes

Cooking Time: 0 minutes

Servings: 3

Ingredients:

- 1 lb strawberries, frozen
- 1 cup orange juice or 1 cup coconut water

Directions:

1. Process the strawberries in your food processor for 2 minutes, or until the fruit turns into flakes. Pour the orange juice, and process it further into a smooth frozen puree.

2. To serve, you may present it either as a chilled soft dessert or as sorbet, frozen after an hour and 45 minutes. You can also serve it like a Popsicle by pouring the soft serve into Popsicle molds and freezing overnight.

Nutrition: Calories: 86, Fat: 2.3 g, Protein: 5.3 g, Sodium: 7 mg, Total Carbs: 20.3 g, Fiber: 9.6 g, Net Carbs: 10.7 g

453. Rum Butter Cookies

Preparation Time: 10 minutes + chilling time

Cooking Time: 5 minutes

Servings: 12

Ingredients:

- ½ cup coconut butter
- ½ cup confectioners' Swerve
- 1 stick butter
- 1 tsp rum extract
- 4 cups almond meal

Directions:

1. Melt the coconut butter and butter. Mix in the Swerve and rum extract.

2. Afterward, put in the almond meal and mix to blend.

3. Roll the balls and put them on a parchment-lined cookie sheet.

4. Keep in your fridge until ready to serve.

Nutrition: Calories: 400, Fat: 4.9 g, Carbs: 5.4 g, Protein: 2.9 g

454. Sherbet Pineapple

Preparation Time: 20 minutes

Cooking Time: 0 minutes

Servings: 4

Ingredients:

- 1 can of 8 oz pineapple chunks
- ¼ tsp ground ginger
- ¼ tsp vanilla extract
- 1 can 11 oz orange sections
- 2 cups pineapple, lemon or lime sherbet
- ⅓ cup orange marmalade

Directions:

1. Drain the pineapple, and ensure you reserve the juice.

2. Take a moderate-sized container and put pineapple juice, ginger, vanilla and marmalade into the container

3. Put in pineapple chunks, drained mandarin oranges as well

4. Toss thoroughly and coat everything

5. Free them for 15 minutes and let them chill

6. Ladle the sherbet into 4 chilled stemmed sherbet dishes

7. Top each of them with a fruit mixture

8. Enjoy!

Nutrition: Calories: 267, Fat: 1g, Carbs: 65g, Protein: 2g

455. Spicy Popper Mug Cake

Preparation Time: 5 minutes

Cooking Time: 5 minutes

Servings: 2

Ingredients:

- ¼ tsp sunflower seeds
- ½ a jalapeno pepper
- ½ tsp baking powder
- 1 bacon, cooked and cut
- 1 big egg
- 1 tbsp almond butter
- 1 tbsp cashew cheese
- 1 tbsp flaxseed meal
- 2 tbsp almond flour

Directions:

1. Take a frying pan then place it on moderate heat

2. Put cut bacon and cook until they have a crunchy texture

3. Take a microwave proof container and mix all of the listed ingredients (including cooked bacon), clean the sides

4. Microwave for 75 seconds making to put your microwave to high power

5. Take out the cup and slam it against a surface to take the cake out

6. Decorate using a bit of jalapeno and serve!

Nutrition: Calories: 429, Fat: 37 g, Carbs: 6 g, Protein: 16 g

456. Strawberry Granita

Preparation Time: 10 minutes

Cooking Time: 0 minutes

Servings: 8

Ingredients:

- ¼ tsp balsamic vinegar
- ½ tsp lemon juice
- 1 cup water
- 2 lb strawberries, halved & hulled
- Agave to taste
- Just a small pinch of salt

Directions:

1. Wash the strawberries in water.

2. Keep in a blender. Put in water, agave, balsamic vinegar, salt, and lemon juice.

3. Pulse multiple times so that the mixture moves. Blend until smooth.

4. Pour into a baking dish. The puree must be ⅜-inch deep only.

5. Place in your fridge the dish uncovered till the edges start to freeze. The center must be slushy.

6. Stir crystals from the edges lightly into the center. Stir thoroughly to mix.

7. Chill till the granite is nearly fully frozen.

8. Scrape loose the crystals like before and mix.

9. Place in your fridge once more. Using a fork, stir 3 to 4 times till the granite has become light.

Nutrition: Calories: 72, Carbs: 17 g, Fat: 0 g, Sugar: 14 g, Fiber: 2 g, Protein: 1 g

457. Strawberry Ice Cream

Preparation Time: 0 minutes

Cooking Time: 5 minutes

Servings: 2 to 3

Ingredients:

- 1 banana, frozen & cut
- 1 cup strawberries, frozen
- 1 tsp vanilla extract
- 2 tbsp coconut milk

Directions:

1. Begin by placing strawberries and banana in a high-speed blender and blend them for 2 minutes.

2. While you blend, spoon in the coconut milk, and the vanilla extract.

3. Carry on blending until the mixture is thick and smooth.

4. Serve the ice cream instantly since it does not keep well in the freezer.

Nutrition: Calories: 78, Protein: 1 g, Carbs: 13.6 g, Fat: 2.7 g

458. Strawberry Orange Sorbet

Preparation Time: 5 minutes

Cooking Time: 0 minutes

Servings: 3

Ingredients:

- 1 cup orange juice or coconut water
- 1 lb frozen strawberries

Directions:

1. Place strawberries in a blender and process until only flakes remain. No more than 2 minutes.

2. Now add the coconut water or orange juice and pulse until the purée is smooth and silky. Make sure you have a spatula on hand in case you need to scrape some puree from the blender's walls.

3. Serve immediately, or place in the freezer for 45 minutes for a sorbet-like texture.

4. You may also freeze the smoothie in popsicle molds for hours or even overnight.

5. Enjoy!

Nutrition: Calories: 118, Protein: 2.88 g, Fat: 2.19 g, Carbs: 23.25 g

459. Strawberry Shortcake

Preparation Time: 15 minutes

Cooking Time: 0 minutes

Servings: 4

Ingredients:

- ¼ cup semi-sweet chocolate chips
- 1 tbsp low-calorie margarine
- 12 hulled strawberries
- 2.3-inch shortcake, quartered

Directions:

1. Using waxed paper, line a cookie sheet.
2. Thread 2 shortcake pieces and 3 strawberries on 4 skewers.
3. In a small deep cooking pan, mix together the margarine and chocolate chips before placing the deep cooking pan on the stove over a burner turned to low heat. Stir until the ingredients are well mixed.
4. Sprinkle the chocolate onto the kabobs and then put them in your fridge for about 4 minutes to cool.

Nutrition: Calories: 40, Protein: 1.85 g, Fat: 2.3 g, Carbs: 3.32 g

460. Sweet Almond and Coconut Fat Bombs

Preparation Time: 10 minutes + 20 minutes chill time

Cooking Time: 0 minutes

Servings: 4

Ingredients:

- ¼ cup melted coconut oil
- 3 tbsp cocoa
- 9½ tbsp almond butter
- 9 tbsp melted almond butter, sunflower seeds
- 90 drops liquid stevia

Directions:

1. Take a container and put in all of the listed ingredients
2. Combine them well

3. Pour scant 2 tbsp of the mixture into as many muffin molds as you prefer
4. Chill for about 20 minutes and pop them out
5. Serve and enjoy!

Nutrition: Total Carbs: 2 g, Fiber: 0 g, Protein: 2.53 g, Fat: 14 g

461. The Most Elegant Parsley Soufflé Ever

Preparation Time: 5 minutes

Cooking Time: 6 minutes

Servings: 5

Ingredients:

- 1 fresh red chili pepper, chopped
- 1 tbsp fresh parsley, chopped
- 2 tbsp coconut cream
- 2 whole eggs
- Sunflower seeds to taste

Directions:

1. Preheat the oven to 390°F
2. Almond butter 2 soufflé dishes
3. Place the ingredients in a blender and mix thoroughly
4. Split batter into soufflé dishes and bake for about 6 minutes
5. Serve and enjoy!

Nutrition: Calories: 108, Fat: 9 g, Carbs: 9 g, Protein: 6g

462. Tropical Fruit Crisp

Preparation Time: 10 minutes

Cooking Time: 22 minutes

Servings: 6

Ingredients:

For the Filling:

- 1 big mango (cut into chunks)
- 1 big pineapple (cut into chunks)
- ⅛ tsp ground cinnamon
- ⅛ tsp ground ginger
- 2 tbsp coconut oil
- 2 tbsp coconut sugar

For the Topping:

- ¾ cup almonds

- ½ tsp ground allspice
- ½ tsp ground cinnamon
- ½ tsp ground ginger
- ⅓ cup unsweetened coconut, shredded

Directions:

1. Preheat your oven to 375°F.

2. To make the filling: melt the coconut oil in a pan on medium-low heat and cook the coconut sugar for a couple of minutes while stirring.

3. Put in the rest of the ingredients then cook for a minimum of 5 minutes. Stir.

4. Take away the contents from heat and move it to a baking dish.

5. For the topping: Combine all ingredients in a mixer and pulse until a coarse meal forms.

6. Put the topping over the filling.

7. Bake for a minimum of 15 minutes or until the top becomes golden brown.

Nutrition: Calories: 265, Fat: 12.4 g, Carbs: 37 g, Sugar: 23.3 g, Protein: 4.3 g, Sodium: 17 mg

463. Tropical Popsicles

Preparation Time: 10 minutes

Cooking Time: 0 minutes

Servings: 6

Ingredients:

- ½ tsp black pepper
- 2 kiwi, cut
- 2 tbsp coconut oil
- 2 tsp turmeric
- 3 cups pineapple, chopped

Directions:

1. First, place all the ingredients needed to make the popsicles excluding the kiwi in a high-speed blender for a couple of minutes or until you get a smooth mixture.

2. After this, pour the smoothie into the popsicle molds.

3. Next, insert the kiwi slices into the molds and then put the frames in the freezer until set.

Nutrition: Calories: 101, Protein: 0.5 g, Carbs: 15 g, Fat: 4 g

464. Turmeric Milkshake

Preparation Time: 5 minutes

Cooking Time: 0 minutes

Servings: 2

Ingredients:

- 1 tbsp ground flaxseeds
- 1 tsp turmeric
- 2 cups unsweetened almond milk
- 2 frozen bananas
- 2 tbsp raw cocoa powder
- 3 tbsp raw honey

Directions:

1. Combine all ingredients into a high-speed blender, and blend until the desired smoothness is achieved.

2. Split between 2 serving glasses, and enjoy straight away.

Nutrition: Total Carbs: 74 g, Fiber: 7 g, Protein: 4 g, Total Fat: 6 g, Calories: 334

465. Vanilla Cakes

Preparation Time: 10 minutes

Cooking Time: 15 minutes

Servings: 8

Ingredients:

- ½ tsp baking soda
- ½ tsp salt
- 1 cup agave sweetener
- 1 cup almond milk
- 1 tbsp apple cider vinegar
- 2 cups whole wheat flour
- 2 tsp baking powder
- ½ cup warmed coconut oil
- 1 tsp vanilla extract

Directions:

1. Ensure the oven is set to 350°F.

2. Prepare 2 muffin pans (12 c) for use by greasing them.

3. Put the apple cider vinegar into a measuring cup that is big enough to hold a minimum of 2 cups. Put in the almond milk for a total of ½ cup. Allow the results to curdle for roughly 5 minutes or until done.

4. Put together the salt, baking soda, baking powder, sugar, and flour together in a big container and whisk well.

5. Separately, mix the vanilla, coconut oil, and curdled almond in its container before combining the 2 bowls and blending well. Put the results into the muffin pans, dividing uniformly.

6. Put the muffin pans in your oven and allow them to cook for approximately 15 minutes. You will know if it's all already cook when you can press down on the tops and spring back when pressed lightly.

7. Allow the cake pans to cool on a wire rack before removing the cakes for the best results.

Nutrition: Calories: 336, Protein: 5.75 g, Fat: 16.25 g, Carbs: 44.15 g

466. Yummy Fruity Ice-Cream

Preparation Time: 20 minutes + 3 to 4 hours freezing

Cooking Time: 0 minutes

Servings: 4

Ingredients:

- ½ cup coconut cream
- ½ peeled and cut small banana
- 1 cup fresh strawberries, hulled and cut
- 2 tbsp shredded coconut

Directions:

1. In a powerful blender, put all the ingredients and pulse till smooth.

2. Put it into an ice cream maker, then process in accordance with the manufacturer's directions.

3. Now, move into an airtight container. Freeze to set for a minimum of 3 to 4 hours, stirring after every 30 minutes.

Nutrition: Calories: 103, Fat: 8.2 g, Carbs: 8.2 g, Protein: 1.2 g, Fiber: 2 g

467. Refreshing Raspberry Jelly

Preparation Time: 10 minutes+ 1 hour freezing

Cooking Time: 40 minutes

Servings: 4

Ingredients:

- ¼ cup water
- 1 tbsp fresh lemon juice

- 2 lb fresh raspberries

Directions:

1. In a moderate-sized pan, put in raspberries and water on low heat and cook for approximately 8 to 10 minutes until done completely.

2. Put in lemon juice and cook for approximately 30 minutes, stirring once in a while.

3. Turn off the heat and put the mixture into a sieve.

4. Position a strainer over a container.

5. Through a strainer, strain the mixture by pushing using the backside of a spoon.

6. Place the mixture into a blender then pulse till a jelly-like texture is formed.

7. Move into serving glass bowls and place in your fridge for approximately 1 hour.

Nutrition: Calories: 119, Fat: 1.5 g, Carbs: 27.2 g, Protein: 2.7 g, Fiber: 14.7 g

468. Citrus Strawberry Granita

Preparation Time: 15 minutes

Cooking Time: 0 minutes

Servings: 4

Ingredients:

- ¼ cup raw honey
- ¼ lemon
- 1 grapefruit (peeled, seeded, and sectioned)
- 12 oz fresh strawberries, hulled
- 2 oranges (peeled, seeded and sectioned)

Directions:

1. Put strawberries, grapefruit, oranges, and lemon in a juicer and extract juice according to the manufacturer's instructions.

2. Put 1½ cup of the veggie juice and honey into a pan and cook on moderate heat for 5 minutes while stirring constantly.

3. Remove it from heat and put in it the rest of the juice.

4. Set aside for roughly 30 minutes.

5. Move the juice mixture into an 8x8-inch glass baking dish.

6. Freeze for 4 hours while scraping after every 30 minutes.

Nutrition: Calories: 145, Fat: 0.4 g, Carbs: 37.5 g, Sugar: 32.4 g, Protein: 1.7 g, Sodium: 2 mg

469. Coconut Butter Fudge

Preparation Time: 10 minutes

Cooking Time: 0 minutes

Servings: 6

Ingredients:

- ¼ tsp salt
- 1 cup coconut butter
- 1 tsp pure vanilla extract
- 2 tbsp raw honey

Directions:

1. Start by lining an 8 x 8-inch baking dish using parchment paper.
2. Melt the coconut butter, honey, and vanilla using low heat.
3. Place the mixture into the baking pan, and place it in your fridge for about 2 hours before you serve.

Nutrition: Total Carbs: 6 g, Fiber: 0 g, Protein: 0 g, Total Fat: 36 g, Calories: 334

470. Comforting Baked Rice Pudding

Preparation Time: 10 minutes

Cooking Time: 20 minutes

Servings: 8

Ingredients:

- ¼ cup almond flakes
- ¼ cup raw honey
- ½ tsp ground cardamom
- ½ tsp ground ginger
- 1 peeled and cut banana
- 1 tsp fresh lemon zest, finely grated
- 1 tsp ground cinnamon
- 2 big organic eggs
- 2 cups cooked brown rice
- 2 cups unsweetened almond milk

Directions:

1. Set the oven to 390 F, then grease a baking dish.
2. Spread cooked rice at the bottom of the readied baking dish uniformly.

3. In a big container, put together the almond milk, eggs, honey, lemon zest, and spices, and beat until well blended.
4. Put the egg mixture over the rice uniformly.
5. Position banana slices over egg mixture uniformly and drizzle with almonds.
6. Bake for approximately 20 minutes.
7. Serve warm.

Nutrition: Calories: 264, Fat: 4.9 g, Carbs: 50 g, Protein: 6.2 g, Fiber: 2.9 g

471. Cookie Dough Bites

Preparation Time: 10 minutes

Cooking Time: 0 minutes

Servings: 2

Ingredients:

- ¼ cup almond flour
- ¼ cup chocolate chips, dairy-free & sugar-free
- ½ cup almond butter or any nut butter
- ½ tsp salt
- 1½ cups chickpeas, cooked
- 1 tsp vanilla extract
- 2 tbsp maple syrup

Directions:

1. First, place all the ingredients excluding the chocolate chips in a high-speed blender for about 3 minutes or until you get a thick, smooth mixture.
2. After this, move the mixture to a moderate-sized container.
3. Next, fold the chocolate chips into the batter.
4. Check for sweetness and put in more maple syrup if required.
5. Serve and enjoy.

Nutrition: Calories: 373 , Protein: 12.6 g, Carbs: 59.1 g, Fat: 10 g

472. Creamy Frozen Yogurt

Preparation Time: 10 minutes + 2 to 3 hours freezing

Cooking Time: 0 minutes

Servings: 3

Ingredients:

- ½ cup coconut yogurt

- ½ cup unsweetened almond milk
- 1 tbsp raw honey
- 1 tsp fresh mint leaves
- 1 tsp organic vanilla extract
- 2 peeled, pitted and chopped medium avocados
- 2 tbsp fresh lemon juice

Directions:

1. Throw all the ingredients into a blender apart from mint leaves and pulse till creamy and smooth.

2. Put into an airtight container then freeze for a minimum of 2 to 3 hours.

3. Take off from the freezer and keep aside for about 15 minutes.

4. With a spoon stir thoroughly.

5. Top with fresh mint leaves before you serve.

Nutrition: Calories: 105, Fat: 1.3 g, Carbs: 20.3 g, Protein: 2.7 g, Fiber: 1.4 g

473. Lemon Vegan Cake

Preparation Time: 10 minutes

Cooking Time: 30 minutes

Servings: 3

Ingredients:

- 1 cup pitted dates
- 2½ cups pecans
- 1½ cup agave
- 3 avocados, halved & pitted
- 3 cups cauliflower rice, prepared
- 1 lemon juice and zest
- ½ lemon extract
- 1½ cups pineapple, crushed
- 1½ tsp vanilla extract
- Pinch of cinnamon
- 1½ cups dairy-free yogurt

Directions:

1. Line your baking sheet with parchment paper.

2. Pulse the pecans in your food processor.

3. Add the agave and dates. Pulse for a minute.

4. Transfer this mix to the baking sheet. Wipe the bowl of your processor.

5. Bring together the pineapple, agave, avocados, cauliflower, lemon juice, and zest in your food processor. Get a smooth mixture.

6. Now add the lemon extract, cinnamon, and vanilla extract. Pulse.

7. Pour this mix into your pan on the crust.

8. Refrigerate for 5 hours minimum.

9. Take out the cake and keep it at room temperature for 20 minutes.

10. Take out the cake's outer ring.

11. Whisk together the vanilla extract, agave, and yogurt in a bowl.

12. Pour on your cake.

Nutrition: Calories: 688, Carbs: 100 g, Fat: 27 g, Protein: 9 g, Sugar: 40 g

474. Dark Chocolate Granola Bars

Preparation Time: 10 minutes

Cooking Time: 25 minutes

Servings: 12

Ingredients:

- 1 cup tart cherries, dried
- 2 cups buckwheat
- ¼ cup flaxseed
- 1 cup walnuts
- 2 eggs
- 1 tsp salt
- ¼ cup dark cocoa powder
- ⅔ cup honey
- ½ cup dark chocolate chips
- 1 tsp vanilla

Directions:

1. Preheat your oven to 350°F.

2. Apply cooking spray lightly to your baking pan.

3. Pulse together the walnuts, wheat, tart cherries, salt, and flaxseed in your food processor. Everything should be chopped fine.

4. Whisk together the honey, eggs, vanilla, and cocoa powder in a bowl.

5. Add the wheat mix to your bowl. Stir to combine well.

6. Include the chocolate chips. Stir again.

7. Now pour this mixture into your baking dish.

8. Sprinkle some chocolate chips and tart cherries.

9. Bake for 25 minutes. Set aside for cooling before serving.

Nutrition: Calories: 634, Carbs: 100 g, Fat: 27 g, Protein: 9 g, Sugar: 40 g

475. Blueberry Crisp

Preparation Time: 5 minutes

Cooking Time: 30 minutes

Servings: 4

Ingredients:

- ¼ cups pecans, chopped
- 1 cup buckwheat
- ½ tsp ginger
- 1 tsp cinnamon
- 2 tbsp olive oil
- ¼ tsp nutmeg
- 1 lb blueberries
- 1 tsp honey

Directions:

1. Preheat your oven to 350°F.
2. Grease your baking dish.
3. Whisk together the pecans, wheat, oil, spices, and honey in a bowl.
4. Add the berries to your pan. Layer the topping on your berries.
5. Bake for 30 minutes at 350 F.

Nutrition: Calories: 348, Carbs: 40 g, Fat: 27 g, Protein: 9 g, Sugar: 40 g

476. Chocolate Chip Quinoa Granola Bars

Preparation Time: 5 minutes

Cooking Time: 10 minutes

Servings: 16

Ingredients:

- ½ cup chia seeds
- ½ cup walnuts, chopped
- 1 cup buckwheat
- 1 cup uncooked quinoa
- ⅔ cup dairy-free margarine
- ½ cup flax seed
- 1 tsp cinnamon
- ½ cup honey
- ½ cup chocolate chips
- 1 tsp vanilla
- ¼ tsp salt

Directions:

1. Preheat your oven to 350°F.
2. Spread the walnuts, quinoa, wheat, flax, and chia on your baking sheet. Bake for 10 minutes.
3. Line your baking dish with plastic wrap. Apply cooking spray. Keep aside.
4. Melt the margarine and honey in a saucepot.
5. Whisk together the vanilla, salt, and cinnamon into the margarine mix.
6. Keep the wheat mix and quinoa in a bowl. Pour the margarine sauce into it.
7. Stir the mixture. Coat well. Allow it to cool. Stir in the chocolate chips.
8. Spread your mixture into the baking dish. Press firmly into the pan.
9. Plastic wrap. Refrigerator overnight.
10. Slice into bars and serve.

Nutrition: Calories: 408, Carbs: 32 g, Fat: 17 g, Protein: 9 g, Sugar: 30 g

477. Apple Fritters

Preparation Time: 15 minutes

Cooking Time: 10 minutes

Servings: 4

Ingredients:

- 1 apple, cored, peeled, and chopped
- 1 cup all-purpose flour
- 1 egg
- ½ cup cashew milk
- 1½ tsp baking powder
- 2 tbsp stevia sugar

Directions:

1. Preheat your air fryer to 175°C or 350°F.
2. Keep parchment paper at the bottom of your fryer.
3. Apply cooking spray.
4. Mix together ¼ cup sugar, flour, baking powder, egg, milk, and salt in a bowl.
5. Combine well by stirring.
6. Sprinkle 2 tbsp of sugar on the apples. Coat well.
7. Combine the apples into your flour mixture.

8. Use a cookie scoop and drop the fritters with it to the air fryer basket's bottom.

9. Now air fry for 5 minutes.

10. Flip the fritters once and fry for another 3 minutes. They should be golden.

Nutrition: Calories: 348, Carbs: 14 g, Fat: 17 g, Protein: 9 g, Sugar: 40 g

478. Roasted Bananas

Preparation Time: 2 minutes

Cooking Time: 7 minutes

Servings: 1

Ingredients:

- 1 banana, sliced into diagonal pieces
- Avocado oil cooking spray

Directions:

1. Take parchment paper and line the air fryer basket with it.

2. Preheat your air fryer to 190°C or 375°F.

3. Keep your slices of banana in the basket. They should not touch.

4. Apply avocado oil to mist the slices of banana.

5. Cook for 5 minutes.

6. Take out the basket. Flip the slices carefully.

7. Cook for 2 more minutes. The slices of banana should be caramelized and brown. Take them out from the basket.

Nutrition: Calories: 234, Carbs: 16 g, Fat: 27 g, Protein: 9 g, Sugar: 20 g

479. Berry-Banana Yogurt

Preparation Time: 10 minutes

Cooking Time: 0 minute

Servings: 1

Ingredients:

- ½ banana, frozen fresh
- 1 container 5.3 oz Greek yogurt, non-fat
- ¼ cup quick-cooking oats
- ½ cup blueberries, fresh and frozen
- 1 cup almond milk
- ¼ cup collard greens, chopped
- 5 to 6 ice cubes

Directions:

1. Take a microwave-safe cup and add 1 cup almond milk and ¼ cup oats

2. Place the cups into your microwave on high for 2.5 minutes

3. When oats are cooked and 2 ice cubes to cool

4. Mix them well

5. Add all ingredients to your blender

6. Blend it until it gets a smooth and creamy mixture

7. Serve chilled and enjoy!

Nutrition: Calories: 379, Fat: 10 g, Carbs: 63 g, Protein: 13 g

480. Avocado Chocolate Mousse

Preparation Time: 10 minutes

Cooking Time: 0 minute

Servings: 9

Ingredients:

- 3 ripe avocados, pitted and flesh scooped out
- 6 oz plain Greek yogurt
- ⅛ cup almond milk, unsweetened
- ¼ cup cocoa powder
- ½ tsp salt
- 2 tbsp raw honey
- 1 bar dark chocolate
- 1 tsp vanilla extract

Directions:

1. Place all ingredients in your food processor

2. Pulse until smooth

3. Serve chilled and enjoy!

Nutrition: Calories: 208, Fat: 4g, Carbs: 17g, Protein: 5g

481. Anti-Inflammatory Apricot Squares

Preparation Time: 20 minutes

Cooking Time: 0 minute

Servings: 8

Ingredients:

- 1 cup shredded coconut, dried
- 1 tsp vanilla extract
- 1 cup apricot, dried
- 1 cup macadamia nuts, chopped

- 1 cup apricot, chopped
- ⅓ cup turmeric powder

Directions:

1. Place all ingredients in your food processor
2. Pulse until smooth
3. Place the mixture into a square pan and press evenly
4. Serve chilled and enjoy!

Nutrition: Calories: 201, Fat: 15 g, Carbs: 17 g, Protein: 3 g

482. Raw Black Forest Brownies

Preparation Time: 2 hours 10 minutes

Cooking Time: 0 minute

Servings: 6

Ingredients:

- 1½ cups cherries, pitted, dried, and chopped
- 1 cup raw cacao powder
- ½ cup dates pitted
- 2 cups walnuts, chopped
- ½ cup almonds, chopped
- ¼ tsp salt

Directions:

1. Place all ingredients in your food processor
2. Pulse until small crumbs are formed
3. Press the brownie batter into a pan
4. Freeze for 2 hours
5. Slice before serving and enjoy!

Nutrition: Calories: 294, Fat: 17 g, Carbs: 33 g, Protein: 7 g

483. Berry Parfait

Preparation Time: 10 minutes

Cooking Time: 10 minutes

Servings: 5

Ingredients:

- 7 oz/200 g almond butter
- 3.5 oz/100 g Greek yogurt
- 14 oz/400 g mixed berries
- 2 tsp honey

Directions:

1. Mix the Greek yogurt, butter, and honey until it's smooth.
2. Add a layer of berries and a layer of the mixture in a glass until it's full.
3. Serve immediately

Nutrition: Calories: 394, Fat: 17 g, Carbs: 35 g, Protein: 7 g

484. Easy Peach Cobbler

Preparation Time: 5 minutes

Cooking Time: 20 minutes

Servings: 6

Ingredients:

- 5 organic peaches, pitted and chopped
- ¼ cup coconut palm sugar, divided
- ½ tsp cinnamon
- ¾ cup chopped pecans
- ½ cup gluten-free oats
- ¼ cup ground flaxseeds
- ¼ brown rice flour
- ¼ cup extra virgin olive oil

Directions:

1. Preheat the oven to 350°F.
2. Grease the bottom of 6 ramekins.
3. In a bowl, mix the peaches, ½ of the coconut sugar, cinnamon, and pecans.
4. Distribute the peach mixture to the ramekins.
5. In the same bowl, mix the oats, flaxseed, rice flour, and oil. Add in the remaining coconut sugar. Mix until a crumbly texture is formed.
6. Top the mixture over the peaches.
7. Place for 20 minutes.

Nutrition: Calories: 194, Fat: 15 g, Carbs: 32 g, Protein: 7 g

485. Salts Peanut Butter Cookies

Preparation Time: 15 minutes

Cooking Time: 0 minutes

Servings: 9

Ingredients:

- 1 cup raw almonds

- ½ cup peanut butter (creamy and unsalted)
- 1 cup pitted Medjool dates
- 1¼ tsp vanilla extract
- Sea salt as needed

Directions:

1. Take a food processor and add almonds, peanut butter, vanilla, and dates and blend the whole mixture until a dough-like texture comes (should take a few minutes)

2. If you want, add some more peanut butter to make the dough sticker.

3. Form balls using the dough and press down using a fork to create a crisscross pattern

4. Sprinkle salt generously

5. Serve immediately.

Nutrition: Calories: 214, Fat: 16 g, Carbs: 32 g, Protein: 6 g

486. Almond Butter Balls Vegan

Preparation Time: 10 minutes

Cooking Time: 0 minutes

Servings: 4

Ingredients:

- 12 dates, pitted and diced
- ⅓ cup unsweetened shredded coconut
- 2½ tbsp almond butter

Directions:

1. Take a bowl and add dates, almond butter, and coconut

2. Mix well

3. Use the mixture to form small balls

4. Store them in your fridge and chill them

5. Enjoy!

Nutrition: Calories: 62, Fat: 3 g, Carbs: 8 g, Protein: 1 g

487. Coffee Cream

Preparation Time: 10 minutes

Cooking Time: 15 minutes

Servings: 4

Ingredients:

- ¼ cup brewed coffee
- 2 tbsp swerve

- 2 cups heavy cream
- 1 tsp vanilla extract
- 2 tbsp ghee, melted
- 2 eggs

Directions:

1. In a bowl, combine the coffee with the cream and the other ingredients, whisk well and divide it into 4 ramekins and whisk well.

2. Introduce the ramekins in the oven at 350°F and bake for 15 minutes.

3. Serve warm.

Nutrition: Calories: 300, Fat: 11 g, Carbs: 3 g, Protein: 4 g, Sugar: 12 g

488. Almond Cookies

Preparation Time: 15 minutes

Cooking Time: 15 minutes

Servings: 12

Ingredients:

- 14 oz/400 g non-wheat flour
- 1 tsp baking soda
- 1 tsp baking powder
- 3.5 oz/100 g tahini
- 1.7 oz/50 g coconut butter
- ½ tsp vanilla
- ½ tsp honey
- Salt

Directions:

1. Mix the flour, soda, salt, and baking powder together.

2. Mix tahini and coconut butter and add 2 tbsp of water in the same bowl.

3. Add honey and vanilla to the tahini mixture and blend it well with a mixer.

4. Preheat your oven (180°C/356°F) and put a baking sheet on it.

5. Add 24 tbsp of the mixture onto the baking sheet and let it bake in the oven for 11 to 15 minutes.

6. Let it get cold a little bit and serve.

Nutrition: Calories: 114, Fat: 16 g, Carbs: 22 g, Protein: 6 g

489. Chocolate Mousse

Preparation Time: 10 minutes

Cooking Time: 0 minutes

Servings: 4

Ingredients:

- Coconut cream scraped from the upper side of 2 pieces of 13.5 oz chilled cans of full-fat coconut milk
- 4 tbsp cocoa
- 3 tbsp agave nectar
- 1 tsp vanilla extract

Directions:

1. Take a large bowl and scoop out the thick coconut cream from the can into the bowl
2. Add nectar, vanilla extract, and cocoa to the bowl
3. Beat it well using an electric mixer, starting from low and going to medium until a foamy texture appears
4. Divide the mix evenly amongst ramekins and chill to your desired level of cold
5. Enjoy!

Nutrition: Calories: 114, Fat: 12 g, Carbs: 22 g, Protein: 6 g

490. Raspberry Diluted Frozen Sorbet

Preparation Time: 10 minutes

Cooking Time: 20 minutes

Servings: 4

Ingredients:

- 14 oz/400 g frozen raspberry
- 4 fly oz/50 g almond milk
- Mint

Directions:

1. Put the almond milk and raspberry in a mixer till it's smooth, and leave the consistency in the freezer for 20 minutes.
2. When serving, put them in ice cream bowls and serve with mint on top.

Nutrition: Calories: 224, Fat: 16 g, Carbs: 22 g, Protein: 4 g

491. Chocolate Covered Strawberries

Preparation Time: 15 minutes

Cooking Time: 5 minutes

Servings: 24

Ingredients:

- 16 oz milk chocolate chips
- 2 tbsp shortening
- 1 lb fresh strawberries with leaves

Directions:

1. In a bain-marie, melt chocolate and shorter, occasionally stirring until smooth. Hold them by the toothpicks and immerse the strawberries in the chocolate mixture.
2. Put toothpicks on the top of the strawberries.
3. Turn the strawberries and put the toothpick in the Styrofoam so that the chocolate cools.

Nutrition: Calories: 205, Fat: 16 g, Carbs: 32 g, Protein: 6 g

492. Coconut Muffins

Preparation Time: 5 minutes

Cooking Time: 25 minutes

Servings: 8

Ingredients:

- ½ cup ghee, melted
- 3 tbsp swerve
- ¼ tsp vanilla extract
- 1 cup coconut, unsweetened and shredded
- ¼ cup cocoa powder
- 3 eggs whisked
- 1 tsp baking powder

Directions:

1. In a bowl, combine the ghee with the swerve, coconut, and the other ingredients, stir well and divide it into a lined muffin pan. Bake at 370°F for 25 minutes, cool down and serve.

Nutrition: Calories: 324, Fat: 31 g, Carbs: 8.3 g, Protein: 4 g, Sugar: 11 g

493. Chocolate Cherry Chia Pudding

Preparation Time: 4 hours 5 minutes

Cooking Time: 0 minutes

Servings: 4

Ingredients:

- 1½ cup any non-dairy milk like coconut or almond milk
- 3 tbsp raw cacao powder
- ¼ cup chia seeds, you can also use chia seed powder.
- 3 tbsp maple syrup or honey

Additional Toppings:

- Raw cacao nibs
- Extra cherries
- Dark chocolate shavings (Preferably 70% dark chocolate or more)

Directions:

1. Use a mason jar or a bowl. If you're using a bowl, just pour in the milk, maple syrup, chia seeds or powder, and raw cacao. Stir thoroughly and place in the refrigerator for 4 hours or more.
2. If you decide to use a mason jar, just pour in the same ingredients, screw the lid on and shake vigorously!
3. Serve in separate dishes and top with any or all of the toppings I listed above.
4. Enjoy!

Nutrition: Calories: 404, Fat: 16 g, Carbs: 12 g, Protein: 6 g

494. Pineapple Cake

Preparation Time: 15 minutes

Cooking Time: 50 minutes

Servings: 8

Ingredients:

- 2 whole medium eggs
- 5 tbsp raw honey
- 1 tbsp almond flour
- 15 frozen sweet cherries
- 3 tbsp melted coconut oil
- 2 slices fresh pineapples
- ½ tsp baking powder

Directions:

1. Prep the oven by preheating it to 350°F.
2. Remove the skin and core of the pineapples. Set aside.
3. Drizzle 1½ tbsp of raw honey in a round cake tin.
4. Layer the pineapple rings and sweet cherries on the honey in a decorative fashion.
5. Bring the cake tin to the oven, then bake for 15 minutes.
6. While all that is going on, mix in the almond and baking powder.
7. In a separate bowl, combine the eggs and leftover honey. Drizzle in coconut oil and stir.
8. Now add the almond mix to the egg mix and stir thoroughly.
9. Take out the cake tin and drizzle batter over the top of the partially baked pineapple rings. Use a spatula to spread it evenly.
10. Put the cake tin back in the oven and bake for an additional 35 minutes.
11. When it's all set, take it out of the oven and leave it to sit for 10 minutes before placing it on a plate.
12. Serve with extra cherries if you like.

Nutrition: Calories: 120, Protein: 2.3 g, Fat: 6.99 g, Carbs: 12.98 g

495. Mediterranean Rolled Baklava with Walnuts

Preparation Time: 20 minutes

Cooking Time: 1 hour

Servings: 12

Ingredients:

- 2 cups walnuts
- 1 lemon zest
- 1 cup cream wheat or plain breadcrumbs
- 8 sheets thawed phyllo dough
- 3 tbsp sugar
- ⅓ cup milk
- 3 sticks melted unsalted butter
- 1 medium lemon
- 3 cups granulated sugar
- 3 cups water

Directions:

1. Mix 3 cups of sugar, 3 cups of water, and lemon slices in a pan and leave to boil

2. Lower the heat, then let it simmer until the sugar completely dissolves. It should take 15 minutes. You should have a nice smooth syrup now. Now leave it to cool for a bit.

3. Chop the walnuts in a blender into bits using short pulses.

4. Pour the walnuts into a bowl along with the cream of wheat, lemon zest, and 4 tbsp of sugar.

5. Stir in milk and set aside.

6. Now, preheat your oven to 375°F.

7. Spread out the phyllo dough and fit it into a baking pan. Trim off the edges that don't fit with scissors. Cover the remaining phyllo sheets while you work so they don't dry out.

8. Place a sheet on a clean flat surface and glaze with melted butter. Do this for all the sheets until it's finished.

9. Arrange the walnut mixture on one side of the sheets and roll them up like you're trying to make a sausage. Do this for all the sheets and walnuts.

10. Arrange the walnut rolls on an ungreased baking pan and glaze with the leftover butter.

11. Bake for about 45 minutes. It's ready when it looks golden.

12. Turn off the oven, then pull out the baking pan. Drizzle syrup over the baklava, making sure the syrup gets everywhere.

13. Bring back the baking pan into the oven, then leave to sit for 5 minutes.

14. Take off from the oven and leave it to cool for a few hours. Slice the rolls into tiny bits and serve.

Nutrition: Calories: 488, Protein: 4.49 g, Fat: 36.89 g, Carbs: 38.21 g

496. Mint Chocolate Chip Ice Cream

Preparation Time: 5 minutes

Cooking Time: 0 minutes

Servings: 2

Ingredients:

- 2 frozen overripe bananas
- Pinch spirulina or any natural food coloring, optional.
- 3 tbsp chocolate chips or sugar-free chocolate chips
- ⅛ tsp pure peppermint extracts
- ½ cup raw cashews or coconut cream, optional.
- Pinch Salt

Directions:

1. Mint or imitation peppermint won't be a substitute for this. Use pure peppermint extract and pour it all at once because a drop is more potent than you realize, so add slowly.

2. Peel and cut the bananas first. Place the slices in a Ziplock bag, then freeze.

3. For the ice cream, put all the ingredients in a blender and pulse. You can skip the chocolate chips and just add them after blending. It'll turn out delicious either way.

4. Serve as soon as it's ready or freeze until it's firm enough, then serve!

Nutrition: Calories: 250, Protein: 6.13 g, Fat: 24.37 g, Carbs: 7.72 g

497. Flourless Sweet Potato Brownies

Preparation Time: 10 minutes

Cooking Time: 30 minutes

Servings: 9

Ingredients:

- ½ cup cooked sweet potato
- 2 tsp vanilla extract
- ½ cup almond butter
- 6 tbsp honey
- ½ tsp baking soda
- 1 large whole egg
- ¼ cup unsweetened Cocoa powder
- 3 tbsp dairy-free chocolate chips, optional.

Directions:

1. Prep your oven by preheating it to 350°F.

2. Line a baking pan with parchment paper, leaving a few extra inches on the sides to make it easier to discard or remove

3. Blend all the ingredients, excluding the chocolate chips, until you get a very smooth and soft batter.

4. Transfer the creamy batter to your prepared baking pan and use a spatula to spread it around so it looks almost even.

5. Slide it into the oven, then bake for 30 minutes or until a knife inserted into the pan comes out clean.

6. Take off from the oven and leave to cool in the pan for 15 minutes before putting it up on a wire rack.

7. If you decide to use the chocolate chip topping, put the chips in a microwave-safe dish and heat until it completely melts. Take off from the microwave and drizzle over the brownies.

8. Serve or store!

Nutrition: Calories: 171, Protein: 5.17 g, Fat: 9.28 g, Carbs: 20.01 g

498.   Paleo Raspberry Cream Pie

Preparation Time: 20 minutes

Cooking Time: 10 minutes

Servings: 12

Ingredients:

For the Crust:

- 1½ tbsp maple syrup
- Pinch salt
- ½ cup unsweetened shredded coconut
- 1 tsp vanilla extract
- 1 cup roasted or salted cashews

Raspberry Filling:

- ¾ cup unrefined coconut oil
- 1½ cup roasted or salted cashews
- ½ cup & 1 tbsp maple syrup
- ¼ cup & 2 tsp fresh lemon juice
- ¼ cup coconut cream from the top solid part of a can of coconut milk that has been refrigerated overnight
- 2 tsp vanilla extract
- 3 cups fresh raspberries
- Pinch salt

Directions:

1. Prepare 12 muffin pans, line them with muffin liners, and set them aside.

2. Make the crust. Set a pan over medium heat and the coconut and stir until it's completely toasted. Stay by the pan because coconuts tend to burn very easily.

3. Transfer the toasted coconuts to a bowl and leave to cool for 5 minutes or so. Honestly, this toasting step isn't essential, but it adds incredible flavor to the crust.

4. To make the crust, put all the ingredients in a blender and pulse at the lowest speed until the mix gets all clumpy. Also, don't pulse for too long, or you might end up with a paste. To know if it's ready, put a bit of the mixture on your fingers and pinch. If it gets clumpy, you're on track. If not, add a little water and pulse at the lowest speed for further minutes.

5. Scoop the mix into the lined tins using your fingers to pack the mix tightly inside the pan.

6. Put the pans to refrigerate while you get to make the filling.

7. In a tiny pot set over low heat, stir in all the ingredients until the oil and coconut cream melts completely. Clean the blender using a paper towel and pour in the filling.

8. Pulse at high speed for like 60 seconds or until it's completely smooth. The only clumps we can forgive are the raspberry seeds.

9. Drizzle a quarter of the filling over the top of each crust. There should be extra filling; you can store and use that in another dish.

10. Place the coated muffins in the fridge to cool. This will take a few hours, like 6 hours, so put it in the freezer if you don't have time for that.

11. To serve, leave them to defrost for 80 minutes or until obviously creamy.

Nutrition: Calories: 565, Protein: 7.74 g, Fat: 43.72 g, Carbs: 42.72 g

499.   Caramelized Pears

Preparation Time: 20 minutes

Cooking Time: 5 minutes

Servings: 5

Ingredients:

- 1 tsp cinnamon
- 2 tbsp honey, raw
- 1 tbsp coconut oil
- 4 pears, peeled, cored & quartered
- 2 cups yogurt, plain
- ¼ cup toasted pecans, chopped
- ⅛ tsp sea salt

Directions:

1. Get out a large skillet, and then heat the oil over medium-high heat.

2. Add the honey, cinnamon, pears, and salt. Cover, and allow it to cook for 4 to 5 minutes. Stir occasionally, and your fruit should be tender.

3. Uncover it, and allow the sauce to simmer until it thickens. This will take several minutes.

4. Soon your yogurt into 4 dessert bowls. Top with pears and pecans before serving.

Nutrition: Calories: 290, Protein: 12 g, Fat: 11 g, Carbs: 41 g

---

500. Berry Ice Pops

Preparation Time: 3 Hours 5 minutes

Cooking Time: 0 minutes

Servings: 4

Ingredients:

- 1 cup strawberries, fresh or frozen
- 2 cups whole milk yogurt, plain
- 1 cup blueberries, fresh or frozen
- ¼ cup water
- 1 tsp lemon juice, fresh
- 2 tbsp honey, raw

Directions:

1. Place the ingredients in a blender, and blend until smooth.

2. Pour into your molds, and freeze for at least 3 hours before serving.

Nutrition: Calories: 140, Protein: 5g, Fat: 4g, Carbs: 23g

Meal Plans

2 Block Menus

Lunch

7 Weeks (49 Days) Meal Plan

Days	Breakfast	Lunch	Dinner	Dessert
1	CHERRY CHIA OATS	GRILLED AVOCADO SANDWICH	TURMERIC RICE BOWL WITH GARAM MASALA ROOT VEGETABLE AND CHICKPEAS	AFTER'S APPLE CINNAMON CHIPS
2	BANANA PANCAKES	CAULIFLOWER STEAKS WITH TAMARIND AND BEANS	ROASTED ROOT VEGGIES AND GREENS OVER SPICED LENTIL	CHOCO CHIA CHERRY CREAM
3	BAKED FRENCH TOAST CASSEROLE	HEALTHY CHICKEN MARSALA	WALNUT ROSEMARY CRUSTED SALMON	AVOCADO CHOCO CAKE
4	WHOLE GRAIN BLUEBERRY SCONES	TUNA STEAKS	ROASTED SALMON WITH SPICY CRANBERRY RELISH	DATE DOUGH & WALNUT WAFER
5	SPINACH MUSHROOM OMELET	AIR FRYER SALMON	ROASTED CAULIFLOWER AND POTATO CURRY SOUP	PINEAPPLE PIE
6	WEEKEND BREAKFAST SALAD	ROSEMARY GARLIC LAMB CHOPS	DIJON SALMON WITH GREEN BEAN PILAF	CITRUS CAULIFLOWER CAKE
7	KALE TURMERIC SCRAMBLE	MUSHROOM FARRO RISOTTO	VEGAN COCONUT CHICKPEA CURRY	SWEET STRAWBERRY SORBET
8	POACHED SALMON EGG TOAST	INSTANT POT BLACK BEANS	CAULIFLOWER TIKKA MASALA WITH CHICKPEAS	CREAMY & CHILLY BLUEBERRY BITES
9	EGG MUFFINS WITH FETA AND QUINOA	POPCORN CHICKEN	SHEET-PAN CHICKEN AND VEGETABLES WITH ROMESCO SAUCE	PISTACHIOED PANNA-COTTA COCOA
10	PEACHES WITH HONEY ALMOND RICOTTA	SPICY CHICKEN AND CAULIFLOWER	GLUTEN-FREE TERIYAKI SALMON	ROASTED BANANAS
11	QUINOA BREAKFAST BOWL	SALMON AND SWEET POTATO MIX	GLUTEN-FREE PINEAPPLE BURGERS	RUM BUTTER COOKIES
12	CREAM CHEESE SALMON TOAST	LEMON ONION MASH	VEGAN MUSHROOMS IN BROTH	SHERBET PINEAPPLE

Days	Breakfast	Lunch	Dinner	Dessert
13	CARROT CAKE OVERNIGHT OATS	CURRIED BEEF MEATBALLS	VEGAN AND MEDITERRANEAN MANGO AND BEAN STEW	SPICY POPPER MUG CAKE
14	MEDITERRANEAN FRITTATA	BROWN RICE AND CHICKEN MIX	COD AND PEAS	STRAWBERRY GRANITA
15	MAPLE OATMEAL	CURRIED SHRIMP AND VEGETABLES	ROASTED VEGETABLES WITH SWEET POTATOES AND WHITE BEANS	STRAWBERRY ICE CREAM
16	TOMATO OMELET	BUTTERED SPROUTS	ROASTED TOFU AND GREENS	STRAWBERRY ORANGE SORBET
17	TUNA & SWEET POTATO CROQUETTES	SHEET PAN ROSEMARY MUSHROOMS	TOFU AND ITALIAN-SEASONED SUMMER VEGETABLES	STRAWBERRY SHORTCAKE
18	QUINOA & VEGGIE CROQUETTES	CHICKEN BREASTS AND MUSHROOMS	SPICED BROCCOLI, CAULIFLOWER, AND TOFU WITH RED ONION	SWEET ALMOND AND COCONUT FAT BOMBS
19	TURKEY BURGERS	CABBAGE WITH APPLE	TEMPEH AND ROOT VEGETABLE BAKE	THE MOST ELEGANT PARSLEY SOUFFLÉ EVER
20	LAMB BURGERS	ROASTED SUMMER SQUASH & FENNEL BULB	GARLICKY CHICKEN AND VEGETABLES	TROPICAL FRUIT CRISP
21	SALMON BURGERS	ROASTED BRUSSELS SPROUTS & SWEET POTATO	TURMERIC-SPICED SWEET POTATOES, APPLE, AND ONION WITH CHICKEN	TROPICAL POPSICLES
22	QUINOA & BEANS BURGERS	POTATO MASH	HONEY-ROASTED CHICKEN THIGHS WITH CARROTS	TURMERIC MILKSHAKE
23	VEGGIE BALLS	CREAMY SWEET POTATO MASH	SESAME-TAMARI BAKED CHICKEN WITH GREEN BEANS	VANILLA CAKES
24	COCONUT & BANANA COOKIES	GINGERED CAULIFLOWER RICE	SHEET PAN TURKEY BREAST WITH GOLDEN VEGETABLES	WATERMELON AND AVOCADO CREAM
25	FENNEL SEEDS COOKIES	SPICY CAULIFLOWER RICE	SHEET PAN STEAK WITH BRUSSELS SPROUTS AND RED WINE	WATERMELON SORBET

Days	Breakfast	Lunch	Dinner	Dessert
26	ALMOND SCONES	SIMPLE BROWN RICE	MISO SALMON AND GREEN BEANS	YUMMY FRUITY ICE-CREAM
27	OVEN-POACHED EGGS	QUINOA WITH APRICOTS	TILAPIA WITH ASPARAGUS AND ACORN SQUASH	REFRESHING RASPBERRY JELLY
28	CRANBERRY AND RAISINS GRANOLA	SIMPLE CARROTS MIX	SHRIMP-LIME BAKE WITH ZUCCHINI AND CORN	CITRUS STRAWBERRY GRANITA
29	SPICY MARBLE EGGS	TASTY GRILLED ASPARAGUS	BROCCOLINI WITH ALMONDS	COCONUT AND CHOCOLATE CREAM
30	NUTTY OATS PUDDING	EASY ROASTED CARROTS	VEGETABLE AND CHICKEN STIR FRY	COCONUT BUTTER FUDGE
31	ALMOND PANCAKES WITH COCONUT FLAKES	DILL HADDOCK	BAKED TILAPIA WITH ROSEMARY AND PECAN	COCONUT MUFFINS
32	BAKE APPLE TURNOVER	TROUT AND SALSA	TOASTED BROWN RICE WITH THYME AND MUSHROOMS	COFFEE CREAM
33	QUINOA AND CAULIFLOWER CONGEE	SHRIMP CAKES	ITALIAN STUFFED PEPPERS	COMFORTING BAKED RICE PUDDING
34	BREAKFAST ARROZ CALDO	ITALIAN CALAMARI	CHICKEN WITH HERB PARMESAN SPAGHETTI SQUASH	COOKIE DOUGH BITES
35	APPLE BRUSCHETTA WITH ALMONDS AND BLACKBERRIES	CHILI SNAPPER	CHICKEN CURRY WITH TAMARIND & PUMPKINS	CREAMY FROZEN YOGURT
36	HASH BROWNS	MASHED CHICKPEA BRUSCHETTA	ZUCCHINI AND LEMON HERB SALMON	DARK CHOCOLATE GRANOLA BARS
37	SUN-DRIED TOMATO GARLIC BRUSCHETTA	PUTTANESCA-STYLE GREENS AND BEANS	PARMESAN AND LEMON FISH	PINEAPPLE CAKE
38	MUSHROOM CRÊPES	MEDITERRANEAN QUINOA BOWLS	CHICKEN LEMON PICCATA	MEDITERRANEAN ROLLED BAKLAVA WITH WALNUTS
39	OAT PORRIDGE WITH CHERRY & COCONUT	PINEAPPLE THREE BEAN SALAD	BLACKENED CHICKEN BREAST	MINT CHOCOLATE CHIP ICE-CREAM
40	GINGERBREAD OATMEAL BREAKFAST	LEEK AND CHARD FRITTATA	CHICKEN MARRAKESH	FLOURLESS SWEET POTATO BROWNIES

Days	Breakfast	Lunch	Dinner	Dessert
41	APPLE, GINGER, AND RHUBARB MUFFINS	GREEK TURKEY BURGERS WITH TZATZIKI	SHRIMP AND VEGETABLE CURRY	PALEO RASPBERRY CREAM PIE
42	ANTI-INFLAMMATORY BREAKFAST FRITTATA	SEARED AHI TUNA POKE SALAD	BANANA AND PEANUT BUTTER DETOX	CARAMELIZED PEARS
43	BREAKFAST SAUSAGE AND MUSHROOM CASSEROLE	ONE-PAN EGGS WITH ASPARAGUS AND TOMATOES	ESCAROLE, PINEAPPLE, AND APPLE SMOOTHIE	BERRY ICE POPS
44	YUMMY STEAK MUFFINS	ANTI-INFLAMMATORY BUDDHA BOWL	GREEN AND LEAFY GINGER-APPLE DRINK	FRUIT COBBLER
45	WHITE AND GREEN QUICHE	HONEY GINGER SHRIMP BOWLS	NUTTY PINA COLADA	WATERMELON AND AVOCADO CREAM
46	BEEF BREAKFAST CASSEROLE	SALMON CAKES	CHAI TEA DRINK	COCONUT AND CHOCOLATE CREAM
47	HAM AND VEGGIE FRITTATA MUFFINS	TUNA SALAD WITH WHITE BEANS	LEMON-MINT GREEN TEA	CHOCOLATE BANANAS
48	TOMATO AND AVOCADO OMELET	CHICKPEA STUFFED BUTTERNUT SQUASH	SPICY CHICKEN VEGETABLE SOUP	WATERMELON SORBET
49	VEGAN-FRIENDLY BANANA BREAD	CLEAN EATING EGG SALAD	LEMON AND GARLIC SCALLOPS	CINNAMON APPLE CHIPS

BONUS:
Introduction to 15 TOP
Anti-Inflammatory Herbs

Below I introduce you to the 15 TOP herbs with anti-inflammatory properties that you can incorporate, if you wish, into your recipes. I know these herbs very well as I have used them on myself, my family and thousands of clients, for several years, getting excellent results. The 15 herbs, due to the concentration of beneficial active ingredients, have the ability to accelerate the healing of inflammatory processes, strengthening the immune system and all the various systems attached to it. This BONUS is a gift that I decided to give you because you have purchased my book and therefore I want you to get the maximum benefits, for your health and that of your loved ones.

1. Turmeric (Curcuma longa) powder: anti-inflammatory properties, useful for various types of inflammation such as muscle pain, toothache and arthritis. It is also useful to counter the inflammation of the digestive and genito-urinary systems. Use: 1 tsp dissolved in a glass of warm water in the morning, on an empty stomach, and in the evening before dinner, away from meals.

2. Ginger (zingiber officinalis) grated or powdered: anti-inflammatory properties useful for osteoarthritis and rheumatoid arthritis. Use: the tip of a tsp dissolved in water, only at lunch, before meals. Also useful to mix with food, in small quantities, to enrich them with flavor and beneficial anti-inflammatory properties.

3. Rosemary (Rosmarinus officinalis) leaves: anti-inflammatory and tonic properties useful to relieve pain, and cramps, oxygenates the blood and regenerates liver and joints, bringing also good mood. Usage: 1 tsp in 1 cup of boiling water. Let stand for 10 min., strain and drink 1 cup in the morning and 1 at lunchtime before meals.

4. Cinnamon (Cinnamomum verum) bark: anti-inflammatory properties useful especially if for many years it has been consumed animal fats, causing inflammations to the digestive apparatus, such as the stomach and intestine. It is also an excellent tonic. How to use it: crumble with fingers a small roll of cinnamon bark, take ½ level coffee spoon and pour it into 1 cup of boiling water. Let it rest for 10 min., strain and drink hot in the morning on an empty stomach and if desired in the early afternoon.

5. Basil (Ocimum basilicum) leaves: anti-inflammatory properties useful for people suffering from arthritis and stomach. The suggestion is to consume it fresh on meals, 2 to 3 leaves are enough. However even dried it can be useful to prepare excellent herbal teas, as follows: pour 1 tsp in 1 cup of boiling water. Let it rest for 10 minutes. Filter and drink 1 to 2 cups per day, just before lunch and dinner.

6. Aloe vera (Aloe barbadensis) juice: remarkable anti-inflammatory properties for the entire digestive and genito-urinary system. I recommend you to use the fresh juice and possibly organic, in the doses of 1 to 2 scoops of 20 ml per day, the Aloe Vera can be found at herbalists and centers of natural products.

7. Olive (Olea europaea) leaves: anti-inflammatory properties useful for the cardiovascular system and the immune system. It is also indicated for diabetic subjects. Use: 1 tbsp in 1 cup of boiling water. Let it rest for 10 min., filter and drink 1 to 2 cups a day, in the morning and in the evening before falling asleep, thanks to the calming effects.

8. Spirea Ulmaria (Spiraea ulmaria L.) leaves and flowers: anti-inflammatory properties useful for kidneys and female genito-urinary apparatus, helps to drain excess fluids, fight gout and rheumatic pains. Use: 1 tbsp in 1 cup of boiling water. Let stand 10 min., strain and drink, 1 to 2 cups per day, away from meals.

9. Cayenne pepper (capsicum annuum): anti-inflammatory properties to fight arthritis and pain. Use: a pinch of crumbled or powdered pepper in 1 cup of boiling water. Leave in infusion for 4 to 5 minutes, filter and drink 1 to 2 cups per day, far from meals. Moderate use, a pinch, over meals as a condiment is recommended.

10. Mallow (Malva sylvestris) leaves and flowers: anti-inflammatory properties for intestines and stomach, thanks to its gelatinous mucilage. Use: 1 tbsp in a cup of boiling water. Leave to infuse for 10 minutes, filter and drink hot, 1 to 2 cups a day, far from meals.

11. Green tea (Camellia Sinensis) leaves: anti-inflammatory properties for stomach, intestines and genitourinary system, facilitates diuresis, activating the metabolism (to lose weight). Usage: 1 tsp in 1 cup of boiling water; leave to infuse for 5 to 6 min, strain and drink 1 to 2 cups per day, away from meals.

12. Thyme (Thymus Vulgaris) flowers and leaves: anti-inflammatory properties for lungs and genito-urinary system; excellent anti-pain in case of arthritis, strengthen the immune system.

13. White willow (salix alba) bark: anti-inflammatory properties to counteract rheumatoid arthritis with widespread pain, including headaches. Usage: 1 tbsp in 1 cup of boiling water; while the water boils set the flame to low and boil for 10 min; then turn off the flame and let stand for another 10 min, strain and drink 1 to 2 cups per day between meals.

14. Serenoa (Serenoa repens) fruits: anti-inflammatory properties for the prostate and the whole inflamed genito-urinary system. Usage: 1 tsp in a cup of boiling water. Leave to infuse for 10 min. Strain and drink 1 to 2 cups daily, away from meals.

15. Pineapple (ananas sativus) stem and fruit: pineapple is very rich in bromelain, a healthy enzyme useful for inflammation of the digestive system; it also aids digestion. You can consume it both as a fruit, in moderation, and as a stem, which you can find in titrated extract, in ready-made capsules, at herbalist's stores and in natural products stores. The stem is excellent for inflammation of the urinary tract and is an excellent activator of the metabolism. Usage: 2 to 3 caps per day, away from meals.

When you start a diet there is usually a period of adaptation of your psychophysical state. The herbs such as rosemary, cinnamon, basil and thyme, being aromatic plants, which affect the limbic system (emotional area of the brain), can help in this process of adaptation by promoting a good mood, in addition to their innate anti-inflammatory properties and beneficial to the immune system.

If your need is also to lose weight, I suggest you use rosemary, pineapple stalk and green tea because they accelerate metabolism and at the same time are useful to fight inflammation of the digestive and genito-urinary system.

Choose the herbs that are best for you. I recommend, especially at the beginning, to use no more than 3 that you can integrate together and create excellent synergistic effects, for the benefit of your health.

I recommend cycles of 3 weeks, then suspend for 7 days and resume another cycle of 3 weeks, repeated for 1 to 3 months, depending on your health needs.

Conclusion

The anti-inflammatory diet is a way to eat delicious dishes at home every day. Recipes created according to the diet's core principles not only look after your health but also your desire to eat tasty food. They can also considerably help you maintain a healthy weight.

It is not easy to change your lifestyle to include a healthy way of eating, but it is possible. Many individuals believe that going on a diet will provide a momentary fix that will lead to long-term results, which is never the case. It's critical to stay focused, have a good mindset, and join support groups, whether online or in person, or both, in order to stay on a healthy diet. If you become disheartened, remember that this is only a temporary setback and that continuing on track for the sake of bettering your health is the most essential thing.

Here are some points to have in mind as you make significant dietary and lifestyle changes:

- Experiment with new foods and don't be afraid to try something uncommon or unexpected. Many exotic fruits and vegetables have unique flavors and health benefits that we aren't aware of. Mangos, guava, jackfruit, and seaweed are just a few of the popular and tasty options to try. Even common grocery store items like avocado, aloe, lentils, and other nutritious and beneficial foods can be simply incorporated into our daily routine.

- Try a different recipe at least once a week, or once every two weeks if you're short on time. It does not necessarily have to be a complicated dish to impress guests; instead, it can be a simple 3-to-4-ingredient dish that you enjoy. It will broaden your culinary horizons and encourage you to try new foods.

- Be active and exercise frequently. One strategy to fight inflammation is to eat healthily. It is beneficial to move around and get into an exercise regimen on a regular basis. Minimal exercise for 30 minutes 3 times a week has been shown to have a positive influence on weight loss and health improvement in studies. Regularly walking, cycling, and experimenting with a range of stretching and strength training routines will help you build muscle and tone while also improving your health.

- If you have a chronic condition that causes inflammation, learn as much as you can about the symptoms, treatments, and things you can take to mitigate the effects. Some illnesses are difficult to treat, but by modifying nutrition, exercise, and daily habits, many of the bad side effects and pain can be considerably minimized.

- If you smoke or drink too much alcohol, it's in your best interest to quit both, or at the very least cut back on your drinking while quitting smoking. Because these behaviors are difficult to break, there are resources online to help you stop your cravings, and eating healthy is one approach to enhance your body's condition while you're at it.

If you become disheartened after a while and see an increase in inflammation-related symptoms, see your doctor or a specialist to monitor your health and any linked conditions (s). Continue to eat healthily, and if you "cheat" every now and again, simply restart. Everyone makes mistakes, and changing one's eating habits can be difficult. Experiences or situations in life might sometimes force us to abandon our dietary intentions, which can make returning to this diet, or any other way of eating, difficult. Always look ahead and consider the advantages of adhering to the diet in the past, as this can motivate you to start over.

Leave a Review

I am an independent author. Reviews are to help other readers learn about my book.

If you liked my cookbook, I would appreciate it if you could leave honest feedback.

I love feedback from my readers, I read every review as it helps me to improve my work, and help others.

Thank you for sharing and for following me.

Customer reviews

★★★★★ 4.9 out of 5

109 global ratings

5 star	████████████	91%
4 star	██	7%
3 star	█	2%
2 star		0%
1 star		0%

˅ How customer reviews and ratings work

Review this product

Share your thoughts with other customers

> Write a customer review